Mergers and Merger Policy

Mergers and Merger Policy

EDITED BY

James Fairburn and John Kay

OXFORD UNIVERSITY PRESS
1989

Oxford University Press, Walton Street, Oxford OX2 6DP
Oxford New York Toronto
Delhi Bombay Calcutta Madras Karachi
Petaling Jaya Singapore Hong Kong Tokyo
Nairobi Dar es Salaam Cape Town
Melbourne Auckland
and associated companies in
Berlin Ibadan

Oxford is a trade mark of Oxford University Press

Published in the United States
by Oxford University Press, New York

British Library Cataloguing in Publication Data
Mergers and merger policy.
1. Companies. Mergers
I. Fairburn, James A. II. Kay, J. A.
(John Anderson), 1948–
338.8'3
ISBN 0–19–877285–8
ISBN 0–19–877284–X (Pbk.)

Library of Congress Cataloging in Publication Data
Mergers and merger policy / edited by James A. Fairburn and John A. Kay.
p. cm.
Bibliography: p. Includes index.
1. Consolidation and merger of corporations—Great Britain.
2. Consolidation and merger of corporations—Government policy—Great Britain. I. Fairburn, James A. II. Kay, J. A. (John Anderson)
HD2845.M475 1988 338.8'3'0941—19 88–16999
ISBN 0–19–877285–8
ISBN 0–19–877284–X (Pbk.)

Set from disc by Parchment (Oxford) Limited

Printed and bound in
Great Britain by Biddles Ltd,
Guildford & King's Lynn

Preface

This book arose out of an Institute for Fiscal Studies project on Competition Policy funded by the Leverhulme Trust. Several of the papers were presented at the IFS conference on Merger Policy held on 16 July 1986. We would like to thank David Thompson for a great deal of help in planning the book, Chantal Crevel-Robinson for typing the manuscript, and Judith Payne for preparing the volume for publication.

J.F.
J.K.

Contents

List of Tables

List of Figures

Introduction

1. The Role of Mergers

Mergers have been an important feature of the British industrial scene since the corporation became the dominant vehicle of business activity in the early twentieth century. Early mergers were generally between firms in related businesses. Their purposes were the suppression of competition, and the rationalization of production through its concentration in larger plants or by sharing common services. These activities were rarely widely admired—Lord Lever's first attempt to establish a near monopoly in the soap industry in 1906 was thwarted at the time by a hostile Press campaign—but did not arouse the political controversy which led to more vigorous enforcement of antitrust legislation in the United States. A legal framework which permitted cartels was equally relaxed in its attitude to merger.

Over time, however, public policy came to take an increasingly sceptical view of restrictions on competition. Judicial positions were less supportive of restraints of trade. Cartels became subject to scrutiny by the Monopolies Commission in 1948 and were generally prohibited after the Restrictive Practices Act of 1956. In 1965 the remit of the Monopolies Commission was extended to allow it to investigate mergers and to recommend, where a merger seemed likely to operate against the public interest, that the Secretary of State should prevent it from going ahead. The Monopolies and Mergers Commission (as it had now become) was expected to balance the advantages of rationalization against the losses from reduction in competition. This type of welfare trade-off was formalized by Williamson (1968).

More recently, however, mergers have come to reflect a rather different facet of the modern corporate economy. The growth of large corporations led to the widely remarked divorce of ownership and control. This in turn generated what Manne (1965) christened the market for corporate control. In its plainest form, the market for corporate control is one in which competing management teams make offers to shareholders for the right to manage the business which these shareholders own. The mechanism by which this occurs in practice is the hostile or contested take-over bid. The market for corporate control has come to replace the atrophied process of formal election at annual general meetings as the way in which shareholders can exert supervision over managers.

The operation of the market for corporate control is subject to essentially the same analysis and criticism as economists apply to other markets. Is it efficient, in that the outcomes are welfare-maximizing in some appropriate sense? What policies are required to ensure that the market for corporate control itself remains a properly competitive market? And the effectiveness of any market rests on the conjunction of appropriate information and incentives, along with a form of organization which enables buyers and sellers to be matched with moderate transactions costs. To what degree do these conditions hold for the market for corporate control?

The evidence and analysis in this book attempt to assess the significance of recent mergers both within the context of the trade-off model and as part of the market for corporate control. The purpose of this introduction is to set out the background and the issues to be addressed.

2. The History of Merger Activity in Britain[1]

The first merger boom occurred at the turn of the century, when there was a string of multi-firm amalgamations. Many of these mergers were in the textile industries, where previously ineffective cartels were replaced by such companies as English Sewing Cotton (formed from 11 firms in 1897), the Fine Cotton Spinners & Doublers Association (31 firms, 1898), and the Calico Printers Association (46 firms, 1899). Huge mergers elsewhere led to the creation of companies like the Salt Union, the United Alkali Company, Imperial Tobacco, Wallpaper Manufacturers, and Associated Portland Cement. In each case many independent firms were assimilated and large shares of industry output achieved (Utton (1972a)). In the soap industry, despite setbacks, Lever Brothers eventually succeeded in acquiring most of its rivals.

In many respects, however, this first merger boom had only limited effect. The firms created were often rambling and ill-coordinated affairs, and were typically small in comparison with the products of the contemporary merger boom in the United States (Payne (1967)). The largest employer at this time was Fine Cotton Spinners & Doublers with 30,000 workers. Moreover, the listing of the largest firms was dominated by brewing and textile companies, with the new sectors such as steel, chemicals, and electrical engineering relatively under-represented. In general, companies remained small, and family control and industrial

---

[1] This section draws heavily from Hannah (1983).

partnerships were the prevalent forms of firm organization. The manufacturing sector showed little resemblance to the economy of today.

In this century there have subsequently been three important merger waves, the first in the 1920s, the second in the later 1960s, and the present one. The activity in the 1920s may be attributed to a change in the nature and organization of industrial activity. More and more firms were gaining public quotations, mass production brought scale economies to many areas of production, and new industries such as vehicles, chemicals, rayon, paper, and electrical engineering were growing rapidly. National marketing and industrial research and development, both of which implied larger scales of efficient operation, were becoming more widespread. Technology transfer through foreign ownership was another new development, providing major competitive challenges to domestic firms.

Mergers in the 1920s had a major impact on most sectors of manufacturing industry. In food and drink, where branding and marketing had become important, firms such as Unilever and Distillers were the product of large mergers. In electrical engineering the three giants GEC, English Electric, and Associated Electrical Industries emerged after a series of amalgamations. The list of major companies created can be extended to such companies as Bass, J. Lyons, Cadbury-Fry, Metal Box, Joseph Lucas, Fison, and Beecham, each of which would continue to figure among the largest British companies for the next fifty years. The most notable merger was the formation of ICI in 1926 from four independent companies. Each of the four—Nobel Industries, Brunner Mond, British Dyestuffs, and United Alkali—had themselves expanded by merger and had attained important positions in dyestuffs, explosives, and alkalis. Although the merger was to complete the domination of several of these markets, its primary consequence was to create a colossus straddling the entire chemicals sector. ICI subsequently placed emphasis upon research and development, and in due course expanded into a range of other chemical industries, particularly pharmaceuticals.

The mergers of the 1920s can now be seen as having largely defined the shape of the British corporate economy for the remainder of the century. The principal firms created then, such as ICI and Unilever, continue to dominate UK manufacturing industry today. The level of concentration in most industries was raised substantially, and every important manufacturing sector was led by at least one firm of international size and significance. Government put no obstacles in the path of these reorganizations, nor, despite a brief flurry of interest at the end of the First World War, was much concern shown about other restrictions on competition.

However, there was equally little direct support for mergers, despite the growing advocacy of 'rationalization' in the later 1920s and in the 1930s as the slump in economic activity persisted and worsened. The rationalization movement saw the root of economic problems as being at the micro- rather than the macro-level. Competition was too intense and led to ruinous price-cutting, bankruptcies, idle capacity, and unemployment. Instead, industries should be urged or compelled to reorganize, adopt new technology, and raise output. Although the government itself did nothing to promote merger, Montagu Norman at the Bank of England established the Bankers Industrial Development Company, a consortium of banks which was to encourage rationalization by threatening not to continue finance to companies which failed to co-operate with plans made for the industry as a whole. The largest of the few mergers which resulted from this intervention was the formation of the Lancashire Cotton Corporation from 96 previously independent firms in 1929–32. The company suffered most of the deficiencies of previous multi-firm mergers. The components continued to operate as largely independent concerns with little central authority or financial control. Some further initiatives of this type, particularly in the steel industry, were subsequently conducted under the auspices of the Import Duties Advisory Committee, following the imposition of tariffs across manufacturing industry in 1932.

The incidence of mergers is strongly related to stock market levels (see King (this volume) for an attempt to account for this phenomenon). The stock market had performed strongly throughout the 1920s, but, with the onset of world depression after 1929, the scale of merger activity fell off sharply. Only in the late 1950s was it to pick up again and approach the peaks of previous waves. The intervening period was characterized by the growth of cartels and restrictive agreements behind the tariff barriers of 1932, and such activity was curtailed only after the restrictive practices legislation of 1956. Although mergers continued, they were not nearly as common or pervasive as before or since. Aggregate and industry concentration generally decreased in these years (Hannah and Kay (1977)).

The pace of merger activity began to increase once again after 1950, rising steadily throughout the 1960s. The largest number of firm disappearances occurred in 1964 and 1965, although the greatest value of assets acquired occurred in 1968. Aggregate concentration and concentration in most industries again increased substantially (Hughes (this volume)). Throughout the period the manufacturing sector was exposed to increasing international competition as other economies recovered from the war, as tariffs were reduced under GATT (General Agreement on Tariffs and Trade), EFTA (European Free Trade Association), and the EEC (European Economic Community), and as newly industrializing countries became a trading force. The motivation of many mergers of this period was to attain large scale, in part because this was seen as necessary to achieve economies of scale and reduce costs, but often less specifically simply to emulate the scale and resources of overseas producers.

Business's own desire for large scale was reinforced by various government interventions to restructure industries. These included *ad hoc* schemes for particular industries, such as the formation of the British Aircraft Corporation in 1960 and the 1967 nationalization of the steel companies to form the British Steel Corporation. More generally, in 1966 the Industrial Reorganization Corporation (IRC) was established to encourage rationalization in the manufacturing sector—which in practice meant to promote mergers. The IRC subsequently had a decisive role in some of the largest acquisitions of the period. The two most notable cases were the formation of British Leyland in 1967 and the merger of GEC first with AEI in 1967 and then with English Electric in the following year.

The formation of British Leyland joined Leyland, the commercial vehicle manufacturer, with the British Motor Corporation, the largest domestic car producer. In so doing, it represented the culmination of a series of mergers over the previous fifteen years which had linked Austin to Morris and then to Jaguar, and Triumph to Rover. The future of the domestically owned British car industry thus rested with the single management of a single concern. With the onset of foreign competition in the following decade, and the failure to establish attractive new product lines and to deal with endemic problems of industrial relations, these hopes were dashed. In 1974 British Leyland was saved from liquidation only by the government's purchase of the major part of its equity. Its market share continued a steady decline from over 50 per cent of the UK car market at inception to around 15 per cent today. By contrast, the creation of GEC proved an initial success. The new company had a substantial monopoly in many areas of electrical engineering, and under the direction of Arnold Weinstock costs were reduced and inefficient production eliminated throughout a group of previously ill-coordinated and unprofitable companies (Cowling *et al.* (1980)). Only in the 1980s did doubts emerge over GEC's strategic judgements in the context of Weinstock's tight financial controls.

These giant mergers should not distract attention from the central characteristic of the 1960s experience, which was the pervasiveness of merger activity, especially in manufacturing. Some of these mergers represented, as in the earlier periods, the growth of a major firm by acquisition of much smaller rivals, suppliers, or customers. Thus Courtaulds undertook extensive vertical integration in the Lancashire textile industry, and the baking and milling, and brewery industries were concentrated into a small number of major firms. By the later phases of the boom, however, many mergers involved the union of two already large players as with, for example, the formation of Allied Breweries, Bass Charrington, Cadbury Schweppes, Rowntree Mackintosh, International Computers, National Westminster Bank, and Ransome Hoffman Pollard.

The largest prospective union of all—between Unilever and Allied Breweries—was never consummated. The reason was that a reference to the Monopolies and Mergers Commission, ultimately benign, delayed the merger until the fashion had passed. The power to make such references had existed since 1965. The Commission was authorized to investigate mergers which were referred to it, assess their effect on the public interest, and advise the Secretary of State whether they should be blocked or permitted. Recommendations as to which proposals should be referred have been made by a non-statutory Mergers Panel, which includes representatives of government departments and has, since 1973, been headed by the Director General of Fair Trading. Although some references have been made of mergers which had already taken place, reference generally postpones the merger, and the rules of the City Takeover Panel require that a bid be abandoned if a reference is made (although, of course, it can be repeated if the Commission's verdict is favourable). This opportunity for an assessment of the implications of merger was implemented during one of the great merger booms of the century, but had little short-term effect. The thrust of policy in the 1960s was the promotion of merger and the IRC its driving force.

In the 1970s, as the boom faded, it became clear that many mergers had not had the desired effects. The most conspicuous demonstration of this was the failure of manufacturing industry to withstand the impact of foreign competition. British Leyland was evidently not a Volkswagen or Toyota, ICL clearly not an IBM. More generally, an increasing number of academic studies showed that these mergers had not generally been profitable nor led to substantial increases in productive efficiency (Meeks (1977), Cowling *et al.* (1980)). The faith placed in large-scale operations was dissipated, and this type of merger proposal became much less common. The IRC was disbanded in 1971, and the Monopolies and Mergers Commission was seen as a more important instrument of policy. In the 1970s, somewhat more references were made, and in decisions such as the opposition to the Beecham/Glaxo proposal of 1972, the Commission showed itself also to be less enamoured with the supposed merits of large scale (Fairburn (this volume)).

In the 1970s, relatively few large horizontal mergers were proposed. This reflected in part the change in fashion, and in part a perception that reference and an adverse report were the likely outcome. Many of the cases referred to the Commission were therefore mergers which were likely to have little or no effect on competition. The public interest issues posed became increasingly diverse, including the personalities of certain ebullient entrepreneurs, the desirability of locating corporate headquarters in Scotland, and the capabilities of alternative management teams. At the same time, competition in the City created advisers—often operating on success-related fees—who were active in promoting mergers and in steering them through the various obstacles to completion. Lobbying for or against references to the Commission became an important part of this activity. It became increasingly difficult to detect the rationale for reference or to predict the likely outcome or the criteria which would be applied.

These elements paved the way for the development of a crisis in the early 1980s. The Commission was involved in a number of much criticized reports. Lonrho was permitted to take a stake in House of Fraser but then prevented from taking full control of the company—at least in part because the management of Lonrho was seen as unsuitable. Opposition to the take-over of companies like Royal Bank of Scotland and Anderson Strathclyde was the result, not of competition arguments—which barely arose—but of other issues such as the loss of local control of Scottish companies. Much of the criticism was actually found within the reports, in notes of dissent penned by members of the Commission. Indeed, in the Charter Consolidated/Anderson Strathclyde case, the Minister of State took the unprecedented step of accepting the minority's views and allowing the merger to proceed.

These developments allowed an increasing politicization of policy. With the Commission prepared to admit arguments about the suitability of management, the impact on the regional economy, and the desirability of foreign ownership, most take-overs raised policy questions of one type or another. It therefore became a viable strategy for an incumbent management to lobby for a reference to the Commission to avert or at least delay an unwelcome bid. This was best illustrated by the case of Sothebys, whose management opposed an American bid for the company and successfully lobbied for a referral to the Commission. The delay allowed them time to arrange a more suitable bid, also from America. No issues of competition were involved in either case, merely the defending management's views of the sensibilities of a very English company.

The Commission itself showed concern that the range of questions raised had become too wide, as was shown by its curt dismissal of any public interest issues in the bid for Sothebys, and its change of mind over the Lonrho/House of Fraser case. Following a departmental review of merger policy, the then Secretary of State, Norman Tebbit, stated: 'my policy has been and will continue to be to make references primarily on competition grounds'. Again—or perhaps for the first time—merger policy became synonymous with competition policy. Most subsequent references have concerned horizontal or vertical mergers, the chief exception being the bid for Allied Lyons by Elders IXL. At issue here was the financing of the bid and whether this jeopardized the future of the company. The Commission concluded that this was a legitimate area of policy concern, although not a valid criticism in the particular case before it.

The contrast between the new focus of merger policy on competition and broader concerns was made more obvious with the onset of a new merger boom in 1985 and 1986. A number of large and vigorously contested bids for major companies emerged. Not only were they not referred to the Commission, but in certain cases the firms were permitted to rearrange their assets in advance to avoid the delay caused by a reference. Both Guinness and Imperial Group planned to sell certain interests if their respective bids for Distillers and United Biscuits were successful, arrangements which were cleared by the Office of Fair Trading. There was nothing obviously wrong with this: if competition was the policy concern and if these arrangements secured effective competition, then all parties were happy. However, the contrast with an earlier phase of policy in which the Commission had given central attention to the details of bids and debates between rival management was marked and obvious. The contrast was re-emphasized when, despite considerable political pressure, the Secretary of State refused to refer the controversial bid by the conglomerate BTR for glass-producer Pilkington.

3. The Economic Effects of Horizontal Mergers

How should proposed mergers be assessed? An influential approach to the analysis of horizontal mergers is the trade-off model of Williamson (1968).

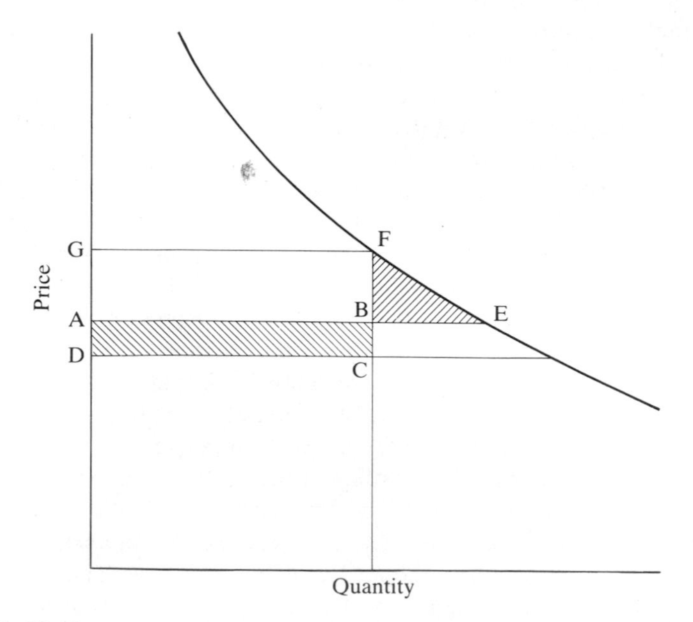

Figure 1. Welfare trade-off when pre-merger price equals cost

A merger, he hypothesized, might both lower costs through economies of scale and raise price by creating monopoly power. In this case, the welfare gains from increased productive efficiency (ABCD) would need to be offset against the welfare losses from reduced allocative efficiency (EBF), as shown on Figure 1.

Nothing can be said on a priori grounds, of course, about the relative magnitudes of the cost reduction (AD) and the effect of market power on price (AG). However, many commentators have been tempted to conclude that the triangle (EBF) looks likely to be small relative to the rectangle (ABCD). One feature of Williamson's analysis which invites this conclusion is that he adopts a competitive starting-point, with initial price equal to cost. If instead price was initially above cost, and a merger subsequently increased market power still further, as in Figure 2 where price rises from Y to Z while costs fall from R to U, then it is necessary to compare the areas RSTU (the efficiency gain) and SVWX (the welfare loss). As market power increases, the benefits of further concentration diminish (because the scale of output is falling) while the costs of further exploitation rise (because the value of lost output is increasing).

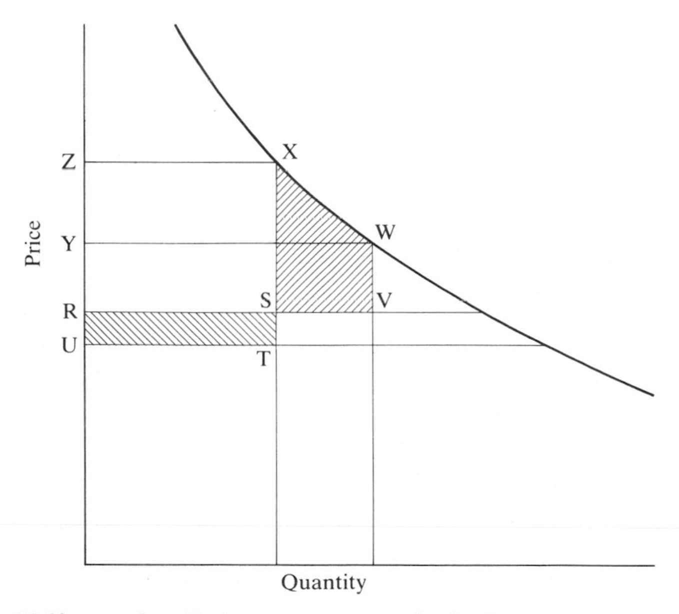

Figure 2. Welfare trade-off when pre-merger price is above cost

Moreover, Posner (1975) has observed that it is worth spending up to the potential profits of monopoly to obtain monopoly. This implies that an amount up to the rectangle DCFG might be an additional social loss attributable to the costs of rent-seeking. We discuss further below the very high levels of fees and commissions associated with take-over activity.

One firm conclusion which can be drawn, however, is that the social benefits of horizontal merger are less than its potential profitability. The cost savings (ABCD) represent both private and social gain. The exploitation of monopoly power yields benefits to the merging companies (DCFG) but costs to consumers (EBF). If a merger is not profitable to the parties to it, it is certainly not desirable; it does not follow, however, that a profitable merger is beneficial.

The value of the Williamson approach lies in the provision of a framework for quantitative analysis. One weakness, however, lies in its essentially static characteristics. Many of the effects of mergers emerge only through time—when cost savings are realized, when reduced competitive pressures diminish efficiency, or when market power is eroded through new entry. It is for these reasons that Littlechild (this volume) argues that the trade-off approach should be applied only where barriers to entry exist.

Williamson's analysis is concerned with horizontal mergers. Vertical acquisitions raise rather different issues. Economies of scale are no longer a possible outcome. However, the vertical merger may yield cost savings through the internalization of transactions which would be less efficiently conducted at arm's length (Williamson (1971, 1975)).[2] At the same time, it may make entry or expansion by competitors more difficult, increasing market power to the benefit of shareholders in the merged concern but to a more general detriment. Although there have been periods when vertical integration was a common motive for merger—as, for example, with the purchase of bakeries by flour millers and regional breweries by national firms in the 1950s, and through Courtaulds's expansion from fibre production into clothing manufacture in the 1960s—few recent mergers have fallen into this category.

Although the work of the Monopolies and Mergers Commission can be seen as—in a very loose qualitative sense—the application of the Williamson approach, in which the detriment of diminished competition is balanced against the benefit of scale economies, the quantitative content of its analysis is low.[3] The relationship between policy and the underlying economic issues is much more readily apparent in the United States. Hay (this volume) describes the policy approach which ruled from the late 1960s to the early 1980s. It drew upon the then growing emphasis on market structure in empirical economic work, and was distilled in the Department

---

[2] For doubts that dealing with an awkward subsidiary is any easier than dealing with an awkward customer or supplier, see Evans and Grossman (1983) and Grossman and Hart (1986).

[3] In his later paper, Williamson (1977) seemed to accept that it was not feasible to conduct a trade-off analysis in a merger case.

of Justice merger guidelines issued in 1968. In the case of horizontal mergers, these guidelines simply stipulated the market share increases which would be challenged by the Department of Justice. These guidelines gave a straightforward and predictable standard, with the consequence that merger proposals likely to infringe the guidelines would rarely progress beyond a gleam in the executive's eye.

Although they became the prevailing legal standards, the adoption of market share merger guidelines was not wholly definitive because there remained the need to define the relevant market for which the market shares would be calculated. Sponsors of mergers could avoid infringing the guidelines by pressing for a broad definition of the market and thus diminishing their market share. Correspondingly, the authorities could succeed in preventing a merger by emphasizing a narrow market definition.

Market definition has proved to be an important issue in many areas of competition policy besides mergers. There are initially two aspects to the problem—the product and geographic dimensions of market definition. The former involves considering which products are close substitutes for each other and finding suitable gaps in the chain of substitution between these products and others. Competition policy investigations and litigation commonly involve much detailed consideration of particular characteristics or end-uses of products in addition to such empirical estimates of cross-elasticities of demand as may be available. The geographic dimension involves determining the scope of the market—whether products are supplied in separate regional markets, nationally, or in international markets—and will involve consideration of transport costs, tariffs, and quotas. Clearly it is possible to go further and consider potential as well as actual competition: are there firms supplying adjacent regional markets which could readily switch supplies to the market in question, or indeed is it feasible for new firms to set up production facilities and enter the market?

These caveats about market definition aside, the original US guidelines offered clear and predictable policy standards. In the later 1970s and early 1980s, however, this received wisdom began to be challenged and the apparently mechanical application of guidelines and arbitrary resolution of market definition issues questioned. These developments reflect major contributions to the theory of competition policy, based on the 'Chicago school' approach which has won growing acceptance from courts and administrators. The Chicago school was deeply critical of prevailing antitrust standards, considering that what were in fact efficient business practices were widely misconstrued as restrictive or exclusionary and condemned by the law. In the light of these criticisms, many areas of antitrust, such as the approach to predatory behaviour by dominant firms and vertical restraints on distributors, have been reassessed and substantial changes made to prevailing legal standards.[4]

One of the central tenets of the Chicago school was that antitrust should revert to a concern of the classic problem where firms are able to restrict output and raise prices. This idea was brought to bear on the field of market definition, and hence on merger policy, in an important article by Landes and Posner (1981). They considered that the standard approaches to this issue failed to get to grips with what should be the central concern—that is, market power, defined as the ability to restrict output and raise prices.

The market should be defined by reference to the observation of market power, rather than market power asserted on the basis of a priori market definition. If firms in region A make sales, however small, in region B then regions A and B form a single market. Similarly, the test of whether commodity X forms a separate market from commodity Y, and, it is argued, the only relevant test, is whether the existence of Y inhibits the pricing policies of the producers of X. Typically, this style of argument leads to the adoption of rather broad market definitions.[5]

These considerations were reflected in the revision of the Department of Justice merger guidelines in 1982. The new guidelines adopted a particular means of implementing the new reasoning, which was to posit a certain increase in price in the market as originally defined and examine the consequences for competition from other products and suppliers. Thus if, in response to such a price increase, the evidence suggested that customers would switch to other products, these products should be added into the market definition. Equally, if outside suppliers were considered likely to commence supplies to the original market, their capacity would also be added. The idea was that it was misleading to consider a particular market definition if that definition represented an area of activity which no firm—abstracting at this stage from the position of existing firms—could profitably control, because if it raised prices it would lose customers to other products or would face new competitors drawn by the lure of the profits it was now making.

An important aspect of these new guidelines is their stress on a view of competition as a process rather than an assessment of static market structure. This conversion was by no means total, however. The guidelines continued to impose restrictions on the extent to which market share might be increased through merger. These now referred to the effect on the Herfindahl index—a statistical measure of concentration—and generally

---

[4] For an assessment of the impact of the Chicago school, see Posner (1979), and for more detail of these arguments, Posner (1976), Bork (1978), and Easterbrook (1984).

[5] A series of responses to the Landes and Posner article were published in 1982 in the *Harvard Law Review*, **95**, 1787–874. See in particular Schmalensee (1982) for a critique of the market share adjustment proposed by Landes and Posner and for alternative means of diagnosing market power.

would have allowed somewhat larger mergers than the previous standards. An important change, however, was the use of constructed market definitions, which might well be very much larger than the 'historic' market definition, with the consequence that market shares would be diminished and more mergers allowed.

The new guidelines sought to take a broader view of competition and the nature of the competitive process, whilst at the same time retaining the clear thresholds and the consequent clarity and predictability.[6] Thus there was still a definite framework for the operation of policy, although the use of constructed definitions must invariably diminish the guidance that is ultimately provided.

4. The Operation of Merger Policy

British policy operates on a two-tier procedure, whereby merger proposals are first selected by the Secretary of State for Trade and Industry and then considered against a public interest standard by the Monopolies and Mergers Commission. The first stage is typically completed within 2 or 3 weeks of a merger proposal becoming known; the standard period for the second is 6 months, extendable up to 9 months. The first-stage selection is advised by the Director General of Fair Trading, who is charged by law with keeping competitive developments in the economy under scrutiny.

One of the tasks at this stage is to establish the basic facts about the merger proposal, and to ensure that it satisfies the necessary preconditions for reference—either that the firm being taken over has assets of at least £30 million or that the merger would create or strengthen a market share of 25 per cent. Although the number of qualifying proposals has varied with revisions in the assets criterion and the level of merger activity (1986 was exceptional, for example), this has tended to mean consideration of some 150 to 250 mergers each year. The information sought by the Office of Fair Trading was described in its 1985 booklet, extracts from which are reprinted as Appendix 1 to Borrie (this volume), and from this it seems that at this stage the authorities will have a good indication of, if not precise information on, the areas of activity of the firms concerned and the extent to which they compete.

What happens in this first stage of assessment? At first sight, there is a considerable similarity between the British process of choosing mergers for reference and the US Justice Department's selection of mergers for legal challenge. In reality, however, there are considerable differences.

First, the screening criteria are not explicit: we know the type of

---

[6] See Hay (this volume) for some doubts on the extent to which this has been successful.

information gathered at this stage, but not how it is used. Thus, for example, there are no simple market share thresholds which guarantee reference. The 25 per cent qualifying criterion should certainly not be interpreted in this light. Therefore, although market share is evidently one factor indicating competitive conditions, it is difficult to know for sure what type of evidence—if any—might work against reference of a merger creating a 40 per cent market share, say.

Second, the procedures of the Commission must give rise to considerable pressure to compress a fuller analysis into the first stage. The Commission's investigations take 6 months or more, which is a long time in the course of any bid, allowing time for considerable shifts in share price—affecting the cost of a bid—or for new bidders to emerge on the scene. This and the costs of dealing with the Commission (principally in terms of executive time used)—factors influencing the high proportion of merger proposals abandoned after reference—might suggest to the authorities that it is unfair to refer any bids but those with the clearest adverse impact. The assessment must also be influenced by the fact that without changes in procedure, it would be difficult to make many more references to the Commission. Thus the situation has developed in which no more than about 10 references are made each year, something under 5 per cent of those satisfying the qualifying criteria.

Further evidence that a fuller-scale analysis is often attempted at the first stage is provided by the existence of the Mergers Panel, a non-statutory body comprising representatives from the government departments interested in a merger proposal. The panel only meets if a proposal is contentious or a reference likely, and can be assumed to be the forum in which any government support for the merger, for example from a department in whose area the two firms operate, will come to the fore. Although the workings of the panel are not public knowledge, some more direct evidence that this fuller analysis is attempted is provided by the fact that the Director General's advice is not always followed. The Director General can be expected to be the party with the most direct interest in promoting competition, and it must be assumed that the rejection of his advice results from the balancing of other countervailing arguments, or political lobbying. The Department of Trade and Industry normally supports projected mergers; other departments may have different views.

It should be apparent that the relationship between the two stages of scrutiny is by no means an easy one. The procedure does not result in the reference of a random selection of mergers—that is obvious. Nor does it result in the reference of only the most adverse—many referred mergers have been approved, and it would be hard to argue that no unreferred merger was likely to have been against the public interest. Perhaps the best characterization is that mergers have been referred if they raise major public interest issues. But this has proved less than satisfactory. It is easy to argue that matters of major private interest are also of major public interest, and hence the policy becomes wide open to lobbying. We noted above that in the early 1980s this had indeed occurred, and that this had led to considerable criticism of the process of referral and examination.

The Tebbit guidelines have defined more clearly roles for the two elements of procedure. Referral is to be based primarily on competition grounds; thus the resemblance to American practice is increased. If referral is made, however, the Commission remains obliged to take account of the full range of factors which might be thought to bear on the public interest—although in practice its own proceedings have tended to give greater weight to these same competition arguments. There is some logic, if also potential tension, in this separation of function. It resembles the explicit separation of the procedure prescribed by the 1980 Competition Act, for another area of competition policy. Here the Office of Fair Trading will first assess whether a firm's conduct amounts to being an anticompetitive practice, and if it does, at the second stage the Commission will also consider any other public interest arguments.

The three principal groups of criticism of this procedure are represented in this volume. One (Swift) stresses the need for predictability in policy, and observes the difficulty of reconciling the establishment of precedent and the creation of certainty with the essential pragmatism of the British policy approach. Another (Littlechild) thinks the range of public interest issues perceived by the Commission inappropriately wide, and argues not only for a concentration on competition issues but for a recognition that potential competition may be as powerful an influence on business behaviour as actual competition. The third strand (George) is influenced by the poor record of post-merger performance and the vacuity of the arguments commonly put before the Commission in justification, or rationalization, of what appear to have been hastily conceived acquisition proposals. This suggests a reversal of the burden of proof, so that prospective merger partners would be required to demonstrate that their proposals were of positive public benefit. In our final section we seek to reach some balanced judgement on these, not wholly consistent, proposals.

5. Conglomerate Mergers and the Market for Corporate Control

The merger activity of the 1960s and 1970s had left a residue of concentrated industries and large firms with often diverse interests, with an industrial structure which neither public nor business policy would now wish to put together. This has influenced merger activity in several ways. An increasing trade in company subsidiaries has developed, largely between companies, but latterly also involving sales of those subsidiaries to consortia of investors, often led by the management of the subsidiary itself (Wright, Chiplin, and Coyne (this volume)). Business strategy has increasingly emphasized the need to concentrate a portfolio of businesses in core areas, and management of that portfolio has increasingly been seen as an executive function.

With industries already concentrated, and the competition authorities often unwilling to countenance further large horizontal mergers, attention has shifted away from the economies of scale and market power arguments so characteristic of the 1960s. The GEC/Plessey proposal of 1986, which reiterated the claims about the need to achieve greater size to become an effective competitor on the world stage, stood out as one of the very few exceptions to the trend. Attention has increasingly been given to arguments about the quality of management, and in particular how the take-over sanction or threat of it prevents the persistence of poor management.

Conglomerate mergers appear to raise no competitive issues, and equally to offer no possibilities of economies of scale, although some economies of scope—due, for example, to common marketing arrangements—may be among the benefits claimed. Diversification may be an attraction of conglomerate merger for managers, but it offers no general benefit to shareholders, who are perfectly able to diversify their portfolios for themselves. Figure 3 illustrates the relevant trade-off here, as formulated by Levy and Sarnat (1970). The different risk characteristics of two companies are described by OA (a company more profitable in state 1 than state 2) and OB (a company more profitable in state 2 than state 1). A shareholder able to invest up to OA in company A or OB in company B can choose a point like C on the frontier AB. The merged concern, however, offers him the

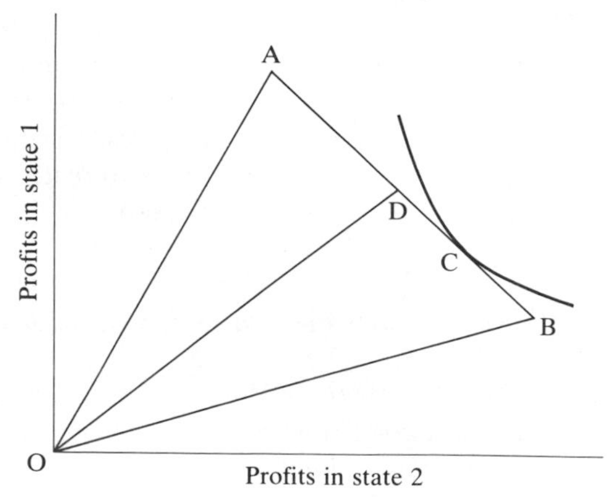

Figure 3. The effect of conglomerate merger on shareholder portfolio diversification

single option of a security D. Able to buy OD of this, he achieves only a lower welfare level than he could attain through a free portfolio choice.

Why then do conglomerate mergers occur? One explanation may be that the share price of one or other of the companies involved is wrong. Although the efficient market hypothesis—which asserts that current values reflect all publicly available information—is the dominant view of stock price behaviour, share price fluctuations appear to be larger than flows of new information would justify. And directors who make acquisition decisions may have access to information which is not publicly available, especially about their own activities or capabilities. A firm whose paper is overrated will sensibly exchange it for assets of tangible value before the market finds out. Or companies which undertake long-term investments may find themselves undervalued by markets excessively concerned with current flow of profits. These opportunities for merger, if they are common, not only lead to acquisitions which offer no public gain but can distort business strategies in ways that are actively detrimental. Puffery and accounting tricks may be used to persuade the markets, for a period, that managers of no special ability are financial geniuses; research and development may be inhibited for fear of an opportunistic bid. Conglomerate merger may also be attractive, and more likely to be of benefit, if the acquirer believes the assets he wishes to purchase are likely to be more valuable under his ownership than in an independent company.

Asymmetric information about the value of assets is a topic which has received considerable attention in the corporate finance literature and which clearly has a bearing on mergers. Another series of explanations with the same antecedents concern the effects of taxation. King (1986 and this volume) is in this tradition of looking at merger as one particular means of investment, the relative attraction of which will depend on the tax regime.[7]

Another distinct motive for conglomerate merger is as a means for firms to enter new industries. Merger offers a speedier way of participating in new markets than does the establishment of new plant. Correspondingly, the impact of such entry is less, and the relative attractions of the two methods are not well understood.

Therefore we do not offer the market power and corporate control arguments as the sole explanations of merger. Nevertheless these two have tended to dominate public debate about merger, particularly the merger of very large firms, and the shift from market power arguments in the 1960s to corporate control arguments in the 1980s has been pronounced. Arguments for mergers based on observations about management style or quality are not, of course, completely new. This type of acquisition grew in significance

---

[7] For discussion of the asymmetric information and taxation arguments, further references, and some empirical assessment, see Franks, Harris, and Mayer (1987).

following legal changes in 1948, which required firms to disclose much fuller information about their activities. In the 1930s, a merger had generally required the full co-operation of the acquired company, since without that the acquirer could not be at all certain what he was buying; and if such co-operation was not forthcoming, as it often was not, that was generally the end of the matter (Hannah (1974)). Greater disclosure made it possible for an outsider to assess the value of a potential acquisition and, with the increasing separation of ownership and control, he could appeal or threaten to appeal to shareholders over the heads of the incumbent management.

So the phrase 'take-over bid' entered the language of the business community and, indeed, the popular Press. An early exponent was Charles Clore's Sears Holdings, and Clore's acquisitions frequently rested on identifying property assets which had value greater than was suggested by their profitability in their existing use. Such opportunism attracted the pejorative label 'asset-stripping'. Acquisitions before the Second World War were normally for cash, but the growing institutional demand for equities enabled companies to issue their own shares in return for newly acquired assets. After capital gains tax was introduced in 1965, share exchanges (which enabled the shareholders in the acquired company to defer their tax liability) were often more popular than cash payments. This facilitated large acquisitions and stimulated a type of merger in which financiers exchanged their own, often overrated, paper for tangible industrial assets. The largest and most successful of these raiders, Slater Walker Securities, engaged in a series of acquisitions, but it was a process which could not continue and, despite a desperate attempt to liquidate its portfolio when markets turned against it in 1973, the company eventually had to be rescued by the Bank of England.

In this type of activity, one can see the beginnings of the development of a market for corporate control. The archetypal weakly managed firm is insulated from direct action by its shareholders by the divorce of ownership from control. They can sell their shares, however; the share price falls and potential raiders see an opportunity to buy the company concerned at a discount to the value of the underlying assets. This triggers the take-over bid. As this mechanism emerged in the 1950s and 1960s, however, its weakness was that the raiders often provided no convincing evidence that their own management skills were sufficiently greater than those of the incumbents to justify the premiums which they paid to gain control of the company. Sears's own performance was persistently disappointing; Slater Walker collapsed. To survive, the market for corporate control had to develop in one of two ways, and in fact it developed in both. One was the emergence of promoters who professed no management ability themselves, but were instrumental in bringing about management changes (arbitrageurs or 'arbs'); the other was the development of companies which were, in a sense, in the business of selling management to undermanaged companies. The first of these was a more common development in the United States. In the UK, the second type of activity was more noticeable, and several companies have made their names and their profits through the business of taking over apparently poorly run firms, the leading examples being Lord Hanson's Hanson Trust and Sir Owen Green's BTR. In recent years, fewer firms have seemed immune to such activity, and the scale and stakes of such take-overs have correspondingly increased. In 1986 there was a series of massive bids, each involving assets of over £1 billion and each fought on the issue of how the target company would best be managed. The targets concerned included such major UK companies as Distillers, Imperial Group, Woolworth, Standard and Chartered Bank, and Pilkingtons.

Although the analogy between the market for corporate control and other markets is an attractive one, there are important differences. The most significant is that the market for corporate control is, by its nature, one which cannot be shared. If I produce a poor product, then I will gradually lose market share, and my competitors will gradually gain it. If I run a company badly, however, the market does not gradually transfer its management to someone else; it leaves me with the monopoly of corporate control until, at the consummation of a take-over bid, it transfers it abruptly and completely. It is this difference in the adjustment mechanism which causes much of the complex regulation which surrounds the process of take-over; and this difference is an important reason why the market for corporate control is less efficient and effective than most other markets.

The indivisibility of corporate control raises a number of issues. Shareholders have an apparent incentive to 'free-ride', to allow others to acquire a controlling interest and incur the costs of bidding and improving management quality while themselves retaining their shares and the full benefit of any profit or share price improvement which may result. Bidders are reluctant to accept less than full ownership of a company they plan to acquire. An opposite consideration, however, is that a minority shareholder has little influence on the affairs of the company, and is afforded little legal protection if a majority shareholder manages it in his own, possibly very divergent, interests.[8] Moreover, the all-or-nothing nature of control invites strategic behaviour by shareholders—or intervening arbitrageurs. A stake that delivers control of a corporation may have a value far in excess of the potential earnings stream to which its owners are entitled, while that stake may have very little value if control can be obtained in other ways. Hence a shareholder's decision may be influenced not only by his estimate of the

[8] A notable analysis of these issues was by Grossman and Hart (1980, 1981), discussed in many of the contributions to this volume.

relative value of his shares under the alternative managements, but also by his assessment of the likely outcome of the bid.

The rules of the Takeover Panel are designed to meet these difficulties. Free-riding is reduced by encouraging bids which are conditional on irrevocable acceptance by shareholders representing 50 per cent of the votes. Thus a bidder need not go ahead unless he is assured of effective control of the company. If he does secure control, he finds that the remaining shareholders will mostly be anxious to tender their holdings to him in order to avoid being locked into a minority position. The scope for strategic activity by shareholders is diminished by limiting the opportunity for discrimination between different shareholders. A company which holds a 30 per cent stake in another is obliged to make an offer for all other shares on the most favourable terms given to any shareholder. If it reaches the 50 per cent mark, it is required to keep the offer open for acceptance by the remaining shareholders. Thus the opportunity for any particular holder to extract rent for a key holding is limited. A shareholder may therefore decide whether to accept a bid or not on merits, without risking loss because other shareholders have chosen to sell.

This detailed regulation of the take-over process is in contrast to the much greater freedom available in the United States, where discrimination between shareholders and the management of strategic stakes are common tactics. The United States has also seen the development of so-called 'poison pills'—devices to protect the interests of company executives, often at the expense of their shareholders. The idea is that you swallow something that is potentially so nasty that it discourages anyone else from swallowing you. The ideal poison pill is one which tastes like sugar in your mouth and cyanide in anyone else's, and American corporate lawyers have invented a number of such devices—for example, rights which become onerous only in the event of a take-over of the company. UK company law, and dominant institutional shareholders, are less sympathetic to these measures, but there are similar tendencies emerging. A simple poison pill is to buy assets which you do not think a predator will want—and if you can buy them at a high price, so much the better. Several companies have restructured their operations in ways in which they would certainly not have done in the ordinary course of business, in order to stave off hostile take-over—Imperial and Distillers, for example, made agreements to dispose of assets at low prices.

The rules of the Takeover Panel have no statutory force, but the need for companies, and particularly their advisers, to gain continued access to the facilities of financial markets ensures that public defiance of them would not be contemplated by major firms. They do not, however, offer any protection against concealed breaches of the rules. The public reputation of the market for corporate control will take some time to recover from the evidence of irregularities in the conduct of Guinness's bid for Distillers. Two companies—Argyll and Guinness—had made share exchange offers for Distillers. It appears that senior managers for Guinness used company funds to provide secret guarantees against loss to certain purchasers of Guinness shares. This artificially inflated the price of the shares and, since the relative value of the two bids depended on the relative share prices of the two would-be acquirers, contributed to Guinness's eventual success. The revelation of these events has stimulated already developing criticism of the operation of the market for corporate control. As these doubts emerged, two major bids—those of Lloyds Bank for Standard Chartered and of Dixons for Woolworth—failed despite substantial premiums to the price before the bid, and BTR was forced by hostile reaction to withdraw its offer for Pilkingtons.

Yet, at first sight, the results of recent conglomerate acquisition seem all to the good. A number of poorly managed companies have been acquired by well managed organizations with a track record of successful diversification. Not only has this increased efficiency in the industries affected, but the example has had beneficial effects elsewhere: P & O, for instance, is a company which has not in fact been taken over but where the threat that it might be has led to substantial management reorganization and improvements in performance.

Yet many remain sceptical about the value of this activity. There are two groups of issues raised. The first involves doubts about the underlying effect of conglomerate ownership on productive efficiency. Other critics allege that the market for corporate control, more or less unique to Britain and the United States, is too expensive and inefficient a means of achieving changes in management structure and performance which could be—and in other countries are—more appropriately accomplished in other ways. We consider each of these questions in turn.

A new owner may increase profits by reducing costs, or by raising prices relative to costs. The first will generally represent a real gain in efficiency. The second may be accomplished by taking fuller advantage of market power, or by retreating from competitive markets and selling to soft customers, such as the government. This may be remunerative for shareholders, but the gains are directly at the public expense and the consequences for industrial structure are adverse. It is clear that conglomerate raiders have squeezed out greater profit from both lower costs and higher prices, and the relative significance of the two is by no means easy for the outsider to detect. The principal control mechanism deployed by companies such as Hanson and BTR is the imposition of tight financial control on the activities of their subsidiaries. Business units are set profitability targets with short time frames, and performance is monitored closely in relation to these targets. There is obviously a danger that this encourages short-term decision-making and inhibits the development of new products and markets which are essential to long-run success. Hanson and BTR have, in the main, concentrated their activities in relatively mature businesses where these considerations are less important. But the management of GEC—a voracious acquirer in the 1960s and a long-term adherent of a similar style of management—has been increasingly criticized for its lack of strategic vision.

Turning now to the second group of criticisms, the direct costs of the market for corporate control, in fees and commissions associated with the process of take-over, are very substantial. In addition to these costs, a successful bid will usually need to be made at a premium to the market price. In some recent major bids—such as those for Standard and Chartered Bank and Woolworth—premiums of around 50 per cent have proved inadequate to gain control of the target company. It follows from this that the gap between potential and actual performance may have to become large before a successful bid is a likely outcome.

There may also be grounds for concern at the long-term results of the market for corporate control. The groupings which result will exhibit no particular industrial logic, if their only common characteristic is a history of weak management. This may not matter if the acquiring firm is ready to dispose of units which do not fit in with its business strategy, and some conglomerates do this. But some of the recent take-over targets have themselves been the—now atrophied—creations of an earlier generation of over-ambitious managers. The market for corporate control may be intrinsically self-exhausting—*quis custodiet custodes?*

The market for corporate control is one in which take-over is the principal discipline on weak or lazy management. As such, it performs an important and useful function, but it does so in a way which raises real problems for both business and public policy. These problems are sufficiently substantial for it to be desirable to seek alternatives. We return to this issue in the final section.

6. Mergers and Merger Policy: An Assessment

Evidence on the performance of mergers is derived from two main sources: the effect on accounting profits and the impact on share prices. It is possible to compare the level of profits in the years immediately subsequent to merger with those of the two merging companies immediately prior to it. In the main, such studies undertaken in the UK have given little support to the view that merger enhances profitability. Hughes (this volume) describes the basis of this evidence.

The considerable difficulties of undertaking such analysis should be noted. The proper comparison is, of course, not with the pre-merger performance of the merging firms but rather with what the post-merger performance would have been if the merger had not occurred. Merger may have been precipitated by the anticipation of changes in performance, either on the part of acquirer or acquiree. The period chosen for comparison may be short—in which case it may give a misleading impression of the effects of the merger, especially since acquisition and reorganization costs will occur early while benefits may take longer to accrue—or it may be long, in which case factors other than the merger itself are likely to be more significant influences on performance. Finally, acquisition itself will distort accounting ratios. Quite apart from the difficulties in interpreting these over the transitional period itself, it is common practice for firms taking control of acquisitions to take a conservative view of the value of the assets they have bought, with the result that profits in the last pre-acquisition period are reduced and earnings in subsequent accounting periods enhanced by corresponding amounts. For these reasons, increasing attention has been given to assessments of how mergers influence share prices.

It has always been clear that a bid increases the value of the shares of the acquired firm. The option of selling their shares or exchanging them for those of the acquirer is one which was available to shareholders of the target company before the merger was ever mooted, and it was one which they had, implicitly, declined. It follows that some bid premium is required to consummate any merger. If the combined firm was worth no more than the sum of the parts, however, this premium would be offset by a corresponding fall in the market value of the acquirer. The analysis of Franks and Harris (this volume) suggests that this is not in fact so.

Since stock markets are forward-looking, and current prices anticipate future growth in earnings and assets, this approach avoids many of the difficulties associated with accounting data. Market expectation may, however, be wrong and markets may over-react to new developments. If the sceptical view of the profitability of mergers is the correct one, then it would be consistent with a view that managers tend to over-estimate the opportunities which they yield—and it is easy to see very human reasons why they should tend to take an excessively optimistic view of their own capacity to run ever larger and more diversified organizations more effectively than those who are doing so at the moment.

It need not follow that they are effective at transmitting this optimism to the stock market, but the possibility that market judgements of the profitability of merger are also mistaken must be considered. Franks and Harris show that acquirers typically *have* outperformed the market in the period immediately prior to acquisition. This outperformance is not continued after the merger but it is not turned into subsequent under-performance either. The implication is that the timing, or possibility, of merger may be influenced by share price behaviour but the gains in value associated with it are sustained.

7. The Future of Merger Policy

We have described above how the Tebbit guidelines of 1984 largely identified merger policy with competition, and thus drew policy back from a diverse set of concerns that had occupied the authorities in previous years. What exceptions should there be to this—to what extent should issues other than competition figure in policy? Equally, could more explicit guidance be given to the assessment of competitive impact, and could the two stages of policy—selection for reference and adjudication by the Commission—be brought closer together? We consider each in turn.

It is difficult to argue that, if the process of public scrutiny of mergers exists at all, it should be exclusively confined to competition matters. Almost all countries have, for example, some process of foreign investment review, and issues of concentration or decentralization of corporate power, or the restriction of financial dealings by persons of dubious character, are legitimate matters of public concern. It is, however, reasonable to ask whether the institutions of competition policy are the most appropriate means of handling these questions.

Several merger references have been made principally, it seems, because of reservations about the activities of senior managers of the acquiring firm. The reputation of Lonrho's chief executive, 'Tiny' Rowland, was a central if implicit issue in the consideration of its attempts to buy House of Fraser, for example. The Commission is an unsatisfactory vehicle for dealing with such a problem—if problem it is. If particular individuals are not suitable persons to run public companies, the issue is relevant to the companies they already manage, not only to ones they might acquire. The Commission was not established to engage in trials of character, and its own embarrassment at being given such a role is evident in a number of relevant reports.

The appraisal of foreign investment has traditionally been dealt with primarily by giving or withholding consents which were required for foreign currency transactions; but these are no longer necessary. Some references have been made—as, for example, with the proposed purchase of Davy Corporation by the American company Enserch or the possible acquisition of the Royal Bank of Scotland by the Hong Kong and Shanghai Bank—in which the desirability of foreign ownership was the main issue. The Bank of England has made clear that it would need to approve of any purchases of a British clearing bank—there is some basis for this in the powers which it enjoys under the Banking Act, but in practice the informal exercise of authority by the Bank is sufficient to achieve its desired result. Several privatized companies have been established with a 'golden share', through which the government could directly veto a take-over of which it disapproved, while in other cases the articles of association have been written to limit the proportion of the equity which can be held by shareholders who are not UK residents.

It is not apparent to us that the nationality of the ultimate shareholders of UK public companies is in fact a matter of great public importance, but it appears that there are many people who think that it is. The mechanisms by which that concern can be expressed seem to be many and incoherent, and the criteria for assessing the basis and legitimacy of the concern undefined. It would be better to have a single procedure which spelt out the public interest issues involved but, until that procedure is devised, it may be that the Commission should continue to play a role. It may even be that review by the Commission should be that single procedure.

It follows that the basis of reference should, as the Tebbit guidelines suggest, be primarily but not exclusively the effect of a merger on competition. In cases where there are public policy issues which do not involve competition—and we are clear that there are such cases—it is desirable to develop alternative mechanisms for review or for the government to accept direct responsibility for political judgement.

What then of mergers affecting competition? Fairburn (this volume) examines the Commission's analysis of horizontal mergers. Although combined market share of the merging parties provides some guidance as to the Commission's verdict—with adverse findings starting at around 40 per cent—other less readily quantifiable factors complicate the picture. Thus the Commission may find market shares give an inaccurate picture of firms' abilities to compete in the industry or ignore important factors such as the ease of entry into an industry or the countervailing power of buyers.

From the point of view of predictability, this is unfortunate. In our discussion of the United States merger guidelines we suggested that there was a tension between the needs of sophistication and predictability. In our opinion there is little to be lost by concentrating on the latter objective and eschewing as a general matter sophisticated trade-offs. Simple standards at the less tolerant end of the Commission's recent spectrum would thus be adopted, although we concede that there is room for debate on details (and on how to extend such principles to non-horizontal mergers). An advantage of this approach is that it enables the bulk of attention to be focused on the initial selection decision, as in the United States. Over time, we would expect few references to be made, and those that were to involve genuinely difficult cases where some sort of trade-off *à la* Williamson would be unavoidable. The overall emphasis would be to admit complications only exceptionally, not as a matter of course.

Alternative recommendations are made by George and by Littlechild in this volume. George prefers a widely canvassed reversal of the burden of proof. The emphasis would then be on the proponents of a merger to establish that their proposal was desirable. This would be part of a regime more sceptical to the merits of merger, involving more reference to the Commission. While sympathetic to the underlying feeling, we suggest a rather different direction below. By contrast, Littlechild is favourably disposed to the merger process. Drawing on a theme evident in the Commission's recent reports, his merger policy would limit mergers only in industries characterized by barriers to new entry which are almost entirely equated with government restrictions on competition. The validity of the argument turns on the speed and direction of corrective competitive processes, and on the transitional costs of higher prices and lower efficiency until these pressures have become fully effective.

What then of mergers that raise few competition issues—in particular, of those that reflect the workings of the market for corporate control? A policy that stresses competition in its criteria for reference will make such acquisitions easier if they are proposed by companies which are not directly in the same business, and will encourage acquirers to minimize the competitive implications of their activities. Swift (this volume) describes how this was the—appropriate—procedure in the contested bids for Distillers and Imperial Tobacco.

It is easy to see reasons why the corporate economy might be subject to excessive levels of merger activity. There is a substantial body of descriptive literature which argues that the managers of the modern corporation, who have only a limited equity stake in their company, are primarily interested in goals other than profitability. Their status, prestige, and remuneration will be influenced more by the size and rate of growth of the company than its rate of return or the value of its shares. Sometimes this is developed in models in which the firm is assumed to maximize objectives other than profit, such as growth or revenues, as described by Helm (this volume). In response, it may be argued that the divorce of ownership and control is often exaggerated and that whatever managers might like to do if given a free hand, the constraints imposed by competitive capital and product markets oblige them to follow a course which can differ only very little from profit maximization.

We feel that a somewhat sceptical view of the motives for merger, and the value of merger activity, is consistent with the evidence we have summarized. The recurrence of merger mania, the disappointing impact on post-merger profitability, the slightly more favourable verdict of the stock market, and the repeated presentation to the Commission of cases which bear the stamp of *ex post* rationalization—all suggest that managers have a very human tendency to over-estimate their own capability to run ever larger organizations. Shareholders individually have little capacity or incentive to constrain such activity. The system is ingrained, and acquisitions are seen to be an accepted reward for good managers. Furthermore there is a substantial financial services business encouraging mergers. Considerable resources are expended in directing management attention away from the areas in which their firms currently operate, toward ones they might occupy in future. There is limited pressure in the other direction, and what there is is provided by the threat of take-over itself.

In the face of this it would seem entirely appropriate that public policy puts obstacles in the path of merger. Review by the Commission constitutes one such obstacle. At one level this seems desirable. Although it is necessary for a firm to explain the reasons for a merger in the offer document and in raising capital, such explanations to shareholders rarely rise above the level of banality and platitude. The obligation to provide a full public interest rationale is attractive and certain of the arguments against it spurious. If there is compelling industrial logic to a merger, it is unlikely that this will evaporate over the 6-month period of an inquiry.

Nevertheless there are substantial costs to this type of public review, and it is at least questionable whether current institutions—designed for competition policy—are fitted to perform it. Extension of such a system—the opposite of what has happened in recent years—would reinforce these problems. (See George (this volume) for contrary opinions on this general issue.) We take the view that there are gains, in terms of clarifying competition policy, from not extending the merger review process in this way, and that such an extension would highlight the deficiencies of this approach.

The general issue of corporate control does, however, deserve substantial attention. There are other industrial economies, more successful than the UK, where the incidence of merger is much lower and where hostile take-overs are unknown. Other means of corporate control are available, and attention should be given to what these are, and how they might be developed with existing UK institutions. As a preliminary to this, we should note the underlying cause of the problem: the increase in the separation between shareholders and managers of large companies. Few large companies now have any substantial individual shareholders. They have been replaced by financial institutions and while there is now considerable attention applied to the revival of the small individual shareholder, growth in such holdings should, if anything, make the matter worse, not better. For the managers of British Telecom, one powerful shareholder has been replaced by many powerless ones. The sense in which this increases the accountability of these managers is far from apparent, the more so since the size and position of BT renders it effectively immune from take-over.

For institutional shareholders, the principal means of indicating disapproval of the management performance of a company is to reduce their holdings of its shares. This will tend to depress the price and make the company more attractive to a predator: if a bid emerges, dissatisfied shareholders will be likely to accept. If effective alternatives are to be found, it is clear that institutions must play a more active part than is implied by the mere signalling of thumbs up or down when their views are canvassed by predators.

The market for corporate control is active in Britain and the United States; Australian and more recently New Zealand entrepreneurs have also been vigorous participants. But in most industrial countries—even ones with a developed stock market, such as Japan, France, Germany, or Switzerland—the hostile take-over bid is legally impracticable or virtually unknown in practice. There the relationship between financial institutions and industry is typically close and continuing, so that action to remedy managerial weaknesses may be taken in a more informal way, and perhaps at an earlier stage. There are several ways in which alternative mechanisms might be developed in the UK which could embody this practice, and so complement, or perhaps ultimately replace, the market for corporate control.

One is direct institutional pressure on company management for change in policies or in personnel. There are certainly cases where this has occurred and it is possible that there are more, unpublicized, instances of this kind of activity. But in the main, institutional investors in Britain do not see this as one of their roles and indeed have little competence to perform it. Nor do they have an incentive to do so. It is unusual for the shareholding of a British financial institution to exceed 5 per cent of the issued share capital—the level at which it must be publicly declared. (The Prudential, the largest institutional investor, owns around this fraction of a wide range of companies.) It follows that over 95 per cent of the benefits of intervention to improve managerial performance would accrue to others. It would be possible to reduce the opportunity for free-riding by other shareholders if the financial institution were to build up a larger stake in the company. There have been instances of this, but the more common response to perceptions of inadequate performance is to sell shares, not to buy them. Non-executive directors, acting either as representatives of particular shareholders or exercising their own responsibilities, may act as a check on management—advising, warning, and, in the last resort, dismissing executive officers. This does occur, but rarely. Many boards are wary about acquiring directors who seem likely to be too independent. Non-executive directors are in practice generally appointed by the executives, and often themselves executive directors of other companies: a sense of self-preservation may make response less vigorous than it might otherwise have been. But the mechanism is one which could be strengthened. One formal procedure for doing so is the German institution of the supervisory board, explicitly charged with scrutiny of the performance of senior corporate managers.

These alternatives to the market for corporate control—shareholder pressure and non-executive action—are complementary rather than competing developments. Each will be more effective if supported by the possibility of the other. To extend them will require changes in City practice and possibly also in company law and in Takeover Panel rules. This should be an important element in the current review of competition policy but it is likely that it is the Bank of England, rather than the existing agencies of competition policy, which will need to bear the main burden of implementation. The objective is to define a closer relationship between companies and those who finance them than is required by passive portfolio management. In few, if any, other countries, is this relationship so tenuous; and there may be reason to think that Britain's industrial performance has suffered from it.

We have argued that the market for corporate control is a decidedly imperfect mechanism for imposing discipline on weak management—expensive and inefficient. But it is the principal mechanism which currently exists. If policy is to restrain such mergers further, it should do so only if other ways of achieving managerial accountability are fostered—and the restraint should proceed only to the extent that this nurture proves successful. We have described what such mechanisms might be—the strengthening of non-executive directors, the more active involvement of institutional shareholders, the possible development of audit committees and supervisory boards. Mere reversal of the burden of proof would not affect mergers motivated by corporate control considerations much. The only proposition on which both parties to the BTR–Pilkington bid were agreed was that whether the bid succeeded or failed would have a substantial impact on the company's behaviour and performance. The dispute was over whether that impact was positive or negative.

We could wish to spare the Monopolies and Mergers Commission the job of arbitration between alternative managerial teams in these circumstances. Anyone who would like to take on that job should not be trusted to perform it. Resolution through the stock market involves the weighting of many diverse opinions, canvassed vigorously by the competing parties. It is probably the least bad means of settling the issue. Rather than seek a better means of settling contested take-over bids, we should try to create conditions in which they are rare events.

1

The Impact of Merger: A Survey of Empirical Evidence for the UK

ALAN HUGHES*

1. Introduction

This paper draws together the results of recent empirical research on the impact of merger on market structure and economic performance in the UK.[1] It concentrates almost exclusively on the post-war period and pays relatively more attention to work not covered in the 1978 Green Paper on Monopolies and Mergers Policy (Department of Prices and Consumer Protection (1978)). The discussion which follows is organized in four sections. In Section 2, possible approaches to assessing the impact of mergers on market structure and company performance and their implications for economic welfare are briefly set out. In Section 3, the principal characteristics of merger activity in the UK are described. Section 4 looks at the relationship between mergers and concentration and diversification as indicators of structural change, whilst Section 5 concentrates on the impact of merger upon corporate performance. The final section draws the discussion of structure and performance effects together and makes some brief points relevant to competition policy.

---

* Currently Acting Head of the Department of Applied Economics, and a Fellow of Sidney Sussex College, University of Cambridge.

The author is grateful to Professor Wynne Godley, Director of the Department of Applied Economics at Cambridge (DAE), for supporting research associated with this paper and to Richard Parkin of Sidney Sussex College for research assistance.

[1] Direct attention is not paid to the determinants of mergers. General surveys which cover this aspect of the literature may be found in Steiner (1975), Hughes, Mueller, and Singh (1980), and Hindley (1972). Specific analyses of the determinants of the time series pattern of merger include King (this volume), Nelson (1959), Geroski (1984), Melicher, Ledolter, and D'Antonio (1983), and Holland and Myers (1979).

2. Frameworks for Assessing the Impact of Merger

The most common approach to assessing the impact of merger upon social welfare is the Trade-off Model (Williamson (1968)). This is based upon a static, partial equilibrium trade-off, of allocative efficiency losses arising from merger-related increases in market power, against any merger-related cost efficiency gains arising from changes in the scale or scope of corporate activity. This has its most natural application in cases of horizontal merger but is in principle extendable to vertical or diversifying merger. There are well-known problems with this approach. In practice, the problem of the second best, divergences between private and social benefits and costs, the exclusion from consideration of distributional issues, and the need to consider possible knock-on effects inducing further mergers must all be taken into account before reaching welfare conclusions. (See, for instance, Cowling *et al.* (1980).) Moreover, the static nature of the trade-off and the implicit assumption of a fully employed self-equilibrating economy which lies behind it have often focused attention away from explicit consideration of many of the issues of investment, technical change, export performance, and regional and national employment effects which so much exercise open-economy policy-makers in this area (Hughes, Mueller, and Singh (1980)). The result has been a preoccupation with the impact of merger on concentration as a proxy indicator for monopoly power (and hence allocative inefficiency) on the one hand, and with studies of the impact of merger on private profitability as a proxy for cost efficiency gains on the other. Neither are ideal indicators. Profitability changes are particularly ambiguous in this respect, since even within the terms of the static trade-off model itself, they potentially incorporate both monopoly power and cost efficiency effects. Limited conclusions can nonetheless be drawn, if from some other source monopoly power changes can be independently identified, and if merging firms' profit changes can be normalized by the experience of non-merging firms within the industry. If all firms in an industry benefit from the merger-induced price changes, profitability differences should reflect changes in efficiency. On these terms, we can interpret the merger's effect on *normalized* profitability as the effect on efficiency.[2] When independent information on market power effects is added, we can begin to make welfare statements. Table 1.1 shows the possibilities.

If increases in monopoly power are separately identified, a trade-off is necessary to deduce welfare losses only where normalized profitability rises. Equally, when normalized profitability falls, a trade-off is only necessary to

[2] In practice, of course, not all firms in an industry group may benefit equally from market power effects, and individual mergers may involve vertical and diversifying, as well as horizontal, components. The spirit of the argument remains clear enough, however.

Table 1.1. Social welfare (ignoring distributional issues)

		NORMALIZED PROFITABILITY		
		Raised	No change	Reduced
MONOPOLY POWER	Raised	?	–	–
	No change	+	0	–
	Reduced	+	+	?

Notes: + Improved.

– Worsened.

? Ambiguous (trade-off required).

0 No change.

deduce welfare losses if monopoly power can be shown to have fallen.

This raises the question of identifying monopoly power effects. By far the most usual indicator of monopoly power used in this connection is some measure of market concentration, and the impact of merger is usually assessed in terms of its relationship to concentration change. Evidence on these market structure effects is discussed in Section 4, along with a discussion of the links between them and monopoly power. An assessment of the corporate performance aspects of the merger trade-off is then presented in Section 5.

The trade-off approach may be contrasted with another, the basic proposition of which is that '. . . the control of corporations may constitute a valuable asset; that this asset exists independent of any interest in either economies of scale or monopoly profits; that an active market for corporate control exists; and that a great many mergers are probably the result of the successful workings of this special market' (Manne (1965) p. 112). Management teams compete for the right to control corporate assets and operating efficiency is ensured by a natural selection mechanism in which the threat and act of take-over by raiders ensure the survival of the fittest teams. Poor past performance due to inefficiency or abuse of managerial discretion leads to weak share prices; potential raiders see the opportunity to alter policies and make capital gains as share prices respond to their improved management of the victim's assets (Marris (1964), Alchian and Kessel (1962), Meade (1968)).

For the stock market selection process to work in this way, a number of conditions must be fulfilled. In particular, share prices should reflect the relative expected profitability of firms; raiders should typically be motivated by the desire to change non-shareholder welfare-maximizing policies and be able to obtain a sufficient pay-off to make their activity worth while.

These conditions may not be realized. Whilst the market pricing mechanism may be 'efficient' in the sense of responding rapidly to changes in information for instance (Keane (1983)), there is not much to suggest that share price movements are systematically related to the current, past, or subsequent underlying performance variables of companies, or to longer-run equilibrium considerations, rather than to those of short-run disequilibrium (Nerlove (1968), Little and Rayner (1966), Shiller (1981), Summers (1986)). This leaves considerable scope for take-overs based on speculative and other motives where corporate control changes hands because of differences of information, or of opinion about the accuracy of stock market valuations, between sellers and purchasers of control, rather than because of proposed changes in management objectives or operating efficiency (Gort (1969), Hughes, Mueller, and Singh (1980), Grossman and Hart (1981)). It also leaves plenty of scope for promoters and arbitrageurs to attempt to manipulate, and benefit from, changes in stock prices associated with take-overs, or the threat of them, in a way unconnected with underlying performance variables (Boesky (1985), Markham (1955)).[3] As one early stock market observer noted: 'Since property here exists in the form of stock, its movement and transfer become purely a result of gambling on the stock exchange, where the little fish are swallowed by the sharks and the lambs by the stock exchange wolves' (Marx (1971)). Equally, mature managerially controlled corporations whose preference for growth may be characterized by the use of a lower discount rate than the market as a whole, will, it has been argued, be faced with a sea of undervalued take-over opportunities (Mueller (1969)). They may then initiate take-overs not to benefit shareholders but to satisfy their own empire-building ambitions (Rhoades (1985), Marris (1964)). Moreover, it has been argued that this 'pursuit of growth may be self-reinforcing; the more managers pursue this objective, the more other managers feel they must conform . . . [thus] rather than deviant managerial behavior being driven out by stockholder welfare-maximizing behaviour, the so-called "deviant" behaviour has more

[3] For another non-standard merger motivation model, see Cable (1977). Here it is argued that, in the case of diversifying merger especially, the search for alternative production possibilities (to allow a company to dissociate itself from an industry or product life cycle) may lead a single bidder to value more highly the investment opportunity information embodied in potential targets than those targets' shareholders themselves do (for example, because the target's own optimal investment programme does not involve using up these opportunities or because the acquiring company perceives possible further search gains on the basis of the information embodied in the targets).

likely driven out the other' (Marris and Mueller (1980) p. 42).[4]

Even where take-overs are stockholder welfare-maximizing in intent, and stock prices are an efficient guide to such action, failures in the market for corporate control may still occur because of transactions cost considerations and because acquiring companies may not be able to capture for themselves all the benefit of the raid.

Disciplinary raids are not costless; the price of identifying mismanagement and the transactions costs of correcting it through take-over can be high so that there will always be some margin of management discretion. The greater the discretionary benefit of control, the more rivalrous the market for control may be, the more raided management may resist, and the higher transactions costs may become. Indeed, since contested take-overs with higher associated legal and advisory costs are more likely to occur in the case of large than small bids (Newbould (1970)), these costs may be greater for larger 'managerial' companies giving more discretion just where it needs to be most curbed. To the extent that the costs of identifying mismanagement are lower for raids within the same industry and the likelihood of contests therefore greater (Halpern (1983)), then where monopolistic structures exist, the costs of imposing discipline will be relatively high, since either the companies involved will be within the same industry but typically large, or the bid will involve an outsider with higher costs of information gathering.

The sums involved are not negligible. A failed diversifying contested bid for a major company in 1986 is said to have cost the raider £54 million in advisers' and other bid fees (Jay (1986)). These transactions costs are in part a function of defensive take-over tactics which are designed to raise either the pre- or post-acquisition costs of gaining control; such methods are well developed in the US and are spreading to the UK. 'Shark-repellent' constitutional arrangements to protect existing directors by staggered elections to the board, or particular voting schemes for bid approvals, 'golden parachutes' to raise the costs of firing incumbent management, and either counter-bidding against the raider, seeking a 'white knight' to contest the unwanted bid, or raiding a third party (Greer (1986)) all throw cost-increasing sand into the works. Whether this is a virtue or a vice depends

---

[4] This hypothesis is not without its critics either. Thus, Hindley (1972) argues that it would appear that the most likely victims of managerial raids would, because of their market valuation, be managerial companies themselves, and therefore auxiliary hypotheses are needed such as that the high capital and transactions costs involved in acquiring the biggest managerially controlled corporations grant them relative immunity. However, this assumes that owner-controlled companies are necessarily more 'efficient', whatever their growth–profit combination. Moreover, the important point remains that the objective of a managerial raid would not be to pursue shareholder-orientated activity after merger. So long as there is slack in the market for corporate control as a result of the factors discussed next, then scope for this sort of behaviour exists. (See also Helm (this volume) and Hughes and Singh (1987).)

upon how genuine raids are from a disciplinary point of view. It also depends upon the terms which shareholders extract from top executives in return for offering them this sort of protection from job loss through take-over. Thus, in principle, many of these devices could be used as part of an overall remuneration and conditions package for the managers which emphasized whatever incentive structure the active shareholders desire (Jensen and Meckling (1976), Knoeber (1986), Hirschey (1986)). This, however, may be expecting rather a lot, given the current structure of governance in the modern corporation in which managers play a leading role in determining their own remuneration and in selecting outside directors to serve on corporate boards (Herman (1981)).

In this respect the growth in importance in the UK of financial institutions as shareholders assumes great significance. For it may be argued that on the one hand they are able to exercise discipline from within companies without the need for raiding, whilst on the other they may impose shareholders' interests as a key factor when bids occur. There are, however, limitations on their potential role. First, with dispersed shareholdings it may not pay a single institution to bear the costs of monitoring and disciplining, the benefits of which accrue to all. The bigger an institution's shareholding, the less of a problem this is, but there remain difficulties of co-ordinating action across shareholders. Even amongst financial institutions, different views about possible, or appropriate, remedies may exist, as well as different philosophies about taking direct action (Cosh, Hughes, and Singh (1986)). Finally, institutions themselves are subject to market and regulatory forces stipulating required portfolio performance which may mean that short-term financial factors dominate their response to raids, in much the same way as other stockholders. Since the incentive to sell out in a bid is lower the lower the transactions costs associated with subsequent portfolio readjustment, and since the effect of Big Bang will be to lower these costs for institutions, they may be even more likely to 'churn' their portfolios.

The market for corporate control may also fail where inefficiency is combined with substantial owner-control at the smaller end of the spectrum of firm sizes. If the valuation placed by owner-managers upon their shares exceeds the marginal valuation ruling in the market, there will be a premium to be paid to effect control which may vary from company to company without any necessary connection with the extent of deviations from value-maximizing policies. As far as small companies are concerned, it means that it may be (for example, in the case of majority ownership) impossible to obtain control, or very costly in the face of a hostile board with large holdings (Davies and Kuehn (1977)). The upshot of these arguments is that effective disciplinary action might be confined to the medium-size ranges of companies.

In addition to market failure problems due to transactions costs, it has also been argued that the incentive structure in bids may lead to too few bids from the point of view of disciplining management (Grossman and Hart (1980)). If each of the shareholders in the target firm in a raid believes that an individual decision to sell out will not prevent the bidder from gaining effective control, then there is for each of them an incentive to hang on to their equity as minority shareholders in the post-bid situation and 'free-ride' on the stock price gains following the new management's efficiency improvements. This prevents the raider from reaping all the benefits, and, in the limit, could prevent successful raids altogether if sufficient shareholders hang on for the free ride.

The implication of this argument is that, *ceteris paribus*, the level of merger activity will be less than is warranted since the private return to the raider is less than the overall return which is split between the raiders and the free-riders. On the other hand it may be argued that if minority rights of sellers are not protected then partial bids (for example, for 51 per cent) will occur followed by exploitation of control at the expense of the remaining minority shareholders. This may occur whether the incumbent management are value-maximizers or not, since in effect the buyer gains complete control whilst paying only half the full purchase price. This could lead to too many 'undesirable' bids, in the sense that they incur transactions costs but merely redistribute wealth between the raider and the oppressed minority rather than create net social value (Yarrow (1985)).

The force of each of these arguments depends upon the institutional and legal constraints within which bidders and potential free-riders must operate during and after the bid process.[5] The problem in principle is how to ensure that there are costs imposed on free-riding minority interests whilst ensuring that there is no undue oppression of minority shareholders after partial bids, or unequal treatment of shareholders in the process of the bid itself. In the institutional context of the UK at least, there are grounds for thinking that the free-rider problem is not a serious deterrent inhibiting the level of merger activity, whilst there is some attempt to deter partial oppressive bids (Davies (1976), Yarrow (1985), Johnston (1980)). In any event, the idea that free-riding has seriously restricted the overall level of take-over activity does not seem very convincing in the face of the huge take-over waves of the post-war period discussed in the following section.

There is thus little doubt that an active market in corporate control exists in the UK. Assessing its impact involves examining not only the change in

---

[5] Thus, corporate charter rules may allow raiders to internalize some of the free-riders' gains by oppressing, or diluting, minority shareholders' interests in the post-bid situation (Grossman and Hart (1980)), or raiders may use two-tier bids with premiums for early acceptance etc. (Brudney and Chirelstein (1978)). The latter are, however, ruled out by the City Takeover Code in the UK (Johnston (1980)).

corporate performance following merger inherent in the trade-off analysis, but also an examination of the selection process itself in terms of the pre-merger real, financial, and share price characteristics of groups of merging and non-merging firms and of the institutional framework within which bids take place. This evidence is surveyed in Section 5 which also draws, where appropriate, on the insights into merger impacts which follow from the other approaches outlined in this section.

3. The Extent and Character of Merger Activity

There are a number of ways of measuring the extent of merger activity. The simplest count the absolute numbers of companies disappearing through merger, or sum the assets, sales, or employment of those companies, or the amounts paid in carrying out the mergers in which they are involved. For comparisons over time, there are obvious shortcomings in relying on current price values of, for example, sales, so deflated series are needed. If the size of the economy is changing then it also would be preferable to express merger activity relative to appropriate population totals. Moreover, for some purposes, for instance comparing the relative importance of growth by merger and growth by investment in new plant and equipment, it would be preferable to measure expenditure on mergers as a percentage of, say, total uses of corporate funds, or of total internal and external expenditure on assets. It is possible to construct series on each of these bases for parts of the economy, especially for industrial and commercial companies, or manufacturing and distribution, and for parts of the post-war period, but there is no long-run comparable series on any of them for the whole economy. Nevertheless, although the series chosen may affect the particular year in which merger activity peaked, the broad picture which emerges is clear enough.

MERGERS 1945–73

Merger activity took off in the late 1950s and early 1960s compared with the previous decade (Brooks and Smith (1963), Bull and Vice (1961), Mennel (1962), Moon (1968)). It accelerated further from 1967 onwards, culminating in twin peaks of activity in the late 1960s and early 1970s. In the peak years 1967–73, the spread of activity encompassed both the financial and non-financial sectors and was at least as intensive as anything previously experienced in the UK (Hannah (1976)). Of the top 200 UK manufacturing companies in 1964, 39 were acquired or merged by 1969, and of the top 200 in 1969, a further 22 were acquired or merged by 1972

(Hughes (1976)). GEC acquired two of its principal rivals, AEI and English Electric; Rowntree Mackintosh and British Leyland were formed; and the Industrial Reorganization Corporation (IRC), as a government agency charged with promoting structural change and efficiency, was directly involved in a promotional or advisory role in 22 mergers involving around £1 billion of net assets between 1967 and 1970 (Cosh, Hughes, and Singh (1980)). Extensive activity occurred in engineering, vehicles, food, drink, textiles, in paper, printing, and publishing, and in distribution (Department of Prices and Consumer Protection (1978), Cowling *et al.* (1980), Cosh, Hughes, and Singh (1980)). There were major banking mergers after 1968 which resulted in a reduction in the number of clearing banks from 11 to 5 and a series of mergers linking clearing and merchant banks (Aaronovitch and Sawyer (1975a)). Mergers were in the main horizontal in direction.

Table 1.2. Expenditure upon, numbers of, and financing of acquisitions and mergers

Period	Within the UK					
	No.	Expenditure (£m.)	Expenditure in 1962 stock market prices[b] (£m.)	Expenditure as a percentage of gross fixed capital formation[c]	Sales of subsidiaries as a percentage of all acquisitions and mergers	
					No.	Expenditure
1967–73[d,e]	954	1 377	822	42.0	–	–
1969–73	988	1 388	777	38.6	21.6	13.0
1974–81	459	947	426	7.7	26.4	16.1
1982–6	529	6 130	933	23.8	29.6	19.4
1982	463	2 206	592	12.1	35.4	36.4
1983	447	2 343	497	12.9	31.8	18.6
1984	568	5 474	976	24.4	29.9	20.5
1985	474	7 090	1 044	31.1	28.3	11.2
1986	695	13 535	1 576	45.2	22.7	10.4

[a]Overseas acquisition activity is likely to be understated because it excludes acquisitions and mergers overseas by existing overseas affiliates and subsidiaries of UK companies, and because Press coverage of overseas activity, on which the data are based, is less full than that of domestic activity.
[b]Actual expenditure (usually the stock market value of the successful offer) deflated by the FT Actuaries Industrial Ordinary Share Index, 1962 = 100.
[c]Actual expenditure as a percentage of gross domestic fixed capital formation at current prices adjusted for leasing.
[d]The first 4 rows are annual averages for the periods shown. Data for 1967–9 are not strictly comparable with data for 1969–86. See note e.

From 1967 to 1969 inclusive, of all proposed mergers falling within the scope of the competition policy authorities, the proportion that were horizontal varied between 79 per cent and 91 per cent by value, and between 80 per cent and 86 per cent by number (Gribbin (1974)). In the period 1970–3 they accounted for 74 per cent by number and 65 per cent by value (Graham (1979)). In many cases mergers had a major impact on the financial structure of merging companies, as the means of financing successful bids tended to raise gearing substantially (Cosh, Hughes, and Singh (1980), Meeks (1977)). Although there is not much evidence bearing directly on the issue, it appears that foreign acquisitions played relatively little part in this wave which was mirrored in an intensification of merger activity in nearly all the major industrial nations (Hughes and Singh (1980)).

by industrial and commercial companies at home and abroad, 1967–86

Percentages of expenditure accounted for by:			Abroad[a]			Total		
Cash	Issues of ordinary	Issues of fixed interest	No.	Expenditure (£m.)	Expenditure in 1962 stock market prices (£m.)	No.	Expenditure (£m.)	Expenditure in 1962 stock market prices (£m.)
–	–	–	–	–	–	–	–	–
30.8	49.2	20.0	66	95.4	54.9	1 054	1 483	832
61.8	33.1	5.1	50	341.4	135.2	509	1 289	561
42.8	47.1	10.2	76	1 247.7	191.4	605	7 377	1 124
58.1	31.8	10.1	95	770.3	206.3	558	2 976	797
43.8	53.8	2.4	58	387.1	82.1	505	2 730	579
53.8	33.6	12.6	74	816.4	145.7	642	6 290	1 122
40.3	52.3	7.4	64	931.5	134.6	538	8 022	1 159
17.9	63.8	18.3	89	3 333.1	388.2	784	16 868	1 965

[a]Data on a consistent basis are not available for the sub-period 1967–73 as a whole since in 1969 the official statistics switched from being collected from company accounts data to being compiled from the Press. For 1969, data are available on both bases. An average of these two sets of data was used to estimate numbers of acquisitions and expenditures in 1969 when calculating the 1967–73 sub-period data. No attempt was made to link series for the other variables shown in this table. For further discussion of the data, see *Business Monitor* MQ7 and references cited there.

Sources: *Economic Trends Annual Supplement*, *National Income and Expenditure*, *Annual Abstract*, *Financial Statistics*, *Business Monitor* MQ7.

MERGERS 1969–86

Table 1.2 takes this period of intensive activity as a base from which to update the story. It provides data on the expenditure upon, numbers of, and financing of domestic and overseas acquisitions of other companies, and of subsidiaries of other companies, by UK industrial and commercial companies. As the table shows, merger activity in terms of both acquisition expenditures and numbers acquired, in the period 1974–81, was around a half its peak level of the years 1967–73. In 1984, however, expenditures rose significantly. By 1986, expenditure in real terms was in excess of the levels reached in the previous post-war peak years of 1968 and 1972. There was no corresponding increase in numbers acquired. The present merger wave is therefore the product of relatively few, relatively massive mergers. At one stage in 1986 there were 4 proposed manufacturing mergers involving one or more bidders worth over £1 billion each (United Biscuits/Imperial/Hanson Trust, £1.2–1.9 billion; GEC/Plessey, £1.2 billion; Argyll/Distillers/Guinness, £1.9 billion; and Elders IXL/Allied, £1.8 billion). Ten per cent of the independent companies acquired in that year accounted for over 85 per cent of total expenditure, whilst the top 10 per cent of subsidiaries acquired accounted for over 60 per cent of total acquisition expenditure on subsidiaries (*Business Monitor* MQ7, 1987 quarter 1). Of the top 200 UK quoted companies by market valuation in March 1982, 23 had been acquired by March 1986 (see further Table 1.6) which is on a par with the experience of the late 1960s.

SALES OF SUBSIDIARIES

The growing importance of giant mergers and acquisitions as a proportion of total activity is paralleled by an increase in the number of, and size of, sales of subsidiaries between companies. This has increased from around 20 per cent by number and 13 per cent by value, to around 30 per cent by number and 20 per cent by value, over the period analysed in Table 1.2. Moreover, whereas prior to 1979 there were few subsidiary sales of absolutely large dimensions (Lye and Silberston (1981), Chiplin and Wright (1980)), since then a number of very large transactions have occurred (Wright, Chiplin, and Coyne (this volume)). Thus in 1984 when the 6 largest independent company acquisitions had an average value of around £100 million, the 3 largest sales of subsidiaries between groups averaged £90 million (*Business Monitor* MQ7, 1986 quarter 4). Promises to sell major divisions posing potential monopoly problems have also come to play a role in a kind of pre-emptive strategy adopted by some would-be acquirers to forestall references to the Monopolies and Mergers Commission.

OVERSEAS ACQUISITIONS AND REGIONAL PATTERNS

The third notable feature of Table 1.2 is the growth in importance of overseas acquisitions relative to domestic ones reaching record proportions in 1986. In annual average terms, in the period 1969–73 around 6 per cent by number, and value, of total independent company acquisitions were made abroad. In the period 1982–6 over 12 per cent by number and 17 per cent by value were.[6] The vast bulk of this activity was outside the EEC (*Business Monitor* MQ7). It is worth noting in passing that the spatial incidence of merger outside the UK is much better documented than spatial incidence within the economy. This is disappointing in view of the emphasis on regional balance as one of the public interest issues relevant to Monopolies and Mergers Commission investigations. Samples of mergers for the early and mid-1970s do, however, suggest a distinct regional imbalance, with the south-east in particular accounting for a share of acquirers (and to a lesser extent acquired companies) substantially greater than would be suggested by its share in, say, total employment (Leigh and North (1978), Goddard and Smith (1978)). The net result has been an increase in the degree to which plants and companies outside the south-east are controlled by companies with headquarters in that region. The possible impact of these effects is discussed in Section 5.

Finally, returning to Table 1.2, an analysis of the medium of exchange used in financing acquisition activity is given. The most notable but not unexpected feature of the post-1973 period is the decline in bond finance, and the corresponding resurgence of cash and equities as prime methods of payment. Although fixed interest securities increased in importance in the 1982–6 boom, as a proportion of total consideration paid it remained at half the levels of the late 1960s and early 1970s.[7]

THE INDUSTRIAL AND SIZE DISTRIBUTION OF MERGER

Table 1.2 relates only to commercial and industrial companies; the companion series relating to financial companies has not been published

---

[6] This mirrors a general increase in the relative importance of investment overseas by UK industrial and commercial companies, which in the period 1979–84 was running at around 12 per cent of total uses of funds, compared with between 5 per cent and 7 per cent in the previous sub-periods 1958–62, 1963–7, 1968–72, and 1973–8 (Hughes (1986)).

[7] The ultimate impact of merger on gearing depends not only upon the way the equity of the acquired company is replaced, but also upon the relative size and gearing of the partners to the deal. These impacts can be very substantial. For the previous UK wave, see, for example, Cosh, Hughes, and Singh (1980). The impact of the current wave has not been systematically investigated.

Table 1.3. The distribution, by industry of target company, of merger proposals falling within the scope of the Mergers Panel, 1978–85

Year	Total number	Total asset value (£b.)	Percentage by number				Percentage by asset value			
			Manufacturing	Distribution	Finance	All services[a]	Manufacturing	Distribution	Finance	All services[a]
1978	229	12.0	50.2	12.2	16.2	37.6	31.4	4.6	51.3	59.2
1979	257	13.1	49.0	16.0	17.9	43.2	28.6	4.7	34.7	44.6
1980[b]	182	22.2	46.7	11.5	28.0	47.8	18.7	4.9	68.1	77.1
1981	164	43.6	43.3	7.3	24.4	45.7	28.1	2.6	60.4	65.6
1982	190	25.9	41.6	8.4	31.6	48.4	23.1	8.5	49.2	62.3
1983[c]	192	45.5	45.3	14.6	17.7	46.9	19.2	7.5	65.8	79.3
1984[d]	259	80.7	43.2	12.0	22.8	52.1	13.2	4.3	54.0	65.2
1985	192	57.5	44.3	13.0	25.0	51.0	35.1	5.6	53.6	64.0

[a] Including distribution and finance.
[b] The assets criterion was raised from £5m. to £15m. on 10 April 1980.
[c] After 1982 the change in the Standard Industrial Classification (SIC) makes the industrial groups not strictly comparable.
[d] The assets criterion was raised from £15m. to £30m. in July 1984.

Source: Annual Reports of the Office of Fair Trading.

since 1980. It showed that financial sector acquisitions fell off sharply after 1973 and had not recovered by 1980. Thus the annual average number of financial companies acquired in the period 1969–73 was 101 and the average current price value of expenditure was £342 million. In the period 1974–9 the respective averages were 47 and £180 million (*Annual Abstract of Statistics* (1985 and 1986) Tables 1750 and 421 respectively). To examine what has happened since then, and to provide an economy-wide industry breakdown of merger activity, we have to make use of the Office of Fair Trading's analysis of proposed mergers falling within the scope of the Fair Trading Act.

This series records merger proposals, a number of which will in the event not be proceeded with, and is restricted to those which would create or intensify a 25 per cent national or regional market share (33.3 per cent prior to 1973) or pass a minimum gross assets size test which was £5 million from 1965 to 1980, £15 million from 1980 to 1984, and is currently £30 million. It therefore excludes a large number of the transactions recorded in Table 1.2. On the other hand its industrial coverage includes insurance, banking and finance, and building society mergers, along with other miscellaneous financial services excluded from the industrial and commercial companies data.

Table 1.3 shows that the financial sector has more than matched the upsurge in merger values for industrial and commercial companies. Target companies in insurance, banking, and finance accounted for around a quarter by number and between one-half and two-thirds by assets of total proposed mergers in the 1980s. The table also shows the significance of distribution as a target sector, especially in terms of numbers.

THE INDUSTRIAL DIRECTION OF MERGER AND THE SIZE DISTRIBUTION OF MERGER DEATHS

From the point of view of the impact of merger upon market structure, it is necessary to look not only at the overall extent and industry spread of activity, but also at its direction and the size distribution of acquirers and acquired companies. There are great difficulties in classifying mergers by type, not least because in many cases elements of horizontal, vertical, and conglomerate expansion coexist. A classification has been attempted by the Office of Fair Trading, however, using the data underlying Table 1.3, and Table 1.4 draws on this. There has been since 1970 an increase in the importance of diversifying mergers. Although this shows up most noticeably in terms of numbers, in 1985 diversifying mergers accounted for over a half of all assets involved in proposed mergers. With that exception, horizontal activity has remained the dominant form even though its position has slipped compared with the peak years of the late 1960s and early 1970s.[8]

Table 1.4. The distribution, by type of integration, of the numbers and value of assets to be acquired in proposed mergers considered by the Mergers Panel, 1965–85.

Period	Total number	Percentage horizontal[a]		Percentage vertical[a]		Percentage diversifying[a]	
		Number	Assets	Number	Assets	Number	Assets
1965–9	466	82	89	6	5	13	7
1970–4	579	73	65	5	4	23	27
1975–9	1 003	62	67	9	7	29	26
1980–4	987[b]	65	71	5	2	30	27
1980	182	65	68	4	1	31	31
1981	164	62	71	6	2	32	27
1982	190	65	64	5	4	30	32
1983	192	71	73	4	1	25	26
1984	259[c]	63	79	4	1	33	20
1985	192	58	42	4	4	38	54
1980–5	1 179	62	57	5	3	34	40

[a]Rows may not sum to 100% because of rounding errors.
[b]The assets criterion for possible referral was raised from £5m. to £15m. on 10 April 1980.
[c]The assets criterion was raised again from £15m. to £30m. in July 1984.

Sources: Annual Reports of the Office of Fair Trading; Department of Prices and Consumer Protection (1978).

[8] This analysis is, of course, based upon large mergers falling within the scope of the Fair Trading Act, which is selecting partly on market share criteria and so may be biased toward identifying horizontal merger. The asset criterion ensures wide coverage, however, and any bias arising must come from different diversification rates for small rather than large acquisition.

As far as sales of subsidiaries are concerned, Chiplin and Wright (1980) report that 60 per cent of purchases in the period 1977–9 were horizontal (i.e. the acquiring company was in the same 2-digit industry as the subsidiary).

Lye and Silberston (1981) on the same basis record 50 per cent as horizontal for the year 1979. Interestingly both studies suggest that the companies selling the subsidiaries were divesting outside their primary industry. Thus 70 per cent of the 1979 divestments are classified as conglomerate by Lye and Silberston.

We have already noted the importance of large mergers in the current wave. Tables 1.5 and 1.6 allow us to examine the relationship between size and death by acquisition more systematically. Table 1.5 looks at patterns of acquisition death prior to 1982 amongst quoted UK non-financial companies ranked in the *Times 1000* list in 1972. The relative invulnerability of the very largest companies is at once apparent. Those ranked 200 to 1,000 have at least three times as great a mortality rate as those ranked 1 to 200. It

Table 1.5. The distribution of numbers and assets of acquired quoted companies, 1972–82, by opening sales size class

Sales rank, 1972	Number of quoted companies	Number acquired	Percentage numbers acquired	Percentage assets acquired[a]	
1–13	10	0	0.0	0.0	
14–25	11	1	9.1	1.2	
26–50	21	2	9.5	2.5	
51–75	22	4	18.2	12.5	
76–100	22	3	13.6	25.9	
1–100	86	10	11.6	4.7	11.2
101–200	75	8	10.7	8.1	
201–300	76	16	21.1	14.6	27.6
301–400	69	24	34.8	35.2	
401–500	70	26	37.1	34.8	35.6
501–600	79	27	34.2	34.4	
601–700	73	28	38.4	38.8	39.0
701–800	68	27	39.7	48.6	
801–900	65	23	35.4	38.0	41.4
901–1 000	68	32	47.1	49.3	
1–1 000	729	221	30.3	10.3	

[a]This column shows the value of the capital employed of quoted companies acquired expressed as a percentage of the total capital employed of the quoted companies in each sales rank class.

Source: Hughes and Kumar (1985).

is interesting to examine the impact on this pattern of the large mergers of the post-1982 period. This is done in Table 1.6, which examines the fate by March 1986 of the top 1,000 UK quoted companies by market value in March 1982. When these figures for numbers acquired as a whole are converted to an annual basis, they come to around the same as for the period 1972–82, but there is a marked shift in the death rate for those ranked 101 to 200. After 1982 they were about the most vulnerable group of all. Whereas their merger death rate was 1.2 per cent per annum for 1972–82, it was 4.2 per cent per annum in the period 1982–6. This did not reflect increased vulnerability to take-overs by smaller concerns (via highly leveraged David and Goliath bids) but by larger ones. Of the 23 merger deaths in the top 200 companies, all but one was of a lower by a higher

Table 1.6. Companies merged or acquired in the period March 1982 to March 1986 which were ranked in the top 1000 UK quoted companies in terms of market value in 1982

Rank in terms of market value	Number merged or acquired	
1–50	1	6
51–100	5	
1–100	6	23
101–200	17	
201–300	11	22
301–400	11	
401–500	14	28
501–600	14	
601–700	14	34
701–800	20	
801–900	12	30
901–1 000	18	
1–1 000	137	

Source: *Stock Exchange Fact Book*.

ranked concern, 10 of the acquirers were ranked in the top 50, and 6 ranked 51 to 100. These death rates for very large companies are comparable to those for the wave of the late 1960s noted earlier, when as in the present wave the medium-sized giants suffered disproportionately (Hughes (1976)).

SUMMARY

In the broadest of terms, we may sum up this section as showing that in the post-war period the UK has experienced two major peaks of activity. Compared with the first (of the late 1960s and early 1970s), the merger wave of the 1980s has been dominated by fewer, larger acquisitions, both of independent companies and of subsidiaries; until 1986, has been financed more predominantly by cash and equities; and has been characterized by a growing proportion of overseas and diversifying mergers. Mergers in manufacturing have continued to play a central role but there has been a very significant level of activity in banking, insurance, and finance as well as in distribution. As in previous waves, increased merger activity has gone hand in hand with an increased vulnerability of the middle-sized giants to raids by their bigger brethren.

In the next two sections we look at the effects of mergers in the UK before, during, and after the first great merger peak. There is little systematic work yet on the current wave.

4. Mergers, Concentration, Diversification, and Monopoly Power

The merger activity described in the previous section has been associated with important variations in both aggregate and market concentration and in corporate diversification. The nature of the relationship between merger and concentration, and the implications of this in turn for competition, have attracted most attention, particularly for the period encompassing the upswing and peak in merger activity in the 1960s. The growth in the importance of non-horizontal mergers has, however, also led to similar questions being asked about the relationship between mergers, diversification, and competition.[9]

---

[9] There has been much less emphasis on the link with vertical integration and its impact on competition. See, however, the case study of Courtaulds in Cowling *et al.* (1980) for a discussion of the issues involved.

TRENDS IN CONCENTRATION AND DIVERSIFICATION

Between 1951 and 1958 market concentration in terms of employment in UK manufacturing industry was rising at about 0.4 per cent per annum.[10] Between 1958 and 1968 it grew on average at double that rate (over 1958–63 at 1 per cent per annum and over 1963–8 at 0.7 per cent per annum) (Hart and Clarke (1980)). Although less well documented, increases in concentration in the late 1950s and 1960s also appear to have occurred in distribution and in the financial sector (Department of Prices and Consumer Protection (1978), Aaronovitch and Sawyer (1975a), Wilson (1980)). In manufacturing, these increases were followed from the late 1960s onwards by a decade of stability. Thus, as Table 1.7 shows, the share of the largest 5 employers in employment, sales, and net output hardly changed from 1970 to 1979.[11]

Table 1.7. Market concentration[a] in the 1970s in UK manufacturing industries

	1970 (%)	1975 (%)	1979 (%)	1970–9 change
Employment	44.8	45.5	45.6	+0.8
Sales	45.5	47.2	46.4	+0.9
Net output	45.7	47.3	47.2	+1.5

[a]Average 5-firm concentration ratios for the 5 largest firms ranked by employment in 93 3-digit industries, 1970–9.

Source: Clarke (1985).

In terms of aggregate concentration, the period 1949–58 saw the share of the top 100 UK manufacturers in net output rise from 22 per cent to 32 per cent (an increase of almost 50 per cent). The next decade to 1968 saw a further rise to 41 per cent but this represented a much slower percentage change than in the previous period (Prais (1976)). Since 1968 aggregate concentration, like market concentration, has shown little tendency to rise either in the manufacturing sector or in the economy as a whole, for which Table 1.8 provides some illustrative data. (See also Prais (1976) and, for

[10] Measured in terms of changes in the average 3- or 5-firm employment concentration ratio for samples of comparable manufacturing industries at the 3-digit level.

[11] A similar picture appears in terms of 5-firm sales concentration ratios at the 4-digit level. Thus, Utton and Morgan (1983) report the average 5-firm sales concentration ratio for 121 product groups in manufacturing as rising from 56.5 per cent in 1958 to 64.8 per cent in 1968 and then remaining at 64.8 per cent in 1977.

estimates based on sales and other measures of size, Hughes and Kumar (1984a).)

Table 1.8. 100-firm employment concentration ratios in the UK economy, 1968–80

	1968	1975	1980
Whole economy	24.7	24.5	25.1
Whole economy private sector	23.2	25.8	25.4
Non-financial sector	25.5	25.1	25.8
Non-financial private sector	24.0	26.5	26.4
Financial sector (top 40)	34.9	39.8	35.1

Source: Hughes and Kumar (1984b).

It is interesting at this stage to note that although concentration has obviously risen substantially since the war and then stabilized, and that merger activity too has shown periods of great intensity followed by periods of stagnation, there is not a simple one-to-one match between the two. Thus although market concentration was rising fastest in the 1960s when merger activity took off, the peak period of acquisition activity between 1968 and 1973 was not reflected in especially fast increases in either market or aggregate concentration. Nor did the period of the fastest rate of change of aggregate concentration in the 1950s coincide with the peak in merger activity in the 1960s. On the other hand the slow-down in concentration after 1973 has been associated with low merger activity. It is too soon yet to evaluate the impact of the latest wave.

These changes in concentration have been accompanied by important changes in the extent to which the largest companies are diversified across a spectrum of different industries, although the nature of the official UK data means that the vast majority of studies for the UK are for manufacturing companies only and relate to diversification *within* manufacturing. This excludes the impact of non-manufacturing output produced by firms primarily operating in manufacturing, and vice versa. This may be a considerable omission in a world in which cigarette manufacturers buy insurance firms and hotel chains. Moreover, in practice only the crudest distinctions, if any, are made between diversification and vertical integration, so that it might be more accurate to term most UK estimates as relating to non-horizontal rather than diversified activity.

It does nonetheless appear that there has been an increase in the post-war period in the extent of diversified manufacturing production in the UK (Utton (1979), Gorecki (1975), Hassid (1975)). However, the bulk of this might be considered narrow spectrum diversification (Wood (1971)); that is to say, outside a primary industry at a fairly fine level of disaggregation (3- or 4-digit) but inside a broader industry order (2-digit) of which it forms a part (Utton (1979)).[12] A more recent study based on a decomposition of census 3-digit employment data using the Herfindahl index measure of diversification (Clarke and Davies (1983)) confirms the tendency for overall *within* manufacturing diversification to rise over the period 1963–8 and suggests that within that there was a decline in the portion attributable to broad spectrum activity, a decline which was accentuated in the period 1971–7. For the 1970s as a whole, the most recent estimate available is based on an analysis of the sales of UK quoted companies (Cosh, Hughes, Kumar, and Singh (1985b)). This includes broad diversification beyond manufacturing and is based on company accounts data. For samples of the largest 100 companies and a further 110 companies drawn from the food, engineering, bricks, pottery and glass, and retail industries, they show substantial increases in diversification on a number of bases, including the Utton and Herfindahl indices and simpler measures such as the number of industries in which sales are made.

What has been the role of merger in these changes in concentration and diversification?

MERGERS AND MARKET CONCENTRATION

The cross-section link between mergers and industry or market concentration may be explored in terms of regression analysis, counterfactual studies, or case studies.

Regression analysis

Hart and Clarke (1980) use company data on merger expenditures as a percentage of opening net assets at the 2-digit level of aggregation in a cross-section regression, along with opening level concentration and logarithmic changes in plant scale, industry size, and the ratio of plants to enterprises, to explain changes in the logarithm of the 5-firm employment concentration ratio for 76 3-digit industries in the period 1958–68. For want of better data, each 3-digit industry is allocated the merger rate of the 2-digit industry to which it belongs. The mergers proxy was statistically significant, but when added to the other variables it increased the explained variation in concentration change by only 4.6 per cent. Similarly, Gratton and Kemp

---

[12] Utton estimates narrow spectrum diversified employment (taking mechanical and electrical engineering, vehicles, and metal goods as one approximately 2-digit group or order) as amounting to 58 per cent of total diversified employment in 1972.

(1977) use quoted company data on the number of mergers per year at the 2-digit level to construct a dummy variable for high, medium, and low merger activity for use in a regression, along with opening concentration levels, sales growth, and advertising intensity, to explain changes in concentration at the 4-digit level for 284 industries in the period 1963–8. The high merger dummy is found to be statistically significant for the producer goods industries, and for the sample as a whole, but not for the consumer goods group. The different levels of aggregation of the merger series and the concentration series are a problem in regression exercises of this type, and it can be argued that using the same values for merger intensity across all 3-digit industries within a 2-digit group will lead to a systematic downward bias in the merger coefficient and in its estimated contribution to concentration change (Hart and Clarke (1980)).[13] There is another problem, however, and that is that the merger series themselves are not well suited for the purpose in hand since they include cross-industry as well as within-industry mergers. Thus an industry with a very high level of expenditure may have a high proportion of it spent outside its primary group, and one with low expenditure may have a high proportion of its members acquired by companies from other industries (see, for instance, Goudie and Meeks (1982), Cosh, Hughes, and Singh (1980)). This problem has unpredictable effects a priori on the estimated importance of merger.

An alternative way of using the company merger data is to combine it with company asset size data at the same level of aggregation. Thus Hughes (1976) correlated merger activity (measured as the percentage of an industry's assets acquired) with changes in the 3-company asset concentration ratio for UK quoted manufacturing companies, both measured at the 2-digit level, and found a significantly positive relationship for the period 1954–68 as a whole and for 2 of 3 sub-periods within it (1960–4 being the odd one out). Taken as a whole, these studies suggest a positive but not always inevitable link between high concentration increases and high merger activity.

Counterfactual approaches

The data on company asset size and acquisition activity have also been used to produce counterfactual estimates of the impact of merger (Utton (1971), Hannah and Kay (1977)). The method used is essentially as follows. Calculate an asset concentration measure on the actual company size distributions in the opening (C_o) and end (C_n) years of the analysis. To

[13] In effect the argument is that the 2-digit level value of merger activity will be higher than it would be for individual 3-digit industries and its variance will be low because the same value is used for all industries within a given 2-digit group. (See Curry and George (1983).)

estimate the impact on concentration of mergers occurring between those years, either demerge the end-year population using end-year size, based on assumed counterfactual growth rates, and calculate a new concentration statistic (C_D); or merge the opening year population as if all the mergers had occurred in the opening year, and calculate an adjusted opening year concentration index (C_m). In the first case the impact of merger is then

$$\frac{C_n - C_D}{C_n - C_o} \times 100$$

and in the second case it is

$$\frac{C_m - C_o}{C_n - C_o} \times 100.$$

Depending upon the counterfactual growth rates assumed in the first method, and the methods of concentration measurement adopted, various estimates can result. Utton, using the variance of logarithms as his concentration measure, at the 2-digit industry level, reports mergers as accounting for between one-fifth and four-fifths of concentration changes between 1954 and 1965, depending upon the industry, and upon whether the first or second counterfactual method outlined above is used. For the period 1957–69 using a variety of concentration measures[14] and the second counterfactual outlined above, Hannah and Kay report the change due to merger in many cases above 100 per cent. This implies that in many industries, concentration would have fallen in the absence of merger. There is plenty of evidence pointing to increases in concentration, at times, and in industries with low merger activity (see further below). This, and the fact that Hannah and Kay themselves, after a simulation analysis of the consequences of the Gibrat effect and internal growth rates, conclude that 'even if there were no merger and if large firms grew no faster than small, significant secular increases in concentration would still be observed' (Hannah and Kay (1977) p. 110), suggest that estimates of the effects of merger over 100 per cent are implausible. In effect the underlying counterfactual is projecting too little concentration growth in the absence of merger.[15] This interpretation is consistent with case study approaches to the problem, which suggest a less dramatic role for merger.

---

[14] As well as calculating concentration ratios they calculate a class of measures such that, in numbers-equivalent form,

$$\mathrm{HK}(\alpha) = \left\{ \sum_{i=1}^{n} s_i^{\alpha} \right\}^{1/(1-\alpha)}$$

For $\alpha = 1$ this corresponds to an entropy measure of concentration, for $\alpha = 2$ to the Herfindahl index.

[15] It is often stated (for example, Curry and George (1983)) that the equal growth rate

Case study approaches

Using the case study approach, Evely and Little (1960) and Walshe (1974) look at high concentration trades in 1951 and 1958 respectively and try to identify the extent to which mergers in the past led to the creation of large firm dominance. Evely and Little concluded that 'there are few firms indeed among the leaders in the trades surveyed which were not created by amalgamation or have not resorted to acquisition and merger at some stage during their development' (Evely and Little (1960) p. 129). They analyse 36 trades with 3- or 4-firm employment or net output concentration ratios over 67 per cent in 1951, and conclude that in 23 of them the leading firms owed their position to a merger or amalgamation (predominantly dating from the turn of the century or 1920s merger waves). Walshe's reworking of these data raised the number to 28. In contrast, his own analysis of 32 products with 5-firm concentration ratios of over 90 per cent in 1958 suggested a lower role for merger, with externally and internally expanded firms each accounting for about half the cases. The difference in his view reflects the dominance of the early merger waves in the Evely and Little sample and the inclusion of younger new technology products in his sample (Walshe (1974)). His reference period of course pre-dates the main post-war periods of merger activity which are captured in the studies of Utton (1986), Hart, Utton, and Walshe (1973), and Hart and Clarke (1980).

Utton analyses long-run trends since the inter-war period in single dominant firm market shares in 19 UK industries. Although the prevailing tendency was for shares to erode, he found that in 7 cases market share had risen or remained constant. In 4 of these, acquisitions had played a role in sustaining dominance. In 2 of these cases the acquisition followed long-standing collaboration or co-operation between the firms involved and in general the acquired companies either invited or did not resist the take-over. He does not report the role of mergers by non-dominant firms in eroding the market shares in the 12 industries where dominance declined, although

---

assumption for acquired and acquiring firms is a reasonable counterfactual assumption to take. Since, as we shall see later, it is often found that acquiring companies are on average faster-growing pre-merger than their victims, it could at least as reasonably be argued that it is biased towards finding a high merger impact, since it may overstate the growth post-merger of the victim had it remained independent, assuming that there is some persistence in growth rates. The same problem affects Utton (1971) to some degree, since the post-merger growth rates attributed to merging firms based on their industry growth rates will be the same for firms merging horizontally within the same Minimum List Heading classification. It is of course the variance of growth that these counterfactuals suppress and which lies behind the apparent paradox in Hannah and Kay's (1977) results discussed in the text above. There is by now a substantial literature on the fine points of this debate, focusing upon the impact that using different time periods, concentration measures, counterfactuals, and company populations has upon reported differences in the role of merger. This debate has focused upon aggregate concentration effects but the principles involved are essentially the same. (See Hannah and Kay (1977, 1981), Hart (1979, 1980, 1981), Prais (1980, 1981), and Sawyer (1979, 1980).)

he notes that in 4 cases the leader's share fell despite its own acquisitions (wallpaper manufacturing, cigarettes, cement, and tyres). Hart and Clarke (1980) provide an analysis of 27 randomly selected product groups over the period 1958–68 and classify them into an increasing concentration with mergers group, an increasing concentration *without* mergers group, and a decreasing concentration group. Over half the sample (14) fell into the first category and they had an average increase in the 5-firm sales concentration ratio of 15.4 per cent compared with 7.8 per cent for the second group (of 6) where internal growth was the norm. The 7 industries in the third group experienced an average fall of 5.1 per cent. On the assumption that in the absence of merger the 14 groups dominated by merger growth would have experienced concentration changes on a par with the non-merger-intensive second group, then concentration would have risen by 4.5 per cent for the sample as a whole. This is around a half of the actual average concentration change experienced (of 8.4 per cent) and therefore Hart and Clarke conclude that mergers in this period probably accounted for around one-half of concentration change.[16] A more sanguine counterfactual distribution of the externally expanded industries towards the concentration decline group would of course raise this estimate.

Mergers have certainly continued to occur in high concentration situations since the late 1960s. Between 1965 and 1978, for instance, 395 proposed mergers considered by the Office of Fair Trading are reported by them either to have created or strengthened a statutory monopoly position in the UK economy (that is, from 1965 to 1973 a market share of 33.3 per cent and from 1973 onwards a share of 25 per cent). These are narrowly defined markets and many of them are extremely small; in 1978, for instance, of 22 such bids, one-third were in markets worth less than £25 million. Another third, however, were in markets worth over £200 million, so that even when in aggregate merger activity is low, significant structural developments in particular industries can occur. It would be interesting to extend the case study approach to the period 1968–73 when, as we have seen, merger activity continued at extremely high levels with a substantial horizontal component but concentration hardly changed at all. As yet this has not been done.

MERGERS AND AGGREGATE CONCENTRATION

This area has been dominated by the counterfactual approach, and the range of estimated merger impacts is as great as when this approach is used

[16] This is higher than the original estimate of Hart, Utton, and Walshe (1973) for the period 1958–63 (using the same methodology). This reflects the higher merger activity of the period 1963–8.

on an industry basis. Table 1.9 illustrates the point for the 1960s[17] as well as covering the period 1969–73.

Table 1.9. Effects of mergers on aggregate concentration

	Aaronovitch and Sawyer			Hannah and Kay					
	1958	1967	Percentage change due to merger	1957	1969	Percentage change due to merger	1969	1973	Percentage change due to merger
CR25	31.4	35.3	110	48.4	60.6	116.4	57.9	60.1	100
CR50	40.9	49.2	62.3	60.1	74.9	102.7	–	–	–
CR100	51.7	62.0	54.3	88.9	97.0	116.0	–	–	–

Note: Aaronovitch and Sawyer analyse the components of concentration change over the period 1958–67 for a population of 233 firms in manufacturing and distribution which were UK quoted companies with net assets of at least £5m., in terms of the effects of (a) the relative growth of firms that survive, (b) disappearances through acquisition, (c) births into the population of companies worth less than £5m. in 1957 but big enough to have been ranked in the top 100 quoted companies in 1967, and, in order to infer trends for the population of quoted companies as a whole, (d) changes in the size of their population relative to the quoted sector as a whole and (e) the interactions between (a)–(d). The table shows the impact of (b) on the same counterfactual assumption as Hannah and Kay (i.e. merging the base year population). Merger growth also affects (a) but the authors conclude that when an attempt is made to separate out the external element in it, neither it nor internal growth differences have a very significant impact on concentration change.

Sources: Cowling *et al.* (1980) based on Aaronovitch and Sawyer (1975b); Hannah and Kay (1977).

Part of the difference between these studies for the periods in the 1960s no doubt reflects the different years covered, but the higher estimates should, in the light of our discussion of market concentration above, be regarded with some reservations. As far as the period 1969–73 is concerned, Hannah and Kay argue that there were few large mergers in their population (which is surprising in view of our earlier discussion of giant firm death rates). They were nonetheless sufficient to prevent concentration falling, whilst there were a large number of smaller mergers which did not register an effect on the concentration ratio but did on their entropy-based

[17] For application to earlier periods see Utton (1971), Hannah and Kay (1977), Hannah (1976), and the literature cited in footnote 15 above.

concentration measure covering the whole distribution. Evidence for the post-1972 period is less plentiful. Hughes and Kumar (1985), however, echoing the findings of Utton (1972b) for the 1960s, report a negative relationship between opening size and intensity of growth by acquisition for 88 surviving companies in the *Times 1000* in the period 1972–81. This, combined with their finding of a negative relationship between opening size and growth, could *ceteris paribus* suggest a downward impact for merger upon the relative dominance of the largest firms.

CONCLUSIONS ON MERGERS AND CONCENTRATION

The broad message that these studies of aggregate and market concentration convey is that in the post-war period in many industries mergers have played a central role in the growth of leading firms and in the development and maintenance of concentrated market structures. They have also been a prime mover in changes in aggregate concentration. However, concentration can, and does, change in the absence of merger although spectacular changes in the UK have nearly always been associated with its presence. This does *not* mean, however, that in general, concentration will always increase substantially in periods of high merger activity, as our discussions of the period 1969–73 make clear.[18] The direction which merger activity takes, its distribution across firms of different sizes, the overall variance and mean of growth rates of different sized firms, the growth of individual industries and the economy as a whole, and the pattern of births and deaths may all independently or together work to prevent that. Successive merger waves in the UK are thus best viewed in their specific historical and institutional context which will condition each of these elements of the overall growth process and hence their structural impact relative to merger.

The basic puzzle remains, however, to account for the failure of concentration to rise in the face of the high merger activity from 1968 to 1973—which had a very significant horizontal component. Assuming that the answer is not to be found in some measurement problem arising from the use of concentration ratios, so that big changes were being wrought in the size distribution beyond the concentration ratio cut-off, then the answer must be sought either in terms of changed relative growth rates of large and small firms which favoured the latter, or in terms of other changes affecting the variance of growth rates. In fact, for continuous quoted companies at

---

[18] Or as the experience of the United States in the post-war period suggests. Despite experiencing a merger wave of enormous proportions in the 1960s, concentration in aggregate hardly changed (see, for example, Hughes and Singh (1980)).

least, size was negatively related to growth in the period 1966–71, and especially in the years 1972–6; if attention is focused on continuing companies in the periods 1964–9 or 1966–9, however, the relationship was positive[19] (Kumar (1984), Meeks and Whittington (1976)). Thus, the merger wave peak and the immediately following years were associated with relatively enhanced small firm growth. The interrelationship between this, the variance of growth rates (which showed no relevant systematic shifts for quoted companies (Kumar (1984))), the size pattern of merger deaths, and the intensity of acquisition growth by size of firm at home and abroad would repay further work.

It may also be speculated that in the relatively depressed years of the 1970s and especially since 1978, merger growth may be more of a substitute for investment than in the 1960s. This, combined with an increase in importance for overseas acquisition and investment, may have reduced the overall mean and variance of domestic growth rates, and therefore induced some stability in domestic concentration trends.

MERGERS AND DIVERSIFICATION

As with concentration, it is easy to point to a broad connection between mergers and diversification. As diversification has risen in the post-war period in the UK, so has merger activity and the proportion of activity that has been non-horizontal. There are, however, very few studies that bear precisely and directly on the link between the two compared with the concentration literature discussed above, and even fewer that deal with vertical integration.

There are a number of reasons for expecting that merger might be a particularly suitable vehicle for diversifying compared with horizontal expansion. First of all, the acquisition of a going concern with an established market position and experienced management is a rapid means of expansion and may avoid important set-up costs associated with entry *de novo* via building new plant. Moreover, initially at least, competition costs may be lower as no new capacity is added to the industry total. Where expansion in market share is planned after entry, advertising costs per unit growth may be lower since there is less need to build up goodwill and market presence. Some support for these ideas comes from Hill (1985). He provides case study material for 12 of the largest most diversified UK firms

---

[19] These results in part also reflect changes in the underlying Department of Trade and Industry population on which the analyses are based.

relating to the 1970s.[20] In all cases he identifies merger as the main vehicle for their diversified expansion, often via the purchase of market leaders in the industries entered. This study does not, however, quantify changes in diversification or the relative importance of different growth strategies towards it. The implication that merger is the principal vehicle for growth in diversification strategies does not appear to generalize to wider samples of firms. Thus Cosh, Hughes, Kumar, and Singh (1985b), using individual company diversification measures, find no evidence of a systematic relationship between acquisition intensity at the individual company level in the years 1971–7 (measured as acquisition expenditure over the period relative to opening net assets) and either diversification levels in 1971 or 1980, or the change in diversification from 1971 to 1980. Thus the simple correlation coefficients relating acquisition activity to the Utton index of diversification for the full sample of 210 firms in 1971 was 0.17 and in 1981 0.07. The growth by acquisition variable had the 'correct' (positive) sign in regression equations seeking to explain changes in diversification (as measured by the Utton or Herfindahl indices or changes in the number of industries operated in) but was never statistically significant (Cosh, Hughes, Kumar, and Singh (1985b)). There are a number of ways these results could be refined, for instance by distinguishing different directions of merger expenditure or extending the analysis to include more industries or later periods. As it stands, however, they suggest that in general the most rapidly diversifying companies have not been especially merger-intensive. This is not to deny that for some companies this has been the case or that some companies with currently very high levels of diversification have adopted merger-intensive strategies in the past, but that diversification and merger need not inevitably go together.

An interesting conjecture which arises out of this literature and our earlier discussion of the direction of divestment[21] is that firms may acquire more extensively diversified interests as a result of merger than they wish, because, for example, their target company is bundled up with others and is not available separately. They may then use the market in subsidiaries to unscramble unwanted parts. This might satisfy a reported desire to keep diversification within relatively related areas (Hill (1985)). Equally, the break-up and sale of the target may be the object of the raid. In either event

---

[20] The firms are Booker McConnell, BTR, Cope Allman, Grand Metropolitan, Arthur Guinness, Imperial Group, Norcros, S. Pearson and Son, Reckitt and Colman, Reed International, Thomas Tilling, and Tube Investments.

[21] Which suggested a high proportion of subsidiary sales were conglomerate whilst purchases were horizontal. The most recently publicized offers of divestment have, however, been horizontally connected subsidiaries of large companies where the divestment has been aimed at avoiding a merger reference.

it means that in assessing the links between merger and diversification, the direction of both acquisition and divestment activity must be relevant.

THE OUTCOME IN TERMS OF MONOPOLY POWER

The impact of mergers on monopoly power cannot be deduced simply from an analysis of their role in the structural changes we have discussed in the previous subsections. We need to trace possible connections between mergers, structural change, behaviour, and the competitive process.

Concentration

As far as concentration is concerned, a proper assessment requires an analysis of the conceptual and empirical links between structure and performance (provided elsewhere in this volume by Fairburn and Geroski) and an analysis of other changes occurring in the competitive environment of UK firms. In my view the evidence for a strong and consistent link between monopoly power and market structure as measured by concentration ratios or other measures of the size distribution of firms in the UK is relatively weak, is primarily based on cross-section static comparisons, and does not readily capture the essence of competitive rivalry as a dynamic process. I have set out the conceptual arguments for emphasizing this last point elsewhere (Hughes (1978)) and will simply make a few observations here on the competitive environment generally. First, the merger waves and changes in concentration which have swept UK industry since the 1960s followed a period of widespread abandonment of restrictive practices, so that part at least of what is observed is a replacement of one sort of market control by another. That is not to say that a decline in such control might not have been preferable, but that in terms of Table 1.1 the structural changes observed do not necessarily imply an *increase* in market power.[22] Second, increased merger activity here as elsewhere has been associated with a growth in the openness of national economies to international competition and direct investment (Hughes and Singh (1980)).

---

[22] Thus Elliott and Gribbin (1977) report that UK industries with terminated price agreements show faster concentration increases in the 1960s than do other industries. They also show that the largest mergers in the 1960s frequently involved companies that were formerly common members of abandoned agreements. In the same vein, Hope (1976) shows how the 1965 Crittal/Hope merger was explicitly designed to replace a faltering agreement. Both Heath (1961) and Swann, O'Brien, Maunder, and Howe (1974) suggest on the basis of questionnaires, interviews, and case studies that merger was a common medium-term response to the abandonment of agreements, although O'Brien, Howe, and Wright (1979) cannot find a significant link between acquisition intensity and abandonment in a cross-section statistical analysis.

It is difficult to argue for a *general* increase in market power of UK firms (manufacturers in particular) in a period when they have consistently lost out in terms of their share of world and UK markets, and of their representation amongst the ranks of the world's largest companies. The downward impact of adjusting for trade on concentration ratios for the UK is now well known.[23] Finally, to the extent that countervailing buyer power constrains producers, the tendency for concentration to increase amongst distributors and their customers may be mutually offsetting. It is difficult to disagree with Utton's conclusion after his analysis of long-term trends in 19 dominant firm positions over the last 30 to 40 years that, although in all cases they retained opening lead positions, 'the forces of erosion have been stronger than those of reinforcement' (Utton (1986)).

All of this is not to deny that in individual cases merger may inhibit the competitive process or prevent the erosion of the dominant firm's market share, but instead to argue that the identification of those cases requires a pragmatic case by case approach. It cannot be presumed that merger-induced concentration change inevitably changes monopoly power in the same direction, and that all assessments of post-merger performance effects in the UK must be predicated upon an assumption that because domestic concentration levels have risen, so has monopoly power. Even in its own terms, that argument would imply no changes in the competitive environment on average between the late 1960s and the early 1980s.

Diversification

By definition, conventional single market monopoly power effects are likely to be minimal in genuinely conglomerate expansion. Nevertheless, potentially adverse impacts on the competitive process may be identified for multi-product growth.

For example, conglomerate firms may impose reciprocal buying pressures upon suppliers to encourage them to use as inputs the products of subsidiaries of the parent conglomerate. Diversified firms may also employ predatory pricing in newly entered markets, and practise mutual forbearance with other conglomerates. More difficult to document are effects arising from reductions in potential competition, where it is argued, for instance, that entry by a large conglomerate firm may deter other likely entrants, or lead to subsequent anticompetitive behaviour which could not, or otherwise would not, have occurred. Where entry of this kind is by merger, it may also be argued that this is at the expense of new investment in

---

[23] See, for instance, Utton and Morgan (1983) and the references therein. As is clear from their work, however, identifying the competitive consequences of these adjustments is not straightforward in view of the possible connections between domestic producers and apparently independent importers.

the market, either by incumbents or the new entrant itself. (See, for instance, Scherer (1980), Steiner (1975), and Markham (1973).)

All of these effects may have implications for market structure. Estimating the nature of them in terms of levels and trends in industry concentration is, however, fraught with difficulties. These arise principally from lack of precise data on the market shares of individual firms in different industries, and the evolution over time of those shares. Similar problems limit attempts to measure the impact of diversifying new entry by either merger or new investment. What evidence we have suggests that conglomerate mergers have had little impact on levels of or trends in market concentration in the US (Goldberg (1973, 1974), Adams and Heimforth (1986)), whilst in the UK and the US neither the presence of diversified firms nor new entry by diversification seems to lead to increased levels of concentration. If anything, the reverse seems to be the case (Berry (1975), Utton (1979)). In structural terms, therefore, the case against conglomerate merger remains unproven. Effects on competitive behaviour, however, especially pricing, are a little better documented. Examples can be found in the US, and to a lesser extent in the UK, of most of the anticompetitive practices referred to earlier. There is little to suggest, however, that these are typical or pervasive features of diversified firms' market behaviour. Where such effects have been most prominent, they appear to be as much due to individual market power as overall diversified strength. Thus in the 7 cases investigated by the Monopolies Commission where the possibility of discriminatory or predatory pricing was examined, the companies involved held extremely dominant positions, the smallest market share being 51 per cent (Utton (1979)).[24] In these terms, the conglomerate merger problem collapses back to the single market monopoly power problem.

There is, however, a broader issue. The growth of conglomerate organization is a replacement of the market by organizational hierarchy. Two questions then arise: is the internal economy of the diversified firm an 'as if' competitive environment; and what impact on competitive stock market efficiency arises from the loss of information inherent in replacing separate accounting units by a consolidated group account?[25]

---

[24] The cases considered involved British Match Company (95 per cent domestic production controlled plus 85 per cent of imports), British Oxygen Company (90 per cent of total UK supplies of oxygen and dissolved acetylene plus trade protection via high transport costs and 30 per cent import duty), Metal Box Company (78 per cent of the market analysed), Courtaulds (over 90 per cent of the UK supply of cellulosic fibres plus tariff protection), Roche Products (over 90 per cent of the market for librium and valium), and Joseph Lucas (51 per cent of the motor vehicle electric wiring harness market and a more dominant position in certain other sectors of the motor vehicle electric equipment market).

[25] For a discussion of these and related issues and some relevant empirical tests, see Cosh, Hughes, Kumar, and Singh (1985b).

The answer to the second question depends on how effective company disclosure rules are. There is not much cause for complacency here. It also depends, however, on how effective the market itself is in evaluating and using such information. In the context of this survey, it is perhaps best to address this question in terms of the market for corporate control; the empirical evidence bearing on this is discussed in the next section. As far as the competitive impact of the internal economy of firms is concerned, we have evidence of considerable variation in its nature (Hill and Pickering (1986a, 1986b)) and some evidence suggesting private profitability gains from superior management organization (Steer and Cable (1978)) but nothing to suggest particular anticompetitive impacts which are not covered by our earlier discussion of product market behaviour.

CONCLUSION: MERGERS, STRUCTURAL CHANGE, AND MARKET AND EXTRA-MARKET POWER

The merger movement has played a major role in transforming the nature of business organization and market structure in the UK in the last two decades, but in my view the problems that this raises are not primarily ones of a *generalized increase* in market power. Such effects in individual markets have occurred, and will occur, as a result of horizontal and non-horizontal merger. A case by case approach is needed to identify them. We should not, however, make a universal background assumption of increased market power in making a net assessment of the average welfare effects of merger. In terms of the matrix presented earlier, we would expect to find individual mergers scattered across all the cells (that is, in some cases without the merger of UK firms less effective rivalry against market leaders and overseas competitors would have been possible[26]) with a concentration, in my view, in the case of the UK in recent years, in the bottom two rows.

There is more at stake, however, than market power. The enormously increased scope of the largest business organizations in the post-war period, and the role that merger has played in creating and restructuring them, raise questions of their extra market power which go beyond the summation of lost consumers' surplus. As Jacquemin and de Jong (1977, p. 198) put it, '. . . big firms represent a concentration of power in private hands rather

[26] It is often argued that a merger could not decrease market power. This view is based on an essentially static conception of market power. Viewed in a dynamic sense, it is intuitively easy to see how an increase in rivalry could be produced by newly merged firms who would otherwise have declined, or left the market altogether. There is plenty of case study evidence to this effect. See, for instance, the discussion below of the international rivalry impact of mergers in bearings, and computers in the UK based on Cowling *et al.* (1980) and Utton's discussion of the possible outcomes of mergers in the glass and plasterboard industries (Utton (1986) p. 65). For the general point, see Hughes (1978).

than in democratically chosen governments. Such private power can cross economic boundaries and poses the threat of an extra-market power which can change the rules of the game in favour of the dominant corporations.' Assessing the force of this argument and appropriate ways of dealing with the problems it raises goes beyond the scope of this paper. It should, however, not be lost sight of in the discussion that follows.

5. Mergers, Efficiency, and Economic Performance

In this section we examine in turn the stock market selection process and post-merger performance, including the impact on real resource use, profitability, investment, trade, technical change, and regional and stock prices.

THE STOCK MARKET SELECTION PROCESS

Analysing the stock market selection process involves looking at the pre-merger financial characteristics of various groups of firms defined by their involvement in merger activity, and in addition examining their post-merger performance. In this section we look at size, profitability, growth, and stock market prices. This is partly for reasons of space, and partly because it is these variables which figure most prominently in discussions of the market for corporate control. Before turning to the empirical evidence, however, a couple of methodological points are worth making. These relate to the choice of control groups, to sample design, and to techniques available for discriminating between groups of firms.

Figure 1.1 summarizes the classification possibilities within a population in any year where companies are identified as either acquiring (AG), or

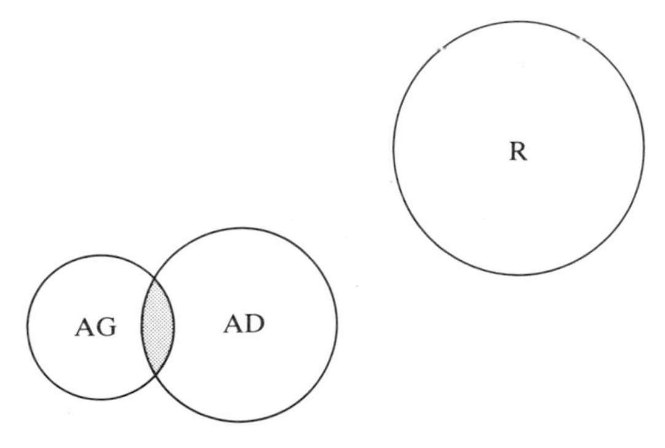

Figure 1.1. Classification of sample

acquired (AD), or neither acquiring nor acquired (R). The possibility that a company may both make an acquisition and itself be acquired is captured by the shaded intersection of sets AG and AD. Since some companies may make more than one acquisition, the AG and AD groups need not be the same size.

In terms of the natural selection model, the most natural comparisons to make are between AG and AD, and between each of these and a control group (C) representing the characteristics of the non-acquiring and non-acquired members of the population respectively. For a comparison with AG, C may be drawn from R or from R plus the unshaded portion of AD; similarly for a comparison with AD, C may be drawn from R or from R plus the unshaded portion of AG. This choice may affect the results significantly if the group characteristics of AG and AD differ from one another and from R. This will become relevant when we discuss studies using different control groups, and which report differing results.

As we have seen, the overall incidence and nature of take-overs, and the institutional framework in which they occur, vary significantly over time and between industries and different sizes of firm. There are also important differences between industries in the average characteristics of firms. There are therefore strong reasons for believing that comparisons of pre-merger (or other) performance characteristics will be subject to aggregation bias unless specific allowance is made for these factors in the sample design. One way of doing this is to choose firms matched by industry, year, and size with the acquiring (MAG) and acquired (MAD) companies. Others are to carry out comparisons on an individual year, or industry, or size class basis, or using individual company data normalized by industry averages. Evidence on each of these bases is available for the UK.

Finally, in seeking to discriminate between groups it is important to bear in mind that statistically significant differences in group averages may conceal very large overlaps between the groups. Moreover, variables which show up well on a univariate basis may prove more or less successful on a multivariate basis when the pattern of intercorrelations between variables is taken into account.[27] Bearing these issues in mind, we can examine in turn evidence relating to the comparative characteristics of acquired and acquiring companies on the UK stock market.

Acquired companies

Table 1.10, drawn from Singh (1975), summarizes the pre-merger characteristics of acquired companies relative to their industry median in

---

[27] For a discussion of these and related issues, see Singh (1971) which remains the most thorough treatment of the subject available.

terms of size, profitability, the short-term change in profitability, and growth in a sample of industries for two periods of take-over activity in the UK—1955–60 and 1967–70. In the period 1955–60 on an aggregate basis, taking all industries together the proportion of acquired firms with below median size, profitability, and growth was significantly greater than 50 per cent. In the period 1967–70 the differences were weaker. Although the proportion of companies with below median value remained above 50 per cent, it was only significantly so for profitability and the change in profitability in the year before merger. Nor were any of the proportions significant on an individual industry basis.

Table 1.10. Percentage of taken-over companies below or equal to their industry median, 1967–70 and 1955–60

Variable[a]	1967-70				All 4 industries, 1967–70	All 5[b] industries, 1955–60
	Non-electrical engineering	Drink	Food	Clothing and footwear		
Size	52.4	61.1	43.8	73.3	55.4	60.5***
Profitability	60.3	55.6	50.0	66.7	58.9**	64.4***
Growth	58.7	52.9	62.5	46.7	56.8	63.3***
Changes in profitability	55.6	61.1	50.0	73.3	58.0*	n/a
No. of companies taken over	63	18	16	15	112	181

Significance levels: * 10%; ** 5%; *** 1%.

[a]Size is measured as net assets. With the exception of the change in profitability, which is measured in *the year before merger*, the remaining variables are averages over the 3 years prior to merger. Profitability is the pre-tax rate of return on net assets; growth is the growth of net assets.
[b]The data for 1955–60 relate to the 4 industries analysed for 1967–70 plus electrical engineering.

Source: Singh (1975).

These results may be compared with those of a number of other studies. The tendency for acquired companies to be smaller than average gets some support from Meeks (1977) in an analysis of 233 acquisitions in the period 1964–72, Kumar (1984) for a sample of 354 mergers in the period 1967–74, and Levine and Aaronovitch (1981) for a sample of 69 mergers worth over £3 million in 1972. Kuehn (1975), however, reports little difference between 1,554 acquired companies in the period 1957–69 and non-acquired companies as a whole. This result probably reflects some degree of aggregation bias because, when size is expressed relative to industry, it becomes a significant variable in explaining the incidence of take-over in a number of industries in his sample (Kuehn (1975) p. 77). Cosh, Hughes, and Singh (1980) compare around 290 acquired companies in the period 1967–70 with all non-acquiring non-acquired companies and find no significant size difference in terms of assets, though in terms of sales the acquired are smaller. In this case the insignificant differences in size arise largely from the deliberate exclusion of relatively large acquiring companies from the control group. Their inclusion would produce results similar to those cited above for other studies using the broader control group concept.[28] In terms of growth, the evidence is also fairly clear-cut. The acquired companies are always less dynamic pre-merger than their respective control groups, even though the difference is not always statistically significant (Kuehn (1975), Cosh, Hughes, and Singh (1980), Levine and Aaronovitch (1981)).

The evidence on profitability is more mixed. Meeks (1977) reports acquired companies as having somewhat below average profitability in the year before merger and somewhat higher profitability in the second and third years before, although none of these differences are statistically significant. He also reports acquired firms in non-horizontal mergers as *more* profitable than the average in their industry for the 3 years prior to merger (though like other victims they had experienced a short-term deterioration in the year before merger). These results are consistent with Singh's (1975) finding of significant short-term deterioration in profitability immediately before acquisition in the period 1967–70. Kuehn's analysis for the period 1957–69 shows the acquired companies as less profitable than the rest, whilst Cosh, Hughes, and Singh (1980) find them less profitable than the non-acquiring non-acquired firms in the years 1967–9. Their result holds for both horizontal and non-horizontal mergers and in 12 of the 14 industries they analyse.

Levine and Aaronovitch (1981), on the other hand, show that acquired companies are *more* profitable than the average for manufacturing and distribution as a whole in 1972. This does not hold for horizontal mergers as a sub-group, which suggests again that non-horizontal victims are relatively profitable. The last result may, however, be affected by aggregation bias, and the authors themselves prefer to conclude that there are no systematic profitability differences. There is not therefore a systematic tendency for the acquired to be less profitable than the average company, and in the case of the victims of non-horizontal acquisitions there is some suggestion that

---

[28] It is worth remembering, however, that, as we saw earlier, the relative vulnerability of different size classes of firm may vary considerably during merger waves, so that different time periods could easily produce different results too.

they are above-average performers. The differences in many cases are in any event weak.

We have so far only discussed financial accounting data, whereas the corporate control theory in effect collapses these underlying indicators, as far as stockholders' welfare is concerned, into a single variable—the market value of the company. Singh (1971), Kuehn (1975), Levine and Aaronovitch (1981), Buckley (1972), and Newbould (1970) have all attempted to discriminate between groups of firms involved in the take-over process in terms of the valuation ratio; that is, the ratio of the stock market value of assets to their reported book value. *Ceteris paribus*, the lower the valuation ratio, the higher the probability of acquisition should be. Singh (1971) found a statistically significant but weak inverse relationship for the period 1955–60; thus 63 per cent of the companies taken over had a valuation ratio less than their industry average and 37 per cent a higher one. Kuehn also found a weak inverse relationship between a company's valuation ratio relative to its industry valuation ratio and the probability of take-over for the period 1957–69, whilst Buckley (1972), for a sample of 65 non-financial mergers in 1971, again reports the acquired as having lower valuation ratios than the non-acquired. Newbould (1970), on the other hand, in an analysis of 64 mergers in the period 1967–8, reports that only 41 per cent of the acquired firms had a lower than industry average valuation ratio and 59 per cent a higher one. Levine and Aaronovitch (1981) report acquired companies as having lower valuation ratios (VR) than acquiring companies but they are not compared with industry averages.

Levine and Aaronovitch and a number of other authors have also compared the acquired and acquiring companies in terms of the related concept of the price earnings ratio (PE) (VR = PE × post-tax rate of return on equity assets). Cosh, Hughes, and Singh (1980), for instance, find no systematic differences for 3 or 2 years before a bid between a sample of 28 acquired and 28 size- and industry-matched non-acquiring non-acquired companies in the period 1967–9, but a significant tendency for the acquired to have a *higher* PE ratio in the year before. Even in that year, however, half the acquired companies had lower PE values. Levine and Aaronovitch report similarly for 1972. Their analysis of a size- and industry-matched sample of acquiring and acquired firms suggests that, whilst the former had higher PE ratios than the latter, they both had higher ratios than the average for companies in manufacturing and distribution industries as a whole. This evidence is inconsistent with a bargain theory of purchase based on low market valuation.

In the very broadest terms, these results suggest that, whilst there is some variation across time periods, the acquired companies have worse short-term profitability growth records and are smaller, less dynamic, and somewhat less highly valued than companies on average. They do not appear to be systematically less profitable on a medium-term basis. What about the acquirers?

Acquiring companies

In terms of growth, acquiring or merger-intensive companies appear to be more dynamic both pre-merger and on a cross-sectional basis over a given time period than those less heavily engaged in merger. Acquirers are also generally larger than non-acquirers. The contribution of merger to overall growth, however, appears if anything to be negatively related to size (Cosh, Hughes, and Singh (1980), Meeks (1977), Kuehn (1975), Kumar (1985), Utton (1972b), Levine and Aaronovitch (1981)).

The picture in terms of profitability is less clear. When the acquiring companies are compared with companies in general, they appear to be as profitable or more profitable (Meeks (1977), Cosh, Hughes, and Singh (1980), Cosh, Hughes, Kumar, and Singh (1985a), Levine and Aaronovitch (1981)). Interestingly, however, in the Cosh, Hughes, and Singh and Meeks studies, disaggregation of the sample into horizontal and non-horizontal acquirers (i.e. making acquisitions across 2-digit industry boundaries) suggests that only the latter have a superior pre-merger profits performance. In fact in the former study the horizontal acquirers were if anything less profitable than comparable non-acquirers. The overlap between acquirers and the rest in terms of profitability again emerges when attention is focused on the performance of acquisition-intensive companies compared over a given period with internal growers (instead of just looking at pre-merger data). Kuehn, in an analysis of a sample of 117 raiders making 3 or more acquisitions in the period 1957–69, finds them as likely to be below the median profitability of their industry as above it. Similarly, Meeks reports that companies with above median growth by acquisition in the periods 1948–64 and 1964–71 are neither more nor less profitable than those relying less on external growth. However, within the former group the 100 most merger-intensive were more profitable in the period 1964–71 than other acquiring or non-acquiring companies.[29]

The acquirers are therefore larger and faster growing but (with the exception of those merging most intensively or involved in diversifying merger) not especially profitable compared with companies in general.

---

[29] Utton (1974) reports 39 acquisition-intensive companies in the period 1961–5 as having lower profits than 39 non-acquirers both in that period and in the subsequent years 1966–70. There may, however, be an aggregation bias here. The samples are not matched by industry. If, as Aaronovitch and Sawyer (1975a) suggest, industry acquisition intensity varies inversely with industry profitability, then acquisition-intensive firms may have lower profit rates. In fact, when Utton does compare profitability between the acquiring firms and their industry, he is unable to distinguish between them (Utton (1974) pp. 22–3).

From the point of view of the market for corporate control, this latter finding is not particularly encouraging, since the non-horizontal acquirers, who appear relatively the most profitable, appear according to our discussion above to have sought out partners who were relatively profitable compared with their industries. The question remains, however, of whether the acquirers can be distinguished from their victims.

Acquired v. acquiring companies

Table 1.11 considers differences between the characteristics of acquired and acquiring companies in the same industries and time periods as Table 1.10. In 1955–60 the acquired companies were significantly smaller, less dynamic, and less profitable than the acquiring companies. By 1967–70, when, as we have seen, the acquired had become less distinguishable from companies on average, so had the gap between them and acquiring companies as a group. They were still smaller and also had a worse performance in terms of profitability growth. They were not, however, significantly less fast-growing or less profitable. The neutrality of the last finding is reflected in other studies for the late 1960s which suggest that sometimes the acquiring and sometimes the acquired have a superior profit performance relative to

Table 1.11. Differences between acquired and acquiring companies, 1967–70 and 1955–60

Variable[a]	1967–70		1955–60	
	$\frac{d}{s}$[b]	t-statistic	$\frac{d}{s}$[b]	t-statistic
Size (logarithms)	−1.35	−6.21*	−1.50	−10.60*
Profitability	−0.29	−1.33	−0.41	−2.93*
Growth	−0.35	−1.60	−0.69	−4.91*
Change in profitability	−0.70	−3.20*	n/a	n/a

* Significance level: 1%.

[a]The variables are defined as in Table 1.10 except that profitability and the change in profitability are measured over 2 years rather than 3 years and 1 year respectively.
[b]*d* is the difference in the means of the acquired and acquiring group, and *s* is their common standard deviation. A minus sign for *d/s* indicates acquired firms had a mean value *below* acquiring firms. When *d/s* is zero the groups are indistinguishable; the larger *d/s* in general the greater the differences between them.

Source: Singh (1975).

each other and that sometimes they are indistinguishable, at least on a univariate basis. Thus, Rose and Newbould (1967) report for a sample of 46 mergers in 1967 that the acquiring are *less* profitable than the acquired. Newbould (1970) for 1967–8 and Levine and Aaronovitch (1981) for 1972 parallel Singh's finding that there is no significant difference between the groups, whilst Cosh, Hughes, and Singh (1980) for the period 1967–9 and Meeks (1977) for the period 1964–71 suggest that the acquiring are either as profitable as or more profitable than the acquired. In terms of growth, the acquiring companies are relatively dynamic pre-merger compared with acquired companies, though not always significantly so (Cosh, Hughes, and Singh (1980), Levine and Aaronovitch (1981)). A more consistent picture emerges in terms of size differentials. Although, as we have seen, the acquired are not always smaller than average, all studies comparing them with the acquirers show the latter to be larger, especially for non-horizontal merger (Singh (1971, 1975), Rose and Newbould (1967), Kuehn (1975), Meeks (1977), Levine and Aaronovitch (1981), Cosh, Hughes, and Singh (1980), Kumar (1984), Cosh, Hughes, Kumar, and Singh (1985a)).

The market for corporate control: an assessment of pre-merger characteristics

In the very broadest of terms, the evidence we have examined suggests that big and fast-growing companies acquire their smaller and less dynamic brethren. The acquirers are not, however, especially profitable relative either to companies in general or to their victims. The non-horizontal acquirers are a possible exception to this rule but, whilst they appear to be relatively profitable compared with other acquirers, there is also evidence to suggest they are selecting companies as victims which are *more* rather than less profitable than the average. In so far as profitability does enter the picture, it appears to be in the guise of short-term adverse *changes* in the year or so before merger for the acquired companies and not in terms of medium- to long-run profit levels.

It has been argued that, if the market for corporate control were working well, then the threat of discipline for poor profitability would in fact produce the results reported for profitability levels. Thus, with a perfectly effective disciplinary threat, all firms would be making maximum potential profits and the remaining take-overs would be occurring for other non-disciplinary reasons. Therefore the data cannot, it is argued, distinguish between the view, on the one hand, that the deterrent is ineffective because the threat is unreal and, on the other, that the deterrent is very effective and so is the threat (Hannah and Kay (1977) pp. 123–5). This is not particularly convincing. In so far as a deterrent is perceived, it must be based on learning from the nature of take-over activity, so that punishment and crime can be connected. If the thousands of mergers that have occurred in the UK have been essentially random, upon what evidence is the notion of the threat of take-over based and what sort of behaviour will it induce? Of course, as we have seen, the incidence of merger is not random when variables other than profitability are considered; this is especially so in relation to size.

Before considering the behavioural consequences of this, it is appropriate to consider the relationship between the incidence of take-over and the various characteristics of companies taken together.

There are essentially two reasons for adopting a multivariate approach to supplement univariate comparisons. First, it may be possible that when variables are considered *together* it is possible to distinguish more clearly between acquiring, acquired, and other firms. Second, many of the characteristics are or may be intercorrelated so that a good discriminator on a univariate basis may fail to be so on a multivariate basis when the pattern of intercorrelations is taken into account. Equally, in a multivariate context the relative importance of discriminators may be assessed. In fact, Singh (1975) and Levine and Aaronovitch (1981) find that when an attempt is made to distinguish between the acquiring and acquired firms on a multivariate basis, the most powerful single discriminator is once again size and *not* a performance variable such as profitability or a stockholder variable like the valuation ratio. Thus, on the basis of size alone, one could expect to classify firms correctly as either acquired or acquiring companies, 75 per cent of the time in Singh's 1967–70 sample and 73 per cent of the time in Levine and Aaronovitch's 1972 sample. This is compared with 50 per cent on the basis of random allocation. Adding other variables to size increases the percentage correctly classified, but not by much. Thus, in Singh's sample, adding the short-term change in profitability raises the figure from 75 per cent to 80 per cent, whilst then adding growth, profitability, liquidity, gearing, and retention raises it only to 83 per cent. Similarly, in the Levine and Aaronovitch sample, adding growth, profitability, liquidity, and gearing raises the correctly classified proportion only from 73 per cent to 80 per cent. If, on the other hand, size is left out, the maximum correctly classified on the basis of *all* other variables taken together is 61 per cent in the Levine and Aaronovitch study compared with 50 per cent achievable on a random allocation.[30] Size rather than profitability or market valuation emerges clearly as the most consistently successful discriminator between

[30] In Singh's 1955–60 sample, size was also the most important single discriminator, followed by growth. In 1967–70, after size, changes in profitability were next most important. In fact, a function taking only profitability, growth, and the change in profits together in 1967–70 would have classified correctly 70 per cent of the time, compared with 75 per cent on the basis of size alone. Tzoannos and Samuels (1972) also report high probabilities of misclassifying companies on the basis of multivariate combinations of financial variables.

acquiring and acquired companies. What kind of behaviour on the part of managers might the *threat* of a take-over based on this sort of selection mechanism induce?

One way of bringing this out is (following Singh (1975)) to compare the actual probability of acquisition by size class of firm and by profitability class. Table 1.12a shows variations in the probability of being taken over by relative size within a firm's own industry in the period 1967–70, and Table 1.12b shows the variations in the same probability by average profitability class.

Table 1.12. The average probability of being taken over within a year, by size class and by profitability class in 1967–70

(a)	Size class							
	Lowest 20%	Next 20%	Next 20%	Next 20%	Top 20%	Top 10%	Top 5%	All
Probability of take-over	3.0	10.1	9.7	6.5	4.5	2.6	1.4	6.7

(b)	Profitability[a] class									
	Lowest 10%	Next 10%	Next 10%	Next 10%	Next 10%	Next 10%	Next 10%	Next 10%	Next 10%	Top 10%	All
Probability of take-over	8.6	11.0	9.8	4.3	5.5	7.4	4.9	6.1	4.9	6.1	6.9

[a]2-year pre-merger profitability.

Source: Singh (1975).

Two things emerge from this: the very largest and smallest quoted firms are the most safe from take-over. In the case of the latter, this may well be because of their relatively highly concentrated and/or family-dominated shareholding patterns (Davies and Kuehn (1977)). Increasing size from the third quintile onwards significantly reduces the probability of take-over.[31] This suggests that if large size is associated with market power, then

[31] This is consistent with our conceptual arguments at the beginning of this section that the sanction might only be effective in the middle ranges. The discussion in the text, of course, relates to quoted companies. The limited evidence for other companies suggests that, for the 1960s at least, similar annual death rates from merger (i.e. 2–3 per cent per annum) characterized the small non-quoted company sector and the lower end of the quoted size range. Attitudes to small firm take-overs are, not surprisingly, less based on questions of management discipline but more on the need to ensure managerial succession and access to financial and other resources (Bolton (1971), Merrett Cyriax Associates (1971), Boswell (1972), Hughes (1987)).

discipline on the stock market may be most restricted in just those cases where the size of the companies involved suggests that product market constraints will be weakest. Table 1.12b, on the other hand, shows that once a company moves out of the bottom 30 per cent of companies in terms of profitability, there is no systematic gain in terms of increased immunity.

This is consistent with evidence that managers of large companies do not link poor long-run profit performance with the threat of take-over. Minimizing the threat of take-over was chosen as the least significant of 10 possible long-run corporate objectives by senior executives of 18 large UK quoted companies in an interview and questionnaire study carried out in the period 1974–6. Moreover, minimizing the risk of take-over was also thought to be the least important of 9 possible reasons for pursuing profits as a long-term objective (Francis (1980)).[32] Even if high profitability and increases in size were both perceived by managers as reducing the probability of take-over, then it is possible to argue that, where they have some degree of internal discretion, they will prefer increases in size. This is because their remuneration status and power are more closely related to size than to profitability. Since size and profit variability over time are also inversely related, increasing size would also help reduce the threat of take-over due to short-term swings in profits. Making an acquisition to increase size might then itself become a tactic to avoid acquisition (Greer (1986)). Interestingly, Pickering (1983) reports that the pursuit of growth (by merger or new investment) rather than enhanced profitability was typical of the post-bid reaction of a sample of UK firms surviving failed take-over attempts in the late 1960s and early 1970s.

For all these reasons, therefore, we should expect that the market for corporate control will be at best a highly imperfect disciplinarian. However, we need to look at post-merger performance before making a final assessment.

POST-MERGER PERFORMANCE

We examine in turn: real resource effects; the impact on profitability and investment; trade, technical change, and regional impacts; and the effect on returns to stockholders.

---

[32] This study relates to a period of low merger activity and managers may respond differently in a take-over boom. Equally, however, the companies sampled had just lived through the 1968–72 merger wave, so that at best the threat complex seems to be highly transient.

Real resource effects

The most detailed study attempting to estimate the real resource effect of merger is that of Cowling *et al.* (1980). They estimate changes in 'unit factor requirements' (K) where

$$K = \frac{P_0}{P_1} \left(1 - \frac{\pi}{R}\right)$$

with P_0 an index of revenue per unit output, P_1 a fixed weight price index of inputs (reflecting an assumption of fixed factor proportions in production), π is total production profits, and R total production revenue. In effect, K is average unit costs deflated by input prices, and changes in it over time are inversely proportional to 'efficiency' in the sense of the ratio of inputs to outputs.[33] Estimates of K are used in the context of individual case study material to evaluate a sample of large primarily horizontal mergers. With one exception, these took place in the period 1966–9 and had been considered by the Mergers panel for possible referral to the Monopolies and Mergers Commission. In general, the combined market share of the merging firms was over 30 per cent and there were significant changes in market share arising from the merger. The size of the mergers meant that in several cases they had been referred to the Monopolies and Mergers Commission for investigation, or the industry in which they operated was the subject of an investigation. In addition a number had been aided and abetted by the Industrial Reorganization Corporation (IRC).[34]

The principal comparison made is between the pre- and post-merger efficiency of the merging firms. Lack of data and suitable comparators meant that in general the authors could not systematically compare the pre-merger performance of the merging companies *relative* to other companies with their *relative* post-merger performance. Instead the impact of merger on the firms merging is compared with an assumed counterfactual growth rate of efficiency of 1.5 per cent per annum, and/or the post-merger

---

[33] This index is sensitive to changes in capacity utilization and to changes in vertical integration and factor proportions. Therefore the authors stress that their assessment of the impact of merger in terms of K is based on its use in the context of particular case studies where the impact of the possible biases in the measure can be evaluated.

[34] In all, 12 individual mergers are analysed (* means merger referred to the Monopolies and Mergers Commission or industry investigated subsequently; + means IRC involvement): London Brick/Marston Valley+; Ransome/Hoffman Pollard+ (RHP); BICC/Pyrotenax*; Tube Investment/Coventry Gauge (TI); Berger Jensen Nicholson (BJN)/British Paint; Rowntree/Mackintosh+; Johnson/Richards Campbell; Thorn/Radio Rentals*; Courtaulds/British Celanese (this merger took place in 1957); Leyland Motor Company/BMH Ltd+ (BL); GEC/English Electric/AEI+; and the formation of ICL+ (K is not calculated for ICL). An industry case study is also provided for the series of mergers affecting the brewing industry, as well as an analysis of Courtaulds's vertically integrating mergers in textiles.

performance of the merged company is compared with industry or comparator firms in the same post-merger period. In 5 of the 11 individual case studies where *K* is calculated, the merging companies showed gains in efficiency considered by the authors to have been in excess of the 1.5 per cent per annum counterfactual.[35] In 4 of these cases, where a comparison with other firms is possible they do at least as well as their comparators.[36] This broadly neutral outcome is mirrored in a study of building society mergers. Barnes (1985) compares changes in the operating cost ratios of merging societies in the period 1970–8 relative to average operating cost changes for other societies allowing for the possible gains to be had by changing size. He finds no tendency for relative unit operating costs to be lower (or for that matter higher) after merger than before, nor for any improvement in growth of assets to accrue from possible improvements in service quality (see also Gough (1979, 1981), Barnes and Dodds (1981)).

These real effect studies suggest that *on average* there is not a systematic efficiency gain, with at least as many cases of no change or deterioration as there are of enhanced performance. There are, however, some success stories and the merit of the case study approach is that some pointers to the reasons why might be found from a close reading of them. I return to this below in considering accounting measures of performance.

The effects of merger on corporate profitability

There are well-known objections to the use of accounting rates of return on

---

[35] This is on the basis of a relatively weak test comparing the best post-merger year with the year of merger itself. In fact, in only one case (BJN) is this test failed on a simple evaluation of the raw data for *K*, and in this case the picture is confused by the fact that the merged company itself was acquired within the comparison period by another company. In 4 cases (BICC, Courtaulds, Radio Rentals, TI) the gains are more than 1.5 per cent but the authors reject the data as either unreliable or misleading, or because the gain is completely reversed after the best post-merger year. BL passes the test set out in the text, but a detailed comparison of averages of *K* pre- and post-merger shows no significant differences. The statement in the text therefore refers to the GEC, London Brick, RHP, Johnson/Richards, and Rowntree/Mackintosh mergers. The indicator *K* was not calculated for the ICL merger but it is clearly regarded on other grounds as successful by the authors.

[36] Thus in the RHP case the authors' opinion is that it is unlikely the merging companies could have kept up with their rivals in the absence of merger (Cowling *et al.* (1980) p. 104). In the cases of GEC and Johnson/Richards, the firms clearly outperformed their rivals in the post-merger period (op. cit., pp. 140–1, pp. 200–1). In the case of Rowntree/Mackintosh the merged firm does at least as well as its rivals (op. cit., pp. 135–6). In the fifth case (London Brick), where a 20 per cent improvement in unit factor requirements occurred in the 5 years following merger, no sensible comparison could be made since, as a result of this and other mergers, the company became the sole supplier of Fletton bricks. The separate case study of the brewing industry suggests that, for the industry as a whole, there was declining efficiency (as measured by *K*) until improvements occurred in the 1970s which took place to the same degree in merger-intensive as well as internally growing firms (op. cit., p. 223). See also Cubbin and Hall (1979).

assets in assessing company performance generally. These arise from their lack of correspondence to economists' concepts such as the internal rate of return.[37] They remain, however, an essential starting-point for internal and external analysts of company performance, and evidence based upon them is therefore of some interest. The usual problems are, however, compounded in the case of take-over by variations in accounting practices and other difficulties arising with respect to consolidating acquired companies in the parent's accounts. There are two principal effects at work here. First, in the merger year, if the acquired company's earnings are incorporated into the acquirer's accounts for whatever proportion of the year remains after acquisition, but only its end-year assets are included in calculating the profit rate on the average of opening and end-year assets of the newly merged combination, then reported profit may be biased either up or down relative to a measure for the merger year which incorporated all the earnings and both opening and closing assets. The direction will depend on the distribution and scale of earnings over the year and the value of the assets. Second, there is a downward bias arising whenever the acquired companies are bought for more than their book value and corresponding 'goodwill on acquisition' is added to the assets of the merging firm. These and other arguments related to the way in which mergers are financed, and in which accounting practices may be harmonized post-merger, lead Appleyard (1980) to conclude on conceptual grounds that there will be on average a downward bias to reported profit following acquisition. Meeks's earlier study (1977) of the problem concurs in this view and he demonstrates the impact empirically for the goodwill point in his careful study. Although on average in the case of a firm making a single acquisition the effect on profitability is small (profitability adjusted for goodwill being, for instance, between 1.3 per cent and 5 per cent higher on average than raw profitability in the second year after merger), in individual cases it could be very large (for example, in the case of the GEC/AEI merger the adjustment amounted to over 20 per cent). Moreover, in the case of multiple acquirers the effect would be cumulative (Meeks (1977)). It is important to bear this in mind in interpreting the results that follow when unadjusted data are used.

---

[37] See, for instance, Harcourt (1965), Fisher and McGowan (1983), and, for a more optimistic view under certain strict assumptions, Kay (1976). Meeks and Meeks (1981) set out a number of objections to other rates of return derivable from accounts (for example, profit margin on sales, and the post-tax return on equity). Their main concern is with the usefulness of these rates as guides to 'efficiency', taking as given that mergers enhance monopoly bargaining power and thus profits, and they consider various biases which might arise in measuring them. Whatever the merits of profitability measures as a guide to 'efficiency', it is clear that the margin on sales and return to equity may have uses in relation to other specific objectives (for example, estimates of monopoly power or of gains to shareholders from reorganizing capital structure) which make them preferable to the return on net assets, notwithstanding any biases in measurement which arise.

There are six studies to which we can refer. Utton (1974) compares the unadjusted pre-tax profit performance of 39 quoted UK companies growing intensively by a series of mergers in the period 1961–5 and then by internal means in the period 1966–70, with 39 randomly selected companies growing primarily without merger over the period 1961–70 as a whole. He found that the merger-intensive firms had lower profitability than the non-merging firms in their merger-intensive period and that the gap widened subsequently. Thus, the average profitability of the merger-intensive group fell from 13.6 per cent to 11.5 per cent and of the control group from 15.4 per cent to 14.2 per cent. However, the industrial composition of the two groups of companies is not the same, so that in addition to any downward accounting biases, there is some aggregation bias (arising perhaps from the fact that mergers occur more frequently in low profit or falling profit industries).[38] Interesting though Utton's counterfactual comparison is as an attempt to measure the effects of merger intensity over a period of time, it does not pick up the profitability effects on the assets of the acquiring and acquired firms under common management after merger, compared with their estimated combined profitability when they were independent. The other studies for the UK (Singh (1971), Meeks (1977), Cosh, Hughes, and Singh (1980), Kumar (1985), Cosh, Hughes, Kumar, and Singh (1985a)) all make attempts to do so, and to deal with the problem of aggregation bias by comparing the profitability of merging companies after merger with their weighted average pre-merger profitability, either relative to their industry average or relative to size- and industry-matched non-merging companies. (In this sense they roughly correspond to the concept of normalized profits shown in Table 1.1 above.) The first two studies (Meeks (1977), Singh (1971)) also attempt to adjust for the accounting bias.

Allowing for accounting biases, Singh found, for a sample of 77 companies making a single horizontal acquisition in the period 1955–60, that a little over 50 per cent of them suffered a decline in their relative pre- and post-tax return on net assets after merger. He did not report the magnitude of the changes but concluded that the impact overall was likely to be neutral.

Some illustrative results of three other studies using methodology similar to Singh's for the later period 1964–76 are shown in Table 1.13. The first two studies relate to large samples of mergers in the whole of manufacturing and distribution, the last to a smaller sample drawn from the largest 100 manufacturing and distribution companies in 1972 plus the food, drink, electrical engineering, bricks, pottery and glass, and distribution

[38] The accounting biases would need to be very substantial to account for the differences observed. Interestingly, the Sturgess and Wheale (1984) share price study reported below, which is based on a subset of the Utton sample, shows that these reported profit differences were not reflected in similar differences in terms of shareholder returns.

industries. (Details of the methodology used are shown beneath the table.) These studies as a whole show negative effects. They are, however, not always statistically significant and a high proportion of mergers show positive effects. Thus, in the period 1964–71, whilst the mean fall in normalized profitability was significantly negative 3 years after merger, 47 per cent of merging companies by then nevertheless showed improvements. Equally, in the period 1967–74, the fall in relative profitability by the fifth post-merger year was insignificant and 40 per cent of mergers showed improvement. The effects are also small and in the case of studies (2) and (3) are biased against finding positive effects because they do not adjust for the

Table 1.13. Changes in normalized profitability[a] after merger in the UK, 1964–76

Post-merger year	(1) Meeks 1964–71			(2) Kumar 1967–74			(3) Cosh, Hughes, Kumar, Singh 1972–6		
	No. of companies (*n*)	Change in normalized profit (ΔNP)	Percentage ΔNP negative	*n*	ΔNP	% ΔNP -ve	*n*	ΔNP	% ΔNP -ve
t + 3	164	-0.06**	52.7	241	-0.08*	61†	66	-0.16	n/a
t + 5	67	-0.11**	64.2†	186	-0.06	60†	18	-0.10	n/a

† Significantly different from 50% at the 5% level.
* Significantly different from zero at the 5% level.
** Significantly different from zero at the 1% level.

[a]Net income/net assets.

Notes: In the case of the Meeks study, the comparison is between the post-merger industry normalized profitability of companies making single acquisitions and the average combined normalized profitability for the merging companies in the 3 years prior to merger. The data are adjusted for accounting bias.
In the cases of Kumar and of Cosh, Hughes, Kumar, and Singh, the methodology is essentially the same except that the pre-merger period is 5 years, multiple acquisitions are included, and there is no accounting adjustment. In each study, the number of mergers compared falls because mergers occurring towards the end of the sample period run out of post-merger years. In addition, in Meeks companies drop out when they make a second acquisition. In each study, the normalization procedure used is to divide the merging firms' profit rate by a weighted average profit rate for their industry (including the profit rate of the merging companies themselves).

Source: Meeks (1977), Kumar (1985), Cosh, Hughes, Kumar, and Singh (1985a).

downward post-merger accounting bias discussed earlier. Thus, in the case of the period 1967–74, for instance, if pre-merger industry profitability was around 16 per cent (as it was in the period 1966–71) then the pre-merger profitability of the merging firms would have been around 19.5 per cent and would on average have fallen by the third year after merger to around 18.2 per cent on an unadjusted, and only 19.2 per cent on an adjusted, basis.[39]

There is not much support here for the view that merger raises relative profitability. The clear impression is of a small, variable, but negative impact. However, in an attempt to distinguish the impact of institutional investors on the merger process, Cosh, Hughes, Kumar, and Singh (1985a) divided the 1972–6 sample into those mergers where the acquirers had substantial institutional shareholder representation and those where they did not. In the former case the post-merger performance was positive (though insignificantly so) in contrast to the negative findings for the sample as a whole and for those mergers where the acquirers had not attracted major institutional shareholdings. This is consistent with a positive role for these investors in influencing, or associating themselves as shareholders with, companies either seeking or more able to achieve post-merger performance improvements. The sample is, however, a small one for a period of low merger activity. A similar test for a later period would be interesting to undertake.[40]

The remaining study of profitability effects, summarized in Table 1.14, presents merger overall in a slightly more favourable light, especially when it is noted that no adjustment is made for the downward accounting bias. It covers a sample of 211 firms in manufacturing and distribution in the period 1967–70 which overlaps with the first two studies of Table 1.13. The years it covers represent the peak of the first major post-war merger wave and exclude the relatively low merger years of the mid-1960s and 1970s. In this study each pair of merging companies is compared with a control group which consists of those companies that were neither acquiring nor acquired in the 5 years prior to and following the merger. The profitability of the merging companies (AGAD) is calculated for 5 years pre-merger and compared with profitability for the average of 3 and 5 years after merger.

---

[39] The figures in the table represent the differences between the ratios of merging company profitability to industry profitability pre- and post-merger. In year $t+3$ the pre-merger ratio in the Kumar study was 1.22 and the post-merger ratio 1.14, giving a fall of 0.08. Hence with industry profitability assumed as 16 per cent, pre-merger profit for the merging companies is $1.22 \times 16 = 19.52$ per cent and post-merger profit $1.14 \times 16 = 18.24$ per cent. Meeks (1977) estimates that profitability adjusted for goodwill for a single merger in the second post-merger year varies between 1.5 and 5 per cent. Taking the upper figure, in view of the inclusion of multiple acquirers in the Kumar study, raises post-merger profitability to $1.05 \times 18.24 = 19.15$ per cent.

[40] For a fuller discussion of this result and its implications, see Cosh, Hughes, Kumar, and Singh (1985a).

Normalization is then effected by comparing the average change for merging firms with that of the unweighted average change for the control group as a whole (*C*) or with that of industry- and size-matched pairs of companies (MAGMAD) drawn from the control group.[41] This differs from the control group used in the studies of Table 1.13 which was the weighted average profitability of the relevant industry population including the acquiring and acquired companies themselves. This difference probably accounts for the bulk of the discrepancy between the studies,[42] which is in any case most marked only for the non-horizontal merging group, which dominate the results for the sample as a whole and form a bigger proportion of the Cosh, Hughes, and Singh sample than that, for instance, of Meeks. The horizontal mergers show no significant changes in profitability either up or down, compared with non-merging firms.[43]

This distinction between the performance of horizontal and non-horizontal mergers is also mirrored in the Meeks study. He reports smaller and less statistically significant falls in profitability for mergers crossing 2-digit industry boundaries (corresponding to the definition of Table 1.14).

If these results for non-horizontal mergers prove robust to further empirical work, they are an interesting finding. It must be remembered, however, that the differences are quite small and high proportions of non-

---

[41] Thus, whilst the data in Table 1.13 refer to differences in the normalized profit ratios, in Table 1.14 the data represent mean changes in actual profit rates.

[42] The profitability change discrepancies hold for both the matched pairs and the overall control group comparisons, which is inconsistent with an explanation based on difficulties of matching for size. Of more relevance is the possible relative downward effect on control group profits in the other studies arising from taking weighted averages (if profits are negatively related to size) and the possible regression towards mean performance of the control group companies in the Cosh, Hughes, and Singh study which were relatively profitable in the pre-merger period compared with *both* the acquiring and acquired companies.

[43] It should be remembered that these profit effects are probably biased downward because they are not adjusted for the accounting problems discussed earlier and they include multiple acquisitions which compound these effects. To the extent that multiple acquisition is associated with learning by doing and persistent success, their exclusion from the Meeks study would bias his results downward and, as we have seen above, there is some evidence that the most intensive acquirers are relatively profitable. However, both the other studies in Table 1.13 included them without dramatically changing the results. Cosh, Hughes, and Singh also report the effects of merger on the sales margin (insignificantly positive for both non-horizontal and horizontal merger) and the ratio of post-tax income to equity assets (significantly positive for non-horizontal and insignificantly so for horizontal). The latter was investigated as part of an analysis of the impact of changes in leverage as a determinant and effect of merger, and gains in this measure reflect the use of debt as part of the purchase consideration to effect capital restructuring. Meeks and Meeks (1981) criticize the sales margin as being biased upwards in the event of vertical merger since some sales are internalized, whilst profits on them are still recorded. The force of this may depend upon the extent to which the control group is vertically integrating. As it happens, the non-horizontal mergers do no better in terms of sales margin changes than horizontal mergers, whilst in terms of the rate of return on assets they do outperform them.

Table 1.14. The change in profitability[a] due to merger, 1967–70

Merger comparison	3-year mean change in profitability				Difference in mean changes	Percentage of industries where difference positive	5-year mean change in profitability				Difference in mean changes	Percentage of industries where difference positive
	Merging		Non-merging				Merging		Non-merging			
	n	$\Delta\Pi$	n	$\Delta\Pi$			n	$\Delta\Pi$	n	$\Delta\Pi$		
All v. C	225	−0.26	1 186	−1.13	0.87*	57	211	0.63	1 185	−0.74	1.38*	71
All v. MAGMAD	225	−0.26	225	−1.78	1.52**	64	211	0.63	211	−0.24	0.87	50
Horizontal v. MAGMAD	109	−0.71	109	−1.89	1.18	64	98	0.47	98	+0.15	0.32	50
Non-horizontal v. MAGMAD	116	+0.16	116	−1.67	1.83**	57	113	0.78	113	−0.58	1.35*	61

* Significantly different from zero at 10% on a 2-tailed test.
** Significantly different from zero at 5% on a 2-tailed test.

Note: For definition of the control groups, see the text.

Source: Cosh, Hughes, and Singh (1980).

horizontal acquirers have negative post-merger performance changes. Nevertheless their relative superiority may be rationalized. It may, for instance, reflect the relative characteristics of the acquiring and acquired firms in this type of take-over compared with others. In both the Meeks (M) and Cosh, Hughes, and Singh (CHS) samples, the acquirers in these mergers were relatively more profitable pre-merger than horizontal acquirers or companies in general. In CHS they acquired significantly below-average profit victims. In M their victims were distinctly above average in profitability. The post-merger evidence suggests that these acquirers were able in the former case on average to turn poor performance around and in the latter more or less maintain good performance. As far as horizontal mergers are concerned, the situation was a bit different. In the CHS sample *both* the acquiring and acquired companies were below-par performers, whilst in M the acquiring were above par and the acquired below. In neither case on average did performance improve after merger and in the M study it fell. If the CHS horizontal mergers were failing firm, rationalizing, or defensive ones, they served only to maintain, not improve, relative performance. One possible explanation for the difference in post-merger performance between the groups is therefore simply that the non-horizontal acquisitions were made by a superior subset of firms (whose relatively superior pre-merger performance reflects superior management skills). This is consistent with a market for corporate control role for diversifying firms. However, as we noted earlier, on average they exercised 'discipline' over the weak only in the CHS case. In M's sample the way to avoid their attention would have been to pursue lower, not higher, profits. More plausibly, the differences between the studies reflect the multi-causal nature of merger motives, in some cases acquirers seeking to turn around poor performers, in others seeking to maintain overall performance by buying into successful ones, the dominant motives varying from time period to time period and company to company. A further question remains, however, and that is, why whatever superior performance horizontal acquirers may have relative to their victims does not lead to gains, or produce losses, whilst the impact for non-horizontal acquirers is more positive.

It may be argued that this reflects the superior ability of diversifying firms to absorb new companies. This in turn depends upon the extent to which they have internally divisionalized management structures more readily adapted to the integration of new concerns. There is little doubt that inadequate post-merger management planning and decision-taking can be a key factor in determining the success or failure of merger and that divisionalized firms may have an advantage in this respect (Kitching (1967, 1974), Newbould (1970), Cowling *et al.* (1980), Grinyer and Spender (1979), Samuels (1971), Hope (1976), Pratten (1970), Hill (1984)). The divisionalized form was, of course, growing in importance in the 1960s, and its adoption is linked to diversification (Steer and Cable (1978), Thompson (1982), Channon (1973)). In the case of the sample of mergers discussed above, any advantage in absorbing acquired companies arising from product-based divisionalization would be strengthened in comparing non-horizontal with horizontal acquirers. This is because the former were typically acquiring companies relatively much smaller than themselves than were the latter (Cosh, Hughes, and Singh (1980), Meeks (1977)). The horizontal acquirers therefore may have experienced greater integration costs both because of inadequate management structures and because of a greater relative size of victim. A further factor may also have been at work. In horizontal mergers there may have been upward wage drift arising from parity bargaining between the plants of newly merged firms in the same industry. Thus Millward and McQueeney (1981), in a case study of 5 mergers in the period 1971–4 where the acquirers employed over 15,000 workers and where there was some degree of diversification involved, found some slight evidence of an increase in parity claims post-merger. They speculate that these would be more widespread in horizontal mergers where the scope for such claims is greater. Moreover if, as Geroski and Knight (1984) argue, the divisionalized form itself is a management response to gain enhanced control over pay and conditions of work, then not only would the parity claims be lower, but the response to them in general might be more effective. In these terms non-horizontal mergers may show superior performance because the internal distribution of income is shifted towards the managers and/or the stockholders. This would reflect a distributional rather than an efficiency impact.

Merger profitability and investment

A further clue to the relative success of the non-horizontal group may be traced to their investment performance. In their case study work, Cowling *et al.* (1980) noted that on a number of occasions where post-merger productivity improvements occurred, this was in association with the introduction of expansionary or restructuring programmes of capital expenditure.[44] They concluded that the link between merger, investment, and improved relative productivity was more than coincidental. Their evidence related to horizontal mergers and would imply, if generalizable, that post-merger success in that group will be related to post-merger investment performance.[45] Equally, if non-horizontal mergers have a better

[44] The cases in question were London Brick/Marston Valley, RHP, and Johnson/Richards Campbell.

[45] In what follows it is implicitly assumed that it is investment which permits the efficiency and profit improvements, rather than better profit performance permitting higher investment.

Table 1.15. Mergers, profitability, and investment

Post-merger year	Number of mergers	All mergers					Horizontal mergers		Non-horizontal mergers	
		Change in normalized profit	Percentage positive	Change in investment share	Percentage positive	Correlation coefficient between (2) and (3)	Change in investment share	Percentage positive	Change in investment share	Percentage positive
	(1)	(2)		(3)		(4)				
$t + 3$	241	−0.008***	39*	0.26	54	+.113***	0.02	53	0.55***	57
$t + 5$	186	−0.06	40*	0.21	58*	+.102**	0.07	55	0.47***	56

* Significantly different from 50% at the 5% level.
** Significantly different from zero at the 10% level.
*** Significantly different from zero at the 5% level.

Source: Calculated from Kumar (1985) Tables 5.3, 5.4, 5.5, 5.8.

post-investment record than horizontal mergers, then as a second hypothesis we might argue that this might help account for their superior profit performance too. Some evidence bearing on these issues is provided in Table 1.15, which shows (for the same sample of companies whose profit changes were analysed in Table 1.13) changes in the share of industry investment for merging firms pre- and post-merger, both in total and for a break-down between horizontal and non-horizontal mergers. It also shows for mergers as a whole the profitability changes following merger and the correlation between them and investment share changes.

A number of points emerge. First, for the sample as a whole there is a small positive change in investment share for merging firms. By the fifth year after merger, 58 per cent show increased investment performance (significantly different from random expectations on the binomial probability test). This is consistent with a number of other studies which have shown on a cross-section basis that there is a positive and significant relationship between growth by acquisition and growth by new fixed investment, and that overall asset growth post-merger is maintained at least at pre-merger rates (Meeks (1977), Cosh, Hughes, and Singh (1980)).[46] The table also shows, however, in keeping with the first hypothesis outlined above, a small but statistically significant correlation between improvements in investment share and changes in normalized profit (column 4). Finally, it is noticeable that when the merging sample is split into horizontal and non-horizontal groups, the former have a negligible investment share change, whilst the latter show a larger and statistically significant improvement. This gives some support to our second conjecture: that these firms may be more successful post-merger because they invest more. At least two possible explanations may be relevant here. The first would emphasize again the superior management form argument. If fewer managerial resources are required to integrate and plan the development of acquisitions in non-horizontal merger, then more are available for planning net expansion. Thus, any trade-off between the two forms of growth may be reduced. Second, non-horizontal merger itself may be the way in which entry into sectors offering new profitable investment opportunities is effected.

However, all of this requires further work to establish both the strength of the underlying relationships themselves and the possible reasons for

[46] Meeks reports, for instance, that in the period 1964–71 the 100 most acquisition-intensive companies also had the highest rate of growth by net investment, and that for 17 industries out of 18 a regression of growth by new investment on growth by acquisition showed a positive coefficient on the acquisition variable. In 9 cases the coefficient was statistically significant. It might be argued that this could reflect the acquisition of dynamic companies rather than an effect of merger. However, the result reported in the text compares pre- and post-merger investment *shares* for both partners, which avoids this problem.

them. Indeed it is a striking feature of the work on merger effects that so little attention has been paid to identifying the relative characteristics of successful and unsuccessful mergers.

Technical change, trade performance, and the regional dimension

With the exception of the discussion of investment effects, the emphasis so far has been essentially static. It has, moreover, focused primarily upon benefits and costs at the level of the individual company. In terms of the wider public interest issues with which economic policy in an open economy is concerned, dynamic and spatial effects are clearly of central interest.

Technical change and trade To the extent that merger has had a positive association with investment performance, it may have improved productivity via embodied technical change, benefits accruing both through the scrapping and replacement of old plant and via net investment. There is some scattered case study evidence to this effect. Thus the London Brick/Marston Valley merger of 1968 led to a gain in efficiency from a post-merger investment and rationalization programme involving a modernization of plant and equipment (Cowling *et al.* (1980)). Evidence that merger may enhance the effectiveness of inputs into the process of technical improvement is also available. The impact of the government-sponsored formation by merger of ICL in 1968 appears to have improved the effectiveness of the UK industry's research and development effort, and of the government's funding, by reducing competitive replication of expenditure. The resulting effect on product quality served to enhance the ability of ICL to match its international rivals in domestic and foreign markets (Stoneman (1978), Cowling *et al.* (1980)). These are, however, particular cases. The merit of the case study approach is the ability to avoid over-simple counterfactuals; its drawback is the difficulty of generalizing results such as these in the face of the limited application of this technique to the UK. It is certainly possible, as some have done, to argue that whatever the evidence suggests in terms of changes in technical performance, the take-over process as a whole might generally inhibit companies from taking a long-term view toward technically enhancing expenditures. If investors' time horizons imply sacrificing research and development expenditures to keep short-term profits and share prices up, then productivity growth and product development may suffer. Apart from the indirect evidence of the relationship between short-term profit changes and the probability of take-over, and possible short-term pressures on institutional and other investors discussed above, there is little beyond anecdotal evidence to support this view for the UK (see, however, Lorenz (1979)).

The evidence on trade effects is also scanty. The case studies of Cowling *et al.* (1980) again suggest some cases where merger enhanced or sustained the ability of the firms concerned to meet international competition. (In addition to ICL, these included mergers in machine tools and bearings where management reorganizations and restructuring played an important role.) Equally, there were others where such claims were made pre-merger but the evidence did not suggest that much improvement materialized subsequently. There is also some statistical cross-section material for individual companies bearing on this issue. Kumar (1984) reports a positive and significant correlation between acquisition intensity and export growth for large samples of continuing quoted UK companies in the periods 1968–72 and 1972–6. The relationship between acquisition intensity and the growth of the export to sales ratio was, however, weaker and not statistically significant. This, of course, does not get directly at the issue of the impact of merger upon subsequent performance. However, for a sample of 311 firms divided into high and low acquisition intensity groups in the period 1965–70, Kumar reports a higher subsequent growth in exports and in export intensity in the period 1971–6 for the merger-intensive group. The differences are not, however, statistically significant.

Regional impacts The impact of merger upon the regional balance of activity and employment is one of the criteria which the Monopolies and Mergers Commission is asked to take into account in its evaluation of the public interest impact of a merger. It has been a significant issue, for instance, in two recent reports where the possibly adverse implications of a proposed merger for the Scottish regional economy were at stake (Charter Consolidated/Anderson Strathclyde, and Royal Bank of Scotland/Hong Kong and Shanghai Bank). It also figured prominently in the campaign to win reference of the BTR bid for Pilkingtons, a bid that was ultimately abandoned. The subject has been relatively neglected by industrial economists. Cowling *et al.* (1980) consider employment rationalization in a general sense in a number of their case studies and provide a specific account of the labour reorganization within GEC following the major mergers involving that company in the late 1960s. Their concern is not, however, with estimating regional impacts as such, but more with considering the extent to which the social costs of community unemployment and job opportunity effects are taken into account in the merger decision. Their answer to which is not a lot.

Massey and Meegan (1979), on the other hand, provide an explicitly spatial analysis of the short-term employment effects, over the period 1967–72, of 14 mergers in the electrical engineering and aerospace industries which the Industrial Reorganization Corporation (IRC) sponsored in the period 1967–70.[47] They stress the historical and industrial specificity of their study and the difficulty of generalizing across space and time in the face of changes in macro-economic conditions and regional policy. The overwhelmingly dominant short-term impact of the mergers they studied was reduced employment, with 38,000 jobs lost and only 4,500 transferred between UK standard regions. The concentration of closed plants in relatively prosperous areas, however, plus the existing strong regional policy incentives to relocate towards the Development Areas, meant that the latter gained most from the limited job switching which occurred. The short-term result was thus a slight decrease in regional unemployment inequality. Similarly, Leigh and North (1978) argue on the basis of an analysis of 263 food, clothing, textiles, and chemical acquisitions in the period 1973–4 that in the Development Areas, superior short-term output and productivity performance following merger may have emerged.

Other studies covering later or longer time periods and different industries are less favourable. They suggest higher closure rates in the Development Areas for externally acquired or controlled plants compared with indigenous ones (Healey (1982), Smith and Taylor (1983), Smith (1979)), and lower rates of employment growth (Fothergill and Gudgin (1982)). Moreover, it has been argued, on the basis of an analysis of plants employing over 100 people in the northern region in the period 1963–73, that where externally acquired plants do show a superior employment growth performance to those which remain independently and locally owned, this may reflect the superior pre-merger growth performance of the acquired plants (Smith (1979)). This would imply a transfer of control outside the region for the most dynamic ones within it. If this could be more securely demonstrated, it could have serious long-term consequences for regional economy growth prospects, when combined with important conclusions emerging from studies of managerial and organizational changes following merger.[48]

On the basis of an interview-based case study of 5 non-horizontal mergers in the period 1971–4, Millward and McQueeney (1981) note a general upward shift of decision-making to the new parent company. This affected in particular capital spending, financing, insurance, legal services, data processing, and clerical and management training functions. In a similar vein, Massey and Meegan (1978) suggest that these and other post-merger restructuring changes in their sample of IRC mergers could give rise to short- and long-run effects weakening growth prospects in the regions outside the south-east. Thus, in the post-merger period the regional branch

---

[47] They included the formation of ICL (under the Industrial Expansion Act (1968)) because of its links with other companies involved in IRC-sponsored rationalization.

[48] For some further informal illustrations of the point see Smith (1986).

plant was left as a production unit with relatively few high-skilled employment opportunities, whilst the higher-level management control, and technical and scientific support functions, were switched elsewhere, especially to the south-east. Supporting conclusions emerge from the analysis by Leigh and North (1978) of 141 acquisitions by 61 companies in the food, chemicals, textiles, and clothing industries in the early 1970s. They show by means of an interview and case study approach that although there was some variation between region, industry, and type of take-over (for example, horizontal or non-horizontal), in general only low-level managerial decision-making (relating to material inputs and production) was retained locally. As a result, in the short term, local economy sourcing for these inputs was maintained in over 80 per cent of cases. On the other hand, over 80 per cent of service linkages affecting marketing, banking, insurance, advertising, legal advice, transport, and security were broken and either internalized by the central parent company or transferred to suppliers in the headquarters region. Nor is this a problem which has spatial effects only across regions. Relocation of headquarters and related staff changes can also have intra-regional implications. It has been argued, for instance, that within the south-east, post-merger changes have contributed to the shift of activity away from inner city to outer ring and suburban locations (Massey and Meegan (1978, 1979), Leigh and North (1978), Gripaios (1977)).

Stock price effects and market returns

The difficulties of estimating changes in accounting profitability and real effects in terms of resource use have led some investigators to emphasize the virtues of using stock price movements as a better guide to the performance impact of merger. There is a growing body of work adopting this approach, though, as I shall argue, it is not without its own important limitations.

Cosh, Hughes, and Singh (1980) complement their accounting data tests with a comparison of shareholder returns (capital gains plus reinvested dividends) in the 5 years before and after merger for 63 acquiring companies and 63 size- and industry-matched non-acquiring companies in the period 1967–9. They find that for the pre- and post-merger periods the acquiring companies had higher shareholder returns. For the pre-merger periods and one year after merger, these positive differences were statistically significant. Thereafter the performance of the acquirers deteriorated relative to the control group. Sturgess and Wheale (1984) compare for each year in the period 1961–70 shareholder returns for two groups of 26 companies which differ in that one experienced intensive merger activity in the period 1961–5 and the other did not. They find no significant differences between the groups in either period. Their results, however, show that in 3 of the years 1961–5 the merger-intensive group significantly over-performed, and in 2 of them significantly under-performed, relative to the non-merging group. In the 1966–70 period this is so in only 1 year. This pattern of performance between periods is consistent with the Cosh, Hughes, and Singh results which suggest post-merger declines for the acquirers.[49]

With these and one or two other exceptions, studies of the impact of merger based on stock price movements have not used return comparisons between merging and non-merging groups but have preferred 'event' study methodology applied to samples of acquiring and acquired companies.[50] A model of stock price returns is estimated excluding data for a period before and after merger and then actual returns for the firms involved are compared with the counterfactual returns based on the estimated equation. The deviation between the actual and counterfactual returns are termed abnormal (AR) and their cumulative sum (CAR) relative to some reference point is taken as the market's reaction to the 'new information' contained in the merger 'event'. Thus positive CARs associated with merger are taken to show that the merger is expected to create value for the shareholders reflecting economic efficiency gains. As Marsh (1986) puts it, 'Quite simply, if acquirees' shareholders gain, and if (at worst) acquirers' shareholders do not lose, there must therefore be net gains to shareholders from acquisition. Put another way, acquisitions have historically allowed companies to reap economic and efficiency gains'.

The most frequently used counterfactual models on which judgements such as this are based are the Capital Asset Pricing Model (CAPM), the Market Model, and the Mean-Adjusted Return Model. Actual returns may also be simply compared directly with a market index. These various models may be set out as follows, where P is the security price, D represents dividends, r_{jt} is the return on security j in month t, $\bar{r}_j$ is its average value over some period of months, rm_t is the return on a market index, rf_t is the risk-free rate of return, and α and β are coefficients of a regression equation used to estimate R^*_{jt} (the counterfactual 'normal' return) so that

$$\mathrm{AR}_{jt} = r_{jt} - R^*_{jt}$$

and

$$r_{jt} = \frac{\{P_t - P_{t-1}\} + D_t}{P_t}.$$

[49] Adjusting their returns for risk using the Sharpe measure reverses the periods, in the sense that the internal growers now outperform the acquirers in the merger-intensive period and vice versa (Sturgess and Wheale (1984)).

[50] Firth (1978), however, combines both. See the discussion of his results below.

R^*_{jt} and hence AR_{jt} may then be calculated using:

1. Mean-Adjusted Return Model $(R^*_{jt} = \bar{r}_j)$

$$AR_{jt} = r_{jt} - \bar{r}_j$$

2. Market Model[51] $(R^*_{jt} = \alpha_j + \beta_j \mathrm{rm}_t)$

$$AR_{jt} = r_{jt} - (\alpha_j + \beta_j \mathrm{rm}_t)$$

3. Capital Asset Pricing Model $(R^*_{jt} = \mathrm{rf}_t + \beta_j(\mathrm{rm}_t - \mathrm{rf}_t))$

$$AR_{jt} = r_{jt} - (\mathrm{rf}_t + \beta_j(\mathrm{rm}_t - \mathrm{rf}_t))$$

4. Simple Market Index Model $(R^*_{it} = \mathrm{rm}_t)$

$$AR_{jt} = r_{jt} - \mathrm{rm}_t.$$

With few exceptions in the UK, the market model is estimated using ordinary least squares (OLS) to obtain the counterfactual values.[52] We can look at the results of these studies for the acquired and acquiring firms separately and then at the net outcome taking both together.

Effects on acquiring companies Barnes estimates the effects of making a bid on 39 acquiring companies in the period June 1974 to February 1976 using a simple index model (Barnes (1978)) and the market model plus an industry index (Barnes (1984)). He reports small positive abnormal returns in the year before merger and offsetting or more than offsetting cumulative negative returns lasting up to 5 years afterwards, although none of these effects are statistically significant. This is in keeping with the declining post-merger results of Cosh, Hughes, and Singh reported earlier using shareholder returns relative to a non-merging control group.

Franks, Broyles, and Hecht (1977) also use the market model plus a market index in a study of 70 mergers in the period 1955–72 in the UK brewing industry. Like Barnes, they find positive abnormal returns in the immediate run-up to the bid announcement that persist for a few months after. There then follow negative effects, chiefly in the period between 5 and 10 months after the bid, so that by the fourth year after merger the CARs

[51] In some cases an industry-specific index may be added to the estimating equation:

$$R^*_{jt} = \alpha_j + \beta_j \mathrm{rm}_t + \gamma_j \mathrm{rz}_t.$$

[52] Recent simulation studies suggest that the simpler estimation techniques and models (such as the mean-adjusted return) are as powerful as the more complex ones in identifying abnormal security performance (Brown and Warner (1980), Malatesta (1986)).

are negative. Similar post-bid results are reported by Dodds and Quek (1985). They analyse 70 acquisitions using the market model in the same period of low merger activity in the mid-1970s as the Barnes sample. They report that after initially positive post-merger effects, the CARs are negative by the fifth year, with 58 per cent of the acquirers showing negative returns. However, as in Barnes, none of this is statistically significant. Franks and Harris (1986b), again using the market model, also report positive abnormal returns over the immediate bid announcement period in a sample of 1,048 mergers in the period 1955–85, a similar result to that of Meadowcroft and Thompson (1986) for 67 mergers in the period 1982–4. In the Franks and Harris study, this is followed by cumulatively negative effects, so that by 2 years after the mergers the CARs are significantly negative and outweigh the pre-merger gains.[53] Finally, Firth (1979, 1980), for samples of 224 successful bids in the period 1972–4 and 434 in the period 1969–75 respectively, reports positive abnormal residuals prior to merger for bidders using equity as the means of payment, substantial losses at the time of bid announcement, and cumulatively negative residuals after the bid, so that for his 1969–75 sample, for instance, by the end of the third year 64 per cent of the acquiring companies have negative CARs. (See also Firth (1976).) Taken as a whole, these studies suggest that acquirers launch their bids when their prices are relatively high (either by accident or design), but that whatever positive short-term effects are associated with the bid, in the longer run they are followed by cumulatively negative effects.

Acquired companies Firth (1979, 1980) reports mildly negative deviations from expected returns in the first 10 months of the year prior to the bid, with around 55 per cent of the acquired companies showing negative CARs. In the 2 months prior to the bid announcement, however, positive abnormal returns occur, becoming very large and statistically significant in the merger month itself, so that by the announcement date 99 per cent of acquired companies show positive CARs suggesting gains of around 22 to 28 per cent due to the merger event. Similarly, Franks, Broyles, and Hecht (1977) report abnormal gains of 26 per cent on average over the 5 months up to and including the offer date; Franks and Harris (1986b) report bid premiums in the 25 to 30 per cent range over the interval from 4 months prior to to 1 month past the first approach or first bid date, and

---

[53] They do not find this result using CAPM, or a simple index model, and speculate that this is due to the fact that if bidders time their bids to coincide with relative highs in their own prices, then the estimated α in the market model will be 'too high' so that there is an inevitable drift downwards after merger compared with counterfactual returns based on the estimated market model. The force of this must depend to some extent on how the estimation period is chosen, and the date from which the abnormal returns are then cumulated. For a critique of the capital asset pricing model itself and possible biases in estimating the counterfactual equations, see Conn (1985).

Meadowcroft and Thompson (1986) report similar gains over a slightly shorter period straddling the bid date.

In the case of Franks, Broyles, and Hecht (1977) and Meadowcroft and Thompson (1986), these gains follow periods of negative residuals which are, however, rarely statistically significant. The picture here is fairly clear-cut: the acquired companies have a mildly below par performance in the year before merger, but as the bid date approaches they gain in performance, perhaps as a result of leaks, insider trading, or the build-up of pre-bid strategic shareholdings. The bid period itself then generates substantial positive premiums.

The net effects Firth (1979, 1980) judges the immediate *short-term* effects on the acquiring and acquired companies together in the late 1960s and early 1970s to have been neutral or negative. That is to say, allowing for the relative sizes of the companies involved, the losses to the acquirers in the 1 month prior to and after the bid matched, or more than offset, the gains to the acquired company over the same period. This neutral or negative impact was maintained up to 2 years post-merger, so that 'The stock market viewed takeovers as having little overall impact on corporate profitability' (Firth (1980)). This view is consistent with the actual profit outcomes discussed above. Meadowcroft and Thompson (1986) and Franks and Harris (1986b), analysing the early 1980s and the period 1955–85 respectively, conclude, on the other hand, that there are net benefits in the short term (that is, 1 month before to 2 or 3 months after the bid). In their samples, the acquirers either gain slightly or at least do not lose, whilst the acquired have substantial positive residuals. (Thus, Meadowcroft and Thompson suggest net gains of around 7–8 per cent on the pre-merger total market capitalization of the companies involved.) These are very short-term effects, however. By the end of the second year, the Franks and Harris acquirers are showing significantly negative residuals at least using the market model (Meadowcroft and Thompson provide no data beyond month 12). It is difficult to argue that these studies taken together and in their own terms suggest that the market expected fundamental long-term gains to occur, and if it did, it revised its opinions as far as the acquirers are concerned. Such gains as did occur accrued to the shareholders in the acquired company.[54]

---

[54] Interestingly, gains of a similar or greater extent seem to be made by shareholders in target companies where the bids fail, as well as those in which they succeed (Firth (1980)). This may reflect pepped-up performance following the bid, and suggests that the threat may be as effective as the fact of take-over. Thus Pickering (1983) reports some target companies as effecting managerial and other changes after surviving bids, and in the majority of his 20 case studies he reports some improvement in performance. It is notable, however, that many of the targets sought purchase by third parties, went for short-term growth, or acquired other companies as ways of reducing future vulnerability, rather than pursuing improved profitability.

The idea that merger has insignificant effects on the processes generating expected returns receives further support from another study by Firth. He estimated the parameters of the market model for 24 months prior to merger, and 24 months after, for 150 merging companies and a similar number of size- and industry-matched non-acquiring companies in the period 1972–4. He could find no systematic significant differences between the merging group and the control group in the mean or variance of stock market returns either pre- or post-merger, or in the estimated parameters of the market model (Firth (1978)).

Even if it were accepted that in the short run the joint effects of merger on abnormal returns may be positive, a fundamental problem of interpretation remains. The underlying methodology of the event studies assumes that demand curves for stocks are horizontal, so that normally trading investors may buy or sell any amount of stock without systematically affecting the price. The marginal price reflects average opinion; when sharp movements in price occur in association with an event (for example, a take-over), they are then interpreted as a response to the 'new information' imparted by it. Positive abnormal returns associated with bids may therefore be interpreted to suggest that the market expects improved performance to follow from merger and shareholders benefit accordingly. The distribution of these gains between the acquired and acquiring is then determined by the competitiveness of the bid market, the presence or absence of rival bids or contests, and so on.

If, however, there are, for instance, divergences of expectations and opinion over security values so that the marginal trading valuation reflects marginal opinion, then the market demand curve slopes downwards to the right and some investors will require a price above that at the margin before selling (Hughes, Mueller, and Singh (1980), Cragg and Malkiel (1982), Miller (1977), Black (1986), Shleifer (1986), Mayshar (1983)). Premiums will therefore be necessary simply to effect the ownership transfer in a take-over, and they may vary with the dispersion of stockholdings and the dispersion of divergent opinion across the various blocks of shares. These premiums will therefore be highly ambiguous guides to expected efficiency gains either when taken on average or in relation to particular mergers. They tell us merely what the short-term windfall wealth effects of merger are, relative to a particular counterfactual for the small number of individuals directly involved as shareholders (or the larger number indirectly involved via changes in pensions and insurance policy premiums following financial institutions' portfolio responses to bids). There is no necessary connection between the direction and magnitude of these premiums and underlying real changes in the management and performance of the assets over which the property rights embodied in the stock give control.[55] All we can deduce is that for *some* reasons the bidders felt it worth while to offer the premiums and the sellers felt it worth while to accept. These reasons, as we saw earlier, may be as much related to the pursuit of monopoly power and empire-building as to enhanced management techniques, scale and scope economies, or other efficiency-enhancing targets. The existing UK stock price evidence does not help us distinguish between them.[56] It is an act of faith to argue on the basis of it alone that acquisitions have in general allowed companies to reap economic or efficiency gains.

6. Conclusions on the Impact of Merger: Structure, Performance, and Policy

Mergers have played a major role in the post-war structural transformation of the UK economy. They have had an impact upon the concentration of market sales, the diversification of corporate output, and the regional and international distribution of corporate activity.

Concentration at the market and aggregate level rose substantially to the late 1960s. This was in large part due to the scale and incidence of merger activity in the decade following the first increases in merger in the late 1950s. The peak years of merger activity from 1968 to 1973 were not, however, associated with contemporaneous or subsequent increases on the same scale. In fact, concentration hardly changed over the decade of the 1970s as a whole. We do not, however, have any systematic studies of the role that merger has played in these years. Reconciling high rates of merger and stability in domestic concentration is possible if, for instance, *inter alia*, a considerable portion of the activity is directed overseas, or contributes either to a faster rate of growth for smaller firms or a reduced variance of growth rates. In the 1960s and early 1970s, we have seen that merger growth and internal growth were if anything complementary. If in the depressed years of the late 1970s and early 1980s net investment has been severely constrained and merger growth has substituted for it at the individual firm level, then extremely high growth rates combining both internal and external expansion might be less frequent, and the drift towards domestic concentration reduced. Similar effects may occur if merger and other forms of expansion by large firms are increasingly diverted abroad.

---

[55] It is interesting in this connection to note that Kuehn (1975) could not find any systematic relationship between the financial and performance variables of acquiring, and acquired, firms and the size of the bid premium.

[56] It is possible, however, by choosing appropriate control group samples, to try to isolate monopoly effects, etc.; for a relevant survey of US evidence, see Jensen and Ruback (1983).

In several instances, changes in concentration may have led to increased market power. It is difficult to sustain the argument, however, that the degree of monopoly in the UK domestic market has increased in the last two decades. At best it might be argued that merger has served to maintain whatever power existed previously, but even that seems overly generous.

Diversifying activity has increased in importance and some firms have grown spectacularly fast by non-horizontal merger. The implication for market power of these changes is ambiguous and probably less important than their broader impact on the nature of resource allocation, in particular for investment goods and productive resources. Much here depends upon how optimistic a view one takes of the virtues of the stock market allocation process versus the internal administrative market of conglomerate firms, and the damage that the loss of information through consolidated accounts causes to the former.

Take-over or the threat of it, as a disciplinary stock market device, leaves a lot to be desired. Except at the height of booms, its discipline appears constrained to the middle size ranges of companies. Moreover, the most favourable route to avoid nemesis is to grow bigger and seek more stable profits in the short run rather than to go for higher medium-term profitability. The disciplinarians are bigger and faster-growing but not on average more profitable, and their shareholders gain little or even lose as a result of their company's acquisitions. The shareholders of acquired companies, on the other hand, make windfall gains that on average have no counterpart in improved resource use or corporate profitability. If these gains are supposed to represent expected performance improvements, then direct evidence on the latter suggests that the market gets it wrong and is on average too optimistic. Neutral net effects on stockholder welfare would be more consistent with observed average post-merger performance effects. All this evidence seems at least as consistent with an inducement to empire-building by growth-minded managers as with discipline in the stockholders' interests.

Within this story, the non-horizontal acquirers appear in a less unfavourable light. They are more successful pre-merger than other acquirers and they improve or sustain performance post-merger better than other acquirers, both in terms of profitability and in terms of post-merger investment, though the differences in either direction are not terribly large. Against this, some information loss might seem a small cost, especially since it is in principle remediable by improved reporting and disclosure requirements. Despite the much publicized success of some conglomerates, not all conglomerates are efficiently run internally and their victims are not always those mismanaging their affairs, so that the growth and success of these acquirers may come to depend on the capture of ever bigger and more successful companies to maintain a given proportionate expansion in size and performance. Nor does the existing evidence tell us much about the sources of the gains in profits for these companies. Some may be consistent with a convergence of private and public gain; others may not, or may represent internal redistributions of income. Moreover, anyone with a memory stretching back to the heady days of the merger boom of the late 1960s will recall how the shining captains of industry today can become tomorrow's over-ambitious failures. And there are always problems of management succession. As with profits, so with growth rates, there is some evidence of regression towards the mean.

Compared with conglomerate mergers, those that have been horizontal have produced neutral or negative performance effects at the micro-economic level. To the extent that horizontal merger activity is more widespread and frequent, it could be argued that neutral results are to be expected since, on average, over long periods of time one sort of expansion (internal) should show the same sort of return as another (external). If in addition there are management diseconomies and industrial relations problems, then over-indulgence in periods of high activity may produce some losses overall. There might be something in this, but it should apply to other forms of merger growth too, so that non-horizontal expansion should be no more successful than other kinds. It is possible to argue here that in fact it too will converge toward the norm, once it becomes the predominant form, and there are more rivalrous predators pursuing the same prey. All this assumes a distribution of entrepreneurial talent and empire-building drive that may, in the UK context, be overly optimistic. In any event, the fact that horizontal mergers are as likely to fail as to succeed, whilst they have obvious potential for market power effects, suggests that on these grounds there should be an appropriate case by case application of existing merger policy powers to them. In the case of non-horizontal mergers where market power effects are suspected, close consideration should be paid to the nature of the company's past success as well as the internal features of its management structure, since these seem likely to be closely connected to the probability of any prospective efficiency gains. In both cases, the power to require undertakings and to monitor post-merger activity should be actively pursued.

All this, however, is very much in terms of private gains and losses, and set in a static context in which efficiency gains are to be traded off domestically against presumed allocative welfare losses (forgone consumers' surplus). There are broader issues. Merger waves bring with them huge windfall gains acquired both legally and illegally by market participants. At the same time, the decisions upon which these redistributions of wealth occur may affect the location of industry and the associated regional distribution of job opportunities and growth prospects within the UK, as well as the ability of industry to compete effectively both domestically and abroad. All of these issues quite properly feature in the list of matters which the Monopolies and Mergers Commission must bear in mind in evaluating the public interest effects of merger, once a reference is made. They have, however, been largely neglected in empirical research which has focused, as we have seen, excessively on the monopoly power–efficiency trade-off and upon an analysis by proxy using stock market returns as a guide to welfare. They have also been ignored most recently in the application of merger policy, where references have been based almost exclusively on competitive effects. Such evidence as we have on these broader issues suggests that there are potentially damaging effects upon regional vitality which may arise after take-over, and on the other hand that in certain circumstances merger can have a central role to play in the reorganization and revitalization of particular sectors. As I have argued at length elsewhere (Hughes (1978)), to be most effective, competition policy must be operated on principles complementary to those adopted in industrial policy generally and be integrated with it. At the very least, the criteria for reference should be consistent with the public interest criteria to be used in evaluating a merger once a reference is made. There is little sense in investigating trade or regional impacts in horizontal merger because a separate market power impact is suspected, but ignoring them in conglomerate mergers because no competition issue is raised.

Finally, it must be recognized that the many issues to which mergers in general, and the current merger wave in particular, give rise cannot be resolved by an appeal to competition policy alone. Much broader questions about the relationship between management and major investors, the internal governance of the modern corporation, and the regulation and organization of capital markets are at issue. As portfolio 'churning' increases in the period of adjustment to Big Bang, it is worth while recalling the views of one well-known market operator.

> As the organization of investment markets improves, the risk of the predominance of speculation does, however, increase. . . . Speculators may do no harm as bubbles on a steady stream of enterprise. But the position is serious when enterprise becomes the bubble on a whirlpool of speculation. When the capital development of a country becomes a by-product of the activities of a casino, the job is likely to be ill done. (Keynes (1936) pp. 158–9)

In the early 1980s in the midst of the latest take-over wave, net capital formation in Britain's manufacturing industry was negative.

2

Take-over Activity in the United Kingdom

MERVYN KING*

1. Introduction

In 1986 the value of mergers and acquisitions in the UK was £13.5 billion.[1] For 1985 as a whole the total was £7.1 billion, for 1984 £5.5 billion, and in no previous year had expenditure exceeded £2.6 billion. Why has there been such a surge in take-over activity?

Simple comparisons of expenditures ignore the change in prices that has occurred, and deflating the figures by a price index for capital goods gives a rather different picture. At 1985 prices, take-over expenditure in the earlier peak years of 1968 and 1972 was £13.3 billion and £11.4 billion respectively. In 1986 take-over expenditure at 1985 prices was £12.9 billion. This is slightly lower than in the previous peak year of 1968. Moreover, as a proportion of the value of the capital stock, take-over expenditure was much higher in 1968 than in 1986.

Nevertheless, the high level of take-over activity witnessed in the last year has prompted renewed doubts about the functioning of the market for corporate control. Recent concern about the conduct of bids and the opportunity for profitable insider trading afforded by take-overs has led many observers to question the value of take-overs as a means of disciplining management. An inquiry into monopolies and mergers policy is being conducted by the Department of Trade and Industry. Three questions are particularly apposite.

---

* Professor of Economics at the London School of Economics and Political Science, University of London.

[1] *Business Monitor* MQ7, fourth quarter 1986, Table 1. *Acquisitions Monthly* (October 1986) reported figures of £13.2 billion for the value of UK public companies acquired and £7.0 billion for UK private companies acquired, giving a total of over £20 billion. These figures include acquisitions by overseas companies and of financial companies, both of which are excluded in the Department of Trade and Industry data. There may be other differences, such as the timing of recorded expenditure, between the two sources.

Firstly, why do take-overs occur in 'waves'? If their role is to replace less efficient by more efficient management teams, then why should this lead to such a volatile pattern for expenditure on acquisitions? I shall argue below that the interaction between movements in the stock market and the structure of corporation tax can help to explain the phenomenon.

Secondly, why is it supposed that the market for corporate control (modified by the existing regulatory framework) generates an economically efficient level and composition of take-over activity? Traditionally, economists have argued that the market provides too *little* rather than too much incentive to engage in take-overs. In contrast, the view is sometimes expressed by industry that the threat of take-over lowers productivity in the long run.

Thirdly, if the take-over mechanism is felt to involve too high a cost, what is the alternative? Managers cannot be allowed to pursue their own interests in an unconstrained manner even if it is costly to monitor their performance. Who is to manage the managers? I shall discuss below the relative merits of the take-over mechanism and some alternative methods of providing an external check on the actions of managers.

2. Take-over Waves in the United Kingdom

Take-over activity is one of the most volatile economic variables. This has

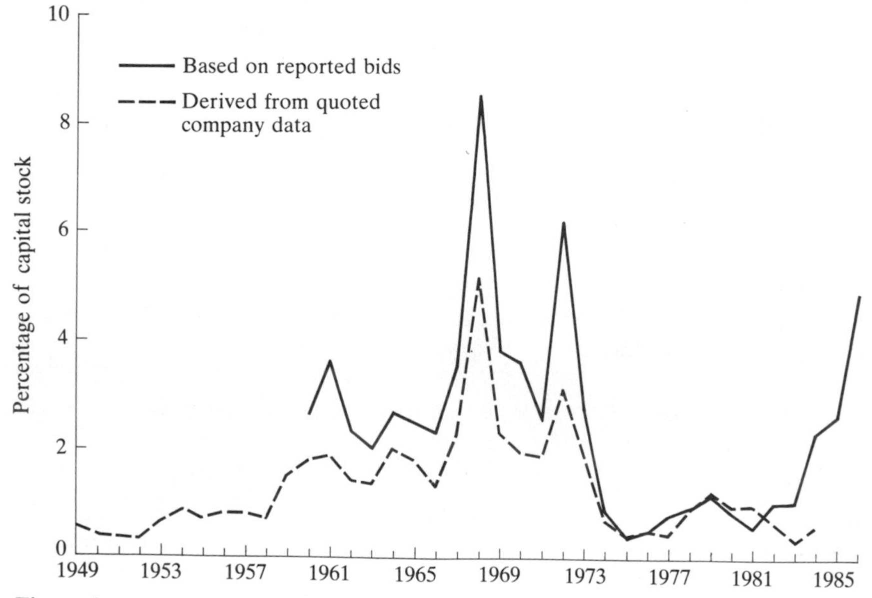

Figure 2.1. Take-over activity, UK 1949–86

led to the idea that take-overs occur in 'waves', with intense peaks of activity followed by troughs of inactivity. If take-over activity is measured by the ratio of expenditure on the acquisition of subsidiaries divided by the value of assets in the corporate sector, then the amount of activity in the peak year, 1968, was over 15 times that in the year with least activity, 1982.

There are two sources of data on the amount of take-over activity in the economy as a whole. The first is the consolidated company accounts published annually by the Department of Trade and Industry (DTI). The second is the data on public announcements of bids which are collected by DTI, followed to completion and published quarterly (in *Business Monitor* MQ7). The pattern of take-over 'waves' in the post-war period is shown in Figure 2.1. Two series are shown. The first is an attempt to construct a consistent series for the post-war period and refers to 1949–83. It is derived from quoted company data and is the series used for the econometric analysis reported below. The second is the DTI series based on reported bids and is available only from 1960. (I have linked the published series which show a break in 1969.) Both series show clearly the take-over waves of 1968, 1972, and (for the series based on announced bids) 1985–6.

3. Puzzles about Take-overs

There are two main puzzles concerning take-over activity. The first is about the timing of take-overs. Why do take-overs occur in waves? The second concerns the issue of whether an unregulated market would generate an efficient level and composition of take-over activity.

As the evidence reviewed in the previous section showed, take-over activity in the UK is highly volatile and occurs in waves. It is also positively correlated with the level of the stock market. But it is difficult to produce a convincing explanation for this observed correlation. The microeconomic determinants of take-overs offer no reason to expect take-overs to occur in waves. And, as Brealey and Myers (1981, p. 679) point out, 'none of the economic motives for mergers . . . has anything to do with the general level of the stock market'. In Section 4 I shall describe a model that explains the relationship between expenditure on acquisitions and the level of the stock market. It is based on the incentive to expand via take-over rather than by investment, which results from the structure of corporate taxation. Empirical tests of this 'trapped equity model' are described below.

The second puzzle surrounding take-over behaviour is the difference between the popular perception of take-over 'mania' as endemic to the Anglo-Saxon capitalist world, and the conventional economic analysis that the market is likely to generate an inefficiently *low* level of take-over activity. What is the source of this apparent conflict and how could it be resolved? The view that insufficient take-overs will occur is based on the difficulty of persuading a dispersed body of shareholders to accept a tender offer at any price that leaves a profit for the offerer. Suppose that a raider could control the assets of a potential target company more efficiently than its existing management. There is a surplus that could be realized to the benefit of all concerned. For simplicity assume that there is no uncertainty about the superior ability of the raider. The problem is to create a coalition to bring about the desired change of control. With a large body of small shareholders, no individual can affect the outcome of a tender offer, and if the offer is expected to succeed there is no incentive to accept unless the offer price exceeds the value of the company under the new management. But the raider would be willing to offer a price no higher than the potential value of the target company less the cost of the bid. Hence any offer price forthcoming will be insufficient to elicit the support of the shareholders of the target company. This is the result of the attempt by small shareholders to 'free-ride' on a successful raid. The problem was analysed by Grossman and Hart (1980).

If the 'free-rider' model is correct then why do we observe any take-overs at all? There are two reasons. Firstly, there may be tax-induced take-over activity of the sort to be explained in Section 4. Secondly, the market finds ways around the free-rider problem. The solution for the raider is to appropriate enough of the surplus to compensate him for the costs of the bid. Since the shareholders would benefit from profitable raids, the dilution of their equity that is necessary to provide an incentive to the raider would be voluntary. There are several ways in which this dilution might occur. One is to allow a successful raider to transfer resources from any remaining minority shareholders to themselves, perhaps by awarding lucrative contracts to another subsidiary. This strategy conflicts with provisions in the Companies Act designed to prevent oppression of minority shareholders. In practice, however, in the UK at least, it is extremely difficult for oppressed minorities to obtain legal redress. Once an offer becomes unconditional, it is normally accepted by the remaining shareholders.

A second solution is to allow the raider to purchase shares in the target company at the pre-bid price before having to reveal his intention to bid. If the raider were allowed to build up a sufficiently large initial stake then the profits on the shares in the target company might be enough to give an incentive to the raider. For example, suppose that the costs of making a hostile bid were 5 per cent of the acquisition cost and the raider would be able to raise the value of the target company by 25 per cent (a little less than the typical premium paid), then the initial stake required would be 5/25 or 20 per cent. It is clear that the provisions of the City Code on disclosure of purchase and declaration of intention by raiders mean that this strategy in itself may not solve the free-rider problem. Under the City Code a raider would be required to disclose his holdings once his initial stake reached 15 per cent. But the effective initial stake that can be built up is probably much less than this figure because the Companies Act compels disclosure of holdings in excess of 5 per cent. And a target company would have an incentive to alert the market to changes in its share register in order to prevent a potential raider from accumulating a large initial stake at the pre-bid price.[2] In the US the threshold that triggers disclosure is 5 per cent, but there is a 'window' of 10 days before the announcement has to be made.

Finally, the raider might collude with a third party who could purchase shares at the pre-bid price, or buy shares after the bid announcement on behalf of the raider in return for a subsequent lucrative contract. At this point arbitrageurs enter the stage. It is very difficult to distinguish between the actions of arbitrageurs in facilitating take-overs that are in the interests of the shareholders, and transactions that are clear examples either of insider trading or of parties acting 'in concert'.

The use of legal and non-statutory restrictions to prevent oppression of minority shareholders and to regulate the behaviour of raiders before a bid is announced, has driven 'underground' the attempts by the parties involved to capture the surplus to be gained from a change in management. There is, therefore, a clash between attempts to prevent the worst abuses of insider trading and the need to find a mechanism to allow efficient take-overs to proceed. In my view the solution is neither to ban or limit take-overs (on the unproven ground that there is no surplus to capture), nor to relax the rules on insider trading, especially those concerning information provided during take-over battles. Instead, alternative means of replacing inefficient by more efficient management should be promoted, and the cause of tax-driven take-over activity should be removed. Some ideas for achieving these objectives are discussed in Section 5.

4. The Trapped Equity Model

There is a tendency to regard merger and acquisition activity as synonymous with hostile tender bids. In view of the publicity surrounding a small number of bitterly contested take-over bids, this is understandable. But in fact, most take-overs, both in the UK and in the US, are not the outcome of hostile bids. For example, in 1982 of 2,400 mergers in the US only 3.9 per cent involved tender offers (American Enterprise Institute (1985)). A satisfactory explanation of take-over activity, therefore, must be able to

---

[2] Roell (1986b) provides a detailed critique of the City Code and its economic effects, including the incentive for raiders to search for potential targets.

account for the large number of acquisitions that are not contested. One possible explanation of take-over waves is that they result from the incentive provided by the corporate tax system to expand via acquisitions.

The existence of a separate tax on companies creates a wedge between the return that can be earned in the corporate sector and the return that could be earned if it were possible to perform the same activity in the unincorporated sector. In most cases the nature and size of the investment required preclude the unincorporated form of organization as a feasible choice. The additional tax burden on companies is capitalized in their share prices. In an 'equilibrium', defined as a state in which the firm wishes neither to expand nor to contract, the value of an unincorporated enterprise is simply the market value of its assets at replacement cost. In the corporate sector the value of the securities (equity, for example) that constitute ownership of the company is the market value of the firm's assets less the present value of the extra taxes levied on the corporate form. The capitalization of the additional taxes on companies means that the ratio of the value of a company on the stock market to the replacement cost value of its assets, known as the Keynes–Tobin q, is less than unity. This view is known as the 'trapped equity model' because money in the corporate sector cannot be distributed to the personal sector without attracting the additional tax burden.

A major implication of the undervaluation property of the trapped equity model is that it is cheaper, *ceteris paribus*, to expand by purchasing companies than by buying new capital goods. In practice, the other costs associated with increasing the size of a firm's operations are very different for the two forms of expansion. The cost of assimilating a new firm into the company's existing operations is likely to be much greater than the adjustment costs resulting from new investment.

I shall now set out a simple version of the trapped equity model of take-overs.[3] To focus attention on the essentials of the model, I shall ignore all differences between raider and target companies. This is in order to demonstrate that take-overs can be driven purely by the effects of the corporate tax system. Differences between raiders and targets can easily be introduced into the model and it can be shown that if the free-rider problem exists then take-over activity is determined solely by the tax effect. It is important to recognize that none of the participants in take-over activity are motivated by tax considerations as such. The influence of taxes comes *solely* through their effect on the level of share prices, and it is these prices that motivate individual take-overs.

Consider a company debating whether to expand by purchasing capital goods or by the acquisition of another company. Most acquisitions are of

---

[3] For a more detailed derivation and discussion, the reader is referred to King (1986).

companies very much smaller than the acquirer, and I shall assume that we can imagine a 'marginal' expansion of the company in either of the two forms. There is a trade-off between the two types of expansion. Take-over is attractive because it is cheaper to buy a company than to buy new capital goods (the undervaluation property) but adjustment costs are greater for take-overs. The company will expand up to the point at which the marginal costs of expansion are equal for both acquisitions and investment. Let the price of a unit of new investment be unity, and the stock market value of a unit of capital be q. If the marginal adjustment costs associated with acquisitions and investment are denoted by c_A and c_I respectively then the following condition holds:

$$1 + (1 - \tau)c_I = q + (1 - \tau)c_A. \qquad (1)$$

This condition states that at the margin the company is indifferent as to whether it expands via acquisition or by investment in new capital goods. Adjustment costs are assumed to be deductible against corporation tax, and the rate of tax is denoted by τ.

Assume that the company has chosen its dividend policy and is indifferent at the margin as to whether it retains a pound and reinvests it, or distributes the pound as a dividend. If the company retains sufficient funds to purchase 1 unit of new investment then its stock market value will rise by q. This must be equal to the market's valuation of the forgone dividend. The cash that the company has to pay for the investment is the direct cost of 1 plus the associated adjustment cost of $(1-\tau)c_I$. But cash in the hands of the company is 'undervalued' by the market because of the additional tax burden on companies. Denote the undervaluation ratio by q^*. In the UK, with its imputation system of corporation tax, the value of q^* is equal to $(1-\tau)/(1-s)$, where s is the basic rate of income tax. Hence the market's valuation of the forgone dividend is $q^*[1+(1-\tau)c_I]$. As argued above, this implies that

$$q = q^*\{1 + (1 - \tau)c_I\}. \qquad (2)$$

From Equations 1 and 2 it follows that

$$c_A = \frac{q}{1 - \tau}\left(\frac{1}{q^*} - 1\right). \qquad (3)$$

Equation 3 describes the optimal pattern of acquisitions activity for a company. It should acquire up to the point where the marginal adjustment cost of acquisition (net of tax) is equal to the value of an extra unit of capital multiplied by the 'undervaluation' percentage. The product of q and the undervaluation percentage is the present discounted value of the taxes that are saved by expanding via acquisition rather than by new investment.

The main implication of the trapped equity model is contained in Equation 3. For a given tax system (described by values of τ and q^*), marginal adjustment costs are, at the optimum, proportional to the level of the stock market, as measured by the value of q. If we make the not unreasonable assumption that marginal adjustment costs are increasing in the quantity of assets acquired, then it is clear that Equation 3 implies that the real volume of take-over activity is positively correlated with the level of the stock market. Take-over activity is driven by the tax wedge between the incorporated and unincorporated sectors. This is proportional to the value of future profits as measured by current share prices. The stock market is high when expected future profits are high, and hence the absolute value of the tax wedge is high also. This creates an incentive for take-over activity.

The next step is to convert Equation 3 into a relationship between observable variables. If we adopt the conventional assumption that marginal adjustment costs are linear in the volume of assets acquired then

$$c_A = \beta_0 + \beta_1 \frac{A}{qK} \tag{4}$$

where A is expenditure on acquisitions and K is the replacement cost value of the firm's capital stock (adjusted for deferred tax liabilities). Equations 3 and 4 together give the following equation for take-over expenditure:

$$\frac{A}{K} = \frac{-\beta_0 q}{\beta_1} + \frac{1}{\beta_1} q^2 + \frac{(1 - q^*)}{(1 - \tau)q^*} \, . \tag{5}$$

In the trapped equity model the principal variable determining the level of take-over activity is the product of the square of the stock market value q and a variable measuring the effect of the corporate tax system.[4] I shall call this variable the 'take-over variable', denoted by TV where

$$\mathrm{TV} = q^2 \frac{(1 - q^*)}{(1 - \tau)q^*} \, . \tag{6}$$

[4] Equation 5 has been derived for an individual firm. To apply the model to the economy as a whole, we aggregate over all surviving firms. The variable measuring acquisitions is then a measure of turn-over in the market for corporate control. In the simple case of an economy of identical small firms, no take-overs in this model would be contested and no individual firm would care whether it engaged in take-over activity or whether it was itself acquired (King (1986)).

The correlation between take-over activity and the variable TV for the UK over the period 1949–83 is shown in Figure 2.2. It is clear from the figure that the model fits the observations rather well, especially after 1955. This suggests that at least part of the volatility of take-over activity is purely tax-driven. Econometric tests of the trapped equity model of take-overs are given in King (1986). The model explains over 75 per cent of the variance in the ratio A/K, and the parameter estimates arc highly significant.

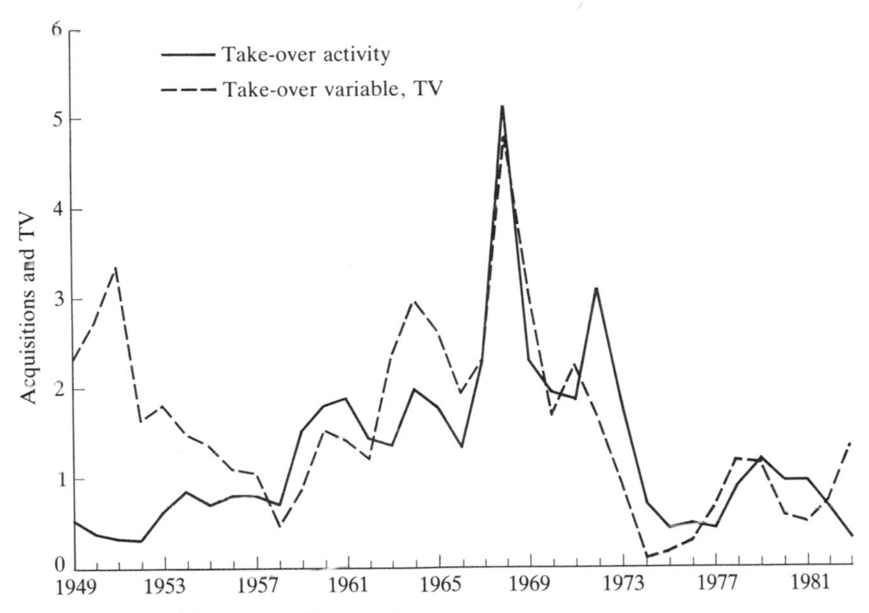

Figure 2.2. Acquisitions, UK 1949–83

The level and volatility of take-over activity would be reduced by a change in the corporate tax system that would raise the value of q^* nearer to unity. This would imply setting the rate of imputation (currently equal to the basic rate of income tax) to be the same as the rate of corporation tax.

In the trapped equity model, cash bids, whether financed by internally generated funds or by issuing debt, are cheaper for tax reasons than bids financed by paper. The model predicts that companies making 'normal' acquisitions will finance them by retentions or by borrowing, and that bids financed by paper will be used only by companies that could put the acquired assets to very profitable uses (such companies have market values of q exceeding unity). Figure 2.3 shows the proportion of total expenditure on acquisitions financed by new equity issues from 1960–86 (unfortunately data are not available for the period prior to 1960). It shows a slight tendency to rise in years of high take-over activity, but the ratio of cash- to paper-financed bids seems independent of the level of activity itself.

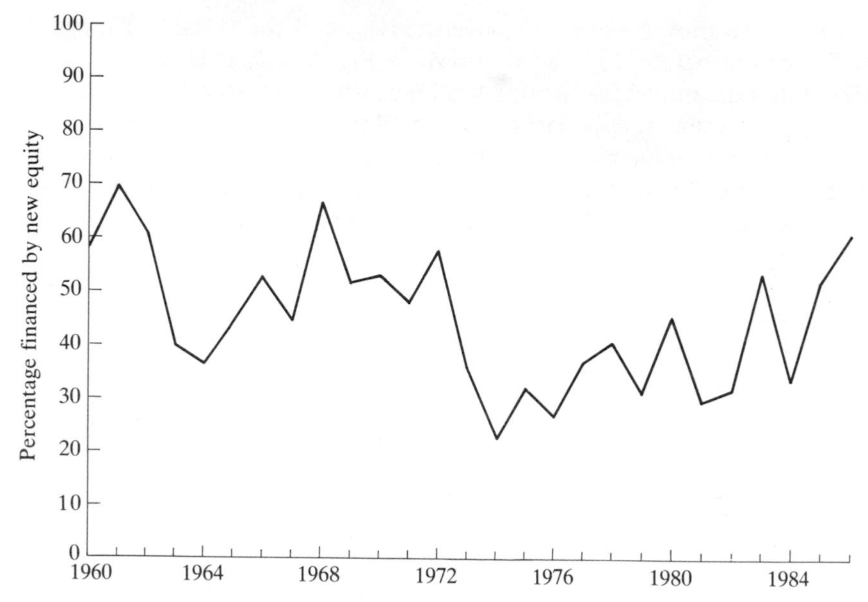

Figure 2.3. Financing of take-overs, UK 1960–86

In the US, cash tender offers exceed paper offers. It is one of the striking features of acquisitions in the US petroleum industry, in which there has been a good deal of take-over activity, that in virtually every case, take-overs were 100 per cent cash-financed (Griffin and Wiggins (1986)). Some share repurchases also took place, but their value was much less in aggregate than the value of stock purchased by other companies in the course of a bid, and in two notable cases (Phillips and Unocal) the repurchases were made only to fend off a hostile bid. Estimates of the values of the assets of individual firms (constructed by the Herold Corporation) make it possible to obtain estimates of q for individual firms in the petroleum industry. Griffin and Wiggins (1986) provide such estimates of q for 10 target firms and 19 non-target firms between 1981 and 1984. The mean value of q for the target firms was 0.51 and for the non-target firms was 0.58.[5] These figures are consistent with the undervaluation feature of the trapped equity model and its implied use of cash-financed bids.

The trapped equity model also throws light on the recent controversy surrounding the use of debt to finance take-overs with very high gearing

[5] Table 1 in Griffin and Wiggins (1986), from which these data are drawn, does not make clear the year to which the figures refer, but from the text it is apparent that for the non-target firms it is 1984 and for the target firms it is the latest year for which data are available (in no case was this earlier than 1981). For only one company, Mesa Petroleum, did the estimate of q exceed unity.

ratios. Debt finance offers raiders the chance to bid for much larger targets than could be purchased from internal equity finance, and is cheaper, for tax reasons, than issues of new equity. The management of even very large companies becomes vulnerable to the threat of take-over.

The use of 'junk bonds' has come under particular attack. In the US, junk bonds are usually considered to be issues rated BB or lower by Standard and Poor's, or Baa or lower by Moody's. The average interest rate on junk bonds is about 5 percentage points above that on AAA rated bonds (although the maturity and call protection of the two types of bond are not strictly comparable). Such high-yielding bonds are naturally attractive to tax-exempt institutions. The default rate on junk bonds over the last 10 years has been 1.6 per cent a year compared with 0.8 per cent on corporate debt as a whole (American Enterprise Institute (1985) p. 47). Public issues of bonds by US corporations increased threefold between 1984 and 1986, and sixfold between 1980 and 1986. The share of junk bonds in this total itself increased by a factor of 3 between 1980 and 1986.

Since junk bonds are defined as issues that have not received the cachet of approval by either of the two major rating institutions, in the UK they might more appropriately be called 'redbrick' bonds. The bid by Elders IXL for Allied-Lyons in 1985 highlighted these issues because the bid was referred to the Monopolies and Mergers Commission on the grounds that 'the financing of the proposed acquisition raises issues which deserve investigation by the Commission' (p. 1). As the Commission stated in its report, 'The reference of this proposed merger is unusual in that its consummation would not appear to represent any material reduction in competition in the markets in which the two companies currently operate' (p. 77). In its evidence, Elders explained that it wished to use debt because 'debt was less expensive than equity'. Presumably the costs associated with a high debt–equity ratio (greater expected bankruptcy costs) were not sufficient to offset the higher tax and other costs of new equity finance.

Opposition to the bid was expressed by several organizations, including the Bank of England, because of the high gearing involved, although no redbrick bonds were involved. Two questions arise. Firstly, would a debt-financed take-over raise the amount of debt in the economy, and if so would this matter? Secondly, is there any 'public interest' involved in a significant change in a company's gearing? The trapped equity model provides a simple answer to the first question. The amount of corporate debt is determined by the wealth of those investors with a relative tax preference for high-yielding securities, and is independent of the actions of any one company. Hence if a large number of take-overs are financed by debt then there will be an equivalent reduction in the amount of debt issued by companies not involved in take-overs. Doubtless this model is too simple, but it makes the important point that the equilibrium amount of debt in total is determined by the desired portfolios of investors. Estimates of the capital gearing of industrial companies in the UK (*Bank of England Quarterly Bulletin*, September 1986) show that there was no increase in 1985 over 1984, despite the sharp rise in take-over activity, and that the ratio of debt to assets was about the same in these years as the average for the decade 1970–9 (at around 20 per cent).

The answer to the second question is more complicated. The Commission concluded that 'The financial aspects of the proposed merger . . . would not affect the future viability of the merged group in a way that would be against the public interest' (p. 86). The Commission declined to say much about the damage that highly leveraged take-overs might produce in other cases, and referred the question of principle back to the Bank of England, the Stock Exchange, and the Department of Trade and Industry. Although not clearly articulated, there seems to be concern that bankruptcy involves costs to third parties which cannot be internalized at the time when the original debt contract is drawn up. Although there is some truth in this view, it has nothing to do with the use of debt to finance take-overs as opposed to other types of investment. Apart from the general monitoring role of the Bank of England, there is no official policy of controlling the level of gearing chosen by companies. It is not clear that take-overs should be treated as a special case.

The motive of the trapped equity model is to provide a systematic explanation of the relationship between take-over activity and changes in the stock market. The correlation between take-over activity in the UK and in the US suggests that there is more to the phenomenon than specific factors (such as the need for restructuring in the oil, gas, and broadcasting industries) identified by some US commentators, which have little relevance to the UK because of State ownership or control of the relevant industries. In the UK, take-over activity in 1985–6 was especially high in the food and retailing industries. For the economy as a whole, take-over activity is a means of getting money out of the corporate sector without incurring the additional taxes levied on the corporate form. In the trapped equity model, the company does not consciously do this when deciding to make an acquisition, but the effect, for take-overs financed by debt or cash, is a withdrawal of funds from the corporate sector.

5. Alternatives to the Current Regime

Market failure is a constant theme of the literature on take-overs. Regulation is based on concern about anticompetitive practices made possible by mergers between firms with large combined market shares. It is surprising, therefore, that so much of the debate on take-overs has concentrated on the profitability of mergers to the participating firms. Accounting studies in the UK (Singh (1971, 1975), Meeks (1977)) typically find that mergers are, on average, unprofitable. Studies of share prices, however, reveal benefits to shareholders. The most comprehensive study of the impact of take-overs on share prices in the UK, an examination of 1,900 mergers between 1955 and 1985 by Franks and Harris (1986b), found that the average bid premium received by the shareholders of the acquired firm was 22 per cent in the bid month and 30 per cent in the 6-month period surrounding the bid. The shareholders of the acquirer earned on average 1 per cent and 7 per cent in the two periods respectively. Similar results for the United States are reported by Jensen and Ruback (1983).

These studies do not resolve the issue of whether the gains come from greater efficiency or the exploitation of monopoly power. Economic integration in Europe means that the scope for domestic monopoly power is narrowing, and competition policy is likely to become more and more a matter for the EEC as progress is made towards completion of the internal market.

I shall, therefore, leave competition policy to one side and restrict my discussion to the market incentives facing the participants in a take-over. On the basis of the analysis presented above, there are four areas in which reforms might be considered.

(a) To eliminate tax-driven mergers it may seem desirable to limit the extent to which the corporate sector is taxed at a rate higher than that which applies to the personal sector. In other words the value of q^* should be close to unity. The 1986 Budget saw the completion of the transition to the new corporate tax regime during which the value of q^* rose from 0.68 to 0.92, its highest value in the post-war period. In the long run this should dampen the responsiveness of take-over activity to swings in the stock market.

A counter-argument is that if the free-rider problem is taken seriously then the tax system offers the opportunity to subsidize take-overs and correct the market failure. The tax would be set at the level required to equate the expected marginal benefit from successful bids to their expected marginal cost. Some very preliminary work suggests that if this approach is taken then the 'optimal' corporate tax rate is about 40 per cent.

(b) The City Code regulates the conduct of bids and restricts the actions of raiders, and associated third parties, as well as those of target companies. It aims to provide protection for shareholders (by prohibiting two-tier bids, for example) and to allow a reasonable period in which a bid may be considered. Its flexibility has ensured that the UK has not experienced the proliferation of defensive measures that has occurred in the US, where poison pills, greenmail, reverse greenmail, and a host of other equally exotically named tactics are either in use or the subject of legal action. For example, in the wake of Distillers's case, the City Code now requires shareholder approval before a target company agrees to meet the costs or expenses of a third party, such as a 'white knight'. Faced with a hostile bid from Argyll, the spirits group Distillers agreed to pay for most of the costs of a rival bid made by Guinness even if this bid were to fail. Such poison pill tactics would now contravene the Code, although the ruling was not made retrospective and in the event Guinness won the battle for control of Distillers. The non-statutory nature of the Takeover Panel, which administers the Code, means that excessive delay through litigation, common in the US where the main instrument of regulation is the 1968 Williams Act, is avoided.

Despite its flexibility, however, the non-statutory nature of the Code has drawbacks. Once a take-over has actually occurred, the Panel is unable to impose sanctions retrospectively. This limits the Panel's effectiveness. The time is ripe for an examination of the statutory position of the Takeover Panel (regulatory issues are discussed in more detail in King and Roell (1987)).

(c) The free-rider problem is the result of a large number of small shareholders acting in isolation and unable to form an effective coalition. If a single large shareholder, or group of shareholders, could be persuaded to take some responsibility for the management then all shareholders would gain. The large shareholder would negotiate directly with the raider. Small shareholders could still free-ride on the large shareholder, but all shareholders would be better off. In the UK the obvious candidates for the role of the 'large' shareholder are the institutions. Rarely does any one institution own a sufficient stake in a company for it to be large in the sense used here. But there is scope for co-operation between institutions, along the lines perhaps of the Council of Institutional Investors in the US which was formed in 1985 with the aim of influencing management. The main problem with this idea is that, *ceteris paribus*, the large shareholder would earn a lower rate of return than the small shareholders who are able to free-ride. This may help to explain why institutions appear so reluctant to be cast in the role that some outside observers would like them to play. Any given institution has an incentive to free-ride on the others.

(d) The reforms discussed above are thought to be necessary because of the failure of internal monitoring of managers within the firm. Would take-overs occur as frequently if the internal control of managers were to be strengthened? This might require the reform of 'corporate governance'. Examples of this include the introduction of 'two-tier' boards and a more powerful role for non-executive directors. Competitive pressures in both product and capital markets, linked to compensation schemes designed to relate managers' interests closely to those of the shareholders, provide a strong incentive for efficient management. Neither a new board structure nor an enhanced role for non-executive directors could supplant competitive market forces. But the costs of relying solely on external competitive pressures are substantial.

Corporate failures, of either whole entities or individual divisions, involve a loss of investment in human and physical capital which can be transferred to other sectors of the economy only at significant cost, and which may have repercussions for the local community and other 'third parties'. If improved internal monitoring could reduce the cost of detecting and replacing weak management, then the social costs of failures might be reduced.

One idea which has been discussed in the context of EEC harmonization is the creation of a supervisory board as part of a two-tier board structure. The impetus for this reform has come largely from those concerned with increasing employee participation in the affairs of their companies. But the danger in the two-tier arrangement is that the supervisory board would have little knowledge of the operations and efficiency of the executive board. The separation of decisions that the two-tier board system entails deprives the firm of the benefits of the contact between inside and outside directors. Non-executive directors appointed to a unitary board would have a much better opportunity of evaluating the abilities of different members of the executive management.

Could stronger non-executive directors play such a role? The argument for non-executive directors received impetus from the dispute over the behaviour of Guinness following its successful attempt to buy Distillers in 1986, despite a rival bid. During the battle, Guinness promised to appoint a Scottish holding company board and non-executive chairman. But after the purchase had been made, Guinness abandoned these plans. City reaction to this change of heart led Guinness to compromise and bring some non-executive directors onto the board. They played an important role in the subsequent dismissal of the chairman, Mr Saunders. Non-executive directors also played a major role in implementing management changes in Beecham's, STC, and Thorn-EMI.

In UK company law, there is no distinction between inside and outside directors. Non-executive directors are appointed by and beholden to the executive directors. Information on the position of outside directors in the UK is meagre. Companies must disclose the names of directors, their remuneration, and financial interest in the company. But companies are not required to distinguish between inside and outside directors. Two questionnaire surveys on the composition of company boards were conducted by the Bank of England in 1983 and 1985 (*Bank of England Quarterly Bulletin*, March 1983 and June 1985). These were sent to companies in the *Times 1000* list. The 1985 survey, covering 344 quoted companies, found that 40 per cent of the companies in the sample had less than three non-executive directors on the board, and only 20 per cent had a majority of non-executive directors. Moreover, only 48 per cent of the top 250 companies in the *Times 1000* list disclosed in their annual report which directors were non-executive.

In the US, outside directors play a greater role. They often outnumber inside directors and the appointment of outside directors is a condition of quotation by the New York Stock Exchange. Quoted companies are obliged to set up an audit committee the membership of which is restricted to non-executive directors. The Securities and Exchange Commission (SEC) requires greater disclosure on the appointment and qualifications of non-executive directors than is usual in the UK.

One of the most important functions of outside directors is to monitor and, if necessary, dismiss the chief executive. To quote a recent study, 'The question to be asked about a board therefore is whether it is sufficiently strong to hold the chief executive (who may be chairman too) in check when necessary' (Charkham (1986) p. 8). A board consisting solely, or even mainly, of executive directors may not be an effective instrument for controlling the chief executive, as the Guinness affair in 1986 demonstrated. But it is not impossible to imagine that an extension of the powers of outside directors might increase the influence of shareholders over inside management. A recent American study (Weisbach (1986)) of 367 companies quoted on the New York Stock Exchange over the period 1974–83 provides some evidence for this view. Weisbach studied the decision to remove the chief executive officer (CEO) of the company. He found that companies with a significant number of non-executive directors (at least 40 per cent of the board) were more likely to remove the CEO, for a given performance level (as measured by published earnings or stock market returns) than were companies with only a small number of outsiders on the board.

One problem with the idea of encouraging non-executive directors to play a more active role in monitoring the performance of executive management is that unless they own a significant stake in the firm, there is no obvious incentive for them to intervene actively when necessary. If the reputation of outside directors as experts in the art of 'managing the managers' were important for their professional future, then the desire to create a good reputation could provide a powerful incentive. For this to be the case, candidates for such positions should neither be at the end of their career nor have another connection with the company. That is not the case today. In the 1985 Bank of England survey, one-third of all non-executive directors were either professional advisers or former executives of the company. Many others were probably retired executives of other companies or employees of a parent company sitting on the board of its subsidiary. Boards with a group of independent and active outside directors who see their role as 'managing the managers' are not yet the norm in British industry.

It might be desirable to encourage, or even enshrine in company law, the practice of an open and contested election for the position of a non-executive director of a public company. At present, approval of non-executive directors by the shareholders is usually a formality. As a first step, company law could be changed to recognize the separate nature of inside and outside directors, and to require companies over a certain size to appoint at least, say, three outside directors. Alternatively, the Stock Exchange, following the American example, could make this a condition of quotation.

To those companies and their management who complain about the destructive nature posed by the threat of take-over, it is worth pointing out that they could signal to the market confidence in their own abilities by appointing several independent and respected non-executive directors, and also by providing more information to their shareholders.[6]

---

[6] A study by the US Securities and Exchange Commission (1985) found no relationship between research and development expenditure, a proxy for 'long-term investment', and either adverse movements in share prices or institutional ownership which is sometimes alleged to focus excessively on short-term earnings.

3

The Market for Corporate Control: The Divestment Option

MIKE WRIGHT,* BRIAN CHIPLIN,†
AND JOHN COYNE**

1. Introduction

1986 saw a number of large contested take-over bids which resulted in considerable attention being devoted to merger policy, including the announcement of a wide-scale review. What is frequently neglected is the fact that many acquisitions are not of previously independent companies, but are purchases of divested activities from other organizations. Indeed, some recent major bids have included an intention to sell off parts of an acquired business once the acquisition is completed. For example, during the battle for the Imperial Group in the first half of 1986, undertakings were given to divest certain activities, particularly where issues of market dominance could arise with possible referral of the bid to the Monopolies and Mergers Commission. Following the acquisition of the Group by Hanson Trust, several parts were in fact divested, the most notable being the sale of Courage to Elders IXL.

Divestment has been a major feature of the corporate sector of the British economy for many years. A few recent examples illustrate the types of change involved. In July 1984 Bowater entered into a demerger whereby it separated itself into two parts—Bowater Inc. based in the USA and Bowater PLC which covered the UK and the rest of the world. By providing

---

* Reader in Financial Studies and Director of the Centre for Management Buy-out Research, University of Nottingham.

† Professor of Industrial Economics and Director of Nottingham Institute of Financial Studies, University of Nottingham.

** Lecturer in Industrial Economics and Director of the Centre for Management Buy-out Research, University of Nottingham.

shareholders with two sets of shares rather than one, the move was claimed to enable the separate entities to be in a better position to fulfil their individual corporate strategies and gain improved access to finance through distinct quotation on two capital markets.

In late 1985, Grand Metropolitan announced its intention to divest itself of its Mecca Leisure subsidiary. The subsequent buy-out of Mecca by its management avoided the possible implications for market dominance had it been acquired, for example, by the Rank Organisation. In September 1986, Guinness sold two of the hotels that it had acquired when it took over Arthur Bell to the Norfolk Capital Group for £23.5 million as part of a continuing appraisal of businesses that were peripheral to the core activities acquired.

These few examples of divestment and demerger illustrate an increasingly noticeable trend in industrial structure, which has important implications for merger policy, but which has received scant attention in the academic literature. It is possible to argue that the main focus of the literature has been unidirectional whereas what is required is a more dynamic perspective on the trading of companies. This perspective should encompass a wider view of corporate strategy and move away from too narrow a focus on the acquisition of independent companies and the simple propositions on concentration which flow from it.

The aim of this paper is to show that such an approach provides at best a partial view of the nature of the firm. For completeness it is necessary to examine decisions and mechanisms of sale as well as purchase. Section 2 considers the circumstances in which divestment may arise and Section 3 analyses the direction of this divestment. Section 4 examines trends in divestment in the context of overall acquisition activity and Section 5 provides a review of the effects of divestment on performance. Section 6 presents a number of policy implications.

It is important to recognize that divestment is an integral part of the market for corporate control. It performs at least three key functions:

(a) it provides a *flexible* mechanism whereby resources can be reallocated both within and between markets;

(b) it provides a *constraint against unnecessary bigness* and enables entrepreneurs to recognize opportunities for gains where the current value of a firm is less than the value of the sum of its parts;

(c) it provides a means whereby past mistakes can be rectified at relatively low cost and is an important part of the *search* for the most efficient structural composition of the firm in a dynamic environment.

Failure to recognize these points frequently leads to unwarranted criticism of the divestment process which is often labelled as 'asset-stripping'.

2. Why Divest?

The transfer of ownership of any set of assets requires an asymmetry in valuation to exist between the buyer and the seller. According to Gort (1969), such asymmetries are more likely to arise when economic disturbances are greatest during periods, for example, of rapid changes in share prices or technology. In analysing the divestment decision it is necessary, therefore, to consider the motives of both the buyer and the seller.

Much of the discussion of the market for corporate control has focused upon the motives of the acquirer and, further, the acquisition is frequently taken to be that of an independent company. Motives for acquisition are considered elsewhere in this volume, but generally it can be argued that the acquirer expects to be able to improve the performance of the assets over and above that obtainable by the previous owner, and in so doing achieve its corporate objectives better than through alternative courses of action. With an acquisition through divestment, the question of a hostile bid, with its associated costs, does not arise although there may be more than one alternative bidder for the assets. In other respects, however, similar considerations apply as in the acquisition of an independent company and further analysis is not necessary here.

Our main focus of attention is on the decision by a company to divest itself of a subsidiary or division. In some circumstances the sale may be regarded as forced, particularly where either the subsidiary or, not uncommonly, the parent faces serious financial problems. In the latter case, rather than sell a poor performer, it may be necessary to sell a highly profitable activity in order to protect the core of the organization. Fears have recently been expressed in some quarters that this kind of divestment may be required where firms make excessive use of highly leveraged financing which they are subsequently unable to service. Although it is possible to overstate this view, and as yet little evidence of the problem has been seen in the UK, the apparent desire of Safeway in the US in December 1986 to dispose of its UK division to ease leveraging illustrates the nature of the problem.

Alternatively, a parent group may take a considered decision to divest itself of a subsidiary. In simple terms, a subsidiary may be a candidate for divestment where it is no longer regarded as fitting within the group. Fit must essentially be interpreted in terms of the entity's contribution towards achieving the parent firm's overall objectives. Such a lack of contribution has several dimensions which are now explored.

Lack of fit may arise from a 'mistake' having been made in the development of a particular product area internally or through an ill-judged acquisition in the past. In addition, an unwanted entity may have been acquired as part of an acquisition 'package', and divestment is a means of adjusting the configuration of assets to more appropriate dimensions. Changing circumstances, for example technological developments, also alter the 'fit' of different parts of the enterprise, and divestment provides an essential means of adjustment. At issue here is the nature of the firm and the boundary between internal and external co-ordination of activities. One or more general principles may be relevant.

(a) Life-cycle behaviour: Stigler (1951) argued that vertical disintegration might be expected during a market's expansionary phase through the spinning-off of decreasing cost activities so as to allow for maximum scale economies. The corollary is that vertical integration is likely to increase during a market's mature phase. Hence, the extent of vertical integration is likely to be related to the phase of the product life-cycle. Tests of the relationship between vertical integration and growth have produced mixed results, but the only direct test of vertical disintegration found no support for the view that such divestment is typical of growing markets (Wright and Thompson (1986)).

(b) Technical change and economies of scale and scope: Failure to achieve economies of scale or scope through internal growth or merger activity, coupled with the impact of technical change, is likely to influence the appropriate configuration of assets for the firm. To a great extent, many mergers carried out to obtain such economies appear to have failed in their objective, partly because the companies acquired have frequently been run as separate entities, and partly because of the impact of technical change and other developments on the optimum size. Technical change may both erode natural monopoly type arguments for economies of scale (Chiplin and Wright (1982)) and modify views about the joint production of certain goods and services (Chiplin (1986)). Hence divestment may become economically efficient, leading to production by two or more separate entities or possibly by means of joint venture.

(c) The economics of internal organization: Williamson (1975), in extending the seminal work of Coase (1937), has developed the argument for preferring internal factor markets over external ones. The benefits are held to derive from the greater informational efficiency to be obtained from internalization, particularly where strategic and operational responsibilities are separated within a multi-divisional (M-form) structure. It is claimed that such a structure permits the best use of decentralized information whilst, at the same time, minimizing the potential for shirking, opportunism, etc. The transactions cost model emphasizes the suitability of internalization where there are frequent requirements for the specialist application of proprietary knowledge, where physical assets are indivisible (Teece (1980)), and where there is a lack of trust in complex transactions (Butler and Carney (1983)).

This model provides both insights with respect to the organization of internally developed activities and, importantly, justification for the acquisition and internalization of primarily separate entities. However, although it has hitherto not received a great deal of attention, the Williamson model also indicates where divestment might be a more appropriate action and, indeed, the M-form structure actually enhances the divestibility of activities. Three major reasons may be advanced in favour of divestment in circumstances of inadequate control:

(i) there may be serious difficulties in the assimilation of acquisitions into a group structure where the corporate cultures of the two entities are incompatible (Arrow (1974), Jones (1985));

(ii) problems may arise in respect of internal trading where the appropriate way to manage one part is not suitable for the other, or where one part of an internal production process is able to exploit an adjacent stage through the benefits of a barrier to entry against outside suppliers provided by common ownership. In such a case, divestment and control through the market may improve overall efficiency (Wright (1986b));

(iii) managers may appropriate gains to themselves rather than shareholders, through lack of commitment or opportunism, problems which may not be easily resolvable because of the difficulty caused by incomplete employee contracts (Wright and Thompson (1987), Dugger (1983), Klein (1983)).

Where divestment does occur, care is required in deciding which part is to be sold, since there may be important spill-over benefits to other parts of the parent organization which are not immediately obvious (Spicer and Ballew (1983)).

DIVESTMENT AND ACQUISITION

To the extent that an acquired activity is perceived not to fit, acquisition and subsequent divestment for some companies may represent an important part of the process of search towards the most efficient corporate structure, which itself is likely to alter with changes in the external environment (Ravenscraft and Scherer (1986a)). An indication of the extent of the two-way acquisition and divestment process in the UK is provided in Table 3.1. Over 10 per cent of acquiring firms made at least one divestment, and in a few cases several, in the period January 1984 to June 1986.

The high level of acquisition activity in 1986 has been accompanied by the emergence of the 'bought deal' whereby unwanted activities are identified by the acquirer before the take-over occurs and sale to another purchaser is agreed in advance. In some circumstances such arrangements can provide an important means by which the acquisition can be funded, and indeed in

Table 3.1. Two-way frequency distribution of parent-to-parent divestments and acquisitions by UK companies which have made acquisitions, January 1984 to June 1986

Number of divestments	Number of acquisitions								
	1	2	3	4	5	6	⩾7	Total no.	Percentage
0	399	104	58	17	7	10	12	607	89.5
1	25	14	3	3	1	2	1	49	7.2
2	4	0	1	0	1	0	1	7	1.0
3	0	1	2	0	0	0	2	5	0.8
4	0	0	1	1	1	0	2	5	0.8
5	1	0	0	0	0	0	1	2	0.3
6	1	0	1	0	0	0	0	2	0.3
7	1	0	0	0	0	0	0	1	0.1
								678	100.0

Source: Derived by the Centre for Management Buy-out Research, University of Nottingham from DTI mergers and acquisitions records.

some cases enable the desired parts of the purchased company to be bought at a substantial effective discount. Concern over the effect of high leverage in the funding of acquisitions has meant that divestment of unwanted elements may be a useful means of allaying such fears. For example, in the bid for Allied-Lyons by Elders IXL (referred to the Monopolies and Mergers Commission) the proposed subsequent sale of the food division would have substantially reduced the high levels of post-acquisition gearing. Such an agreed sale may also be sought as a means of avoiding a reference to the Commission, particularly if the element which would be most likely to receive the attention of the Office of Fair Trading is not the main reason for acquiring the whole group.

The relative fit of a subsidiary may not be independent of its size. A study by Duhaime and Baird (1985) for the USA showed that in about one-quarter of cases the divested unit accounted for over 5 per cent of the parent group's sales turn-over. With smaller subsidiaries one might expect a disproportionately higher incidence of divestment where the costs of control and of effecting any necessary turnaround outweigh the benefits to be obtained. For larger subsidiaries it may well be worth while investing effort to control them and solve the problems. Hence to the extent that divestments of larger subsidiaries are observed, they are more likely to be associated with poor performance of either the subsidiary itself or the parent.

This section has examined why a firm may wish to divest itself of a subsidiary or division. The increased level of divestment in recent years may be explained by various factors which may differ depending upon whether the divestee stands in a horizontal/vertical or conglomerate relationship with its parent. Poor performance of either the parent or the divestee and the need to reassess corporate direction, which involves the sale of poorly fitting entities, are perhaps the main explanatory factors involved. Divestment may be part of a parent's search activity to find an optimum configuration of assets. However, there are good reasons for thinking that divestment may be appropriate in integrated cases, particularly where economies of scale and scope are unable to be realized. The failure to achieve these economies, and also obtain effective performance in conglomerates, may be due to the difficulties of internal organization in large complex structures. Divestment offers a solution to this problem which may be more effective and cheaper than attempts to design a better organizational framework, particularly for small subsidiaries (Wright and Thompson (1987)).

3. Divestment to Whom?

Divestment may take several forms, although some may be encountered more frequently than others. The appropriate purchaser may not necessarily be the bidder who offers the most money, since other important issues may be involved.

For *asset swaps or strategic trades*, few if any funds change hands. Transfer of ownership is effected by exchanging some of the assets of one firm for some of those of the other. The process is subject to the difficulties traditionally associated with barter. Thus, severe problems can arise since a match is required, not of what one company has to sell with what another is prepared to pay, but of what one company has to trade with what part of another company it is prepared to accept, and vice versa ('coincidence of wants'). Consequently, some of the most notable examples of asset swaps have occurred in the US brewing industry (Davis (1986)) and have been enforced divestitures as part of antitrust policy. For example, Pabst and Stroh were required to exchange breweries in different regions so as to improve competition. In the UK, brewers have been required in some areas to exchange public houses in order to reduce distribution monopolies. Though difficult, an asset swap may be a preferred route where bilateral strategic fits can be identified and where it may be strategically dangerous to sell off one part to a competitor without ensuring simultaneous acquisition.

Spin-offs or demergers involve the effective splitting of one organization into two (or more) parts, and may take the form of either two roughly equal entities or the spinning-off from the parent of a relatively small element (Lawton (1984)). In the former case, shareholders receive a new set of shares in both of the demerged parts pro rata to their original holding. Subsequently, shareholders are able to trade in the parts rather than just the whole. The case of Bowater referred to above is the prime example of this arrangement in the UK. It was argued by the company that one of the major sets of reasons for a demerger related to the problems in agreeing strategic direction as the demands of one half of the firm for investment funds, the US paper interests, had direct adverse consequences for freighting and forwarding activities in the UK and the rest of the world. Sell-off would have created a major problem in this instance because of the problem of how to absorb and reinvest a large volume of funds and maintain the level of shareholders' returns (Wright (1986a)).

In the latter form of spin-off, a smaller part, perhaps involving a recently developed product, is distanced from the parent by introducing new equity-holders often including the incumbent management (Garvin (1983)). The parent retains an equity interest, gaining advantages from capital gain without the problem of direct day-to-day managerial involvement. To date in the UK this kind of spin-off is rare, although in October 1986 ICL announced such an arrangement for its Active Memory Technology department, a producer of array processors. Such spin-offs may occur in areas of peripheral interest to the parent, but which may subsequently yield high returns. Although the UK capital market is becoming increasingly interested in these ventures, present trends suggest an unwillingness by UK companies to sell in this way.

Sell-offs have been the traditional means of disposing of a subsidiary, though parents may prefer to close down marginal operations rather than sell capacity to competitors. Activities involved in sell-offs may not, in themselves, be earning low returns, for reasons outlined in the previous section. An example of a significant sell-off where the parent wished to exit from a particular product area is the case of the sale of the soft drinks business of the Beecham Group in November 1986. The proceeds amounted to £130 million, £120 million of which was achieved through the sale of the bulk of the activities to Britvic with the balance being received from Cadbury–Schweppes.

The growth of *management buy-outs*, whereby the subsidiary is sold to its incumbent management and becomes an independent entity, offers an alternative source of purchase (Coyne and Wright (1986b), Wright (1985)). A parent may prefer to sell to management where speed of sale and local reputation are important. The threat not to co-operate with an external purchaser may also reinforce management's hand, as may its ability to control information relating to the subsidiary. Management's threat not to co-operate may carry more force where it forms a substantial, difficult-to-replace, element of the subsidiary's value. Management's control over information relating to the subsidiary may produce an asymmetry in its favour which may deter an external purchaser whilst at the same time allowing incumbents to purchase at an advantageous price (Wright and Coyne (1985), Wright, Coyne, and Mills (1987)). However, for managers lacking substantial funds of their own, to be able to buy requires that the transfer can be financed from external sources. The development of funding for management buy-outs over the last 5 years, together with legal relaxations on the taking of security on loans contained in the Companies Acts, has enabled larger, and a larger variety of, buy-outs to take place (Coyne and Wright (1986c)). As with the funding of some mergers, concern has been expressed that the gearing levels involved are becoming excessive, though this view may be overstated (Chiplin and Wright (1987)). A typical example of a buy-out on divestment is Metsec from TI, which required

Table 3.2. Acquisitions, divestments, and buy-outs, 1969–86

Year	Acquisition of independent industrial companies			Sales of subsidiaries between industrial parent groups			Management buy-outs		
	No. acquired	£m.	Average £m.	No.	£m.	Average £m.	No.	£m.	Average £m.
1969	742	961	1.30	102	100	0.98			
1970	608	954	1.57	179	126	0.70			
1971	620	745	1.20	264	166	0.63			
1972	931	2 337	2.51	272	185	0.68			
1973	951	1 057	1.11	254	247	0.97			
1974	367	459	1.25	137	49	0.36			
1975	200	221	1.11	115	70	0.61			
1976	242	348	1.44	111	100	0.90			
1977	372	730	1.96	109	94	0.86	13		
1978	441	977	2.22	126	163	1.29	23		
1979	414	1 438	3.47	117	186	1.59	52	26	0.50
1980	368	1 265	3.44	101	210	2.08	107	50	0.47
1981	327	882	2.70	125	262	2.10	124	114	0.92
1982	296	1 373	4.64	164	804	4.90	170	265	1.56
1983	302	1 783	5.90	142	436	3.07	205	315	1.54
1984	396	4 253	10.74	170	1 121	6.59	210	255	1.21
1985	339	6 281	18.53	134	793	5.92	229	1 176	5.02
1986 Q2	185	8 082	43.69	51	389	7.63	140	710	5.07

Sources: Acquisitions and divestments: *Business Monitor* MQ7; buy-outs: Wright and Coyne (1986).

major rationalization but which was successful and achieved a USM (unlisted securities market) flotation in 1985 (Wright *et al.* (1987)).

Sell-offs, management buy-outs, spin-offs, and demergers are thus all seen to have merits in specific circumstances (Coyne and Wright (1986a)). In the following section the actual trends in divestment are examined.

4. Divestment Trends

To place divestment activity in context, data on ownership transfers generally are presented in Table 3.2. The first set of figures relate to the acquisition of independent industrial companies, the second set to the sales of subsidiaries between industrial groups (that is, where one group's acquisition is another's divestment), and the final set to management buy-outs.

The acquisition of independent firms accounts for the largest element in ownership transfer, both in number and value terms, between 1969 and the first half of 1986. Indeed, in value terms these acquisitions have consistently exceeded the other two routes combined in each year.

Parent-to-parent divestments vary greatly over time in number and value, but are most important relative to acquisitions in 1975 and 1982. Since 1982 the sales of subsidiaries between parents have represented about 20 per cent of the total of all ownership transfers by number. It is evident from examination of the whole series that divestments have been a permanent feature of the corporate scene and are not simply recession-related.

Management buy-outs have increased in number and value since the late 1970s. For the last 4 years there have been more buy-outs each year than parent-to-parent divestments, although their average size has generally been much lower. Parent-to-parent divestments are in turn smaller on average than acquisitions of independent companies.

Wide dispersions around these averages are worth noting. As can be seen from Table 3.3, 17.9 per cent of the acquisitions of independent firms were at values of £10 million or more, whereas the figures for sell-offs and management buy-outs were 11.9 per cent and 12.6 per cent respectively. In value terms, not shown in the table, this size category accounted for 84 per cent of independent company acquisition values, 52.9 per cent of sell-off values, and 80 per cent of buy-out values in 1985. At the other end of the size spectrum, buy-outs were more likely to be below £0.5 million in value. The relative proportions of buy-outs and sell-offs occurring in the largest size category have equalized during the last 2 years as the buy-out marketplace has developed. Financing institutions are now willing and able to fund much larger transactions than hitherto (Coyne and Wright (1986c)). The largest buy-out to date has been Lawson-Mardon Packaging, which was sold by BAT Industries to its management for £273 million. In contrast, Hanson Trust sold Courage, the sixth largest brewer in the UK and part of its recently acquired Imperial Group, to Elders IXL for £1.4 billion in September 1986.

Table 3.3. Size distributions of independent acquisitions, sell-offs, and management buy-outs compared, 1985

Size band (£m.)	Independent acquisition		Sell-offs		Buy-outs	
	No.	%	No.	%	No.	%
Less than 0.1	39	11.5	17	12.7	8	5.3
0.1 to 0.499	71	20.9	22	16.4	52	34.5
0.5 to 0.999	46	13.5	19	14.2	15	9.9
1.0 to 4.999	90	26.5	45	33.6	45	29.8
5.0 to 9.999	33	9.7	15	11.2	12	7.9
10.0 or more	61	17.9	16	11.9	19	12.6
Total	340	100.0	134	100.0	151	100.0

Source: *Business Monitor* MQ7, 1986 Q2.

Acquisitions of independent companies, sell-offs, and buy-outs are found across all sectors of industry. There is no apparent difference in the relative spread across industrial sectors between independent company acquisitions and sell-offs (Chiplin and Wright (1980)).

Given that divestment is a well-established part of corporate strategy, it may be used, as is the case with acquisition activity, more intensively by some firms than others. The intensity of divestment activity may be influenced by the number of product and geographical markets occupied by a firm, and by the urgency and strength of the need for corporate strategic adjustments. Where acquisitions are simultaneously being conducted, divestment may be a convenient way of disposing of those parts of a recently purchased group that are peripheral to the main areas of interest. It is not uncommon for acquisitions of large groups to be structured in such a way that unwanted parts are already pre-sold by the time the deal is completed. In some circumstances the initial purchaser may acquire the business that is really desired for a small net cost.

In respect of sell-offs Chiplin and Wright (1980) show that during the 2-year period from the second quarter of 1977 to the first quarter of 1979, some 26.5 per cent of 268 divesting firms engaged in more than one divestment, with 4 per cent undertaking at least four sales of subsidiaries.

Multiple divestments as management buy-outs are also observed, with some firms also pursuing both types. For 1985 Coyne and Wright (1986c) found 22 parents which sold two or more subsidiaries to an incumbent management. Three firms (Hanson Trust/US Industries, Unilever, and Sears Holdings) disposed of four or more subsidiaries in this way during the year.

Simultaneous acquisition and divestment activity was monitored by Chiplin and Wright (1980), with a quarter of divesting firms also making one or more acquisitions in the same period. For more recent trends see Table 3.1.

From the point of view of merger policy, the direction of divestment in relation to the main activity of the parent may be important. One might expect that peripheral activities rather than core businesses are likely to be divested. However, as discussed earlier, there may be important reasons why horizontal or vertical disintegration may be observed. Evidence from UK divestments (Chiplin and Wright (1980)) suggests that about one-third of divestment activity is horizontal in nature, a fifth is conglomerate, a tenth vertical, and the remainder relates to divestment by financial companies, breweries, hotels, etc. For the US, Duhaime and Grant (1984) found that sell-offs were likely to involve the more peripheral business units, with vertical disintegration being unusual. A recent study by Ravenscraft and Scherer (1986a) provides support for this view and shows that many divested units were previously acquired rather than having been generated internally, an indication of the search process involved in acquisition and divestment activity.

With reference to management buy-outs, Wright (1986b) showed that 47 per cent of 68 buy-outs on divestment from parents still trading had business relationships with their former parent, though for the most part these links accounted for a relatively small proportion of the buy-out's sales or purchases.

Of course, the sale of a subsidiary does not necessarily imply that the divestor is exiting completely from a market, especially if it has several subsidiaries operating in a particular sector. But whether partial or complete exit reduces market concentration depends upon the nature of the purchaser. The evidence from sell-offs (Chiplin and Wright (1980)) suggests that horizontal or vertical divestments by one firm are likely to augment horizontal integration in the new parent.

5. Empirical Studies of the Effect of Divestment on Performance

Empirical studies of the performance effects of different types of divestment on both vendor and acquirer have only appeared to any great extent over the last few years, and relate predominantly to American experience. The principal focus of attention in these studies has been the impact of announcements of sell-offs and spin-offs on shareholder wealth. The literature in this field has examined both voluntary divestments and those which have been enforced as part of antitrust policy. Some attention has been given to the strategic decision-making processes involved in divestment and, more recently, the issues concerning management buy-outs have been addressed (de Angelo, de Angelo, and Rice (1984)). The 'announcements effects' approach adopts an efficient markets framework and examines abnormal share price behaviour around the time of the announcement of a spin-off or sell-off. Different reasons for divestment may be expected to produce varying impacts on shareholder wealth, particularly if the divestment is being enforced as part of antitrust policy. Voluntary sell-offs or spin-offs might be expected to result in an upward movement in the share price of the divestor as the action should have an expected positive net present value in comparison with retaining the activity. In the case of spin-offs there are several potential sources of gain to shareholders including: improvements in the efficiency of productive organization; an increase in the opportunity set of shareholders as they are able to adjust their holdings in the demerged entities; a possible transfer of wealth from bondholders if the equity in the spun-off company is distributed solely to shareholders, leaving bondholders with no claim on the assets of the new entity; and possible relaxation in rate regulation following any break-up (Hakansson (1983), Galai and Masulis (1976)).

For enforced divestitures it can be argued that if a dominant firm has been enjoying its market power, the firm's shareholders will lose from the removal of that power. However, a possible counter-effect in terms of a relaxed regulatory framework also needs to be taken into account. Studies of the effects of enforced divestitures have produced conflicting results. Burns (1977, 1983) found positive shareholder wealth effects, whilst Kudla and McInish (1981) and Boudreaux (1975) have observed a negative impact. Negative effects on shareholder wealth may, of course, be insufficient to outweigh large positive abnormal returns accumulated over the years prior to divestiture (Ellert (1976)). Montgomery, Thomas, and Kamath (1984) found the consequences of enforced divestiture on shareholders to be insignificant.

Tests of voluntary spin-offs have generally shown them to have a positive effect on announcement. Boudreaux (1975), Miles and Rosenfeld (1983), Schipper and Smith (1983), and Hite and Owers (1983) all appear to support the view that shareholder gains are attributable to an improvement in the efficiency of the new structural arrangements.

The studies of voluntary sell-offs have produced similar findings. Alexander, Benson, and Kampmeyer (1984) found some evidence of positive announcement effects. Rosenfeld (1984) showed that the positive effect of both spin-offs and sell-offs was stronger than that found by Alexander *et al.*, and that spin-offs outperformed sell-offs in terms of market reactions on the day of the event. Jain (1985), whilst confirming the positive effects, found that gains to buyers were smaller than those to sellers.

The study of sell-offs by Montgomery *et al.* (1984) found that the reason for sale was more important than the act of sale itself. The significant effects were related to the underlying corporate strategic reason for the divestment. Sell-offs linked to clearly defined strategic decisions were valued positively by the market, whilst those that were apparently the sale of unwanted assets without clear strategic goals were valued negatively. Divestments arising as a response to liquidity problems did not give rise to significant announcement effects. Sell-offs are thus seen as firm-specific events, their effects depending on various underlying strategic motivations, a view also supported by the work of Hearth and Zaima (1986).

Klein (1986) has attempted to resolve some of the differences between previous studies, and points to the important implications of the relative size of the divestiture and whether the transaction price is initially announced. If the transaction price is initially announced or the divestment is relatively large, abnormal returns are found to be significant and positive. Where price or relative size are not specifically isolated, smaller or insignificant announcement day effects are evident.

It may be concluded that the studies of sell-offs find the same direction of abnormal returns to shareholders as do those of acquisitions of independent firms. In these latter studies, acquiree shareholders generally experience large positive returns, whilst the shareholders in the acquirer are much less likely to benefit (Chiplin and Wright (1987)).

However, it is important to bear in mind the limitations associated with this type of study (Halpern (1983), Brown and Warner (1980), Givoly and Palmon (1985), Hite (1986)). Specifically in the case of sell-offs, the market may be expected to have an informational problem. Unlike the acquisition of public limited companies whose stock market quotations ensure that the market has information for valuation purposes or where accounting data are readily available, performance information relating to subsidiaries is much harder to access. Moreover, a press release about a sell-off may be expected to contain less information about the transaction itself than may be gleaned from the generally more public acquisition of an independent firm.

The performance effects of management buy-outs on divestment have received far less attention than is the case for sell-offs and spin-offs, though the evidence indicates that substantial benefits are realizable from achieving independence (Wright and Coyne (1985)). Of 111 management buy-outs studied, 62 per cent were from parents still trading. Reorganization after buy-out involved development of the management structure, changes in employment, improvements in cash and credit control systems, and movements into new product areas which had previously been difficult to enter. These kinds of improvement were generally found to have been occasioned by problems which arose from being part of a parent organization or by the impossibility of resolving such difficulties from within a group structure. Given the relative newness of the phenomenon in the UK, a more rigorous study of the longer-term performance effects of buy-outs has not been possible to date. However, by late 1986 some 98 buy-outs had already achieved a stock market flotation, of which three-quarters had previously been subsidiaries of parent groups.

US experience as analysed in a study by Scherer (1984) mirrors the results found for the UK. He examined 15 cases of sell-offs of subsidiaries that had a conglomerate relationship with their parent. Of this group, 4 were acquired to augment the new parent's horizontal integration and appeared to result in improvements in efficiency which could not be attained under the previous relationship. Eight of the group were sold as leverage buy-outs, with post-sale improvements in efficiency also in evidence, especially with respect to the exploitation of cost-cutting opportunities. Benefits also seemed to be derived from the removal of delays and distortions in decision-making and the draining away of resources to other parts of the larger conglomerate organization. However, the danger was that after the sale, particularly in the buy-out cases, heavy debt financing placed restrictions on investment. These funding arrangements were often accompanied by pressure for short-run cash flow maximization and rapid exit. Such potential problems have also been noted in respect of UK buy-outs (Wright, Coyne, and Mills (1987)) and cause one to take a rather less sanguine view of some kinds of buy-out funding arrangements than advocated by others (for example, Jensen (1986b)).

6. Conclusions and Policy Implications

A good deal of the merger activity in the late 1960s and early 1970s was promoted by a view that economies of scale (and to some extent scope) would thereby be achieved, with a consequent improvement in the overall performance of the UK economy. In practice, there is little evidence that substantial economies of scale or scope were actually realized and frequently acquisitions continued to be managed as independent entities (O'Brien (1978)). At the same time, technological change has altered the appropriate configuration of assets required to obtain technical economies of scale and scope across a wide spectrum of industries. A redrawing of the boundaries of the firm is an essential part of the market process and it has been shown that divestment has had a major role to play for many years.

The respecification of the activities of a firm can be effected in several ways. Parts that are peripheral to the main business may be sold to a new parent or the subsidiary's management. Where trading relationships exist, divestment, or contracting out, is possible. If this action is carried out so that the divested part is sold to a specialist in a particular activity, economies of scale benefits may be obtained to outweigh any resulting costs of externalization. Alternatively, divestment to management may take place through a management buy-out. Under such circumstances, competition between suppliers may become more effective as the barrier to entry of common ownership is removed. Together with the equity stake in the firm that management now has, such a change may increase the performance stimulus to ex-divisional management.

Planned divestment of parts of an enterprise has featured prominently in a number of recent major acquisitions. Hanson Trust, which acquired the Imperial Group for £2.6 billion in April 1986, had realized £1.7 billion through the disposal of subsidiaries by October of the same year. Thus, Lord Hanson argued that the company had recouped almost 65 per cent of the total cost of the acquisition by selling companies which had been forecast to contribute only 45 per cent of the Imperial Group's profit.

Similarly, the Elders IXL bid for Allied-Lyons in late 1985 had contained a planned intention to dispose of the food division of the acquired enterprise. This bid was referred to the Monopolies and Mergers Commission whose report in September 1986 provides evidence of the Commission's thinking on the implications of divestment.

The Commission noted that the immediate effect of any such sale would be to reduce the overall size of Allied-Lyons with possibly detrimental implications for economies of scale and internal cross-trading and cross-financing. The Commission did not pronounce directly on this point, but by implication did not consider any detriment to have major consequences. It was recognized that whilst the original intention had been to sell the food division intact, practical necessity had forced the company to break up the division and dispose of it to as many as 10 different purchasers. The effect on competition would clearly depend on the identity of the eventual purchasers, and, as the Commission noted, any such acquisition would be subject to the normal merger review procedures of the Director General of Fair Trading. The Commission also specifically referred to assurances given by Elders IXL that it wished to sell to those who would preserve the businesses as going concerns.

In conclusion, a reading of the report would suggest that the Commission found nothing particularly disturbing in this specific case of divestment on acquisition. Indeed, recognition of the potential value of divestment suggests considerable scope for the development of clearer guidelines on merger policy incorporating the ability of companies effectively to negotiate with the Director General of Fair Trading about the scope of the enterprise following acquisition and its likely competitive effects. If such a course were to be followed, it would be necessary to provide a more adequate procedure for ensuring that any assurances on divestment are actually carried out (Chiplin and Wright (1987)).

4

Mergers, Take-overs, and the Enforcement of Profit Maximization

DIETER HELM*

1. Introduction

The case for a *laissez-faire* policy towards take-overs and mergers is typically founded upon two separate arguments—that they enable economies of scale to be reaped from increases in concentration (Williamson (1968)) and that they prevent managers from deviating away from profit maximization towards the pursuit of managerial objectives, which would permit inefficiencies to arise (Alchian and Kessel (1962)). Thus take-overs and mergers assist the allocation of resources either by reducing costs or by allocating resources to the control of efficient managers. In this paper, I shall concentrate on the second argument, and show that it suffers from a number of theoretical weaknesses.[1]

For the take-over mechanism to guarantee efficiency, the capital market must be perfect. In practice, market failures arise in the transactions costs of the take-over and the information required to identify deviations from profit maximization. In this paper, the traditional managerial models of the firm are re-examined as the potential explanation of deviations from profit maximization, and the imperfection of the take-over mechanism as a constraint in these models is shown to depend upon the extent of these costs and information failures.

---

* Research Fellow at the London Business School, Fellow in Economics at Lady Margaret Hall, Oxford, and a Research Associate of the Institute for Fiscal Studies.

This article draws heavily on a chapter of the author's D.Phil. thesis (Helm (1984a)). Thanks for earlier comments are due especially to Amartya Sen, John Hicks, and George Yarrow, and on this version to David Thompson, Jim Fairburn, John Kay, Martin Slater, and Colin Mayer. The usual disclaimers apply.

[1] See Winter (1964) for an early theoretical treatment of the selection argument, and Singh (1975) for an empirical investigation.

An alternative mechanism for the enforcement of profit maximization has been suggested to lie in the managerial market (Jensen and Meckling (1976)). This hypothesis is also examined, and a number of failures in the managerial market are identified, weakening the constraint on managerial behaviour. Thus the paper shows that the argument for *laissez-faire* in take-over and merger policy is weak, and hence the case for an interventionist policy strengthened. There is market failure in the capital and managerial markets.

Finally, since profit maximization may encourage the exploitation of monopoly power in the product market, the pursuit of managerial objectives by lower price strategies may actually be desirable (especially if combined with technical efficiency), and hence the enforcement mechanism in the capital and managerial markets may even be undesirable.

The paper is structured as follows. Section 2 sets out the traditional theory of managerial behaviour. The origins and implications of the separation of ownership and control are traced, to show how this institutional feature may give rise to non-profit-maximizing behaviour. Though the classic models associated with Baumol (1959), Williamson (1963), and Marris (1964) have now become somewhat unfashionable, I shall here draw out the key features of these models that might lead one to expect non-profit-maximizing behaviour. Section 3 sets out the simple take-over mechanism incorporating transactions costs and imperfect information. In Section 4, the failures associated with the capital market are considered and a theoretical result concerning imperfect information is presented to show that the enforcement of profit maximization under uncertainty in the capital market is fraught not only with empirical and institutional obstacles, but also with logical difficulties. I shall argue that capital markets at best place satisficing boundaries upon the pursuit of managerial objectives. Section 5 looks at the managerial theory of corporate control, and questions the extent to which competition in the managerial market might enforce profit maximization. While there are a number of reforms that might aid managerial incentives, such as pensions and profit-related bonuses, there are a number of key theoretical obstacles. These arise in the theory of team production and associated free-rider problems. Finally Section 6, the conclusion, considers the relationship between profit maximization and product market efficiency, and indicates the problems that arise from profit maximization for incentives towards increased concentration and oligopolistic strategic deterrents to entry.

2. Managerial Theories of the Firm Revisited

THE SEPARATION OF OWNERSHIP AND CONTROL

The separation of ownership and control, the source of the problem of a divergence between the objectives of shareholders and managers, is the norm for the modern industrial corporation in the UK. It has its origins in the nineteenth century, but it was in the inter-war period that the distinction became marked (Hannah (1983), Chandler (1977)).

There were three crucial components which brought about this transition. The institutional innovation of the joint stock company allowed risk to be spread and thus greater sources of capital to be tapped (Hicks (1982)). It formally separated directors from shareholders. The second contributory factor was one of size. The growth in the absolute size of the firm, in part because of supply-side technological and organizational changes, led to greater problems of co-ordination and the need to delegate authority. Finally, the growth of information and knowledge percolated through to management with the development of 'management science' and financial skills.

While firms remained comparatively small in absolute terms, owners could satisfactorily call upon family labour to manage their day-to-day affairs. The need for capital was correspondingly small and the market in equities relatively thin, and thus the attractiveness of equity sales over debt as a means of raising capital remained slim.

The coming of modern manufacturing techniques in the inter-war period, first in the US and then in Europe (Chandler (1977)), spurred on the growth of the professional managerial function. As firms grew in size, the possibility of comprehensive management by the single entrepreneur diminished. Control was necessarily decentralized, and specialist functions increasingly passed to those with particular knowledge and skills. The growth of 'managerial science', or 'Taylorism' as it was then sometimes called, aided this process.

THE MANAGERIAL THEORIES OF THE FIRM

With the separation of ownership and control in the modern corporation, the simple black-box profit-maximizing theory of the firm was increasingly recognized as inadequate. Berle and Means (1932) pioneered the study of this separation, while in the same period Coase (1937) proposed the novel idea of considering the firm as itself the response to an imperfection or market failure—the existence of internal economies of scale. With the emphasis shifted to internal organization, it was soon recognized that the interests of shareholders and managers might diverge. For although in the neoclassical paradigm, utility- and profit-maximizing behaviour were synonymous, the pursuit of utility by managers was reflected in their total income from the firm, itself related directly to salaries and bonuses and only indirectly to profits. Thus in order for managers to maximize their utility, it might turn out to be beneficial for them if the company diverged from profit maximization towards some other goal more closely connected with salaries, or indeed, as Hicks (1935) suggested, if they were permitted to pursue 'the quiet life'.

The subsequent debate divided between three schools of thought. The first held on to the neoclassical black-box model. Friedman (1953) argued that the realism of the assumption of profit maximization was irrelevant in modelling the behaviour of firms, provided the predictions of the theory were 'successful'. As I have argued elsewhere (Helm (1984b)), this approach is methodologically mistaken. The second school, the behaviouralists, took a more radical approach, denying the possibility of maximization. Simon (1955) argued that the inherent limitations on human rationality and the imperfection of information ruled out maximization. Individuals were only capable of 'satisficing'. Cyert and March (1963) argued that internal organizational conflict led to compromises which reflected a balance of interests rather than maximization of profits. The third school, the managerial theorists, argued that firms continued to maximize an objective, but replaced profit by a single and well-defined alternative goal which might best deliver the maximum utility to managers. The most important of these models are associated with Baumol (1959), Williamson (1963), and Marris (1964), who respectively proposed sales, managerial utility, and growth maximization. In order to explore the take-over mechanism, I shall concentrate on this third set of managerial models.

Already, in these early models, constraints on the deviation from profit maximization were explicitly recognized. The firm could not sacrifice everything for growth, and hence there was a limit or constraint upon the boundary of the objective. Managers themselves had an interest in limiting the deviation, being concerned with salary, but salary that was likely to continue. Hence they were not prepared to sacrifice profits if shareholders were likely to intervene and replace them. They could therefore be assumed to be risk-averse.

Marris's (1964) model explicitly recognized the take-over constraint. It assumed that managers' utility depends upon their salaries, and these were best maximized by maximizing the growth rate of the firm, i.e. $U = U(G_d)$. The demand for capital by managers is therefore determined by the components of G_d. These include the rate of diversification and the proportion of successful new products. The supply of capital is determined by the shareholders' utility function, and this consists of the security and profits that the potential investment offers them. The equilibrium growth path is then determined by equating the supply of capital from shareholders with the demand from managers. Though an endogenous theory could be constructed of the take-over mechanism should firms stray from the equilibrium path, i.e. from the supply of capital schedule, the take-over constraint was in these early models typically simply assumed exogenous.

The early models were unsatisfactory in a number of respects. First, empirical evidence failed to provide support for any simple relationship between salary and the assumed objective of the firm in these models.[2] Second, the new theories themselves had little by way of explanation as to why the selected goal should be chosen by managers. This led to increased emphasis on internal theories of the structure of organizations. One strand has been the transactions approach developed by Williamson (1975), focusing on how managers pursue their aims in organizational terms, drawing in part on earlier work on internal organizational theory. Another internal approach is that of the principal/agent literature, which considers the relationship between the shareholders and managers in terms of the incentive mechanisms set to control managers (see Section 5 below).

The third area of dissatisfaction stems from the implicit assumption of non-increasing costs of growth-diversifying strategies. The faster the rate of growth of the firm, the greater the internal disruption caused, and hence proportionally higher costs are incurred. Penrose (1959) addressed this problem directly,[3] and Solow (1971) explored the extent to which growth maximizing is best pursued by profit maximization.

The fourth and final dissatisfaction with the early managerial models arose with the constraint assumed. This was, as noted above, typically exogenous. The modern theory of the take-over mechanism is essentially an attempt to provide an endogenous account and it is to this that I now turn.

3. Enforcement in the Capital Market

THE SIMPLE TAKE-OVER MECHANISM

If the capital market were perfect, then the take-over mechanism would operate instantaneously whenever managers deviated from profit maximization. The perfect and freely available information would alert

---

[2] See Cosh (1975), for example.

[3] See in particular Slater's introduction to the second edition of Penrose (1959), and Slater (1980).

shareholders in the capital market immediately of any deviation from profit maximization. The share price would instantaneously fall to reflect this, and the absence of transactions costs would make intervention costless. As the actual price falls below the potential price, the profit maximization motivation of shareholders would ensure that arbitrage captured this potential economic rent.

Only if these strong assumptions of perfect competition are met will enforcement guarantee product market efficiency. Since these markets are in fact riddled with market imperfections, we know immediately that the take-over mechanism will be imperfect. The relevant question is thus not whether the take-over mechanism guarantees efficiency, but rather how much inefficiency, in the sense of the pursuit of managerial objectives, it permits.

Throughout this paper, I shall assume for simplicity that the raider is a profit maximizer. In practice the raider could, like the target, pursue other managerial objectives, as might those involved in the take-over process, such as merchant banks and regulatory agencies. This would further weaken the constraint as a guarantee of efficiency in the product market.

The two most important sources of failure in the capital market are transactions costs and information cost asymmetries. These can be incorporated in the take-over constraint upon the pursuit of managerial objectives, first with respect to transactions costs (following Yarrow (1976)) and second with respect to information costs (following Helm (1984a)).

Transactions costs

Transactions costs arise in a number of ways, associated with the administration of share transactions, the costs of forming a coalition of shareholders sufficiently large for the bid to have a chance of success, and the post-take-over reorganization of the management and resources of the target company (net of synergy benefits). Following Yarrow (1976), the take-over constraint can be written:

$$V^* - V \leqslant C$$

or:

$$V \geqslant V^* - C$$

where V^* is the maximum potential market value of the firm's ordinary shares, V is the actual market value of the firm's ordinary shares, and C is the costs of take-over.

The condition is therefore the standard optimality one, stating that deviations from profit maximization by managers are possible without take-over up to, but not beyond, the point where the marginal benefits of take-over become greater than the marginal costs, capitalized in the share value. In Yarrow's formulation, these costs depend on the size distribution of shareholdings and the parameters of the enforcement cost function. The general problem for the wealth-maximizing manager can then be set up as:

Maximize $U(X)$

subject to $V(X, Y) > V^*(Y) - C$

where X is a vector of utility-yielding variables and Y is any parameter affecting the market value of the firm's equity.[4]

The outcome then depends on the costs of enforcement of take-overs and the extent to which the interests of managers and shareholders vary; that is, if shareholders desire profits, the extent to which the components of $U(X)$ for managers do not depend upon profits. I return to these below.

Information costs

The second market imperfection to include in the take-over constraint is information costs (though these may not in practice be completely distinct from transactions costs). Shareholders are typically not perfectly informed, and can be assumed to know the actual share price of the firm (V), but not the maximal potential value (V^*). V^* is a matter of conjecture and estimation. It requires the estimation of the hypothetical counterfactual—what the firm would be worth if it pursued the hypothetical best feasible alternative policy to its present one. Typically, there exist a large number of potential strategies, each countered in oligopolistic markets by rivals' responses, and each involving the shareholders in information gathering. Standard search theory suggests that shareholders will only gather information up to the point at which the expected benefits exceed the expected costs. Thus managers can deviate from profit maximization free of the fear of take-over until this information search constraint binds. (Managers are here assumed not to control information; though of course in reality there may be a strategic game in information revelation.)

The constraint upon managers now depends on actual transactions costs and the expectations of both managers and shareholders.

---

[4] The first and second order conditions are set out in Yarrow (1976).

4. Further Theoretical Problems with the Take-over Enforcement Mechanism

The simple take-over constraint set out in the previous section suffers from at least two theoretical difficulties. These further weaken its ability to guarantee efficiency, and hence the case for a *laissez-faire* policy. The first difficulty arises directly from the simple model, and is associated with the estimation of future costs and benefits. The second adds a dynamic element to the simple static model, and concerns the process of buying up shares in the target company.

UNDEFINED OPTIMIZATION

Standard optimization where information is costly and imperfect treats the acquisition of information like that of any other ordinary goods. A person will gain (in profit or utility) from the acquisition of information up to the point where the marginal cost of acquiring one more piece of information is just equal to the marginal benefits it is expected to yield, *ex ante*. Thus the problem of gathering information under uncertainty is reduced to a standard optimization form.[5]

Despite its simplicity, this solution is, as I have shown elsewhere (Helm (1984a) Chs. 5 and 6), unfortunately no more than an evasion of the informational problem. For I here assume that although the person lacks complete information, he or she does know the marginal costs and benefits of search. However, there is no good theoretical reason for assuming that if the information itself is unknown, nevertheless the marginal costs and benefits are known a priori. And if they are not, then the person has a second-order search problem in order to optimize. The marginal costs of calculating the marginal costs of search must be equal to the marginal benefits of calculating the marginal costs, and also, the marginal costs and benefits of calculating the marginal benefits must be equated. But again, why should we assume that the person knows these marginal costs of

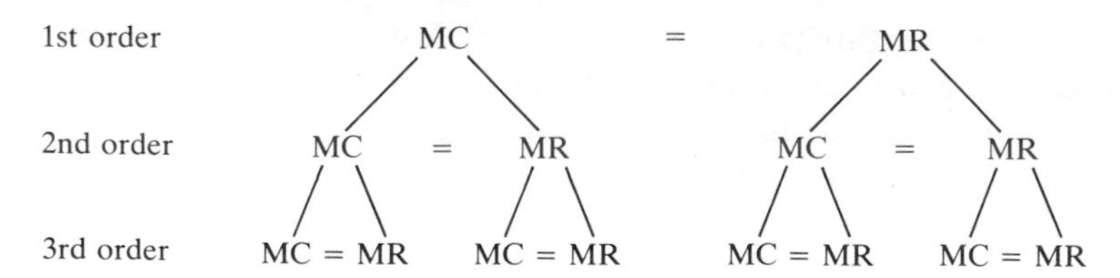

Figure 4.1. The search optimization infinite regress

[5] See Hirschleifer and Riley (1979) for a survey of the literature, especially pp. 1396–9.

calculating at the second order? And if not, then we retreat to the third order. The general problem can be set out diagramatically as in Figure 4.1.

Indeed this problem is in fact what is termed in philosophical literature an infinite regress (see Winter (1964), Helm (1984a), Elster (1984), and Hamlin (1986)). Such an argument has no solution and it follows that optimization search behaviour under uncertainty is hence undefined. But if the optimization search solution is undefined, then the shareholder cannot obtain an optimum estimate of the maximum potential share price (V^*), and the simple take-over mechanism set out in Section 3 above is itself incomplete.

Such a radical result has strong implications. We can either attempt to overcome the regress within the optimization framework or consider alternative non-optimizing rules of judgement under uncertainty.

Retaining the optimization approach

There are at least three ways of retaining the optimization approach to informational problems faced by shareholders in estimating V^* and C. These are the assumptions that the search costs and benefits are known, that the regress tends to zero, or that the probability distributions over V^* and C are known.

First, the regress will not affect the optimization procedure if the costs and benefits at the second order are known. In the capital market, the costs of search might be reasonably well known. Information gathering is often a standardized procedure amongst brokers. However, it is hard to argue that the benefits are known, *ex ante*, since these tend to be more diffuse and require the simulation of alternative scenarios for the firm.

Second, the regress might be assumed to tend to zero. Thus it might be argued that in practice the search costs tend to be negligible after the first round, and therefore that the optimization description is a good enough approximation. The argument does, however, allow the logical regress argument to stand, and hence the optimum to be strictly undefined. Furthermore, the empirical claim that the costs do tend to zero is open to dispute in at least some circumstances. These include areas where primary research is needed to assess the probability of alternative strategies, and where the firm is exposed to substantial external risks which the search procedure needs to estimate. But whether or not costs do tend to zero, it is clearly implausible to rely on this assumption for benefits. Benefits from future projects are typically more speculative, especially where a degree of innovation is required.

The third option, to assume probability distributions, requires the provision of a theory as to where they come from. It is thus derivative on the first two claims, and hence again unconvincing.

Alternative non-optimizing rules for decisions under uncertainty

The alternative reaction to the regress argument is to accept it, and to examine how managers and shareholders might behave as a result. In practice, detailed planning of the amount of resources allocated to search are rare, and a procedural satisficing decision is adopted (Simon (1976)). Rules-of-thumb decisions are made, and these are typically revised if evidence comes to light of unsatisfactory attainment of objectives. Managers are, in Simon's (1955) terms, constrained to satisfice under uncertainty, precisely because maximization is undefined.

Thus an understanding of the take-over constraint relies on the procedural rationality of those estimating it—the actual rules and methods employed by shareholders and their agents in estimating V^*. These involve comparisons with relatively similar firms and the use of financial indicators such as price/earnings ratios, beta coefficients, debt/equity ratios, and so on, to identify prima-facie evidence of managerial 'inefficiency'. When a firm is deemed to have departed from a 'satisfactory' performance on these standard criteria, further investigations (and hence costs) are undertaken, and a potential intervention considered. The substantive decision to initiate a take-over emerges from a procedural investigation, where V^* is unknown.

This approach is not only more in tune with casual observation, but also accords closely with much recent evidence concerning reasoning under uncertainty. The expected utility-maximizing hypothesis has been undermined by experimental evidence. Studies reported in Kahneman, Slovic, and Tversky (1983) document this evidence, as does Shoemaker (1982). Recent alternative theoretical models to expected utility maximization include those of Kahneman and Tversky (1979), Loomes and Sugden (1982), and Heiner (1983). These in part derive from the much earlier work of Keynes (1921) and Shackle (1949) on probability, and of course Simon's (1955) satisficing model. It is not the purpose of this paper to survey these approaches, but rather to draw attention to the fact that there are a number of other non-utility maximization approaches to decision-making under uncertainty, which reinforce the case for a procedural rather than a substantive account of the take-over decision. Furthermore, to the extent that these accounts are consistent with the logical problem of the infinite regress, they provide additional support for the notion that the take-over mechanism does not necessarily enforce profit maximization upon firms.

FREE-RIDING AND THE GROSSMAN AND HART PROBLEM

The simple take-over mechanism set out in Section 3 is a static one. It provides no account of the process by which a take-over occurs. This process is complex and hedged with rules and regulations. It can itself create market failures which further impede the efficiency of the take-over mechanism.

One major difficulty that arises in this context is referred to in the literature as the Grossman and Hart problem (1980). This problem refers to the ability of existing shareholders to free-ride on the potential raider in the take-over process. In the Yarrow (1976) model of the take-over discussed above, one of the costs of the take-over is the formation of a coalition just large enough to execute the take-over. The Grossman and Hart paper examines the problem from the point of view of the shareholder owning shares in a company where $V < V^*$ and from whom the raider seeks to purchase shares. Grossman and Hart point out, *ceteris paribus*, that an offer of V' where $V^* > V' > V$ is typically assumed to be accepted. However, since the existing shareholder attaches a positive probability to the likelihood of the take-over, he or she expects that after the take-over the price will rise to V^*. Hence the expected future value of V tends to V^* as the expectation of success rises. Furthermore, the raider, and not the existing shareholder, bears most of the costs (C) incurred in the take-over. Hence our shareholder, expecting the price to rise to V^*, will not accept an offer of V'; rather, he or she will free-ride on the raider bearing the take-over costs, and reap the rewards of V^*.

Now, with incomplete information, the probability of a purchase offer representing a credible take-over bid depends on the number of shares held by the raider, and thus the size of the coalition. Therefore, as the number of shares held by the raider or coalition rises, the expectation of approximation towards V^* rises; hence the price demanded by the seller also rises. Hence the share price at V tends to that at V^*, and the gap between them decreases as the size of the raider's coalition holding rises. At the limit, V^* is the only acceptable price to the seller.

The implication of this result is that the take-over constraint is considerably weakened, and that the gains to the acquirer are likely to be small. It thus accords with recent empirical evidence on share price movements and the gains from mergers reported most notably by Firth (1979) and Franks and Harris (1986a).[6]

The capital market constraint as a method of enforcing profit-maximizing behaviour on managers is thus rather weak. It selects out

[6] Some solutions to this problem have been suggested in the literature, relating to the institutional procedures that give bidding rights to the raider. Most notably, Yarrow (1985) suggests that compulsory acquisition provisions of the 1948 Companies Act, when combined with the rules in the City Code on Takeovers and Mergers protecting minority shareholders, combine to provide 'a regulatory environment which allows the takeover mechanism to function in a way closely approximating that traditionally assumed in the theory of the firm' (pp. 4–5). The issue of minority shareholdings is, however, complex, and the Yarrow argument is at best an approximate solution. See Meadowcroft and Thompson (1987).

inefficiencies that are greater than the satisficing targets that shareholders implicitly set for firms, and then only succeeds if the free-riding problem can be overcome. Managers are thus only weakly disciplined by the take-over constraint, and we cannot therefore rely on the capital market to enforce profit maximization.[7]

5. The Managerial Market Constraints

If the take-over mechanism provides a weak constraint on managers, it has been suggested that an alternative method of enforcing profit maximization on the firm lies in competition in the market for managers.

MANAGERIAL COMPETITION

In a famous article, Jensen and Meckling (1976) shifted attention from the traditional concern with the separation of ownership and control directly, to the problems of control and incentives in the managerial market. In subsequent articles by Fama (1980) and Jensen and Ruback (1983), attention shifted to competition between rival groups or teams of managers for the control of corporate assets.

This competition, it was argued, acts to eliminate by arbitrage the potential rent which arises because of divergences from the maximization of shareholders' wealth, and hence profit-maximizing procedures. As Jensen and Ruback (1983, p. 44) put it, 'Competition from alternative managerial teams in the market for corporate control serves as a source of external control on the internal control system of the corporation'. One implication of an efficient managerial market is thus that the rent from corporate control is reduced to the normal profit rate, which is equivalent to the pursuit of profit-maximizing objectives. Such a market must, of course, meet the standard requirements for efficiency.

As with the take-over mechanism and the capital market, the Jensen and Ruback managerial constraint fails to enforce profit maximization where market failures arise. In practice, the managerial market displays a number of such failures. The market is heterogeneous, and to a varying extent is often informationally inadequate, relatively thin, and characterized by considerable immobility due to housing market imperfections, educational considerations for children, two-jobs requirements, and so on. Managerial

---

[7] The counter-argument here is that the impact of a large penalty, even where the probability is small, may be a strong deterrent to risk-averse managers. See Mirrlees (1976) and Calvo and Wellisz (1978).

jobs often require specialist firm-specific skills and have non-negligible entry costs.

Thus institutional characteristics of the managerial market provide little support to the argument that managerial competition is a strong mechanism for the enforcement of profit-maximizing behaviour. But there are also theoretical difficulties with this approach, to which I now turn.

TEAM-WORK, MEASURING RESULTS, AND FREE-RIDING

The selection in the managerial market of the most efficient management to control corporate assets depends on the relationship between rewards and effort, and the ability of the market to judge the individual marginal product of each manager or worker. Frequently, however, marginal products cannot be separated for each individual, since the production and management are joint products (Alchian and Demsetz (1972)). Management is typically a team function, differentiated by a hierarchy of control. Competitive selection operates on that team, not on the individual components of it. Two teams may have some efficient and some inefficient members in each. If A beats B in the managerial market, some inefficient workers may be selected for rather than against because the efficient members outweigh them in yielding the total product. The reason for this relates to the difficulty in directly measuring these individual marginal products, either because of combined inputs or because of the costs of measurement. The team is a co-operative solution to the attainment of an objective, be it profits or some proxy for managerial utility.

Within the team, because the marginal products cannot be individually measured, each individual may have the incentive to free-ride on his or her associates. As long as the team output is greater than that of rivals, the individual can put in less effort without being detected.[8] Thus where selection and enforcement bear upon teams, managerial competition will still permit individual inefficiencies to arise.

DEFINING MANAGERIAL OBJECTIVES

Proper monitoring of free-riding behaviour would reduce the inefficiencies that result, but there would still be an efficiency loss represented by the monitoring costs (Alchian and Demsetz (1972)). But of perhaps greater direct impact on the effectiveness of managerial competition is the internal organizational problem of getting the agreement of managers to a single

---

[8] But see Radner (1985) on incentive mechanisms within firms.

objective and its implementation. Managers in firms, as Cyert and March (1963) noted, represent different interests—be they sales and marketing, financial, production, or some other functional representative. Maximizing the salaries of managers implies different policies depending upon the individual's place in the firm. Profit maximization may produce the best financial performance, whilst higher sales may better promote the interests of the sales manager. The solution to this conflict of interests lies in a negotiated organizational approach, with trade-offs between the various interests. Such organizational solutions fit the satisficing paradigm better than the maximizing one.

In both the Jensen and Ruback model and that of Grossman and Hart, the precise institutional arrangements can have considerable impact on the efficiency of the market enforcement mechanisms. These include both external organizational arrangements of regulatory authorities and codes of practice, and the internal arrangements within the firm. Thus general theoretical models can often give a misleading guide to practice.

6. The Interaction of Market Failures: Product Market Competition and Profit Maximization

Thus far the principal obstacles to the enforcement of profit maximization upon firms through the capital and managerial markets have been shown. In particular, the assumption that either of these markets can guarantee profit maximization is misplaced. The question that then arises is whether this should matter for policy. Is it really important that the capital market, in particular, enforce discipline upon firms? I shall in conclusion suggest that this assumption may also be misplaced.

Profit maximization is only synonymous with welfare maximization in an economy characterized by perfect competition. This result is captured in the fundamental theorems of modern Paretian welfare economics.[9] Under all other circumstances, the pursuit of profits will lead to a divergence from Paretian optimality. In particular, the presence of market power tends to increase price above marginal cost. The smaller the number of firms in the industry, the greater is the possibility of collusive behaviour and the potential to engage in strategic entry-deterring behaviour. To the extent, therefore, that the enforcement of profit-maximizing behaviour tends to induce firms to exploit market power, it will, *ceteris paribus*, tend to lower economic welfare.

Consider now the behaviour of the managerial firm. The objectives of these firms may be complex. Nevertheless, size and growth rate seem to be

[9] See Helm (1986) for an exposition of the Pareto principle and of market failure.

the typical objectives. The question that then arises is what differing policies these firms might adopt to their profit-maximizing alternatives, and what the welfare consequences are of these policies. There are two aspects to this: what pricing policy is pursued and whether the firms tend to technical inefficiency.

The managerial firm sacrifices profits in the pursuit of its management objective. One method by which it may achieve this is by lowering its price. If price falls towards the competitive level, then welfare rises. Price is now closer to marginal cost than it would have been if all the market power had been exploited. Thus managerial behaviour may enhance welfare, provided technical efficiency is maintained and the price does not fall too low, beyond the welfare optimum.

Despite the popular belief that managerial objectives tend to be conducive to cost inflation and hence technical inefficiencies, it is hard to see why managerial firms should have this incentive structure, unless 'the quiet life' or leisure maximization enters directly into their utility function (Hicks (1935)), or these additional costs substitute for direct salary as tax-advantageous perks.[10] In other circumstances, technical inefficiency will distract from the growth and output performance of the company, and hence reduce managers' utility. Thus the worry about technical inefficiency in the managerial firm may be misplaced. Indeed, in the classic case of state enterprise, where the technical inefficiency argument is most popular, Rees (1984) has used an output maximization model to map managers' objectives, and shown that under this plausible model, production is technically efficient.

Thus it is not at all clear that the substitution of profit for other managerial objectives through the discipline of the take-over mechanism unambiguously tends to increase welfare. Indeed, there exist a plausible set of circumstances where the imposition of profit maximization may tend to diminish welfare. Perhaps then it is fortunate that the capital and managerial mechanisms for enforcement of profit maximization are typically far from binding on the firm.

[10] Williamson (1963) formalizes this managerial behaviour as an 'expense preference' to include in his managerial utility function.

5

Shareholder Wealth Effects of UK Take-overs: Implications for Merger Policy

JULIAN FRANKS* AND ROBERT HARRIS†

1. Introduction

The purpose of this paper is threefold. First, we offer an overview of UK merger activity and the role of the Monopolies and Mergers Commission in take-overs. Second, we estimate costs to shareholders arising from referrals of proposed mergers to the Commission. Finally, we discuss broader concerns about the aggregate level of merger activity, and how institutional changes might be more effective alternatives to merger as a way of removing inefficiencies.

In the empirical section, we examine a sample of mergers from the period 1965–85 in order to answer three questions. First, what costs do shareholders bear when a bid is referred to the Commission and is subsequently permitted to proceed? We compare value changes to shareholders in referred mergers with those measured in a large sample of 1,900 successful mergers. Second, does the rejection of a merger by the Commission involve the loss of a bid premium which shareholders would have realized in a successful merger? Third, do bids that fail because of management and shareholder discretion perform better or worse than bids that fail as a result of rejection by the Commission?

In Section 2 of the paper, we provide historical statistics on merger activity in the UK and briefly describe the role of the Commission and the level of its intervention. In Section 3, we describe data, methodology, and

---

* National Westminster Bank Professor of Finance, London Business School.

† Professor of Finance, University of North Carolina at Chapel Hill.

The authors wish to thank the Leverhulme Trust for financial support, and Colin Mayer, Paul Bloom, Jim Fairburn, John Kay, Martin Howe, and Barry Roberts for suggestions and comments. All remaining errors are their own. An earlier version of this paper appeared in *Oxford Review of Economic Policy* (Franks and Harris (1986a)) and the authors appreciate permission to use substantial portions of it here.

results for our analysis of referred mergers. In Section 4, we explore some of the policy issues that are raised by the recent high level of merger activity. In particular, we discuss some institutional changes that might reduce the level of merger activity by providing a less costly means of capturing perceived merger benefits.

2. Merger Activity and the Role of the Commission

PAST MERGER ACTIVITY

Table 5.1 reports statistics from the Department of Trade and Industry (DTI) on the level and value of UK merger activity from 1963 to 1985. From

Table 5.1. UK acquisitions and mergers, 1963–85

Year	Number acquired	Value (£m. historic prices)	Value (£m. 1985 prices)
1963	888	352	2 429
1964	940	505	3 371
1965	1 000	517	3 295
1966	807	500	3 077
1967	763	822	4 928
1968	946	1 946	11 145
1969	846	1 069	5 794
1970	793	1 122	5 730
1971	884	911	4 255
1972	1 210	2 532	11 023
1973	1 205	1 304	5 197
1974	504	508	1 749
1975	315	291	806
1976	353	448	1 064
1977	481	824	1 690
1978	567	1 140	2 159
1979	534	1 656	2 763
1980	469	1 475	2 087
1981	452	1 144	1 447
1982	463	2 206	2 569
1983	447	2 343	2 608
1984	568	5 474	5 806
1985	474	7 090	7 090

Source: Department of Trade and Industry.

Table 5.2. Acquisitions of UK quoted companies

Year	Number of acquisitions
1955	24
1956	26
1957	39
1958	42
1959	71
1960	83
1961	43
1962	44
1963	38
1964	37
1965	42
1966	41
1967	59
1968	108
1969	67
1970	55
1971	58
1972	56
1973	45
1974	37
1975	84
1976	100
1977	125
1978	86
1979	80
1980	57
1981	69
1982	62
1983	70
1984	93
1985[a]	52

[a]First half of year.

Source: From data described by Franks and Harris (1986b). These represent UK companies that disappeared from the London Share Price Database (LSPD) due to merger and for which share price data were available around the merger date. For years prior to 1975, LSPD only contains about two-thirds of all UK quoted companies and includes the larger firms.

these time series, it is apparent that the value of acquired firms' assets is more volatile over time than is the number of acquisitions. In 1968, one of the peaks of merger activity, the pound sterling value of mergers (at 1985 prices) is more than 13 times the value of acquisitions transacted in the trough of 1975. In comparison, thc number of acquisitions in 1968 is only 3 times that recorded in 1975. The level of merger activity can be put in a different perspective if one considers that in 1985 the value of merging firms' assets was about 5 per cent of total non-financial corporate assets calculated on a replacement cost basis; in 1968 it was nearer 8 per cent. The result is that merger activity has been a formidable force in changing the ownership of British industry. An interesting question is whether these ownership changes have greatly influenced the restructuring of industry.

The figures in Table 5.1 refer to the acquisitions of any UK company, whether privately or publicly held. In Table 5.2, we provide the annual acquisition statistics for UK publicly quoted companies for the period 1955 through to June 1985. There were approximately 1,900 acquisitions for the

Table 5.3. Number of acquisitions in selected countries

Year	Canada	Germany	Netherlands	United States
1975	264	445	n/a	2 297
1976	313	453	n/a	2 276
1977	395	554	n/a	2 224
1978	449	558	n/a	2 106
1979	511	602	n/a	2 128
1980	414	635	n/a	1 889
1981	491	618	296	2 395
1982	576	603	328	2 346
1983	628	506	296	2 533
1984	641	575	370	2 543
1985	712	709	318	3 001

Sources: Data for Canada, Germany, and the Netherlands are from annual reports submitted by each country's delegate to the meeting of the Committee of Experts on Restrictive Practices, June 1986, OECD. They constitute only a sample of mergers, since they include mergers that come within the jurisdiction of the regulatory body. Data for the US come from W. T. Grimm and Company. They record completed and pending transactions as of the end of the year. Grimm includes transfers of ownership of 10% or more of a company's assets or equity, and hence includes divestitures. The latter constitute about 37% of the total.

30-year period.[1] Since currently there are only about 2,000 UK companies quoted and traded at any one time (excluding the unlisted securities market), the death-rate from merging has been substantial. Because acquirers have been on average about 8 times the size of acquirees in value terms, the smaller company has had a higher probability of disappearing through merger.

This level of merger activity is not confined to the UK. In the US, similar levels of merger activity have been seen. Table 5.3 documents the last decade of merger activity in 4 western countries and the rising trend of that activity.

ROLE OF THE COMMISSION IN MERGER ACTIVITY

The Monopolies Commission was established in 1948 by Act of Parliament, its name subsequently being changed, in 1973, to the Monopolies and Mergers Commission. Merger control, as we know it today, was introduced in 1965, although some new provisions were introduced in the Fair Trading Act (1973).[2] A primary responsibility of the Commission has been the investigation of mergers. Currently, the Commission only investigates mergers that are referred to it by the Secretary of State for Trade and Industry (the Minister), who usually (but not necessarily) acts on the recommendation of the Director General of the Office of Fair Trading (OFT). The OFT completes a preliminary study of announced bids, and as a result the Director may recommend a referral. If the Minister agrees to a referral, the bid is investigated by the Commission. In fact, both bids and consummated mergers can be referred, although the latter is a rare event. In addition, the OFT can provide confidential guidance to individual companies prior to any referral. Such guidance may include information on whether a referral is likely, possibly before a bid is publicly announced. Such 'guidance' is given in an increasing number of cases.

Criteria for referral are broad. Any bid is eligible if the combined market share of the merged firms exceeds 25 per cent, or if the assets of the acquired company are greater than £30 million (raised in 1984 from £15

---

[1] The figures in Table 5.2 tend to understate significantly the total number of successful acquisitions as reported by Roell (1986a). Using statistics from the Takeover Panel, she reports a total of successful acquisitions of 116 for 1983–4 and 160 for 1984–5. The corresponding statistics for Franks and Harris's (1986b) database are 81 and 99, respectively. Possible reasons for the differences are (a) that the Takeover Panel includes USM (unlisted securities market) acquisitions whereas Franks and Harris do not, and (b) Franks and Harris's exclusion of UK acquisitions of foreign companies. There may also be a mismatching of figures arising from different definitions of when a merger is consummated.

[2] For a discussion of the UK merger legislation and the role of the Commission, see Office of Fair Trading (1985).

million). As a result, only a small proportion of the mergers reported in Table 5.1 qualify; up to 1985 the number was about 200 each year.

On the basis of the report, the Minister makes the decision to accept or reject the merger. The Minister does not have to accept the report of the Commission, and in a number of cases has not done so. The Minister can, however, only disallow a merger if the Commission report makes an adverse judgement with at least a two-thirds majority.

Once a referral is made, three possible results may ensue. The bid may be rejected, accepted, or laid aside. In the last case, no report is made because the bid lapses, usually because the acquiring company has indicated that it does not wish to proceed with the acquisition. In considering a bid, the Commission must take into account the general public interest. An important criterion is the effect of the bid on competition. Such a consideration embraces not only mergers that would lead to horizontal and vertical integration, but also conglomerate mergers. However, current policy is that vertical and conglomerate mergers are unlikely to be referred unless they raise 'special' concerns of wider public interest. Other considerations may also play a role, such as those of employment (and regional considerations), international competition, foreign ownership and its implications for the national interest, and the survival of failing firms.

Up to November 1985, only 93 mergers have been referred to the Commission (excluding newspaper mergers which are considered under

Table 5.4. Timing and number of referrals and outcomes

	1965–9	1970–4	1975–9	1980–4	1985	Total
Total referrals	13	19	21	36	4	93
Acceptances	7	5	7	14	2	35
Rejections	5	5	7	15	0	32
Laid aside	1	9	7	7	1	25
Report awaited					1	1

Notes: Where a merger is rejected by the Commission but the majority (of Commissioners) is less than two-thirds, we have classified the outcome as a rejection (at least 1 case).

Where 2 acquiring companies bid for the same company and both bids are referred, we have classified them as 2 referrals.

In 1 case at least, the Minister has accepted a merger when two-thirds of the Commissioners recommended rejection.

Results for 1985 are through 12 November.

Source: Office of Fair Trading (1985).

separate provisions). Although the rate of referral has increased in recent years, referrals represent only about 2 or 3 per cent of those mergers eligible for consideration by the Commission. Table 5.4 documents the timing, number, and outcome of Commission referrals. Though only about one-third of referrals lead to rejection, the rejection rate understates the Commission's deterrence capability since it is possible that bids laid aside would have borne a high probability of rejection. Furthermore, an unknown number of bids have not materialized because the OFT has given informal advice that a referral would be likely to be recommended. While a minority of mergers were rejected, the average value of a rejected bid was more than 5 times the size of an accepted bid (using equity market value of the target firm as the bench-mark).

3. Mergers, Shareholder Value, and Commission Decisions

Neoclassical economic theory holds that a voluntary decision by market participants to merge is based on some perception of shareholder benefits. Activity by the OFT and Commission to monitor, and at times prohibit, mergers may deprive shareholders of these benefits—the social calculus being that undesirable anticompetitive effects will occur if the merger is undertaken.

Important questions arise about the nature and magnitude of shareholder benefits forgone when a merger is referred and rejected. Accounting studies (Meeks (1977), Singh (1971, 1975)) of UK mergers have generally concluded that, on average, mergers produce zero or negative shareholder benefits; only a study by Cosh, Hughes, and Singh (1980) suggests an increase in post-merger profitability. In addition, UK studies of share price performance have produced conflicting results. Franks, Broyles, and Hecht (1977) found mergers were value-creating, but their work was restricted to a single industry. Firth (1979, 1980), on the other hand, found that any gains to acquiree shareholders were more than offset by losses to acquirers, and concluded that mergers are most likely 'motivated by maximization of management utility reasons' (1980, p. 235). Using a sample of 39 mergers from the period 1974 through to 1976, Barnes (1984) found small gains to the acquirer around the merger announcement date but greater losses during the subsequent 6 months. Dodds and Quek (1985) used a larger sample for the same period and found residuals around the announcement date similar to those of Franks *et al.* (1977) and contrary to those of Barnes.

Recently, in a more comprehensive study, Franks and Harris (1986b) have measured the gains and losses to shareholders in almost 1,900 UK mergers that took place during the period 1955–85. Their results show that acquiree shareholders gained substantially with bid premiums of 22 per cent in the month of the bid. At the same time, acquirer shareholders gained 1 per cent. As a result, the authors concluded that mergers were value-creating for shareholders. This evidence is similar to evidence for US mergers, as reviewed and summarized by Jensen and Ruback (1983).

Even if one concluded that mergers generally were not value-creating for shareholders, would it be reasonable to assume that the referral of bids to the Commission and their eventual rejection would be costless to shareholders? Indeed, if this were the case, it could be argued that a rejection by the Commission might prevent the dissipation of shareholder wealth as a result of management hubris. However, such a conclusion would not be reasonable, despite some empirical evidence casting a negative light on merger activity in general. Those mergers that are rejected by the Commission presumably are motivated (in part, at least) by a reduction in competition. The latter should be anticipated to produce supernormal profits that are capitalized in share prices. Indeed, if this were not the case, the neoclassical logic for opposing mergers on anticompetitive grounds would be suspect. Anticompetitive effects leading to supernormal profits are a benefit to shareholders even though there are net costs imposed upon society in the form of reduced efficiency in resource usage.

SAMPLE AND METHODOLOGY

To provide evidence on shareholder wealth effects in mergers and the impact of Commission decisions, we obtained a comprehensive list of mergers (excluding newspaper mergers) referred to the Commission through early 1986. For each merger we obtained the following key dates: the *bid date*, when the acquirer announced its bid; the *referral date*, when the merger is referred to the Commission; and the *report date*, when the Commission publishes the report, accepting or rejecting the merger. When the merger is laid aside, no report is published although the 'laid aside' date was collected. Mergers are typically referred to the Commission within a month or two of the bid. Over 90 per cent of all referrals come within 2 months of the bid. The lag between referral and the final reporting date could be up to a year, but a 6- or 7-month lag is more typical. In cases where all three dates exist in our sample, the median lag between bid date and report is 8 months. These lags show that, subsequent to initial bids, shareholders are subject to uncertainty and possible delays in both referral and the ultimate fate of the merger.

For our analysis of effects of Commission decisions on shareholder wealth, we require share prices which we obtained from the London Share Price Database (LSPD). LSPD includes all UK companies quoted since 1975, in addition to a large sample of companies from 1955. Although there were over 90 mergers referred in the period examined, the sample used in this study was smaller. Some companies were not quoted (because they were private or foreign), while in other cases share price data were not available in the LSPD. Finally, in other cases we were unable to obtain necessary information on key dates. As a result, for companies with return data we had bid dates for 86 mergers, referral dates for 82, and report (including laid aside) dates for 75 companies.

To measure the impact on shareholders, we use a model to predict how share prices would have performed if a merger had not taken place and then subtract this predicted return (control return) from the realized return. The difference between the prediction and the realization is a measure of the percentage shareholder value gain attributable to the merger.

Value gain = Realized return - Control return

Returns include both dividends and capital gains (or capital losses). We calculate these value gains on a monthly basis with time defined relative to a particular event. The particular event is referred to as 'month zero' (since monthly share price data are being used) for all companies in the sample. Thus month 'minus one' for a company is 1 month before the event for that company, irrespective of the actual calendar date. To measure value gains arising from the bid announcement, we define month zero as the bid month. Alternatively, when we study the effects of Commission decisions, month zero could be defined as the report date. In the latter case, the value gain in month zero is interpreted as the effect of the Commission report on shareholders' wealth. Due to possible anticipation by the market of forthcoming events, we also report value gains accumulated over periods of months surrounding the event date.

The approach described above requires a control or predicted return. We use the so-called 'market model' which controls for general equity market movements, adjusting for both company risk and the company's expected performance given movements in a market index. If a company were of similar risk to the market index and, prior to the event, had average stock returns equal to returns on the market, the control (or forecast) return would be defined as the return on an equally weighted index of all stocks covered in LSPD. If the control return is less than the return actually realized in a month, we can say the security has outperformed the market. If in the event month, on average, a sample of companies (for example, acquirees) outperforms the market, we attribute the 'value gain' to the event. Our procedures are described in more detail in the Appendix.

Why use share price data rather than accounting data? The accounting methodology measures rates of return on assets before and after the merger. The advantage of this method is that *realized* rates of return are being measured, which should reflect actual changes in the profitability of assets employed. The major disadvantage is that accounting rates of return are rarely equal to economic rates of return (see Kay (1976), Solomon and Laya (1967)). Not only are accounting profits different from free cash flows, but more important, the initial and final book values of assets may be poor proxies for their economic values.

Given the measurement problems in accounting studies, share price studies offer an alternative to measuring the effects of merger. Provided that share prices reflect the underlying economic values of assets, changes in equity values will properly capture *expected* changes in the economic profitability of the firm. Notwithstanding the substantial empirical evidence supporting the efficiency of the stock market, efficiency is still a controversial proposition (see Summers (1986)). Furthermore, stock market prices reflect both current levels of profitability and anticipated changes. As a result, it is difficult to disentangle expectations from realizations.

Even if share prices do not properly anticipate changes in the profitability of assets, it may still be possible to make statements about whether mergers add value to shareholder wealth. However, it would not be possible to claim that these changes in shareholder wealth reflect changes in the underlying profitability of the firm's assets associated with the merger. In this study, we rely on share price data.

RESULTS

Proposition 1: Do mergers in general create value for shareholders?

The evidence from share price studies has been controversial. Firth's studies, mentioned earlier, have examined a relatively short period of time (1969–75) whereas Franks, Broyles, and Hecht examined mergers in only one industry. However, the latest study by Franks and Harris (1986b) includes a much larger data set and a much longer time series than previous studies.

Franks and Harris (1986b), using methodology similar to that described earlier, examined nearly 1,900 UK mergers with the results shown in Table 5.5. Acquiree shareholders have significant positive gains as a result of mergers. There are 22 per cent value gains to acquirees in the bid month and 30 per cent gains over the 6-month period beginning 4 months prior to the bid. The higher gain for the 6-month period may reflect the market's anticipation of a bid. Acquirer shareholders obtain a small value increase in the bid month and a 7 per cent gain over the 6-month period, with almost two-thirds of the individual acquirers showing gains for the period. To some extent, the acquirer gains prior to the bid may reflect positive earnings trends or other favourable developments which coincided with the bid or which influenced the acquirer's timing of a bid. As a result, it is not clear how much of the 7 per cent gain is attributable to the anticipation of merger benefits by the acquirer. What is clear is that there is no evidence of acquirer shareholder losses. Franks and Harris also show that gains to acquiree shareholders are larger in contested and/or revised bids than in the single bid case, but that there is no reduction in returns to acquiring firm shareholders. This evidence suggests that contested and/or revised bids are more a manifestation of larger merger benefits than of an increase in competition for corporate control. In summary, Franks and Harris's work shows positive gains to shareholders in merging firms, with most if not all of the gain going to acquiree shareholders.[3]

Table 5.5. Average value changes

	Average value changes		Percentage of firms with value increases	
	Bid month	6 months (−4 to +1)	Bid month	6 months
Acquiree	22%*	30%*	86	85
Acquirer	1%*	7%*	50	65

* Significantly different from zero at 95% confidence level.

What is the post-merger performance of these acquiring firms? In an efficient stock market, we would expect the market to price the anticipated gains from merging in an unbiased way; thus we would expect no abnormal performance post-merger (positive or negative). Franks and Harris (1986b) examine acquirer shareholder returns for 2 years subsequent to merger, beginning after the bid becomes unconditional. Their results show that acquirers, on average, outperform the market prior to the merger but that this abnormal performance does not continue post-merger; thus, a bench-mark for acquirers based on pre-merger performance produces losses of 10 to 13 per cent over a 2-year period.[4] However, if the bench-mark is altered

[3] Franks and Harris (1986b) report that on average the acquirer is 7 to 8 times as large as the acquiree, based on market value of equity; thus, a direct comparison of percentage value gains does not give a full picture of the split of value gains. They show, however, that value gains still go largely to the acquiree after controlling for the relative size of merging firms.

[4] Franks and Harris (1986b) show that acquirer shares appear to outperform the market in the 5- to 6-year period prior to making a merger bid. This corresponds to high pre-merger α values in the model market (see the Appendix). They suggest that this may, in part, indicate

to represent the performance of all firms (i.e. a market index) then acquiring firms outperform the market by about 4 per cent over the 2 years subsequent to merger. It should be apparent that the post-merger performance of acquiring firms is very sensitive to the bench-mark used.

Proposition 2: Do Commission rejections deprive shareholders of value?

Grossman and Hart (1981) draw a distinction between 'acquisitional' take-overs, motivated solely by inside information held by the acquirer, and 'allocational' take-overs where the prospective merger benefits require a reallocation of real resources. If a take-over is 'acquisitional', the bidder's incentive to acquire and process information is based on gains to be reaped when the information is released and the currently 'undervalued' target company is revalued upwards. Why is a merger required to realize these benefits? Grossman and Hart point out that any small shareholder's incentive to gather and process information about a company is limited by the ability of other shareholders to free-ride. Shareholders free-ride if they gain from the revelation of new information but do not bear the costs of gathering it. To avoid this free-rider problem, at least in part, a single bidder may be motivated to acquire an entire company. Thus, purely acquisitional take-overs may play a role in improving information reflected in financial market prices.[5]

On the other hand, 'allocational' take-overs involve changes in real asset markets (such as cost savings or increased monopoly power). In allocational take-overs, increases in financial market value reflect planned changes in real asset markets, not just changes in the market's information about those markets.

If an acquisitional merger is referred to the Commission and rejected by it, would the value added by the acquirer's information be eroded as a result of the rejection? We would not expect any erosion if the information gathered and processed by the acquirer is revealed by the bid process. Alternatively, if the information is retained by the acquirer and is never made public, then the value added would be eroded by the rejection. We

---

managers' timing of take-over bids following favourable developments in their stock price, perhaps to capitalize on what they perceive as advantageous financing conditions. It may be that the management of acquiring firms have superior information to other market participants about the economic value of their assets and therefore about the value of their financial securities.

[5] There is a further question of how much value gain a bidder can reap, given that a bid may reveal some of the inside information. This may explain why bidders often obtain sizeable 'toe-hold' interests prior to making a formal bid. Rules about disclosure of such toe-hold interests thus can be interpreted as ways to limit a bidder's profit from inside information. Such rules may discourage acquisitional take-overs which improve the efficiency of the information market.

believe the former is the more realistic case, since information (such as an undervaluation of the assets) would be revealed by the announcement that a bidder had gathered and processed information, and was intending to bid. Moreover, the time delays and investigation surrounding Commission deliberations would be likely to reveal the information.

If mergers referred to the Commission are allocational, two outcomes of Commission rejection are possible. If the value-creating resource reallocation is not unique to the proposed merger, Commission rejections may not significantly erode shareholder wealth if another merger (where rejection by the Commission is not anticipated) can accomplish the same reallocation. On the other hand, if the real resource reallocation is unique to the proposed pairing (or to any merger that would be rejected by the Commission), shareholder wealth would be eroded upon Commission rejection.

In Commission referrals, we would expect the proposed merger to be allocational rather than acquisitional. Furthermore, in Commission rejections, we would expect a likely benefit of merger to be enhanced market power. Such market power enhancement is likely to be unique to the merger (or to that set which would be referred to the Commission). As a result, we would expect value gains to be eroded as a result of Commission rejection.

Table 5.6 reports value changes around the bid month for Commission referrals. (Bid month is month zero.) For all Commission referrals, average value changes in target firms are 15 per cent in the bid month and 26 per cent over the 6-month period. These are somewhat lower than Franks and Harris's (1986b) estimates of acquiree value changes in mergers generally, but are still significantly positive, suggesting that the market does place

Table 5.6. Bid value changes to shareholders in mergers referred to the Commission in the announcement month

	Bid month value changes		6-month (−4 to +1) value changes		Percentage of firms with bid month value increases	
	Target	Bidder	Target	Bidder	Target	Bidder
All referrals	15%*	0%*	26%*	1%	70	43
Accepted	26%*	2%	32%*	6%	88	50
Rejected	5%*	−2%	20%*	−1%	48	33
Laid aside	14%*	−1%	26%*	2%	68	53

* Significantly different from zero at 95% confidence level.

value on the prospective merger. At 20 per cent, initial value gains to acquirees are lower for bids ultimately rejected than those accepted (32 per cent). This pattern of gains around the bid month may result because the market is, at least in part, successful in discriminating between bids that are likely to be referred to and rejected by the Commission and those that are not. For example, suppose a merger would produce a £1 million value gain if the market knew it would be consummated. The value gain at the bid would, however, be less than £1 million and could be approximated as the product of the £1 million and the perceived probability of the merger taking place. Thus the lower bid month gains realized in our sample may reflect perceptions of possible Commission rejection and hence lower probabilities of an actual take-over.

Turning to bidders in Commission referrals, value gains to bids that are ultimately accepted or laid aside appear comparable to those in mergers generally—about zero in the bid month and small positive gains over a 6-month period. Given our sample size, these figures are not, however, significantly different from zero. For rejected bids, there are no bidder gains; this again suggests market anticipation of Commission referral and rejection. In general, Table 5.6 shows that proposed mergers eventually referred to the Commission are viewed at the bid date as value-creating for shareholders. However, the market's capitalization of those gains is likely to be attenuated by the perception of a relatively high probability of the merger not taking place (compared with those mergers that are not referred).

To see how OFT and Commission decisions affect shareholder value, we examined value changes in the referral and report months, with the results shown in Table 5.7. In all categories, value gains are eroded on the referral date by approximately 8 per cent to targets and 1 per cent to bidders. There is significant further erosion to acquirees when the bid is rejected (–9 per

Table 5.7. Value changes on referral and report

	Value changes in referral month		Value changes in report month	
	Target	Bidder	Target	Bidder
All referrals	–8%*	–1%	–3%*	1%
Accepted	–9%*	–1%	2%	2%
Rejected	–8%*	0%	–9%*	1%
Laid aside	–9%*	–2%	(No report)	

* Significantly different from zero at 95% confidence level.

cent in the report month) and a small positive (though statistically insignificant) gain to the target upon acceptance. Value changes to bidders are small in both the referral and report months and are generally not significantly different from zero.

There are two possible interpretations of our results for rejected mergers. The first is that a value-enhancing merger has been rejected, and the costs of the rejection by the Commission are borne by the shareholders of the target company. The second is that the merger was not value-enhancing and the loss to the target is simply the disappearance of (an undeserved) bid premium. The latter explanation is not easy to sustain, however, because if it held, we would expect to see value losses to bidders in the bid month. In a merger that is not value-enhancing, a target's gain should be equal to a bidder's loss. However, in Table 5.6 we do not find any appreciable losses to bidders around the bid month. The evidence thus indicates a cost to shareholders of Commission deliberations and rejections—a cost that falls upon target shareholders.

A difficulty in measuring value changes in Commission referrals and rejections is that information about a merger is revealed by a series of events rather than by one single event. In Table 5.8, we report an estimate of the entire effect of the three events (bid, referral, and report) for the period from 12 months prior to the report date, through to 1 month thereafter (a total of 14 months). Given lags between bid and report dates, this corresponds to a beginning date for our analysis, on average, 4 months prior to the bid date.

Table 5.8. Value changes over whole inquiry

	Average value changes through report date (−12 to +1)	
	Target	Bidder
Commission accepted	38%*	6%
Commission rejected	9%*	−6%

* Significantly different from zero at 95% confidence level.

The results show markedly different patterns based upon the Commission's decision. For Commission acceptances, as expected, value increases arise as the result of the consummated bid. Furthermore, these value changes are quite comparable to value gains in successful mergers generally. In contrast, Commission rejections ultimately erode a large part of value gains initially manifested at the bid stage. The 9 per cent figure for target shareholders in rejections is well below the bid premiums measured in Table 5.6; furthermore, half of the rejected targets experienced value losses over the 14-month period. Since a large part of the initial value gain is eroded, at least part of the merger benefits are likely to be unique to the merger (and allocational in the Grossman–Hart sense). However, partial erosion suggests that some part of the anticipated merger benefits are not unique; either because the benefits are acquisitional or because other companies are expected subsequently to bid for the target.

Proposition 3: Do value changes in Commission rejections differ from those in failed bids generally?

We have argued that erosion of value gains in Commission rejections is a sign that the perceived benefits are unique to merging and that those benefits derive from changes in real resource allocation. Evidence on value changes in failed bids provides an interesting comparison. It would be logical for managers and shareholders to terminate merger plans if an alternative to the proposed merger provided a superior means of reaping the merger benefits. In such a case, despite the failed bid, we would not expect an erosion of value.

Studying failed bids in the US, Bradley, Desai, and Kim (1983) show that targets in unsuccessful bids do not show an erosion of value when the bid fails; however, this result holds only when the target is subsequently acquired by another bidder. Bradley *et al.* conclude that such a pattern implies that merger benefits are unique to merging but not necessarily unique to a specific merger. In cases when the target is not subsequently taken over (about one-quarter of the US sample), all value gains are eroded within 2 to 4 years following the bid.

Though limited, UK evidence also shows a persistence of value gains in failed bids generally. For a sample of 60 failed bids supplied to us by an investment banking house (for the period 1981–4), we found no erosion of initial value gains in the 10 months following the bid. We did not, however, trace whether a firm was subsequently acquired. Indeed, part of our sample is too recent to test for a subsequent acquisition.

Commission rejections appear different from failed bids generally, supporting the notion that in Commission rejections part of the merger benefits are more likely to be unique to the particular merger.

Our results suggest that mergers referred to the Commission are anticipated to be value-creating to shareholders, with essentially all gains accruing to target shareholders. For Commission acceptances, the Commission imposes costs on shareholders in terms of time delays and value reductions due to uncertainty about the final disposition of the case.

When a favourable report is released, however, shareholders ultimately reap value gains comparable to those in successful mergers generally. In contrast, Commission rejections lead to erosion of part of the value gains estimated around the initial bid. This value erosion is different from the pattern for failed bids generally, which suggests that many of the merger benefits anticipated in Commission rejections require a merger and are not captured by independent action on the part of the target. This would be consistent with mergers motivated by planned reallocations of real resources, such as exercise of market power or achievement of economies of scale. What is clear is that Commission rejections impose costs to shareholders in the form of forgone benefits. This is an expected outcome if Commission rejections are based on neoclassical analysis of the effects of anticompetitive behaviour.

Indeed, there is some evidence that the Monopolies Commission had some limited success in eroding the dominance of some companies that were investigated in the period 1959–73 and became subjects of dominant firm or 'complex monopoly' reports (see Shaw and Simpson (1986)). Such an erosion of market position presumably resulted in losses to shareholders. It is beyond the scope of this paper to measure the net benefits to the public resulting from Commission actions.

4. Public Policy towards Mergers

The results of the previous section of this paper suggest that the current policy of investigating mergers is costly to at least one party—the shareholders. Of course the benefit of the Commission's actions is the deterrence of increased market power which certain mergers would produce. Over and above the costs isolated in our empirical section, there may be additional costs to the economy in general, purely because of the possibility of an investigation. The source of the costs is that an investigation reduces the incentive for bidders to gather and process information about prospective acquisitions, if the possibility of investigation increases the likelihood that private information collected by the bidder will be revealed to other potential bidders.

Furthermore, the delays accompanying an investigation (regardless of the outcome) may permit other companies to become bidders, thereby reducing the prospective profits of first processing the information. Such free-rider problems will discourage mergers where the benefits of the merger are either informational or require resource reallocations (for example, the target management is inefficient) not unique to one bidder. The potential for such free-rider problems may be large since share price evidence in both the US and UK suggests that merger benefits are usually not unique to one bidder.

However, due to the relatively small number of investigations by the Commission and the evidence presented here suggesting that Commission referrals are more likely to involve some benefits unique to the merging firms, current Commission activity is not likely to create large disincentives for gathering information.

Drastic changes in the Commission's mandate may, however, lead to such disincentives. Concerns about the levels of merger activity are widespread and are not simply confined to those of market power. Some politicians have suggested a much stronger investigative role for the Commission, where the onus of proof that merger benefits exist would fall upon the bidder. If a new policy were implemented which changed the criteria for referral and increased the number of investigations, the incentives of bidders to gather and process information could be much reduced. Thus, some mergers that are profitable to shareholders and possibly to the economy would not take place.

In this section, we describe some of the wider concerns expressed about the level and motivation of merger activity. We try to trace possible malfunctions in markets (financial or managerial) which form the basis of these concerns, with the objective of finding institutional solutions. Such solutions may be preferable to a more wide-ranging regulatory role for the Commission envisaged by some parties, where the prospect of investigation may inhibit worthwhile mergers.

THE MERGER MARKET WHEN FINANCIAL AND MANAGERIAL LABOUR MARKETS ARE WELL FUNCTIONING

If managerial labour markets are well functioning, managers will be motivated (by both pecuniary and non-pecuniary benefits) to work in shareholder interests. Further, in such a sublime state, equity market prices will give unbiased estimates of value gains to shareholders. As a result, mergers would only be pursued by management if they were value-creating to shareholders. Multiple bidders might compete for a target firm, but we would not expect to observe target management opposing value-creating bids.

In such a stylized world, there would still be concerns about merger activity. Shareholder gains in a merger could be a direct result of those anticompetitive effects which raise product prices and distort resource allocation. Since mergers could also be motivated by cost-reducing measures, there might also be concerns about effects on non-shareholder interest groups regarding lost jobs or stranded customers or suppliers. Such non-shareholder concerns might be broadened to include regional issues or concerns about the aggregate concentration of economic power and its effects on the political process.

It is precisely these sorts of concerns that are appropriately dealt with by a body such as the Commission which applies a social calculus to weigh costs of merger. It has responsibility to assess anticompetitive effects as well as to weigh factors such as employment or regional concerns. However, the case for the Commission's giving high weight to job losses as a reason for obstructing a take-over may be limited. Given international competition, attempts for short-term job security may come at long-term costs of wholesale employment loss if British industry were supplanted by foreign competitors. It is perhaps for this reason that so few mergers have been prohibited on these grounds.[6]

Certainly in the 1960s there was a great concern that mergers would increase the rate of concentration and thereby reduce competition (see Opie (1982)). Such concerns led in the UK to the passage of the 1965 Monopolies and Mergers Act. There were similar concerns in the US. However, existing legislation and the size of the resulting institutions were simply not designed to act as a 'public conscience' for aggregate merger activity. Moreover, in recent years, governments in both countries have been more pro-business and less interventionist than previous administrations.

Despite recent increases in the number of Commission referrals and investigations, it is probable that neither the Monopolies and Mergers Commission in the UK nor the Federal Trade Commission and Justice Department in the US have significantly dented the merger boom in recent years. Greater international competition has not only reduced the fears of increased concentration, but has sustained the impression that UK firms must grow larger if they are to compete internationally.

The previous discussion does not imply complacency over mergers and competition. Rather, it simply recognizes that much stronger anticompetition legislation against mergers would be unlikely to reduce the level of merger activity substantially.

IMPLICATIONS FOR POLICY WHEN FINANCIAL MARKETS ARE NOT WELL FUNCTIONING

The *Financial Times* (3 July 1986) has stated that 'Take-over bids and bull markets go hand in hand.' This is a controversial proposition since there is some empirical evidence that the level of merger activity is not correlated

[6] A suggestion often made as a means of addressing non-shareholder interests is to make managers responsible to a board of directors that includes representatives of various constituencies including employees. Effective working of such a scheme has difficulties, however, since small board representation may have little ultimate effect if the non-shareholder interest is always outvoted.

with stock prices (see Geroski (1984)). However, both practitioners and academics remain unconvinced, if not sceptical, about the lack of a relationship. We discuss in this section some theories about how financial markets may motivate mergers and what concerns this motivation may give rise to.

One model, described by King (1986), suggests that merger activity has historically been correlated with stock market prices due to a tax-induced distortion in the pricing of financial assets. King claims that this distortion arises from the extra tax burden on corporate income compared with personal income, a burden that increases with rising corporate profits and resulting bull markets. However, the Finance Act of 1984 has reduced this tax wedge in the imputation system. In effect, the 1987 corporate tax rate of 35 per cent and the income tax rate (for standard rate taxpayers) of 27 per cent imply that the additional tax burden on corporate income is now 8 per cent only. As a result, King's argument predicts that merger booms are a thing of the past, at least those motivated by tax distortions in financial markets. In this respect, the source of a market malfunction has been removed.[7]

A second source of market malfunction will occur if markets mis-price equities. If that mis-pricing provides an incentive to merge, then it is a matter of public concern since such a malfunction would disrupt the role of mergers in allocating resources. If a significant proportion of mergers were motivated by inefficiencies in the capital market, then very different regulatory policies from those charged to the Commission would be sought.

Mis-pricing may occur because it may be necessary for management to retain valuable information on the economic value of real assets if its release to shareholders would result in a deterioration of the company's competitive position (see Myers and Majluf (1984) for a discussion). If some equities are overpriced, this may provide the management of those companies with an incentive to finance acquisitions of properly priced companies with their overpriced equity. Indeed, the opportunities to acquire may encourage management or its agent to release information which would lead to overpricing. Until recently, UK rules have severely restricted the sale of equity to anyone other than existing shareholders, and thus the only method of selling equity to external or new shareholders was through an acquisition.[8] Shareholders of the prospective acquisition may

---

[7] We note that King's argument depends on strong assumptions about the pricing of assets in the corporate and non-corporate sectors. For example, King assumes companies cannot be liquidated and reincorporated on a regular basis to reduce the burden of corporate taxes. Important additional assumptions are also required, and we refer the interested reader to the original paper.

[8] Even though UK companies may now issue new equity to shareholders (via, say, a placing) this may not remove entirely the incentives to acquire to capitalize on overpriced equity. First,

not recognize the overpricing, if they cannot distinguish between equity-financed mergers motivated by mis-pricing and those motivated by, say, capital structure reasons.

Low-cost remedies for such mis-pricing are difficult to construct. One drastic one would be to force companies to finance mergers with cash only. If companies did not have sufficient liquidity, they would have to issue equity to their shareholders. To the extent that current shareholders purchased new equity, there would no longer be an incentive to issue overpriced equity to benefit existing shareholders. Further, such a market discipline would require shareholders to vote with their cash. There is an impression gained from some market participants that shareholders have a smaller incentive to express disapproval when management is using internally generated funds. However, such a new measure would add to the transactions costs of merging.

Mis-pricing may also create incentives for take-over based on underpricing of potential acquirees. Acquirers may be performing the role of arbitrageurs buying up underpriced securities. If such take-overs are 'acquisitional' in the Grossman–Hart sense and provide incentives for gathering and processing information, such mergers may provide benefits in the form of superior information flows to financial markets. The Grossman–Hart argument depends, however, on financial markets' properly pricing securities, given the information available. If financial markets are not efficient in pricing equities, take-overs of 'underpriced' securities may well produce undesirable effects. The management of would-be acquirees may forgo profitable investment opportunities or cut research and development if it is perceived that the market does not properly price such opportunities. If financial markets were well functioning, management time devoted to mergers may be well spent, but if there is substantial mis-pricing, mergers (and attempts to avoid take-over) may lead to dissipation of long-term economic benefits.

Remedies for various sources of mis-pricing are beyond the scope of this paper.[9] They are certainly made more difficult by the lack of theory as to

---

such fund-raising activities require a motive, and the issuing management could hardly declare the motive to be 'to sell overpriced equity'. Second, higher levels of corporate income may make it more profitable to acquire assets already in the corporate sector (via merger) than to raise cash to purchase newly produced assets or financial assets (see King (1986)).

[9] One possible remedy is to introduce rules and laws that delay the speed of take-over, the rationale being that such procedures give financial markets more time to digest important information. However, we have already referred to the disincentive effects of delays. A more drastic step, proposed by some in the US, would be to change the traditional link between share ownership and voting rights, for example, by requiring a shareholder to have owned shares for a certain period of time before voting rights can be exercised. The intent of such measures, at least in part, is to delegate authority to those shareholders with 'long-term' horizons. The assumption is that financial markets are influenced too much by short-term factors and too little by the long term. As a result, management may have incentives to take measures which

why such mis-pricing should occur and the lack of empirical evidence of its sign and size.

Our final concern about the operation of the financial market concerns transactions costs incurred in the merger process. Kay (1986) has estimated that the annual fees paid to third parties in the merging process might be £500 million. The DTI data suggest that the value of acquisitions in 1985 is about £7 billion. Simple arithmetic therefore suggests the costs of merging may average about 7 per cent of acquisition value; and this excludes the cost of management time expended by the merging parties. Some examples of costs incurred in particular mergers suggest that Kay's figure may be conservative for 1986. Argyll's unsuccessful bid for Distillers may have resulted in £47 million in fees, with 75 per cent being paid for underwriting fees for the separate bids. Some of these costs (£13.9 million) were offset by profits on the sale of Argyll's share stake, but this should not be used to justify the transactions costs. In another contested take-over, Dixons spent £12 million in its unsuccessful bid for Woolworth, while the latter spent £20 million in repulsing the bid. (All these figures are taken from the *Financial Times*.)

The question as to whether these costs are excessive depends upon several considerations. The most important is, what alternatives are there to merging as a way of obtaining the benefits that would arise? If many of these bids are simply vehicles for removing weak and inefficient management, then it seems very expensive to spend millions or even tens of millions to remove the chairman or part of the board of directors. It is like buying an entire football team when only one player is wanted.

We do, however, have several cautions regarding the previous argument. First, the little evidence we have suggests that a large part of these transactions costs occur in hostile bids which account for only a small fraction of acquisition activity. Second, the transactions costs we have described consist of two very different kinds of costs. One, such as advertising and fees to merchant banks for managing the take-over process, are pure costs to the economy as well as to the company. However, underwriting fees which may account for a large proportion of total costs are of a very different nature. Underwriting fees are made for the purchase of short-term financial assets (they are 'side-bets' on the future price of the acquiring company's stock made between underwriter and company). Such fees should not be classified as costs to the system; rather, they consist of

increase reported profits at the expense of longer-term profitability. The difficulty with an approach that limits voting rights is that it may also insulate current management from desirable financial market discipline.

the purchase of insurance which changes the risk borne by the company.[10] If these risks are properly priced, then they are no more of a cost to society than the purchase of insurance against fire risk. It is the fire risk that is the source of the cost, not the insurance. In this respect, the estimate of £500 million attributed to the cost of merging may be an excessive estimate of the costs to the system of the merging process. It could certainly be undesirable to inhibit merger activity in general because of these high costs, if most are incurred in only a few hostile bids.

INTERNAL VERSUS EXTERNAL DISCIPLINES ON MANAGERS: ALTERNATIVES TO ACQUISITIONS

Many authors, for example Mueller (1969), have questioned the ability of shareholders to monitor and control the conduct of management. They have argued that, as a result, management is able to follow policies that maximize the wealth and status of the managers rather than that of shareholders.[11] According to this view, many take-overs would dissipate shareholder wealth as acquiring firm managements overbid for acquirees. However, to the extent that financial markets are well functioning, the weight of US and UK evidence (see Franks and Harris (1986b), Jensen and Ruback (1983)) would not support this view.

Starting from similar concerns about shareholders' monitoring of managers, Grossman and Hart (1981) provide a role for the acquisitions market in disciplining management. As described earlier, they argue that where share ownership is widely dispersed, it does not pay individual shareholders to bear the costs of monitoring and gathering information in order to increase the efficiency of management. By separating (and dispersing) ownership and control, a free-rider problem has been created. All shareholders share the benefits if one shareholder disciplines management, but that one shareholder is forced to bear all the costs of so doing. Thus, acquisitions play a pivotal role in the market for corporate control.

What are the alternatives to acquisitions as a disciplining process? One way would be for shareholders to elect a body of professionals to represent them, whose sole purpose would be to monitor the performance of management. In another form, this is surely part of the role of the non-executive director, except that in the UK those directors are usually

[10] The cost of underwriting has been analysed as the purchase of a put option by the company from the underwriter. Marsh (1980) has raised questions as to whether underwriting fees have been properly priced.

[11] These agency costs have been analysed in a more formal setting by Jensen and Meckling (1976).

appointed by and responsible to executive management. It may be that non-executive directors should be appointed by nominating committees directly representing shareholder interests. This form of appointment has been increasingly adopted in the US. This monitoring role performed by non-executive directors does overcome the free-rider problems described earlier; all shareholders now pay for their information processing costs.

The important role played by non-executive directors has been widely discussed in the changes in senior management brought about in companies such as Beechams, STC, and Thorn-EMI. In the US, the Chairman and Chief Executive of Alleghany International recently resigned after public criticism described him as an extravagant and careless executive. An Alleghany shareholder filed a class action lawsuit against the company's directors charging them with 'waste of corporate assets and grossly improper business decisions'. It is of some interest that there are a number of well-known non-executive directors on the Alleghany board. It could be argued that the presence of such directors hastened the disclosures and ultimately the change in top management; alternatively, it may be said that the presence of those non-executive directors did not restrain top management from an apparently excessive lifestyle. It may be that the role and duties of the non-executive directors should be more clearly defined, just as is the role of the external auditor. The question remains, however, as to whether the role should be defined by legal apparatus, institutions acting collectively, or on a company by company basis.

An alternative suggestion to the appointment of non-executive directors would be for institutions to play a more active role in changing the management of a company. The free-rider problem could be mitigated if institutions formed shareholder groups which would investigate companies that appear to stumble and falter. As a result, they would play a more prominent role in the election of directors at shareholder meetings. This is an interesting alternative, but it requires co-operation among otherwise competing financial institutions. Furthermore, the skills of portfolio managers may not be suitable for pronouncing on the fitness of incumbent management. It may be that a prerequisite for more active institutional shareholders is a somewhat differently educated portfolio manager.[12] As a result, we suspect that increasing and strengthening the role of the non-executive director will prove to be the preferred option.

---

[12] Direct stockholder interest may not be the only answer to a more efficient managerial labour market. It is important that managers' compensation provides an appropriate incentive structure. Therefore, managerial compensation plans should be related more directly to the profitability of the organization. However, compensation schemes on their own will not be sufficient if there is little provision for the removal of inadequate management.

5. Conclusion

In this paper, we have analysed the costs to shareholders that result from Commission investigations. We show that Commission rejections lead to substantial erosion of value gains that were capitalized at the bid date, suggesting that the prospective shareholder benefits involved some reallocations of real resources unique to merging. The neoclassical economic argument is that the costs of such forgone shareholder benefits are more than offset by the Commission's deterrence of increased market power. We suggest that Commission investigations may introduce further costs in terms of reduced incentives of prospective bidders to investigate inefficiently run companies. Since the number of companies investigated by the Commission is small, such disincentives should be similarly small. However, a much wider role in merger regulation, envisaged by some, could alter the size of these disincentives.

Concerns about mergers have substantially increased, rising with the level of merger activity, and these concerns go well beyond the types of anticompetitive behaviour which may be deterred by the Commission. As a result, we have examined potential sources of those concerns and described institutional changes that may be appropriate. The problem is to find possible sources of market malfunction and, where possible, correct them rather than to turn immediately to governmental mechanisms for counterbalancing such malfunctions.

Appendix: Estimation of Value Gains

To implement our measure of value gain, for any company j we construct 'abnormal returns' calculated as:

$$\mathrm{AR}_{jt} = R_{jt} - C_{jt}$$

where R_{jt} is the realized return in month t (dividends plus capital gains) and C_{jt} is the control return. These abnormal returns are estimates of value gains. To focus on the effects of a particular event, we define time relative to an event date. For example, $t = 0$ can be defined as the bid month, the month of referral, or the reporting month. Methods of estimating control returns have been widely studied in the finance literature. Here we use the so-called market model where control returns are defined as:

$$C_{jt} = \alpha_j + \beta_j \mathrm{RM}_t$$

where RM_t is the return on the equally weighted index of all stocks covered in LSPD and α and β are parameters estimated by regressing R_{jt} on RM_t for the 60-month period beginning at $t = -71$. The market model thus controls for general market movements adjusting for both company risk (β) and the company's performance over and above the market (α) prior to the event being studied. Brown and Warner (1980, 1985) provide extensive discussions of 'event study' methodology. For a more complete discussion as applied to mergers, see Franks and Harris (1986b). Average values for target firms are $\alpha = .004$ and $\beta = .93$. For bidding firms, the average values are .006 and .99 respectively.

We also test the sensitivity of our results to two alternate methods. The first controls only for market movements ($C_{jt} = RM_t$) for all companies. The second is an empirical adaptation of the Capital Asset Pricing Model as described in Franks and Harris (1986b). Our conclusions are not materially affected by the choice of model. We use continuously compounded (log) returns in all cases.

To assess returns for a portfolio of companies (for example, target firms when there is a Commission rejection) over a number of months, we calculated company-specific multi-period returns by summing AR_{jt} over time. These returns are then averaged across companies into portfolio cumulative returns (PCAR) defined as:

$$PCAR_t = \frac{1}{n} \sum_{j=1}^{n} \sum_{i=t_b}^{t} AR_{ji}$$

where n is the number of companies in the portfolio ($j = 1, \ldots, n$), and the cumulation process begins at time t_b and includes those monthly abnormal returns that are observed up to and including month t. These portfolio returns ($PCAR_t$) thus measure the average excess (or short-fall) in shareholder returns relative to the market model bench-mark, which estimates what shareholder returns would have been if the company's returns had maintained their normal return relationship to equity markets in general.

We have considered two statistical tests for the significance of $PCAR_t$. The first uses a t-statistic calculated as $T = PCAR_t/s$ where s is calculated as

$$\{\sqrt{(t_b - t + 1)}\}\ SD$$

and SD is the standard deviation of 1-month PCARs for a time period assumed to be unaffected by merger (in this case the period used to estimate the market model). The second significance test is non-parametric and uses the percentage of the multi-period company-specific returns that are positive. For a detailed discussion of these and other statistical tests, see Franks and Harris (1986b) and the references therein. Significance levels in the text (indicated by an asterisk) are determined using the t-statistic (two-tailed tests for 95 per cent confidence level).

To test the significance of differences between value gains for different groups of companies, we use a t-statistic calculated as

$$(M_1 - M_2) \ / \ \sqrt{(\sigma_1^2 + \sigma_2^2)}$$

where M denotes a cell mean, subscripts 1 and 2 the two portfolios, and s is defined as above.

In 10 cases, bid and referral months coincided. This would have the effect of biasing downward our estimate of gains at the bid date (since some bid month returns would also contain negative reactions to referrals) and biasing downward in absolute value our estimate of losses at the referral date. Where possible we estimated the effects of such contamination. The losses at referral date were about 10 to 11 per cent for each of the three categories of referrals, and gains at the bid date increased only modestly. The adjustment thus changed none of our basic conclusions.

6

The Empirical Analysis of Market Structure and Performance

JAMES FAIRBURN* AND PAUL GEROSKI†

1. Introduction

In evaluating any horizontal merger, a central concern is the likely effect of that merger on industry performance. Although many performance criteria might be thought relevant—levels of costs and efficiency, standards of inventiveness and innovation—much attention is typically given to the apparently more direct and tractable effects on prices and thence profits. Will the reduction of competition arising from the merging of competing firms, and the corresponding changes in the concentration of sales within an industry, elevate prices over costs and thus increase profits?

A potentially fruitful approach to this question is to consider the past performance of a range of industries which differ in their configuration of firms and in other attributes, and to isolate and measure the general effect on observed prices or profits of varying levels of sales concentration. Research of this type is the subject of this paper.

The paper is structured as follows. In Section 2 we set out the common framework of this type of analysis, which is known in the industrial economics literature as the 'structure-conduct-performance' paradigm, and we examine and assess the British evidence. Dissatisfaction with this basic approach has led in recent years to a number of modifications to and developments of the underlying framework, which are discussed in Section 3. Although as yet subject to only limited empirical testing for Britain, these new approaches nevertheless offer a number of insights into industry performance. Section 4 contains our conclusions.

---

* Temporary Lecturer in Economics at the University of Southampton.

† Senior Lecturer in Economics at the University of Southampton, currently visiting the Centre for Business Strategy at the London Business School.

2. Structure, Conduct, and Performance

Analysis of inter-industry variations in performance commenced with the work of Bain in the 1940s and 1950s, and the essence of the 'structure–conduct–performance' approach was also established by him. The approach views the structure of the industry, or 'market structure', as the major exogenous variable of interest, determining the extent to which firms in a particular industry are able to achieve a long-term elevation of prices over marginal costs, and therefore earn persistently high returns. The manner in which structure affects performance is through its effect on firms' behaviour or 'conduct', i.e. the ways they interact with each other and the way in which prices and output levels are chosen. The basic 'structuralist' hypothesis that structure is the important determinant of performance follows from the view that the range of conduct it is possible to observe in an industry with a given structure is extremely limited. Hence structure determines conduct, and performance follows directly from this. Indeed, in much of the literature we are to discuss, conduct is suppressed almost entirely, and little is lost by concentrating one's attention on the structure–performance link alone.[1]

Of the many possible 'structural' characteristics of industries, that which has been the subject of most persistent attention is the level of industry concentration. Concentration indices are summary measures of the number of firms within an industry and the distribution of their sizes.[2] The most widely used index in both official statistics and empirical work is the *k*-firm concentration ratio, which gives the proportion of industry sales accounted for by the largest *k* firms. (The 5-firm concentration ratio, CR5, is most commonly available in the UK.) Much recent work has, however, favoured the Hirshmann–Herfindahl index, the sum of squared individual market shares for all firms in the industry. The attributes of an industry captured by concentration indices are generally thought to characterize the extent to which it will be able to raise prices. Thus, an industry with relatively few

---

[1] A classic exposition of the basic structuralist view is given in Bain's (1959) textbook. Scherer's more recent text (1980) argues that a range of possible behavioural patterns can in principle be observed in markets with a given structure. In more modern work—see Waterson (1984)—prime attention is given to conduct and the structure–performance link down-graded. For arguments that question the exogeneity of market structure to pricing decisions, see Clarke and Davies (1982), Geroski (1982a), and Donsimoni, Geroski, and Jacquemin (1985).

[2] There is a large literature on the properties that a concentration index should embody and on the relative merits of those available, see, e.g., Hart (1975), Hannah and Kay (1977), and Davies (1979). (For discussion of the impact of merger on concentration, see Hughes (this volume).) Many of the indices are highly correlated, suggesting that as an empirical matter the choice between them may be of little consequence. For alternative approaches stressing the importance of making the correct choice, see Schmalensee (1977), Kwoka (1979, 1981), and Geroski (1983).

firms, or one with several firms much larger than the remainder, is generally thought more likely than a relatively unconcentrated industry to achieve high prices in equilibrium. This outcome does not depend on firms making a collusive agreement, and hence is sometimes termed 'tacit' collusion. However, it may be that the probability of overt collusion does additionally increase with increasing concentration, a factor which, if true, will strengthen the observed relationship between concentration and profits.

Testing the basic structuralist hypothesis has taken the form of looking for a systematic and stable positive association between average industry price–cost margins or rates of return on capital, and levels of industry concentration. However, Bain (1956) argued that in examining the concentration–profits relationship, one must hold constant industry cost and demand conditions, and make allowance for the condition of entry into the industry.[3]

Bain's own approach was to examine individual industries in detail, and make a necessarily subjective assessment of the height of individual and overall barriers to entry. Following the influential paper of Comanor and Wilson (1967), the far more common approach has been to find statistical proxies for entry barriers. Thus one can derive estimates of the minimum efficient scale (the importance of economies of scale in relation to the size of the industry) from the actual scale of operation of existing firms, and one can take the industry advertising–sales ratio as a proxy for product differentiation advantages. Such proxies are then added to measures of concentration in regressions explaining profits, together with additional conditioning variables, such as the growth of industry sales, the level of imports, etc. Entry barriers normally seem to exert a positive influence on profits, with a significant positive correlation almost invariably being observed between advertising intensity and profit margins.[4]

Following Bain's first study (1951), this type of exercise has formed the basis of a huge number of studies covering a number of different countries.[5] Most researchers have detected a positive correlation between industry

---

[3] In addition to using proxies for entry barriers to explain profitability, it is also possible to use them in the explanation of actual rates of entry. For a survey of models of this type, see Geroski and Masson (1987).

[4] This finding has attracted considerable controversy. There are questions of whether current advertising expenditure or the accumulated stock of advertising capital is appropriate, and whether the positive coefficient reflects a barrier to entry. See Comanor and Wilson (1979) for a survey. There are also reasons to expect advertising expenditures to be determined by concentration (Waterson (1984) Ch. 7), so that it would be inappropriate to regard advertising as an exogenous determinant of profits. However, simultaneous equations models suggest that it can in fact be taken as exogenous for the purposes of estimation (Strickland and Weiss (1976), Geroski (1982b), Martin (1979, 1980)). We return to this below.

[5] Surveys of the literature include Weiss (1974), Scherer (1980, Ch. 9), and Schmalensee (1986). The studies covered often involve modifications we discuss in the remainder of this section.

concentration and average industry returns. However, the relationship is typically rather weak, and is often estimated with a fair amount of imprecision. Although dwarfed by research on the US, there have now been some 14 published studies relating to the British manufacturing sector. We have chosen to focus on the more recent studies, which have examined the period from 1968 onward.[6]

The most common specification of the structure–performance model is an equation which is linear in the relevant variables or, less frequently, linear in their logs. Hart and Morgan (1977) produced results for this model on a sample of 113 MLH (3-digit) Census of Production industries for 1968. Their first step was to carry out a log-linear regression of their chosen measure of profits, the ratio of gross profit to value added, on a constant term and the 5-firm concentration ratio. This yielded a positive, significant relationship, which implied that a 10 per cent rise in concentration would be associated with a 1 per cent increase in industry profits. However, less than 10 per cent of the variation in industry profits was explained in this way. Further variables were then added: the import–sales ratio (MS), a measure of the efficient scale of operation in the industry (MED), the growth of industry sales (G), the advertising–sales ratio (AS), and a proxy for the capital–labour ratio (KL). AS and MED are fairly common proxies for the product differentiation and economies of scale entry barriers identified by Bain. A variable such as KL is often added to correct for the fact that the profits variable does not include the cost of capital, which varies with capital requirements across industries. Finally, measures of growth and imports are often added as conditioning variables to reflect disruptions caused to the concentration–profits relationship by rapid growth in demand (and the consequent need for capacity adjustment) or by the influx of imports. Equation 1 shows the results of these extensions.

Equation 1

(Equation 5 from Table 1, Hart and Morgan (1977) p. 183)

$$\text{PCM} = \text{constant} + 0.0021\,\text{CR5} + \underset{**}{0.1562\,\text{KL}} + 0.0397\,G + \underset{**}{0.0746\,\text{AS}}$$

$$- 0.0047\,\text{MED} + 0.0285\,\text{MS}.$$

---

[6] The earlier studies excluded from consideration are Shepherd (1972), who found an insignificant positive profits–concentration relationship for 1958 and 1963; Phillips (1972), who revealed a significant positive relationship for 1951; Holtermann (1973), with an insignificantly negative relationship for 1963; and Khalilzadeh-Shirazi (1974) with an insignificantly positive relationship for the same year. Caves, Khalilzadeh-Shirazi, and Porter (1975) present modifications of the latter study which lead to a significant positive relationship. The studies are reviewed, and their specifications and data discussed, in Hart and Morgan (1977).

n = 113;
R^2 = 0.432;
** indicates significant at 5% level;
PCM log of gross profit as share of value added (value added minus employee compensation all divided by value added);
CR5 log of 5-firm employment concentration ratio;
KL log of ratio of gross capital expenditure to labour;
G log of proportionate change in money sales;
AS log of ratio of advertising to sales;
MED log of median size of enterprise by employment;
MS log of ratio of imports to domestically produced sales.

Advertising intensity and the capital–labour ratio are positive and significant, but the remaining variables are not significant, and MED and MS have unexpected signs. The non-significant coefficient on concentration would appear to be due to the inclusion of the capital–labour ratio, which is collinear with concentration. Introduction of KL dramatically lowered the coefficient on CR5. Hence, one can only conclude that highly concentrated, capital-intensive industries earn relatively high profits, *ceteris paribus*.[7] The problem of multicollinearity makes it difficult to isolate the effects of each variable on profits and is common in these studies, particularly with the concentration and minimum efficient scale measures.

More recently, Clarke (1984) has applied a similar model specification to the period 1970–6. Using the 7-year panel data at his disposal, Clarke derived the level, trend, and variance of profits in each industry, and examined relationships involving each of these measures. (We focus on the approach comparable to Hart and Morgan.) Clarke began by regressing the level of profits against dummy variables for a number of different industrial sectors, a procedure which explained approximately 60 per cent of the inter-industry variation in profits, with significant positive coefficients for the food and drink, and chemicals sectors. Further variables were then added, and a typical result is shown as Equation 2.

Equation 2

(Equation 8 from Table 1a, Clarke (1984) p. 61)

$$\begin{aligned} \text{PCM} = \; & \underset{(22.0)}{45.8} - \underset{(1.55)}{0.06}\,\text{CR5} + \underset{(3.02)}{0.52}\,\text{AS} + \underset{(2.81)}{3.40}\,\text{KS} + \underset{(1.84)}{0.012}\,G \\ & + \underset{(1.22)}{0.05}\,\text{MS} + \text{Sectoral dummies.} \end{aligned}$$

---

[7] Hart and Morgan also tried replacing the concentration ratio simply with the number of enterprises as an indicator of the degree of competition. The variable attracted the expected negative coefficient, which was significant despite the inclusion of the other variables.

n = 105;
R^2 = 0.666;
t-statistics in parentheses;

PCM	measure of average profit margin (net output minus wages and salaries divided by net output, expressed as percentage), 1970–6;
CR5	5-firm employment concentration ratio for 1970;
AS	advertising expenditures divided by value added, 1968;
KS	net assets at order level, allocated to industries on basis of proportions of total capital expenditures, then deflated by value added, 1970;
G	market growth in sales, 1970–6;
MS	import–sales ratio as percentage, 1970.

The findings of central interest here are that concentration appeared to have only a negative and insignificant relationship with profits, and that only advertising intensity and capital intensity were significant. Noting the significance of capital intensity, and comparing these results with those of Hart and Morgan, leads one to suspect that capital intensity (and perhaps the industry dummies) may to some extent obscure the relationship between profits and concentration. The results did, however, prove robust to alternate specifications, including ones where advertising and capital expenditures were netted out of profits, and advertising and capital intensities omitted from the equation.[8]

One clearly interesting feature of a relatively small, open economy like Britain is that profits are likely to be affected by trade. Consideration of this topic has been somewhat peripheral in the studies covered so far, and import variables have perversely attracted positive (though not significant) coefficients. By contrast, Lyons (1981) derived a more precise theoretical relationship between profits and import intensity, and estimated this on a sample of 118 MLH industries for 1968. Equation 3 is one of his estimated equations.

Equation 3

(Equation R5 from Lyons (1981) p. 291)

$$\begin{aligned} \text{PCM} = {} & \underset{(0.43)}{-\,0.017} + \underset{(1.93)}{0.180\,H} + \underset{(3.69)}{0.154\ \text{DDM}} + \underset{(3.68)}{0.136\ \text{XS}} \\ & + \underset{(4.60)}{1.06\ \text{AS}} + \underset{(2.96)}{0.050\ \text{HET}}. \end{aligned}$$

[8] Clarke also found that the variation in profits was positively associated with concentration, thus rejecting the hypothesis that slightly lower profit rates in concentrated industries might be compensated for by less profit variation.

n = 118;
R^2 = 0.3123;
t-statistics in parentheses;

PCM	value added less wages and salaries divided by sales, 1968;
H	Herfindahl index by employment for domestic production;
DDM	domestic industry's share of the domestic market (production less exports plus imports);
XS	proportion of domestic production which is exported;
AS	advertising-sales ratio;
HET	imports plus exports less the difference between them, all divided by imports plus exports (see text).

A significant negative impact of imports on profitability is shown by the coefficient on domestic industry's share of home sales (DDM), which of course falls as imports rise. Product differentiation was proxied by the conventional advertising-sales ratio and more interestingly by a measure of the heterogeneity of traded goods (HET). This measure was derived from the assumption that if an industry both imports and exports goods, those goods are likely to be differentiated. Equally, if goods are differentiated, they are likely to be less directly competitive with home production, and will therefore exert less of a discipline on pricing and profits. Both AS and HET attract significant positive coefficients as hypothesized. More important for our purposes is that the chosen measure of concentration, the Herfindahl index, is significant.[9] Note that Lyons does not include capital intensity or minimum efficient scale, which, as we have seen, have obscured the concentration-profits relationship.

A question which arises with the models discussed thus far is whether estimating just a single equation will yield consistent and unbiased estimates of the coefficients of interest, particularly the coefficient on concentration. Can concentration and the other explanatory variables reasonably be taken as exogenous? The fear that they cannot has led researchers elsewhere to estimate simultaneous equations systems, in which, for example, concentration, advertising intensity, and profitability are simultaneously determined by the exogenous variables. Indeed, several models with a very large number of equations have been estimated.[10]

Clearly there are good reasons to suspect that many of the right-hand side

---

[9] In previous work on the traded sector, Hitiris (1978) had similarly found that modelling the effects of trade variables—in his case, the degree of protection of home production—led to a significant positive concentration-profits relationship for 1963 and 1968, for smaller samples of industries of around 40 observations. Following criticism of his original work, new estimation suggested a significant positive relationship for 1963 which collapsed in 1968. See Lyons, Kitchen, and Hitiris (1979).

[10] Caves, Porter, Spence, and Scott (1980) is an example, which contains a good discussion of this way of modelling structure and performance.

variables are endogenous. First, high profitability is likely to attract new entry (thus affecting concentration) and imports, as well as itself being explained by concentration, imports, etc. Second, several variables are likely to be the simultaneous result of firms maximizing profits through the contemporaneous choice of advertising expenditures, capital stocks, and output levels. A natural procedure to follow is then to test for exogeneity, and this is done by Geroski (1982b). Using techniques which fortunately do not require that all the equations in the system be fully specified, he concluded that the variables which are most probably endogenous are imports and exports. His results suggest that the estimated effect of import competition on profits is biased down when imports are erroneously assumed to be exogenous, i.e. taking imports to be exogenous when they are in fact endogenous understates their effect on profits. However, as with other work in this area, the estimates of simultaneous and single equation models appear to be generally similar.

Some dissatisfaction with the simple linear models used in the literature has arisen from the feeling that they lack a solid theoretical formulation. This defect was remedied by Cowling and Waterson (1976), who showed that the price–cost margin was proportional to the Herfindahl index and to a conjectural variation term, and inversely proportional to the industry elasticity of demand. The conjectural variation term captures the extent to which firms think that competitors will react to their output changes, and therefore describes the type of equilibrium in the industry. Estimation of this relationship is hampered by the lack of good estimates of industry demand elasticities at the correct level of aggregation. As a way round this, the authors proposed taking ratios of the relationships at different points in time. Assuming elasticities of demand and the conjectural variation term to be constant over time, one can then obtain an estimate of the association between changes in concentration and changes in price–cost margins. Cowling and Waterson also anticipated that the degree of collusion would increase with concentration, and to capture this specified a log-linear form for the equation linking price–cost margins to the Herfindahl index. The relationship was then estimated for 94 industries using data from 1968, 1963, and 1958. No other entry barrier variables could be included due to the paucity of data, but a unionization variable and a durable goods dummy were included. (This had little impact.) The result is given as Equation 4, which shows a positive and significant relationship between margins and concentration.[11,12]

---

[11] Hart and Morgan (1977) were unable to replicate this result, finding no significant relationship with a smaller sample of industries which they considered to be comparable over the same period.

[12] Waterson (1980) used the same procedure when examining the effect of concentration at

Equation 4

(Equation 3 from Table 1, Cowling and Waterson (1976) p. 272)

$$\log(\text{PCM}_{68}/\text{PCM}_{63}) = \underset{(0.683)}{0.0333} + \underset{(2.942)}{0.2957} \log(H_{63}/H_{58})$$

$$+ \underset{(1.480)}{0.4985} \log(\text{TU}_{63}/\text{TU}_{58}) + \underset{(0.619)}{0.0344} \text{ DG.}$$

n = 94;
R^2 = 0.096;
t-statistics in parentheses;
PCM value added minus wages and salaries divided by sales revenue;
H Herfindahl index;
TU proportion of total employees who are union members;
DG dummy variable with value 1 in industries producing durable goods, 0 otherwise.

The studies reviewed so far typically find only rather weak relationships between concentration and profits. One reason for this is that the usual assumption of a linear relationship might be erroneous. In his original study, Bain argued that the important variation in market structure '. . . is not between industries of oligopolistic and atomistic structure, but between the more highly concentrated oligopolies and all other industries' (1951, p. 194). This idea translates into what has become known as the critical concentration ratio hypothesis. When concentration in an industry exceeds some critical level, profits will be increased, whereas if concentration lies below that level, a competitive pricing outcome will be observed. Bain found such a break to occur when the 8-firm concentration ratio exceeded 70 per cent. In general, modifications of the basic structuralist hypothesis of this type have had some success in yielding a more comprehensive description of the data, and revealing a stronger, though more complex, profits–concentration relationship than suggested by linear regressions.[13] Cowling and Waterson, as just noted, chose a log-linear specification to capture any change in the coefficient on concentration, induced by a

---

successive stages of production, and again found a significant and positive relationship between (seller) concentration and margins. The coefficients on margins in this and the earlier paper do suggest perversely that the degree of collusion falls with rising concentration. However, Dickson (1982) has shown that when a conjectural elasticity is used, collusion as now defined does indeed seem to increase with concentration.

[13] White (1976) is a well-known example of this type of work. It is, of course, possible to posit a more complex formulation than a single break in the relationship. Indeed, Bradburd and Over (1982) suggest two critical thresholds according to whether concentration is rising or falling.

changing propensity to collude, as concentration levels altered.

Geroski (1981) was led by similar concerns to build up the relationship from the data, rather than imposing on the data any specific linear or non-linear functional form. He followed a number of approaches to this issue, the preferred one being to insert a series of dummy variables for different concentration levels.[14] The resulting equation, Equation 5 below, also included a concentration–growth interaction term to examine whether industry growth tended to weaken the concentration–profits relationship in addition to increasing profits directly as previous studies had found. Geroski discovered that margins rose gently with the 5-firm concentration ratio up to a level of 35 per cent, then stayed roughly constant to 75 per cent, fell sharply to 85 per cent, and rose sharply thereafter. It was also observed that the concentration–profits relationship was weaker in fast-growth industries (as hypothesized) and in advertising-intensive industries. Unlike earlier studies, inclusion of a capital intensity variable did not completely obscure the effect of concentration, although the effect was weakened.

Equation 5

(Equation 5 from Table 1, Geroski (1981) p. 283)

$$\underset{(4.03)}{\text{PCM} = 0.186} - \underset{(1.12)}{0.528\,\text{CR5}} + \underset{(0.897)}{0.359\,\text{Z1}} + \underset{(1.14)}{0.473\,\text{Z2}}$$

$$+ \underset{(1.17)}{0.515\,\text{Z3}} + \underset{(1.80)}{0.780\,\text{C8}} + \underset{(1.27)}{0.565\,\text{C15}} + \underset{(1.33)}{0.604\,\text{C19}}$$

$$+ \underset{(1.48)}{0.634\,\text{C20}} + \underset{(2.49)}{0.130\,G} - \underset{(2.01)}{0.156\,G.\text{CR5}} + \underset{(2.41)}{0.241\,\text{AS}}$$

$$- \underset{(1.48)}{0.292\,\text{AS.CR5}} + \underset{(0.066)}{0.001\,\text{KS}} + \underset{(1.02)}{0.063\,\text{XS}} - \underset{(1.52)}{0.0102\,\text{MS}} + \underset{(0.731)}{0.095\,\text{DV}}.$$

n = 52;
R^2 = 0.459;
t-statistics in parentheses;
PCM gross output less wages and salaries divided by gross output, 1968;
CR5 5-firm sales concentration ratio, 1968;
G average industry sales growth rate, 1963–8;
AS advertising expenditures divided by sales, 1968;
KS capital stock divided by sales, 1968;

---

[14] This is a generalization of the critical concentration ratio, allowing the data to reveal a number of thresholds and discontinuities.

XS exports divided by industry sales, 1968;
MS imports divided by industry sales, 1968;
DV Berry index of diversification, 1968.
Remaining terms are dummies for particular intervals of CR5. Twenty equal-sized intervals constructed, C1 = 0.00 to 0.05, C2 = 0.05 to 0.10, etc. Four intervals then omitted due to missing observations and to avoid perfect collinearity, and remaining 16 grouped into 7 classes:
Z1 = C4 + C5 + C6; Z2 = C7 + C9;
Z3 = C10 + C11 + C12 + C13 + C14 + C16 + C17; C8; C15; C19; C20.

The studies described above have each used data at industry level drawn from the official Census of Production. One of the problems with such data is the paucity of information on the level of industry costs, particularly the costs of capital. In an attempt to circumvent this problem, Nickell and Metcalf (1978) examined a sample of products which were available as both proprietary brands and supermarket own-brands. They hypothesized that own-brand prices were linked directly to costs, and used the ratio of own-brand prices to proprietary prices as their (inverse) measure of margins. The data were obtained simply by perusing the supermarket shelves. The cost–price ratio was then regressed against market structure variables at the product group level (where the concentration ratio was used) and at the MLH level (where the Herfindahl index was also available). As hypothesized, a negative relationship with concentration was obtained, suggesting that proprietary brands are relatively more expensive at higher concentration levels. The relationship was generally statistically significant, and a significant relationship with advertising was also observed. An example is given as Equation 6.

Equation 6

(Equation 6 from Table 1, Nickell and Metcalf (1978) p. 264)

$$\begin{aligned} \text{Po/Pp} = {} & \underset{(14.8)}{1.01} - \underset{(2.93)}{0.206}\,\text{CR5} - \underset{(3.66)}{1.28}\,\text{AS} + \underset{(1.30)}{0.062}\,G \\ & - \underset{(0.93)}{0.044}\,B + \underset{(2.02)}{0.022}\,\text{MES} - \underset{(2.43)}{0.062}\,\text{NF}. \end{aligned}$$

n = 29;
R^2 = 0.564;
t-statistics in parentheses;
Po/Pp ratio of own-brand to proprietary brand prices, 1976;
CR5 5-firm concentration ratio at product group level, 1968;
AS advertising expenditure as percentage of sales, 1975–6;
G 5-year growth in sales, 1963–8;

B	average size of all establishments in MLH employing over 25 people, value added, 1968 (proxy for absolute cost barrier to entry);
MES	minimum efficient scale as a percentage of industry size;
NF	non-food industry dummy variable.

Although these various studies provide some support for a positive correlation between industry profits and concentration, there remains the important question of interpretation. According to the traditional view, market structure determines profits through its effects on pricing behaviour. This may be labelled the 'market power' hypothesis. An alternative explanation of the same correlation is associated with Demsetz (1973, 1974). This 'efficiency' hypothesis suggests that relatively efficient firms will tend to achieve large market shares and high profits. One would still observe a positive correlation between concentration and profits, but the interpretation placed on it would be different and considerably less malign.[15]

There is no reason to prefer either the market power or the efficiency hypothesis on purely theoretical grounds, and attention has consequently turned to empirical work. Initial research, including Demsetz's own, centred on the reasoning that if the efficiency hypothesis were true, one would expect to observe a positive relationship between firms' market shares and their levels of profitability within concentrated industries. By contrast, the advantages of market power were thought to benefit all members of an industry, and thus no intra-industry relationship of this kind would be expected. Some support for these observations was found with US data.

Tests of the efficiency hypothesis on British data have recently been undertaken by Clarke, Davies, and Waterson (1984). The authors first examined the price–cost margins of large and small firms, and found no significant difference between them either in industries of above-average or in industries of below-average concentration.[16] If anything, small firms' margins were somewhat higher than large firms' margins. This clearly offered no support for the Demsetz view. They then developed a more detailed model, which involved regressing individual firms' price–cost margins on their market shares within each industry, and examining the slope of the fitted relationship. A steep slope would favour the efficiency viewpoint, a flat slope the collusion interpretation. Using data derived from the Census of Production size–class distributions and pooled for the years 1971–7, Clarke, Davies, and Waterson examined this relationship for 104

[15] However, even if true, the limited diffusion of efficient techniques is clearly sub-optimal.

[16] On one measure, small firms' margins were higher in industries of above-average concentration, suggesting a collusive effect.

industries. Their first conclusion was that only 29 industries showed a positive linear relationship, which meant that only this minority of the sample fell into a pattern amenable to discriminating between the two hypotheses. In 13 further cases, economies of scale appeared to be the factor making any distinction impossible, and in the remainder the complications were perhaps caused by the effects of product differentiation. For the 29 industries consistent with the model, their measure of collusion could be recovered. A spread of results was observed: in some cases it was high, but in others low, leaving a role for efficiency. The estimates of the degree of collusion were then regressed against measures of concentration for these 29 industries, and the positive and significant relationships found were taken as further support for the collusion hypothesis.[17] Overall, then, one can reject the extreme Demsetz view that efficiency is all, but retain some role for efficiency in explaining the profits–concentration relationship.

The market power or efficiency dispute has also become associated with another line of research in industrial economics, which compares inter-industry and intra-industry variation in profits. The traditional story here is that all firms in an industry gain from output restriction and the consequent rise in product price. Thus high levels of concentration identify broad pools of excess profits across industries. An alternative is that the larger firms may be sufficiently insulated from their smaller rivals that in restricting output only they attain higher profits. In this scenario, high levels of concentration identify only narrow pockets of market power. To discriminate between the two, one might therefore wish to explore the relationship between market share and profitability. Although this approach shares with the Demsetz approach the desire to look within industries, it is more concerned with the distribution of profits within the industry than with the origin of those profits in terms of collusion or efficiency.

A number of studies for the United States have followed this approach.[18] The authors have examined the variation in firms' profits, and have discovered that the firm's market share is an apparently far more important determinant of its profits than is the level of concentration in industries where it operates. Although market shares and concentration are interrelated, these results would seem to describe the distribution of gains

[17] The overall relationship between industry margins and the Herfindahl index for these industries was implied to be positive but with declining slope.

[18] Recent studies have typically used one of two rich and relatively new data sets: the Strategic Planning Institute's PIMS data or the Federal Trade Commission's Line of Business data. They include Gale and Branch (1982), Martin (1983), Ravenscraft (1983), and Kwoka and Ravenscraft (1986). Schmalensee (1985) attempts to distinguish the relative importance of industry and firm effects on profitability.

within an industry, leading one to the conclusion that it is the larger firms which derive most of the benefits. The 'shared asset' of monopoly power is not shared very evenly within industries.

Utton (1986) has recently conducted some intra-industry analysis on British data. Using a sample of about 50 markets examined by the Monopolies and Mergers Commission, he found that the average profits of market leaders (relative to the manufacturing industry average) were notably higher when the leader was 'dominant' than in a 'concentrated oligopoly'. (Dominance is defined as a leading firm having a market share of about 50 per cent and its nearest rival having less than half the leader's share; a concentrated oligopoly is where the two leading firms have a combined market share of 50 per cent.) Leading firms' profits in concentrated oligopolies were in turn higher than those in the remaining industries. Using a sub-sample of 42 firms for the period 1972–4, Utton then regressed relative profitability on market share, and most of his specifications produced significant and positive correlations between the two. Although the Commission sample is definitely not random and the analysis here confined to partial correlations (excluding the influence of barriers to entry, growth, etc.), there seems to be no reason to think that further experiments in the UK will not produce the type of results commonly found in the United States.

The natural extension of this line of approach is to examine why the gains from market power are uneven, and this has led to the analysis of strategic groups and mobility barriers (Caves and Porter (1977)). Whereas entry barriers describe obstacles to movement *into and between* industries, mobility barriers comprise similar obstacles *within* the industry. Mobility barriers are thought to emerge from the selection of competitive strategies by firms within the industry (to produce highly differentiated products, to integrate into distribution, etc.). Those which select the same strategies form relatively homogeneous strategic groups, which are then protected from challenges from outside and are thought able to develop within-group patterns of collusion. The evident empirical problem with this analysis is quite how to identify strategic groups. No work of this type has yet been attempted for Britain.[19]

To conclude, the British evidence does give some support for a positive profits–concentration relationship. However, the relationship is weak, probably complex and non-linear, and is often estimated imprecisely. Moreover, even thus qualified, a positive relationship has not been observed in the 1970s with British Census of Production data. Attempts to distinguish the effects of collusion from the effects of efficiency have had

---

[19] Empirical work for the US includes Newman (1978), Porter (1979), Caves and Pugel (1980), and Oster (1982).

some success, but have indicated that a simple model of such effects may not be rich enough to explain the data. We have indicated one further avenue which has been pursued with new data sets in the United States, and the limited attempts thus far to follow this line in Britain. In the following section we shall describe two rather different paths which have been followed in recent empirical work in industrial economics.

3. New Developments in the Analysis of Market Performance

The analysis of market performance has evolved considerably since Bain's early study. The previous section indicated some advances achieved within the framework laid out by Bain: the use of other independent variables such as barriers to entry, the estimation of systems of equations, the examination of the shape of the profits–concentration link, and efforts to probe the market power or efficiency debate. In this section, two rather different approaches will be outlined: the examination of the pattern of competition within individual industries, and the examination of the persistence of market power.

The first of the new approaches we consider could be regarded as having emerged from concern with the dependent variable typically used in the structuralist studies. As we have seen, a correlation between market structure and average profits (the rate of return on capital or the price–cost margin) may be interpreted as reflecting either collusion or the superior efficiency of market leaders. The problem arises because one is using rates of return to make inferences about pricing behaviour. Theory suggests that prices will be raised relative to costs, but since it is difficult to observe prices and costs, various profits measures are used as proxies. (There is continuing controversy over which of the available profit measures, if any, best fits the purpose.[20]) Ideally one would wish to examine the effect of market structure on prices, holding marginal costs constant. Profits are not really the appropriate variable to use in examining this type of conditional prediction, since they do not satisfactorily hold constant the various influences that market structure might have on costs. Bias is bound to result if variations in marginal costs across industries are correlated with the market structure variables of interest.

One response to this problem is to consider the effects of market structure on prices. Here, one needs to consider single industries with differing

[20] Weiss (1974) and Scherer (1980, Ch. 9) cover the issue. Controversy has been regenerated by Fisher and McGowan's (1983) strong claims about the inadequacy of using accounting data to describe economic returns; see Kay and Mayer (1986) for a response. A comparatively recent attempt to overcome the difficulties is to use Tobin's q, e.g. Salinger (1984).

structural characteristics, as with a series of regionally distinct markets for a particular product. Studies of this type in the United States (for example, Geithman, Marvel, and Weiss (1981)) have often found stronger relationships than those studies focusing on measures of profit.

However, one can push further with this type of data and try to infer from prices, costs, and market structure the conduct which underlies any observed discrepancy between prices and marginal costs. The starting-point for an exercise of this kind is the observation that a profit-maximizing firm chooses output to equalize marginal revenue and marginal cost. At any level of output, marginal revenue depends upon the demand curve facing the firm and on the pricing behaviour of its rivals. In exactly the same way that one uses information on outputs and inputs to make inferences about the parameters of a production function, or data on prices and quantities to test restrictions on the parameters of consumer demand functions, one can use basic data on prices, outputs, costs, and demand, together with the marginal cost equals marginal revenue condition, to infer what the conduct of industry members must have been in order to have generated the observed data. Since different types of behaviour (for example, dominant firm pricing, Cournot behaviour, competitive price taking) generate observably different price–output configurations in equilibrium, one can infer which of these conduct types appears to have occurred.[21] Notice in addition that one is able to 'correct' for correlations between market structure and costs in such an exercise: the 'collusion or efficiency' ambiguity does not cloud interpretation of the results.

To date, the only example of this type of work on UK data is the recent paper by Borooah and van der Ploeg (1986). In contrast with the American literature which focuses on specific industries, Borooah and van der Ploeg examine a series of broad industries (food, mechanical engineering, textiles, etc.) over the period 1954–79. For each industry, they estimate input demand and output demand functions, and from the resultant estimates of price elasticity and conjectural elasticity they derive a measure of monopoly power. The ranking of these measures across their 10 industry groups was unrelated to the ranking of aggregate concentration across industries, suggesting quite different areas of policy concern. Although an interesting exercise, we imagine that a wide variety of industry cost and demand conditions are suppressed within the group aggregates. To investigate individual industries requires extensive gathering of data. In principle, such empirical work could form part of merger and monopoly investigations,

---

[21] For recent examples, see Gollop and Roberts (1979), Appelbaum (1982), and Roberts (1984). Geroski, Phlips, and Ulph (1985) survey the literature. An extension of the approach is to model how conduct changes over time (e.g. Porter (1983), Geroski, Ulph, and Ulph (1987)) or to predict the conduct consequences of a merger (Baker and Bresnahan (1985)).

although we acknowledge that such an approach bears little resemblance to current policy.

The final new approach we shall mention concerns the dynamic performance of industries. Attention is here shifted from the consequences of market power at any one point in time to the question of whether high prices and profits persist over time. Clearly, relatively transitory positions of market power are unlikely to arouse much concern. Therefore, what matters is how rapidly monopoly positions and their associated returns are eroded by the threat or fact of new entry.

Recent work in this area has aimed to develop time series descriptions of the profitability of firms, either in isolation or grouped together to capture common industry effects. One can then determine how rapidly above-average rates of profit converge toward long-run levels, and attempt to explain this intertemporal performance. It emerges from recent studies that although profits in British industries are not, on average, particularly high by American or European standards, positions of above-average profitability tend to persist for relatively longer than elsewhere.[22] It also seems to be the case that there is a notable variation in performance within industries, and therefore industry characteristics can explain only part of the observed patterns (Cubbin and Geroski (1987)).

The picture of a sluggish competitive process, which the persistence of profits suggests, is mirrored by studies of the stability of leading firms' market shares (Shaw and Simpson (1986), Utton (1986), Geroski (1987)). Whilst it is not obvious that market shares ought necessarily to decline—if leaders are more efficient or have continued access to some specialist resource, for example — the very slow pace of observed decline suggests that even when leading firms lose their edge, their replacement by relatively more efficient rivals can take an extremely long time.

4. Conclusions

We observed at the outset that one reason for interest in the type of work surveyed in this paper is that it might provide clear guidance for policy. If concentrated industry structures are found to be directly related to high profits, an important policy objective should be to reduce levels of concentration or at least to prevent their increase. The work surveyed in Section 2 provides limited support for such a policy: the concentration–profits relationship in the UK is weak, non-linear, and dependent on other factors; it seems to have disappeared in the 1970s.

---

[22] Geroski and Jacquemin (1986) compare the UK with France and West Germany; for the United States, see Mueller (1986).

Nevertheless the subsequent work surveyed in this paper suggests that it would be unwise to conclude on this point. The material covered in Section 3 suggests two important further issues. First, the growing awareness of limitations with previous approaches and of the need for sound theoretical underpinnings in empirical work has led to a move from cross-sectional work to close studies of particular industries. Such studies certainly validate concern that the impact of market power is more complex than is allowed for in simple concentration indices, but in many cases market power most certainly does exist. Second, there has been a broadening of perspectives from examination of the current level of market power to investigation of its duration. On this score, empirical work has indeed found that whatever the current dimensions and determinants of profits, a speedy competitive process should not be relied upon.

This type of work does, however, forsake the direct lessons about industry structures which were suggested by the original cross-sectional studies. Can anything be retained from the original approach, or modifications of it? We would suggest that the chief lessons to be learned here are from those studies which emphasize the impact of *market share* on profits—a lesson the duration of profits studies took on board from the outset. Thus, although concentration does not appear to have a clear impact on profits, more recent studies from the USA suggest that market share does. Factors which augment large market shares and remove the dampening effect on profits of large *rivals'* market share—i.e. factors such as mergers—may well have substantial impact on profits. A merger policy based on this premiss may therefore seem more justified than one relying on the concentration doctrine, even though there has been only limited confirmation of such results for Britain.[23] Since horizontal merger policy in Britain has never been based on opposition to all increases in concentration, a weakening of policy could not therefore be justified by reference to empirical work in industrial economics.

---

[23] The extent to which the market share arguments can be tested is severely limited by the nature of data currently available.

7

The Evolution of Merger Policy in Britain

JAMES FAIRBURN*

1. Introduction

The aim of this paper is to provide an overview of the operation of merger policy in Britain from the introduction of controls on mergers in 1965 to the end of 1986. The structure of the paper broadly reflects the two-stage procedure characteristic of British policy, whereby a limited number of the many merger proposals falling within the scope of the legislation are first selected by the authorities for further consideration, and these few are then examined by the Monopolies and Mergers Commission against a broad public interest standard. Thus, following a brief description of the legislation, Section 2 will examine the initial selection decision: which types of mergers have been referred to the Commission, and how the types and number of references have changed over time. The section is concerned with establishing the broad pattern of policy. Section 3 then focuses on the operation of the Commission: how it has dealt with the various issues it has been required to consider, for example, how it establishes the effect of a particular merger on competition. Section 4 contains some concluding comments on the overall operation of this two-stage policy, and offers some tentative policy recommendations.

2. Merger Policy

INHERITED INSTITUTIONS

The first modern competition legislation preceded the institution of controls over mergers by some 17 years. The 1948 Monopolies and Restrictive

---

* Temporary Lecturer in Economics at the University of Southampton.

Practices Act set up a Commission (composed of prominent lawyers, economists, businessmen, and trade unionists) to inquire into the effects of restrictive agreements and monopoly firms in the manufacturing sector. The Commission had to establish whether such practices and situations operated against the public interest, a loosely defined criterion incorporating business efficiency and competition among other considerations. The Commission investigated in depth individual industries referred to it by the Board of Trade. Its reports showed a general hostility to the effects of agreements between firms to restrict prices, share markets, and deal only with agreed customers. However, little direct government action resulted and the number of industries considered was tiny in comparison with the estimated pervasiveness of such restrictions. As a consequence, new legislation was introduced in 1956. The Restrictive Practices Court was established to consider restrictive agreements of certain types. The presumption was that such agreements were harmful and would be outlawed unless they could be shown to be justified according to certain specified criteria, the so-called 'gateways'. In practice the new Court interpreted the generous gateways tightly, and as a consequence many agreements were abandoned and overt cartelization of manufacturing industry rapidly diminished in the early 1960s.

During the years in which the new legislation was becoming effective, the Monopolies Commission continued to operate, albeit on a diminished scale, examining industries where there were single monopolists or groups of jointly dominant firms. Certain of its reports showed that one important way of establishing or strengthening a monopoly position was by means of merger with competing firms, for example Wall Paper Manufacturers had repeatedly countered its diminishing market share by multiple mergers with rivals, and in the tobacco industry the leading firm Imperial Tobacco was found to have a substantial interest in its rival Gallaghers. At the same time the pace of merger activity was quickening and in some cases clearly replacing recently condemned agreements with tighter links. Other contemporary events highlighted the importance of merger, the most notable example being ICI's hostile, and ultimately unsuccessful, bid for Courtaulds, the other principal domestic manufacturer of man-made fibres, in 1961–2.

The antipathy to large-scale take-over battles, and the growing realization that the monopolies legislation provided only a belated and ineffective response to mergers, led to agreement on the need for further legislation. The Conservative government's 1964 White Paper included proposals for the control of mergers, and these measures were largely adopted in the incoming Labour government's 1965 Monopolies and Mergers Act. The Act adopted the administrative means of control familiar from the monopoly legislation. Mergers, like monopolies, were to be referred to the Commission by the relevant government department, at that time the Board of Trade. The Commission would then have 6 months, or exceptionally up to 9 months, to ascertain whether the merger proposal would be expected to operate against the public interest, the vague standard set out in 1948. The Act provided the government with the means to halt a merger proposal while the investigation was underway (a provision absent in the preceding White Paper).

The adoption of the public interest investigation by the Commission rather than a more specific prohibition enforceable in the Court—as with the restrictive practices legislation—indicated the lack of a clear stance on horizontal mergers. Furthermore, the legislation was to apply to mergers creating or strengthening a one-third share of supplies, or where the book value of assets acquired exceeded £5 million. Thus vertical and conglomerate mergers, as well as mergers between competing firms, could be referred.[1] The general and flexible nature of the provisions was indicated in the government's introduction of the legislation:

> Mergers involving large firms are not, of course, necessarily harmful to the public interest—I should like to make the point—but the power of a giant, especially of two giants united, might be such as to stifle competition, or the empire created might be too large for the most efficient use of resources. In judging all these cases, however, I would propose always to remember what mergers can in certain cases do to achieve greater strength for our economy at home and abroad.[2]

This latter feeling, that mergers were often a powerful means of restructuring British industry, was further emphasized in contemporary policy developments. In particular, in 1966 the Industrial Reorganization Corporation (IRC) was established to promote rationalization, a manifestation of the feeling that British firms were frequently too small to compete effectively on world markets. The IRC was staffed largely by businessmen and little constrained by formal procedures. Its principal role proved to be the encouragement of mergers in industries it determined to be

---

[1] In speaking on the second reading of the bill, Douglas Jay, then President of the Board of Trade, commented on likely candidates for referral:

> One obvious case, I think, is where competition in a vital industry might be markedly reduced. That is why we have provided, as an alternative to the criterion of monopoly, the size of assets test, so that what are called vertical or diversifying mergers could be investigated if the public interest required.

(Reprinted in the 1978 Green Paper, *A Review of Monopolies and Mergers Policy* (Department of Prices and Consumer Protection (1978)).)

The specific concerns with non-horizontal mergers are not evident from this statement.

[2] Douglas Jay, reprinted in the 1978 Green Paper.

too fragmented. It typically proceeded by determining in its opinion the most efficient firm in an industry, and promoting mergers around that base. This prompted Caves's (1968, p. 321) caricature of British industrial policy: 'In order to achieve industrial efficiency, find the most efficient firm in Britain and merge the rest of them into it'. Clearly the ethos behind the establishment of the IRC, and the direct actions of that body, would have an important influence over the early phases of merger policy.

THE FIRST PHASE OF POLICY, 1965–73

In this and following parts of this section, the operation of merger policy will be sketched out principally using information on the references made to the Commission. Table 7.1 gives the details up to 1973, thus taking us through the intensive merger activity of the late 1960s and early 1970s, and stopping before the first full year of operation of the Office of Fair Trading (see below).

The most notable feature of Table 7.1 is the paucity of references, and the reference question merits further attention. In 1969 a Board of Trade pamphlet noted that between July 1965 and April 1969 only 10 of the 350 mergers falling within the scope of the legislation had in fact been referred. The same pamphlet also gave details of the referral process, revealing the existence of the Mergers Panel. The Panel was a non-statutory body comprising representatives of the Board of Trade and other government departments which had an interest in the particular proposal at issue. Its task was to assess the information gathered by the Board of Trade about the merger proposal and decide whether to recommend a referral to the Commission.[3] Although the Minister was not bound by the Panel's recommendation, this was evidently the forum in which most of the contentious issues would be discussed. The pamphlet listed many criteria relevant to the reference decision, including questions of efficiency as well as competition, but gave no indication of how the various factors were weighed against each other. The Panel's procedure was evidently no simple screening process, but rather in contentious cases might amount to the *de facto* public interest inquiry when no reference was ultimately made. However, the Panel's investigations were completed in a much shorter interval: it typically took no more than a few weeks to come to a decision, compared with the Commission's standard 6-month inquiries.

---

[3] Knowing of the existence of a merger proposal did not prove a major difficulty. Although there was no formal notification procedure, the time limit within which a reference must be made began when the proposal became public knowledge. In practice, voluntary notification became common to expedite the referral decision.

Table 7.1. Merger references to the Commission, 1965–73

Year	Reference	Public interest finding
1965	BMC/Pressed Steel	Not against
1966	Ross Group/Associated Fisheries	Against
	Dental Manufacturing/Amalgamated Dental	Not against
	Dentists' Supply Co/Amalgamated Dental	Not against
	GKN/Birfield	Not against
	BICC/Pyrotenax	Not against
1967	UDS/Burton	Against
1968	Barclays/Lloyds/Martins[a]	Against
	Thorn/Radio Rentals	Not against
1969	Unilever/Allied Breweries	Not against
	Rank/de la Rue	Against
	Marley/Redland	Abandoned
1970	Burmah Oil/Laporte Industries	Abandoned
	British Sidac/Transparent Paper	Against
1971	(Pulp paper and board-making activities in UK of) Reed International/Bowater Paper	Abandoned
1972	Beecham/Glaxo	Against
	Boots/Glaxo	Against
	Sears Holdings/William Timpson	Abandoned
1973	Tarmac/Wolseley-Hughes	Abandoned
	Glynwed/Armitage Shanks	Abandoned
	Whessoe/Capper-Neill	Abandoned
	British Match/Wilkinson Sword	Not against
	Bowater/Hanson Trust	Abandoned
	Davy/British Rollmakers	Against
	Boots/House of Fraser	Against
	London & County Securities/Inveresk	Abandoned

[a]The Commission objected to the proposed mergers between Barclays and Lloyds and between Barclays, Lloyds, and Martins. It stated that it would not object to either large bank merging with Martins. The findings were not by the requisite two-thirds majority but were none the less complied with.

Note: A listing of completed reports is contained in the Appendix to this book.

Source: Annual Reports on the Monopolies and Mergers Commission, various years, HMSO, London.

The clearest evidence of conflicting objectives arose through the parallel operation of the Commission and the IRC. Mergers between competing firms were likely to be a central concern of the Commission and the majority of early references did indeed involve horizontal mergers. (The Commission's analysis is considered below.) In the same period, the IRC sponsored approximately 50 mergers (Hindley and Richardson (1983), Hague and Wilkinson (1983)). These included the formation of British Leyland, and the merger of GEC with first AEI and then English Electric. In addition there were a whole string of mergers, many of which showed similar characteristics to those which were referred. Indeed in one case, the IRC sponsored a merger of the trawling interests of the Ross Group and Associated Fisheries, a full merger of the two companies having previously been found against the public interest by the Commission. More generally, it has been suggested that the prime role of the IRC, certainly in those cases where it did not directly provide finance, was to establish that a merger proposal would not be referred to the Commission.[4]

This first phase of policy therefore confirmed the impression established on enactment of the merger legislation, that relatively few mergers were thought to give rise to public interest concerns, and saw the parallel operation of a policy clearly antagonistic to merger control. What of the mergers actually referred to the Commission?

The earliest references involved mergers with an impact on competition. The majority were horizontal, i.e. concerning competing suppliers of a product, although the first reference (*BMC/Pressed Steel*) and certain subsequent ones (*Dentists' Supply Co/Amalgamated Dental*, *Thorn/Radio Rentals*) involved vertical issues through the merging of firms at successive stages of the production process. Certain of the initial references were also characterized by the fact that the Board of Trade had not used its power to halt the merger, and thus the Commission was confronted with a completed transaction. Although this did not seem to affect the finding in *GKN/Birfield*, in *BMC/Pressed Steel* considerable emphasis was placed on assurances given by the company not to discriminate in supplies, and in *BICC/Pyrotenax* the Commission seemed clearly hostile to the merger but reluctant to carry this through to the breakup of an established concern.

The reports failed to show much evidence of a consistent approach by the Commission. Of the early horizontal mergers, the Commission objected to *Ross/Associated Fisheries* and *UDS/Burton*, and as noted was clearly hostile to *BICC/Pyrotenax*. In each case it emphasized the impact of the merger on parts of the fish, menswear, and cable markets. In other cases

[4] Young and Lowe (1974) refer to the close working relationship between the IRC and the Mergers Panel, and Hindley and Richardson (1983) cite the example of GEC/AEI where a merger had previously been contemplated but where IRC sponsorship ensured that no reference to the Commission would be forthcoming.

where the impact on market share was just as substantial (*GKN/Birfield*, *Dental Manufacturing/Amalgamated Dental*, and *Thorn/Radio Rentals*) it cleared mergers, having placed emphasis on such factors as the buying power of customers—the motor manufacturers and Ministry of Health—and imminent technical and demand changes in the television industry. The lack of predictability clearly weakened the contrast between merger policy and other policy initiatives: one could not say with certainty that the IRC had encouraged mergers to which the Commission would have taken exception. The point remains, however, that the characteristics of the two sets of mergers were similar, and consistency would require that they at least be referred.

In the early 1970s, as shown in Table 7.1, the Commission's stance on this type of merger strengthened considerably, with adverse findings in each of *British Sidac/Transparent Paper*, *Davy/British Rollmakers*, *Boots/House of Fraser*, and the Glaxo mergers. In the latter two cases, this was despite fairly low shares of industry output, and the *Beecham/Glaxo* case in particular showed the Commission resisting an argument that an increase in scale was required for the domestic drug companies to compete effectively in what was an international market. Instead, the Commission stressed the importance of there continuing to be a number of decision-making centres in the allocation of research expenditures. Yet at the same time as the toughening of policy was shown by this case, the potential for anomalies in the referral process was also displayed. The original bid for Glaxo by Beecham had initially been cleared: only when the rival bid by Boots emerged was it decided to make the reference to the Commission.

The last feature of the early phase of policy to which attention will be drawn is the commencement of referrals of conglomerate mergers. Given the concern expressed at the scale and nature of earlier bids, such as ICI/Courtaulds, it was not surprising that the merger procedures would be applied to this type of proposal. Equally the Commission had already been drawn to comment on conglomerate issues in previous references, for example its discussion of the likely impact of the *UDS/Burton* merger on management capabilities. In outright conglomerate mergers, such issues would form the heart of the Commission's inquiries. The first such references were *Unilever/Allied Breweries* and *Rank/de la Rue*, referred and reported on in parallel in 1969. Although the Commission did not see any exceptional merits in the huge, agreed Unilever/Allied Breweries proposal, it opposed only the contested Rank/de la Rue bid. A take-over was thought likely to have an adverse effect on the management of de la Rue, with the probable loss of personally established technical exchange agreements, and this was the central reason for the Commission's opposition. This report was important in that it drew the Commission firmly into an involvement with the mechanics of take-over bids and a potential role as arbitrator in disputes between the companies involved. The lack of any other clear stance on conglomerate mergers was evident in *General Observations on Mergers*, published as an annexe to these two reports. Here the Commission noted the increased size of recent proposals, and expressed concern at the buildup of giant firms through equity-financed acquisitions and at the financial instability and managerial weaknesses which might result. Its only specific recommendations, however, concerned post-merger disclosure of accounting information, and these were not followed up. Thus the early referrals marked the beginning of a policy of conglomerate references, in which the object of the inquiries was by no means clear at the outset. Although there were few other conglomerate references in the period covered in Table 7.1—only *British Match/Wilkinson Sword* of those resulting in reports—this was to be an important facet of merger policy subsequently.

THE MIDDLE YEARS, 1974–83

The initial phase of policy had then established the ground rules on which subsequent policy would operate. The net of merger policy was cast widely, bringing many mergers of diverse types within the scope of control, but it was evident from the outset that relatively few cases would be drawn in. It was clear that the selection of references was as important a part of policy as subsequent consideration of particular mergers by the Commission. Within this framework, the 1960s and early 1970s had indeed seen the referral of diverse types of merger—horizontal, vertical, conglomerate—and a broad range of issues considered by the Commission, from a merger's likely effect on prices to its impact on the morale of incumbent management.

The atmosphere in which policy was to operate was to be different in several respects from 1974 onwards. Overt official encouragement of large-scale mergers had ceased with the disbandment of the IRC in 1971, and the high level of merger activity of the late 1960s and early 1970s had given way to the gentler pace of activity which characterized the next 10 years. This had limited impact on the workings of policy, since there continued to be a fairly constant stream of proposals falling within the scope of the legislation each year.[5] Yet although the amount of work faced by the Panel and the Commission did not decline, the background against which they worked would be less frenetic and it remained to be seen whether policy standards would be clarified as a result.

The early 1970s had also seen an important change in the institutional setting of policy. The 1973 Fair Trading Act, in addition to modifying the

[5] More detail on numbers of qualifying references and mergers is given in the final part of this section.

market share and public interest criteria of the competition legislation,[6] established the Office of Fair Trading (OFT) to oversee competition and consumer protection legislation. In the competition sphere, the head of the OFT, the Director General of Fair Trading ('the Director General'), took over the duties of the Registrar of Restrictive Practices, and became responsible for referring monopolies to the Commission and overseeing any subsequent actions that were called for. In the area of mergers, there were fewer changes. The Director General was not given primary responsibility for making references, as with monopolies, but was simply charged with keeping informed of current merger proposals. He took over as the head of the Mergers Panel, but recommendations made were still not binding on the Secretary of State. Although the operation of policy became somewhat better documented, it was not then essentially altered by the 1973 Act.

Table 7.2 gives details of references in the period. The table first shows a general increase in the rate of referral in the early 1980s compared with the mid- and late 1970s, 1977 apart. One consequence of this was that in the early 1980s there was a sufficient number of reports on horizontal mergers that one could begin to ascertain the Commission's criteria of judgement in a way that is less true of the intermittent reports of the first half of the period. This question will be taken up in Section 3.

Yet in this period, in particular, the competitive ramifications of mergers were only part of the story. There was also a series of referrals of conglomerate mergers. The hostile bid of Amalgamated Industrials for Herbert Morris was referred, and when that was prevented, the resultant bid by Babcock and Wilcox was also directed to the Commission. Lonrho's efforts to control House of Fraser were the subject of three separate references from 1978 to 1984, and take-overs of Anderson Strathclyde, Illingworth Morris, and Sothebys were each the subject of notable references. The last example was the foremost case of a reference being courted by an incumbent management and proving the crucial element in its defence against an unattractive bid which did not, however, raise any competition issues. Sothebys was faced by a bid from an American company. Following a substantial lobbying effort, the reference was made, against the advice of the Director General. The consequent pause gave Sothebys a chance to find a 'white knight', A. Alfred Taubman. Although that bid was also referred, the first bid was soon abandoned, and following a token clearance of the Taubman bid by the Commission, the way was thus cleared to proceed.

---

[6] The market share criterion was reduced from a one-third to a one-quarter share of supplies. The new public interest criteria placed somewhat more emphasis on competition than previously—the exact wording is given in the Appendix to Borrie (this volume) and further discussed by Swift (this volume)—but the specified criteria remained only factors 'among other things' which the Commission had to consider.

Table 7.2. Merger references to the Commission, 1974–83

Year	Reference	Public interest finding
1974	Eagle Star/Sunley/Grovewood	Not against
	Charter Consolidated/Sadia	Not against
	Sears Holdings/The Nottingham Manufacturing Company	Abandoned
	NFU Development Trust/FMC	Not against
	Dentsply International/AD International	Not against
1975	Weidmann/Whitely	Not against
	Norvic Securities/W Canning	Abandoned
	Eurocanadian Shipholdings/Furness Withy/Manchester Liners	Against
	Amalgamated Industrials/Herbert Morris	Against
1976	Pilkington/UKO	Against
	Babcock & Wilcox/Herbert Morris	Against
	Fruehauf/Crane Fruehauf	Not against
	BP/Century Oil	Against
1977	Provident Financial Group/Cattle's (Holdings)	Abandoned
	Associated Engineering/Serck	Abandoned
	Sketchley/Johnson Group Cleaners	Abandoned
	Smith Bros/Bisgood Bishop	Not against
	Rheem International/Redfearn National Glass	Abandoned
	Rockware Glass/Redfearn National Glass	Against
	United Glass/Redfearn National Glass	Against
	Derritron/British Electronic Controls	Abandoned
1978	Lonrho/Scottish & Universal Investments/House of Fraser	Not against
	Hepworth Ceramic Holdings/H & R Johnson-Richards Tiles	Abandoned
1979	GEC/Averys	Not against
	FMC Corporation/Alginate Industries	Not against
	Merck/Alginate Industries	Not against
1980	Hiram Walker-Gooderham/Highland Distillers	Against
	Blue Circle/Armitage Shanks	Not against
	S & W Berisford/British Sugar Corporation	Not against
	Compagnie Internationale Europcar/Godfrey Davis	Not against
	Grand Metropolitan/Coral Leisure Group	Abandoned

Table 7.2 contd.

Year	Reference	Public interest finding
1981	Enserch Corporation/Davy Corporation	Against
	Lonrho/House of Fraser	Against
	European Ferries/Sealink	Against
	British Rail Hovercraft/Hoverlloyd	Not against
	Hongkong & Shanghai Banking Corporation/Royal Bank of Scotland	Against
	Standard Chartered/Royal Bank of Scotland	Against
	BTR/Serck	Not against
	Argyll Foods/Linfood Holdings	Abandoned
1982	Rowntree Mackintosh/Huntley & Palmer	Abandoned
	Nabisco Brands/Huntley & Palmer	Not against
	ICI/Arthur Holden	Not against
	Great Universal Stores/Empire Stores	Against
	Charter Consolidated/Anderson Strathclyde	Against
	Sunlight Service Group/Johnson Group Cleaners	Against
	Initial/Johnson Group Cleaners	Against
	Prosper de Mulder/Midland Cattle Products	Abandoned
	Linfood Holdings/Fitch Lovell	Not against
	The Enterprises of Alan J. Lewis/Illingworth Morris	Not against
1983	London Brick/Ibstock Johnsen	Not against
	Redland/Ibstock Johnsen	Abandoned
	Hepworth Ceramic Holdings/Steetley	Against
	GFI/Knoll International Holdings/Sotheby Parke Bernet	Abandoned
	A. Alfred Taubman/Sotheby Parke Bernet	Not against
	Pleasurama/Trident Television	Against
	Grand Metropolitan/Trident Television	Against
	Trafalgar House/P & O	Not against
	GKN/AE	Against

Source: Annual Reports of the Director General of Fair Trading, various years, HMSO, London.

The elements present in these examples were also evident in other references where some competition issue might also be involved. A majority of references involved contested take-overs, with the parties involved taking full opportunity to set out what they considered to be public interest issues.

Other elements which repeatedly featured were foreign take-overs, as with the bids by Eurocanadian Shipholdings, Hongkong and Shanghai Banking Corporation, and the Enserch Corporation amongst others, and the regional question, where a series of bids for companies based in Scotland—Alginate Industries, House of Fraser, Highland Distillers, the Royal Bank of Scotland, Anderson Strathclyde—were referred between 1978 and 1982. The following section will examine how the Commission responded to this diverse set of concerns.

THE RECENT PAST, 1984–6

Table 7.3 outlines references made between 1984 and 1986. The first entry in the table, Lonrho/House of Fraser, was the last of a kind. This was the third time the bid had been referred. In the first case, in 1978, the two companies had been linked by Lonrho increasing its share in House of Fraser through a bid for Scottish and Universal Investments. The Commission had cleared this stake, but explicitly noted that a greater level of control might give rise to public interest issues. When Lonrho did increase its shareholding, in 1981, a further reference had been made and the Commission in turn had found increased control likely to operate against the public interest. The third reference arose as the bitter boardroom disputes between Lonrho and House of Fraser continued and Lonrho attempted to increase its representation on the House of Fraser board.

Soon after the reference, an internal Department of Trade and Industry review of the operation of mergers policy concluded with what has become known as the Tebbit guidelines: 'my policy has been and will continue to be to make references primarily on competition grounds'.[7] Henceforth, it seemed clear that hostile conglomerate bids of the Lonrho/House of Fraser type would no longer be referred. Indeed, the House of Fraser saga was to provide confirmation of this change. When the Commission's investigation was extended for a further 3 months, the Lonrho stake was sold off to the Alfayed Investment Trust. Despite the heat engendered by the previous contest, and despite the fact that very little was known of the new owners of this prestigious British company, no reference of the new merger situation was made, despite considerable political clamour for this to be done.

The Tebbit guidelines then marked a change of emphasis in reference policy, although the elements of that change—consistent referrals of horizontal mergers and an awareness of the difficulties of providing an opportunity to refer contested bids—had been apparent some time before

[7] For further discussion, see Borrie and Swift, both in this volume.

Table 7.3. Merger references to the Commission, 1984–6

Year	Reference	Public interest finding
1984	Lonrho/House of Fraser	Not against
	Scottish & Newcastle/J. W. Cameron	Abandoned
	Dee/Booker McConnell	Not against
	BET/Initial	Not against
1985	Imperial Group/Pernaflex	Abandoned
	Scottish & Newcastle/Matthew Brown	Not against
	British Telecom/Mitel	Not against
	McCorquodale/Richard Clay	Abandoned
	Elders IXL/Allied Lyons	Not against
	BET/SGB	Not against
1986	GEC/Plessey	Against
	Imperial Group/United Biscuits	Abandoned
	Guinness/Distillers	Abandoned
	Cope Allman/Cleveland Strip	Abandoned
	Norton Opax/McCorquodale	Not against
	Hillsdown Holdings/S & W Berisford	Abandoned
	Tate & Lyle/S & W Berisford	Against
	London International/Wedgwood	Abandoned
	P & O/European Ferries	Not against
	Feruzzi/S & W Berisford	Against
	Strong and Fisher (Holdings)/Garnar Booth	Abandoned
	Trusthouse Forte/assets of Hanson Trust	Not against
	Gulf Resources and Chemicals Corporation/Imperial Continental Gas	Abandoned

Source: As Table 7.2.

then. Subsequently the majority of references have indeed focused on competition issues. For the most part, these have been involved horizontal mergers, often in fairly small or regional markets, although much larger mergers (for example, *GEC/Plessey*) and vertical mergers (for example, *British Telecom/Mitel*) have also been referred.

The Tebbit guidelines retained the option that some mergers not involving competition issues might be referred to the Commission, and inevitably subsequent attention has focused on what the scope of this exception might be. The first evidence was produced by the 1985 reference of the Australian company Elders IXL's bid for the huge food and drink manufacturer Allied Lyons. This was notable for the relative size of the two companies, and the consequent facts that the bid was highly leveraged—Elders would have to borrow heavily to finance the acquisition—and that to pay off this debt, Elders planned to sell off certain parts of the Allied Lyons group. These were evidently thought to be issues involving the public interest, and although the Commission cleared the bid in autumn 1986, another highly leveraged bid (Gulf Resources/Imperial Continental Gas) was also referred later that year.

This pattern of references and these exceptions, however, meant that merger policy had limited impact on the merger boom of 1985 onwards. No matter how large or bitterly contested a bid was, if no competition issues were involved a reference was unlikely. A final feature further limited the overlap between merger policy and the merger boom. The Imperial Group/United Biscuits and Guinness/Distillers bids were initially perceived to arouse competition concerns in the snack food and whisky markets respectively, and both were referred to the Commission. These references clearly reduced the bids' chances of success, since Hanson Trust and the Argyll Group had rival bids for the Imperial Group and Distillers respectively. However, in both cases the initial bids were then abandoned, and arrangements made to sell off certain interests in the markets of concern, should the revised bid succeed. These arrangements were cleared by the competition authorities, and the contests allowed to continue. Although United Biscuits subsequently lost out to Hanson Trust, Guinness won control of Distillers and duly sold off the specified whisky interests.[8]

These arrangements were clearly consistent with the newly declared goals of policy. If the authorities were concerned with the impact of a merger on competition, and if that part of a bid which gave rise to such a concern could be removed to the satisfaction of the authorities, the objectives of all parties would be achieved. Such arrangements did, however, reinforce the recent changes in policy. Two or three years previously, a contested bid could have been referred to the Commission and the arguments of the competing parties analysed in detail. Now, bitterly contested bids involving large public companies were not only not examined, but furthermore the policy concerns were dealt with in an abrupt manner to ensure that the bids could proceed with minimal interruption.

Most of the large bids of 1985 and 1986 were not then subject to scrutiny by the Commission. The resistance to this new stance was apparent at the close of the period, in the latest of the £1 billion plus bids. This involved BTR, one of the most notable of the new conglomerates, and Pilkington, a family-controlled glass manufacturer located in the north of England and

---

[8] Similar proposals were adopted in Dixons's and Mills and Allen International's bids for Woolworth and London and Continental Advertising Holdings; see 1986 Annual Report of the Director General of Fair Trading, p. 28. For further discussion, again see the contributions by Borrie and Swift in this volume.

noted for a record of intensive research and innovation and of good labour relations. The bid arose as the controversies surrounding Guinness's take-over of Distillers threw new doubts on the ethics and merits of take-over, and in an atmosphere in which the short-term focus of the City—typified by its favourites, BTR—was widely and adversely contrasted with the long-term needs of industry, as represented by Pilkington. Despite considerable pressure for a reference from the company, its work-force, and MPs of all parties, the proposal was not referred to the Commission, and considerable relief was apparent when BTR subsequently retired from the contest as Pilkington's value was revised upward by the market.

REFERRAL POLICY: CONCLUSIONS

The preceding discussion has described how referral policy has progressed through a number of phases to the current one of primary concern with competition issues. It remains to gather together here some overall figures and general discussion.

Tables 7.4 and 7.5 illustrate a central facet of referral policy, namely that it has always selected from the large number of proposals satisfying the qualifying criteria only a very few for further consideration by the Commission. Table 7.4 gives the annual figures, and shows how the total varied with the overall level of merger activity in the first 10 years covered, but has subsequently kept at a fairly continual 160 to 260 proposals per year (to this extent justifying a comment made in the text above), until 1986. This has been accomplished by twice raising the qualifying assets criterion, from £5 million to £15 million in April 1980 and then to £30 million in July 1984, as shown in the table.[9] The absolute number of references made, and the proportion of qualifying mergers referred, has varied substantially from year to year. However, Table 7.5 makes it clear that the proportion remains low, and fairly consistent over longer periods at around 3 per cent.

[9] Although with an assets criterion in place, this procedure is clearly justified in principle by the inflation of asset values, in practice it has been applied erratically (reducing qualifying proposals by over a half—on the basis of the 1978–9 overlap—for the increase to £15 million, and by about a third—using 1981–3 figures—for that to £30 million). Moreover, the presence of the criterion is ultimately questionable. It clearly brings proposals with no competitive ramifications within the scope of the legislation, and as Hughes's discussion (this volume) of the OFT evidence illustrates, these have constituted an increasing proportion of the total. With the shift in attention to competition, this could clearly be revised, although large mergers will continue to be the subject of what non-competition concern remains. For competition mergers, an assets criterion—certainly one which focuses on the large firm as opposed to, say, combined size—is a less obvious requirement. However, as a practical matter it would continue to be easier to make references on the basis of assets, as has been the case in the past, rather than to use more contentious market share figures. Clearly the decision on such matters depends on the type of regime in place—as discussed in the remainder of the text—and the capacity allocated to the enforcement agencies.

Table 7.4. Merger proposals qualifying for consideration by Mergers Panel, 1965–86[a]

Year	£5m. criterion	£15m. criterion	£30m. criterion	Actually considered	References made[b]
1965 (part)	48			48	1
1966	63			63	5
1967	96			96	1
1968	133			133	2
1969	126			126	3
1970	80			80	2
1971	110			110	1
1972	114			114	3
1973	134			134	8
1974	141			141	5
1975	160			160	4
1976	163			163	4
1977	194			194	8
1978	229	103		229	2
1979	257	131		257	3
1980	182	140	115	182	5
1981		164	105	164	8
1982		190	122	190	10
1983		192	129	192	9
1984			223	223	4
1985			192	192	6
1986			313	313	13

[a]The assets criterion was raised from £5m. to £15m. on 10 April 1980, and to £30m. in July 1984. The back projections show how many mergers would have qualified had the higher criteria prevailed in preceding years.

[b]Including more than one bid each for: Amalgamated Dental, Glaxo, Redfearn National Glass, Alginate Industries, Royal Bank of Scotland, Johnson Group Cleaners, and Trident TV.

Source: As Table 7.2.

Two related factors are relevant here. First, the approach initially taken by policy-makers, and continued to date, was to assume only 'special' cases merited examination, rather than, say, referring large classes of horizontal merger. Second, the Commission's capacity is somewhat fixed, and the referral authorities must be conscious of this fact. Although the Commission has been able to cope with the sort of numbers experienced to

Table 7.5. Merger references and abandonments, 1965–86

Period	Total qualifying mergers	Referred to Commission	(2) as percentage of (1)	Referred mergers abandoned	(4) as percentage of (2)
	(1)	(2)	(3)	(4)	(5)
1965 (part)–70	546	14	2.6	2	14
1971–5	659	21	3.2	9	43
1976–80	1 025	22	2.1	7	32
1981–5	997	37	3.7	8	22
1986	313	13	4.2	7	54
Total	3 540	107	3.0	33	31

Source: As Table 7.2.

date—in addition to examining monopolies and anticompetitive practices and conducting efficiency audits of nationalized industries—any substantial change in referral policy would entail adding to its capacity.[10] Thus there are considerable forces placing bounds on current referral policy.

Table 7.5 also illustrates that a substantial proportion of referred mergers are subsequently abandoned by their participants (a factor obviously easing demands on the Commission's time). To discuss the reasons for this requires further consideration of the Commission's approach, its predictability, and cost in terms of time taken and resources expended. Are proposals abandoned because participants recognize they will be opposed by the Commission? I shall return to this question (with no clear answer) subsequently: suffice at this stage to note that, to the extent that this is true, it suggests that merging firms consider they still have a chance of averting reference altogether, or else would have dropped the proposal at birth.

Given the wide scope of the qualifying criteria, it may not be surprising or interesting that so low a proportion are referred. Of more concern is the treatment of particular classes of merger, specifically substantial horizontal mergers. At the outset it must be admitted that accurately characterizing mergers not reported on by the Commission is difficult, because the report itself tends to throw much light on the exact nature of the firms and the markets in which they operate, information which is not generally available elsewhere. Nevertheless there are three sets of evidence which suggest that

[10] As discussed in subsequent sections, reforms of merger policy need not necessarily take this route, but might choose instead to simplify the analysis of mergers and thus reduce or even generally eliminate the role of the Commission.

there have been important ambiguities in the referral process.

First, there is the existence of the IRC in the early years of merger policy. As noted above, there is little doubt that IRC-sponsored mergers were often similar to those considered and sometimes prevented by the Commission in the 1960s. The sources cited earlier give further details.[11]

Second, there are some data available giving the market share breakdown of merger proposals satisfying the qualifying criteria. Gribbin (1974) provided this for the period 1965 to mid-1973, and the 1978 Green Paper (Department of Prices and Consumer Protection (1978)) extended it through to the end of 1977. Table 7.6 displays the two sets of figures, and extracts data for a period in the mid-1970s. Unfortunately, no subsequent data are available.

Table 7.6. Qualifying mergers which qualified on the basis of market share

	Total	Total as percentage of all qualifying mergers	Total for which specific figure available	Market share created			
				25–50[a]	50–80	80–100	50–100
1965–mid-1973	281	281/798 = 35%	239	118	74	47	121
Mid-1973–1977	92	92/764 = 12%	87	46	34	7	41
Total	373	373/1 562 = 24%	326	164	108	54	162

[a]Market share criterion was changed from 33% to 25% in November 1973.

Sources: Row 1: Gribbin (1974) Table 6; row 3: Green Paper (Department of Prices and Consumer Protection (1978)), Appendix Table 6, p. 111.

Table 7.6 can first be used to modify the impression given by the overall breakdown of merger proposals into horizontal, vertical, and conglomerate categories given annually by the OFT and reported by Hughes (this volume). Horizontal mergers have accounted for the majority of the total (albeit a declining majority in recent years), or typically over 100 such mergers per annum. Table 7.6 shows (column 2) that if a minimum market share is introduced into the calculations, this proportion declines to around a third for the 1960s and early 1970s, and further to only 12 per cent in the mid-1970s. (This decline is obviously of some intrinsic interest, given the indication that the policy stance altered and the Commission's attitude appears to have hardened around this period.) Moreover, these figures also modify a common presumption that to resort to a guidelines approach, whereby any merger satisfying a minimum market share might be referred,

[11] Ellis (1971, pp. 286–95) discusses referral policy in the early years.

would put unbearable strain on the system of control. Thus, on the mid-1970s basis, adopting a 25 per cent market share guideline would increase references to about 20 per year, a substantial but hardly earth-shattering increase.[12]

The figures in Table 7.6 can next be compared with the actual operation of policy. In the period to 1977, only 25 horizontal mergers were in fact referred (using the Green Paper definitions to ensure comparability: p. 111, Appendix Table 7). This is evidently still only a small proportion of the total given in the table (326) and, more worryingly, only a fraction of those mergers creating or strengthening a market share of 50 per cent or more (162). Clearly not even all mergers creating market shares of 80 per cent or more (54) were referred, possibly not even those 7 in the mid-1970s, as policy strengthened.

These figures suggest that in a substantial number of cases, mergers creating a strong presumption of danger of monopoly abuse were not even put before the Commission. It is apparent from Gribbin's (1974, p. 72) analysis that one reason for this is that many of the mergers were very small. Thus of the 281 proposals in the top row of the table, 70 per cent (193) did not separately satisfy the assets criterion, and as a class had average target firm assets of £1.9 million. More precise figures would be needed to increase our understanding of referral decisions, and would also be valuable on a continuing basis.[13]

The third set of evidence relating to anomalies in the referral process concerns the Director General's advice to the Secretary of State. The Director General is charged by law with keeping the state of competition in the economy under review: of those contributing to the referral process (the parties to the bid, other government departments represented on the Mergers Panel, the Secretary of State), he is the one most likely to advocate the cause of competition, an issue which is a principal concern of the legislation. Therefore the referral process can be criticized when his advice

---

[12] Of course, all this conjecture depends on how mergers are subsequently treated. If the Commission were to make no move toward such presumptions, a great many wasteful reports would be produced: I return to this in Section 4. Alternatively, if the guidelines became the centre of policy, i.e. no merger was allowed which infringed them, the figure would fall from 20 to zero as proponents of merger declined to waste their time planning mergers which would certainly be outlawed. See Hay's discussion in this volume of the 1968 US guidelines.

[13] It should again be noted (see footnote 9) that it is not obvious that because a merger is small it deserves no policy attention. There is obviously not much sense in applying an expensive policy procedure to a market which would not possibly justify it in terms of monopoly profits or welfare loss averted. To the extent that small markets are liable to be swamped by the effect of a large new entrant, or a rush of foreign competition, this conclusion is reinforced. However, policy based on guidelines, for example, need not be costly in this sense.

is rejected, particularly when that advice is to refer a merger.[14] There have been 10 such instances to date.[15] To cite the explanation of the most recent:

> The Secretary of State accepted that some detriment to competition could result from the acquisition, but took the view that in the particular circumstances of the case this was not serious enough to outweigh the employment and efficiency benefits to be gained from the probable strengthening of the United Kingdom fibreglass industry. (Annual Report of Director General of Fair Trading for 1986, pp. 26–7)

As is clear from the legislation, it is this type of trade-off which the Commission is there to perform, and which it is given 6 months to do. If the fairly common pre-emption of such an inquiry before reference suggests that the Commission's procedures are too slow, then an obvious direction of policy reform is indicated. If it suggests that the Commission would not have come to the same conclusion, an obvious question as to the Secretary of State's particular expertise in these matters is raised. The doubts surrounding these issues are perhaps sufficient to consider giving the Director General sole charge of making competition references. As noted above, this is essentially the procedure with monopoly inquiries. Complementary changes in the remainder of policy and extensions on this general theme will be pursued in Section 4.

The evidence above leaves some doubt as to the extent of anomalies in the referral process. Do the Director General and Secretary of State simply sometimes differ, but essentially pursue the 'correct' policy, or do they and the system conspire to neglect dozens of mergers which are harmful to competition? It does not seem sensible to address this question without first considering the other half of policy: what the Commission does with the references it receives. This is the purpose of Section 3.[16]

---

[14] There are two known instances—A. J. Lewis/Illingworth Morris, GFI/Knoll/Sothebys (and by implication a third, consequent on the latter, A. Alfred Taubman/Sothebys)—when a reference was made contrary to the Director General's advice. Given that these did not involve competition, and that a case *can* be made for public scrutiny of *specific* non-competition issues, the criticism of these is less.

[15] Since 1978 details have been given in the Annual Report of the Director General of Fair Trading. The 1978 report (p. 10) cited Imperial Group/broker chicken business of J. B. Eastwood Ltd as the third, and other sources (e.g. Whish (1985, p. 519)) suggest Tate and Lyle/Mandre Garton and Woolworth/Dodge City were the previous two. The subsequent cases, including referrals against advice, are (with year of annual report and page reference): Thorn Electrical Industries/EMI and Calor Gas/Clogas (1979, p. 41); A. J. Lewis/Illingworth Morris (1982, p. 29); GFI/Knoll/Sothebys, Blue Circle Industries/Aberthaw and Bristol Channel Portland Cement, Dalgety/agricultural division of Rank Hovis McDougall (1983, p. 29); Nestlé SA/UK subsidiary of Carnation Company (1984, p. 30); Cannon Group/Screen Entertainment, and Owens-Corning Fibreglass Corporation/two fibreglass plants of Pilkington Brothers (1986, p. 26).

[16] To pre-empt the following discussion somewhat, the Commission has rarely shown concern at mergers creating market shares below about 30 per cent. On this basis, research at the Institute for Fiscal Studies by Andrew Bird could not find many instances of substantial

3. Mergers and the Commission

The previous section has established that British merger policy has gone through several phases. The policy began in an atmosphere clearly supportive of mergers and industrial restructuring, with the consequence that few mergers were referred to the Commission and attention in large part lay elsewhere. As support for merger subsided in the 1970s, policy was left unfocused, a characteristic emphasized by the fact that policy had been extended to cover mergers involving no competition issues. This lack of clarity as to why mergers were referred in turn allowed an increasing politicization of policy in the late 1970s and early 1980s, as supporters and opponents of particular mergers saw the chance to use this state of affairs to their own advantage, seeking to win or avoid a reference to the Commission. This in turn brought its own reaction when in 1984 the Tebbit guidelines pulled policy sharply back to a concern with the impact of mergers on competition.

These changes have meant that the Commission has been presented with a broad array of issues to consider, against a changing background of public and political attitudes toward merger. This section considers how the Commission has responded. What gives importance to these questions, and ultimately what has allowed such changes in priorities to occur, is that the Commission's deliberations are little constrained by the legislation. The Commission is required to establish whether a merger is expected to operate against the public interest, and the ways in which this is so, but in so doing must take into account 'all matters which appear to [it] in the particular circumstances to be relevant'. Thus it is fully able to pick up the particular issues in any given proposal, and base its findings upon them.

A broad distinction can be made between those mergers that involve questions of competition and those that do not. There are several obvious types of competition issue, such as when actual or potential competitors merge or when a supplier of a product or input merges with one of its customers. I shall begin with issues not involving competition.

---

horizontal mergers which had not been referred in the early 1980s. Using market research and trade journal sources, a picture of many merging industries was built up. These drew attention to the cement merger noted above (footnote 15), but no other merger appeared to create as much as a 20 per cent market share, and many were in these terms trivial. The deficiencies of such research are the accuracy of the sources used—reaffirming the desirability of the authorities themselves revealing more data on non-referred cases—and the coverage. Thus the study could not mimic the referral process by confirming information on all cases which were referred. The impact of sales of subsidiaries, less well covered in the financial press, is partly to blame.

NON-COMPETITION ISSUES

In a number of reports, non-competition issues have been to the fore. Often the question evidently at issue here is one of management efficiency: whether the incumbent management or the acquiring management will run the company better. Other distinct issues suggested by various references are whether the merger will have an adverse impact on the regions, whether a foreign take-over would be desirable, and whether the financing of a merger might give cause for concern.[17] Attention has primarily been given to those cases where the Commission has indeed considered that a merger should be prevented on such grounds, and we examine these presently.

A more general point to make first is that even if the Commission does not ultimately reject a merger on the basis of these issues, its analysis will still be conditioned by such matters. This is best illustrated by the growth of references of contested bids. Very few of the earlier references concerned contested bids, but a much higher proportion of references in the 1970s and early 1980s were opposed by the target firm's management. Indeed, as indicated in Section 2, obtaining a reference to the Commission came to provide an important potential defence against an unwanted bid. This had the consequence that much of the Commission's time was spent accepting, qualifying, or rebutting the various contentions of the parties involved. However the arguments are ultimately treated, this process tends to give shape to the Commission's inquiries and reports. The point is that the impact of non-competition considerations should not be measured solely by the number of mergers prevented on such grounds: the availability of such defences has meant they have been a principal preoccupation of the Commission.

This leads to the first of the non-competition issues, the question of management efficiency. Given both the prominence of evidence submitted by the parties involved and the broad scope of the public interest criteria, it is not surprising that the Commission has been drawn into this question. If two companies are vigorously disputing which of them is best suited to managing a group of assets, it is tempting for the Commission to express its view.

On several occasions the Commission has objected to mergers which were thought likely to have adverse effects on management efficiency and morale. The argument was first used in *Rank/de la Rue*, and has subsequently been used to protect the management of Glaxo against Beecham, Herbert Morris against both Amalgamated Industrials and Babcock & Wilcox, and House of Fraser against Lonrho.

[17] The balance of payments and employment are two other considerations which have been mentioned. However, conclusions on these matters have not generally been independent of those on efficiency.

The regional question has surfaced on a number of occasions, with one particular 'region', Scotland, being a central concern in a series of reports in the period 1979–82. The Commission showed itself to be concerned with employment and career prospects in Scotland and the need to prevent Scotland becoming a branch economy, and this led to the prevention of Standard Chartered's bid for the Royal Bank of Scotland, and a majority finding against the Charter Consolidated/Anderson Strathclyde proposal. The latter became notable because it was not accepted by the Minister of State.

In three further reports the Commission has perceived foreign ownership to be undesirable, at least in part because of the nature of the industries involved. Thus the Commission accepted that it was 'advantageous' to have a British owned and controlled transatlantic shipping company (*Eurocanadian Shipholdings/Furness Withy/Manchester Liners*). (The benefits consisted of having a close knowledge of, and paying particular regard to, the interests of British traders.) It was thought necessary for a contract engineering company to be perceived to be British controlled because of the importance of national identity in securing overseas contracts (*Enserch/Davy*). Finally, the foreign take-over of a British clearing bank was thought likely to impair the Bank of England's control of monetary policy (the Hongkong and Shanghai Banking Corporation/Royal Bank of Scotland proposal).

The most topical of the non-competition issues to be considered is the impact of the financing of a merger. Whereas referral policy and the stance of the Commission currently suggest that the issues outlined above have been down-graded, this particular issue has been the subject of recent concern. It was the reason behind the referral of the first conglomerate merger proposal since the Tebbit guidelines, *Elders IXL/Allied Lyons*.

In its report, the Commission accepted that the financing of a bid might be a public interest issue. If a bid for a major public company were likely to lead to severe financial weakness in the new group, it was not sufficient simply to rely on the market to patch things up after the group had contracted or even collapsed. The particular issue at hand was where a bid was largely financed by debt, so that the group would have a high level of gearing and be exposed to a risk of further borrowing and financial constriction if profits did not subsequently live up to expectations.

The Commission examined the levels of gearing and interest cover of Elders's bid on two different projections, and concluded that in this case there was little risk of financial problems. The company had plans to reduce the gearing ratio, in part by selling off Allied Lyons's food division. The Commission also seemed reassured by Elders's recent connections with Broken Hill Proprietary Company and by the reputation of the consortium of banks financing the bid, which had put limits on how far Elders could borrow. The proposal was therefore cleared, but the Commission conceded that less desirable bids of this type might emerge, and invited the Bank of England and the Stock Exchange to consider what might be an appropriate response. One alternative is clearly that further bids might be referred to the Commission for a similar type of analysis, and this therefore remains an active issue.

One final issue should be mentioned, even though it has not been the central concern of any inquiry in the way that those outlined above have. This is the loss of information which results when one company's accounts are submerged within another's, with the consequent danger that poor post-merger performance can be concealed from investors. The disclosure issue was first mentioned in *General Observations on Mergers*, the annexe to the first two conglomerate merger reports. On some subsequent occasions, the Commission has required assurances that separate disclosure of the results of specified activities be given after a merger (*British Match/Wilkinson Sword*, *Berisford/British Sugar*), although in *Blue Circle/Armitage Shanks* it thought this would be an unfair obligation to place on the company. Nevertheless, the latter report did include recommendations for changes in company law to reduce management discretion in making disclosure decisions.

COMPETITION ISSUES

The impact of a merger on competition seems the clearest subject of public policy concern. Within this area there are, however, a number of diverse issues ranging from minor overlaps between two companies' fields of operations to the outright merger of two (or more) substantial and direct competitors. This section will commence with the less direct cases.

A general worry with a merger might be that it enables the new group to subsidize certain of its activities from the profits made elsewhere. This has not been a common concern, with the Commission usually accepting firms' arguments that they run activities as separate profit centres and that it would be irrational to cross-subsidize. One exception was *Blue Circle/Armitage Shanks*, the merger of powerful producers of cement and ceramic sanitary-ware. Before allowing the merger to proceed, the Commission required assurances that the group would not grant special discounts to builders' merchants on certain products if they took other products from the group, and that it would not generally use cement profits to reduce the prices on other lines. It was clearly suspected that the group might engage in predatory activity designed to harm Armitage Shanks's competitors. A clear alternative here—and perhaps a necessary alternative, given the unclear force of the assurances—would be to examine any instance of such conduct under the anticompetitive practice provisions of the 1980 Competition Act.

A more common, but related, issue arises from vertical mergers which join together suppliers and customers. For example, firm A might be a producer of a product which is used by firm B. If they merge, firm B might be required to use firm A's product rather than take its supplies from firm A's competitors, although it would otherwise have chosen not to do so. Implicit in such a change is that firm A's product is being subsidized within the new firm, perhaps to the detriment of A's competitors.

Such interlinkages are common in modern diversified firms. In certain cases they may seem almost incidental and the merger would not generally be called vertical. In *Lonrho/House of Fraser* (1981), Lonrho was seen to produce textiles of the type sold in Fraser department stores. One of the Commission's objections to the merger was the danger that Lonrho's textiles would be promoted unfairly in this way, and assurances that this would not be done were not accepted.

In other cases the vertical links between firms have been a more central concern.[18] However, vertical mergers remain comparatively rare, and the Commission's attitude to them has not been clear. One prerequisite for any objection to such a merger is the presence of market power in the activities concerned. In the Boots/Glaxo proposal, for example, the question arose of whether Boots could use the control of a drugs wholesaler to its advantage by discriminating in supplies away from other retail chemists. Since drug wholesaling was fairly competitive, this was not thought to be a danger. By contrast in *Pilkington/UKO*, UKO was the only domestic producer of mass-produced lenses, and one of the Commission's objections to the merger was that UKO would be required to take more of its supplies of lens blanks from Pilkington than it would otherwise choose to do. However, market power does not constitute sufficient grounds for an objection: *BMC/Pressed Steel* involved the take-over of a substantial producer of vehicle bodies by one of its customers. Here the Commission was content to rely on assurances that Pressed Steel would continue to supply the other vehicle producers.

The most recent such case, *British Telecom/Mitel*, was also the largest to come before the Commission for some time. This concerned BT's backward integration into the manufacture of telecommunications equipment through

[18] Competition law's hostility to vertical mergers and vertical restraints more generally, particularly the foreclosure and leverage arguments (the idea that a monopolist can extend or leverage its market power into other markets), has been one of the central concerns of critics of antitrust in the United States, for example Bork (1978). Krattenmaker and Salop (1986) suggest there may sometimes be a basis for concern in such practices. See also Williamson (1983) for the argument that vertical mergers involving concentrated industries may enhance entry barriers by requiring simultaneous entry into the two activities; Williamson also describes the US Department of Justice guidelines' approach to the issue.

merger with Mitel, a Canadian-based manufacturer of private automatic branch exchanges (PABXs). There was no doubt of BT's dominant position as telecommunications network operator, and the Commission thought it very likely that BT would be able to divert business to such a subsidiary, given its influence over technological specifications for links with the network and the favourable position of its staff as routine contacts with customers and sole source of advice on equipment. The case was also complicated by the fact that BT's main business was regulated, and thus the distortions in favour of a manufacturing subsidiary might have provided a means of exercising BT's market power which it would not otherwise have. The Commission recommended that the merger should be prevented unless severe restrictions were placed on BT's ability to favour Mitel. In the event, only much weaker restrictions were sought by the Secretary of State (Gist and Meadowcroft (1986)).

The final category to be considered involves the merger of competing firms. This is the largest category, and to keep the analysis tractable and topical, the paper will concentrate on the Commission's reports produced from 1980 onward.[19] As indicated in Section 2, there were few clear guidelines from the earlier period. In the 1960s the Commission had objected to some mergers involving large combined market shares but let others pass. The Commission's stance seemed to toughen in the early 1970s with its objections to the merger of both Boots and Beecham with Glaxo, but the signals from later in the decade were less clear. Charter Consolidated was allowed to merge with Sadia and Weidmann with Whitely despite high market shares, whilst the Boots/House of Fraser merger was prevented despite low ones. More generally there was only an intermittent flow of reports and an increasing propensity to consider issues other than competition. Both of these complications have been mitigated in the 1980s.

The first step in such inquiries is to determine an appropriate market definition. This entails a certain amount of simple gathering of facts, establishing what the firms' interests are and how they overlap, but where firms are diversified or products complex there may be many such overlaps and this stage of the inquiry consequently prolonged.

Beyond this basic stage, market definition will have both a product and a geographic dimension. Thus the Commission will have to consider which products are close substitutes for the output of the merging firms, and over what area competition extends.

Product market definition involves looking for a gap in the chain of substitutes between products. However, such a gap may not be obvious. In *Nabisco/Huntley and Palmer*, for example, the Commission considered

[19] For further discussion of earlier periods, see Rowley (1968), Sutherland (1969), Ellis (1971), Pickering (1974, 1980), Pass and Sparkes (1980), Colenutt and O'Donnell (1978), and Utton (1975).

markets for biscuits and savoury snack foods (crisps, nuts, and snacks). These two products were seen to be distinguished from each other and from confectionery by such factors as price, taste, place of sale, child or adult appeal, size, and nature of wrapping. But the Commission also had to consider whether the biscuit market should be subdivided into markets for savoury, plain, or chocolate biscuits (it decided not), and precisely where the boundary between biscuits and confectionery lay. To cite some well-known brands: is a Penguin or a Club a biscuit? What about a Kit-Kat?

Another example is provided by *British Rail Hovercraft/Hoverlloyd* and *European Ferries/Sealink*. These reports placed hovercraft in the same market as cross-Channel ferries. They also distinguished several types of demand for such ferry services: accompanied vehicle traffic, through passengers to Continental destinations, and excursionists. Survey analysis suggested that the various routes were often regarded as close substitutes by travellers with vehicles, and in particular that the Anglo-French crossings should not be considered separately from Anglo-Belgian crossings. For through passengers, a further dimension came into play, and here the Commission outlined market shares for travel to Paris and Brussels, with air transport showing the largest share.

Product market definition therefore presents a number of conceptual problems and requires a considerable amount of time and attention. Where there are difficulties in distinguishing a product, the Commission may stress supply characteristics, i.e. factors specific to the industry rather than the market. For example, *GUS/Empire Stores* concerned firms conducting catalogue mail-order selling. Clearly the products here will face close substitutes in corresponding products—clothes, shoes, household goods, etc.—sold in the shops. Nevertheless the Commission stressed factors to some extent specific to the mail-order industry—the use of agents and catalogues, the provision of credit, the right to return goods—and focused subsequent analysis on firms operating here.

Geographic market definition involves considering how competition is localized by transport costs or the immobility of the goods or services produced. The two situations which command particular attention are when markets are highly localized and when products are traded on world markets, although in principle there is a complete spectrum between the two extremes. Examples of the first were found in *Dee/Booker McConnell*, which considered local competition between cash and carry wholesaling depots, and *Scottish and Newcastle/Matthew Brown*, which involved competition between pubs in Cumbria. Rather than precisely analyse each local market, of which there may be dozens or hundreds, the Commission's approach here has been to examine the typical distance a customer will travel, and on this basis measure how many local monopolies currently exist and how many more would be created by the merger. A less satisfactory

Table 7.7. Market definitions

Reference	Market definition
Hiram Walker/Highland Distillers	Malt whisky distilling
Godfrey Davis/Europcar	Car rental
British Rail Hovercraft/Hoverlloyd	Cross-Channel ferry services; ferry services to Northern Ireland
Nabisco/Huntley and Palmer	Biscuits; savoury snack foods
GUS/Empire Stores	General catalogue mail-order selling
Sunlight/Initial/Johnson	Textile maintenance: laundry dry-cleaning linen rental cabinet towel rental
Linfood/Fitch Lovell	Cash and carry wholesaling; grocery retailing
Pleasurama/Grand Metropolitan/Trident Television	London casinos
Hepworth/Steetley	Refractories: high alumina bricks basic bricks dolomite bricks sliding gate systems
Trafalgar House/P & O	Deep-sea passenger shipping; cargo shipping (Europe–Australasia)
GKN/AE	Engine components: pistons piston rings cylinder liners plain bearings
Dee/Booker McConnell	Cash and carry wholesaling; grocery retailing; grocery purchasing
BET/Initial	Textile maintenance: workwear rental cabinet towel rental dust mat rental
Scottish & Newcastle/Matthew Brown	Beer retailing in Cumbria
GEC/Plessey	Telecommunications equipment: public switches transmission systems PABXs various other products;

Table 7.7 contd.

Reference	Market definition
	defence electronics: radar avionics systems underwater defence systems communication systems
BET/SGB	Access industry: off-shore scaffolding industrial and petrochemical scaffolding other major projects hire and sale of equipment
Norton Opax/McCorquodale	Personalized cheques; lotteries and promotional games
P & O/European Ferries	Anglo-Continental freight transport; Northern Ireland freight transport

approach, evident in the retailing side of *Linfood/Fitch Lovell* and *Dee/Booker McConnell*, is simply to measure regional as well as national levels of concentration, rather than pressing further to consider the state of local competition of particular shops.

At the other end of the spectrum, although the impact of imports will be acknowledged, international markets have been considered less often than might be imagined. Where markets are not to some extent insulated by transport costs, other factors may impinge. Thus in *GEC/Plessey*, the Commission was willing to concede that there was an international market in public switches (telephone exchanges), but in other sections of telecommunications equipment and more particularly in defence electronics, the purchasing policies of the Post Office (less so under British Telecom) and the Ministry of Defence had meant that effective competition extended only among domestic producers. Thus for truly international markets one had to look to such cases as passenger cruises (where the competition was potential rather than actual, see below) in *Trafalgar House/P & O*, and the scotch whisky market, characterized of course by the fact that all production was within the UK, although 85 per cent of output was exported.

Table 7.7 presents a summary of the market definitions used in the Commission's reports since 1980. This emphasizes the fact that in many cases, most obviously *GEC/Plessey*, a range of different markets were involved. Clearly it is not possible to discuss each in detail here. Indeed the Commission may not be able to conduct as full an inquiry as one might wish. Examples include the localized markets noted above, and *Godfrey Davis/Europcar*, where distinctive local, national, and international markets were discussed but data presented only for the aggregated total market.

Table 7.8. Combined market shares of merging firms

Merger	Combined market share	Against public interest	Market definition
Linfood/Fitch Lovell	7.3%		Grocery retailing in south
Europcar/Godfrey Davis	8.5%		Cars available for rental
British Rail Hovercraft/Hoverlloyd	19.5%		Accompanied vehicle traffic
BET/SGB	22.5%		Access industry
Hiram Walker/Highland Distillers	28%	Yes	Quality malt whisky distilleries
Hepworth/Steetley	39%	Yes	Refractories
BET/Initial	41%	[a]	Combined workwear, cabinet towel, and dust mat rental
McCorquodale/Norton Opax	43%		Personalized cheques
Nabisco/Huntley and Palmer	43%		Savoury snack foods
Initial/Johnson	45%	Yes	Cabinet towel rental
GUS/Empire Stores	47%	Yes	General catalogue mail-order
P & O/European Ferries	52%		Continental freight ferry services
GEC/Plessey	59%	Yes	PABXs
Sunlight/Johnson	60%	Yes	Linen rental in London
Trafalgar House/P & O	66%		Passenger cruises from UK
Pleasurama/Grand Metropolitan/Trident Television	67%	Yes	London casino takings
GKN/AE	71%	Yes	Various engine components
Sealink/European Ferries	71%	Yes	Accompanied vehicle ferry traffic to Continent

[a]The Commission clearly regarded the merger as having adverse effects on the public interest, speaking of 'a *prima facie* detriment to competition' (para. 8.40) and of this outweighing any benefits from the merger (8.40). However, due to BET's existing shareholding, these consequences were seen to be 'inherent in the existing situation' and 'not properly attributable' to a full merger (8.41), and the merger was therefore not prevented.

Having defined the market, the Commission will then begin to assess competition within it by computing the market shares of the merging firms and their competitors. Two questions then arise. Do market shares adequately describe the state of competition and the merger's effect upon it? If they do, then what levels of market share are liable to lead to the prevention of a merger? It will be convenient to address these issues in reverse order.

Table 7.8 presents the Commission's estimates of combined market share of merging firms, in particular markets considered relevant. The table should be interpreted with considerable caution, since it illustrates only particular markets from those analysed by the Commission. Thus the overall refractory, engine components, and access industry shares are presented for *Hepworth/Steetley*, *GKN/AE*, and *BET/SGB* respectively, whereas for *Sunlight/Johnson*, *Initial/Johnson*, and *GEC/Plessey* certain specific markets are given. Some other reports are omitted due to the approach to the local markets outlined above. Finally in certain cases the market definitions seem somewhat arbitrary, although these definitions figured in the Commission's conclusions; for example, *Hiram Walker/Highland Distillers* shows the share of quality malt whisky distilleries excluding those owned by Distillers (since Distillers was considered to be self-sufficient in malts, and unlike other whisky suppliers did not operate in the market for whisky fillings). The table would give a somewhat different impression if the whisky share were adjusted downward, or if different sectors of the textile maintenance or access industries were considered.

Keeping these caveats in mind, can any general statements be made about the Commission's treatment of market share in these reports? Beyond the fact that mergers involving low market share—say under 30 per cent—are likely to be allowed, and those involving very high combined market share—over 60 per cent—will probably be prevented, it would seem not. Clearly such statements are imprecise and leave a broad range of market share where the Commission's finding is unpredictable. This contrasts somewhat with the position found in an earlier paper (Fairburn (1985)), where although there was an uncertain intermediate range, this was narrower (20 to 40 per cent) and the Commission would typically prevent mergers creating or strengthening the largest market share in any reasonably concentrated market. Thus mergers involving a combined market share of over 40 per cent would normally be blocked. Such an impression is reinforced by the Commission's statements in reports of the time, for example in *GUS/Empire Stores* (para. 8.23):

It seems to us that where a company in an already highly concentrated market or market sector further strengthens its position by acquiring a competitor, this may be expected *prima facie* to be inconsistent with the objective of maintaining and promoting effective competition in that market.

Subsequent findings such as those in *Trafalgar House/P & O*, *BET/SGB*, *McCorquodale/Norton Opax*, and *P & O/European Ferries* clearly do not take such a strong position against increases in concentration, and this leads to the other of our questions. When do market shares fail to give an adequate representation of the state of competition within a market?

Market shares may give a fairly good representation of the state of competition when they truly reflect firms' underlying capacities to produce for that market, and where those capacities are largely fixed through time. They are liable to be less informative when these conditions do not apply, where output can be readily expanded, and where other firms can transfer capacity from elsewhere or establish new capacity in the market. Thus an obvious extension to the analysis of concentration would be to consider the process of new entry and possible barriers to new entry. (For further discussion of the Commission's analysis of barriers to entry, see Littlechild (this volume).)

In each of the cases where the Commission has cleared mergers which would produce a combined market share of over 40 per cent, new entry has been considered to provide an important discipline on any attempts by the group to restrict output and raise prices. In *Trafalgar House/P & O*, the merged firm accounted for 70 per cent of cruises from UK ports and 45 per cent of fly-cruises from the UK (where passengers are flown to foreign ports from which cruises begin), about which the Commission remarked, 'These are large market shares, which in most cases would give us serious concern about a proposed merger' (para. 7.12). However, it continued: 'An even more important feature of this market is the ease of entry into it. Ships, which are the principal capital assets used by cruise operators, are by their nature very mobile and readily redeployed in response to market demands' (para. 7.13).

Likewise, the costs of marketing such cruises—the only cost in the case of fly-cruises—were seen to be low, and some recent new entry had in fact been detected. Similarly, in the personalized cheque printing market the Commission found that the requisite technology was readily available and entry by other security printers was feasible, and in the freight ferry markets examined in *P & O/European Ferries* new entry was again considered practicable and some evidence of recent entry presented in support of this. (In each case the Commission also considered whether the new firm could successfully engage in predatory pricing, i.e. cutting prices to deter entrants or eliminate existing competitors, and concluded that it could not.)

In the personalized cheque printing and freight ferry markets, a further factor thought likely to limit any danger of increased prices was the buying power of the banks and hauliers' associations. Buying power has often featured in the Commission's reports, although precisely what is at issue is unclear. (In these reports the Commission indicated the ability to bargain with suppliers for better prices: hence the presence of alternative suppliers rather than existing market shares was thought relevant.) A similar argument was used in the majority finding in *Nabisco/Huntley and Palmer*, which allowed the merger despite the high share of savoury snack foods. The buying power of the British Steel Corporation and the car producers was not, however, deemed important enough to mitigate the effects of the *Hepworth/Steetley* and *GKN/AE* mergers on the refractory and car components industries respectively.

Finally, *Dee/Booker McConnell* was in part concerned with the other side of the coin, a merger possibly increasing buying power. The merged firm would be the largest purchaser of groceries if its retailing and wholesaling interests were combined (there was some question as to whether this would be done). Despite the concern expressed elsewhere about the buying power of multiple retailers, this was not considered a major issue and the merger was allowed to proceed.

One further area in which market shares have been considered deficient indicators of the state of competition is where there are indivisibilities on the demand side. This has been illustrated in two recent reports. In *BET/SGB* a combined market share of 46 per cent of the off-shore scaffolding sector (which 'would normally imply a considerable degree of market power') was seen to reflect the firms' current holding of a few large contracts. In fact there were a number of firms—around a dozen—actively competing for such contracts, and hence the market share was a measure of success rather than strength. (Buying power was again seen to be an element in this market.) In *GEC/Plessey* similar arguments were used to opposite effect. Thus in different defence electronics markets—various radar and communications systems, torpedoes, and sonar—one of the firms held current contracts and thus had large market shares whilst the other had none. What the Commission emphasized was that the firms had in the past competed for contracts and were among few domestic firms that could do so in future. On the basis of this loss of potential competition, the Commission objected to the merger. (The Commission also objected to various actual reductions in competition in telecommunication products, and to the reduction in competition in research and development.)

Therefore potential competition has been considered important on a number of occasions, most often where it is seen to diminish any adverse impact of a merger on competition. *GEC/Plessey* represented an exception in that here, potential competition itself was harmed. Although a reduction in potential competition was also used as an argument against the mergers in *Sunlight/Initial/Johnson*—where the firms owned laundry facilities which might in the absence of merger be used as the basis of expansion into a number of the product markets—it has not been used elsewhere. Of course, any conglomerate merger represents a diminution of potential competition, since the acquiring firm could enter the market directly rather than by take-over. However, it would seem most relevant in mergers which just miss the horizontal classification, i.e. where the firms supply similar but not identical products or where they supply the same product in different geographic markets (often called product-extension or market-extension mergers). Nevertheless in reports such as *London Brick/Ibstock Johnsen*, where the firms produced different types of bricks, and *Standard Chartered/Hongkong and Shanghai Banking Corporation/Royal Bank of Scotland*, where the bidders were banks outside the clearing bank system, potential competition was not stressed. Given the large market shares required for prevention of horizontal mergers, more frequent objections on the more uncertain basis of reduced potential competition would seem unlikely.

One issue which has not been mentioned so far is the possibility of increases in market power being offset by any cost savings attained through merger.[20] Although the Commission has on a number of occasions looked quite closely at potential cost savings, for example in *Nabisco/Huntley and Palmer*, it has not generally considered this type of trade-off. This may seem surprising in view of the wide scope of the legislation and the prevalence of arguments about rationalization when it was enacted. The principal reason seems to be the lack of quantification of the degree of market power following a merger.[21] The Commission appears to ask whether or not a merger would have an effect on competition, and its answer is never sufficiently precise to then enter into a subtle calculation of the net effect of market power increase and cost reduction combined.

THE COMMISSION AND MERGERS

Three brief points can be made in conclusion to this section before proceeding to some overall analysis of British merger policy. First, the diverse merger reports show the Commission attempting to establish a broad range of 'public interest' standards on issues which have been presented to it. Questions such as the suitability of foreign ownership in particular areas, the general impact of a merger on a regional economy, or the implications of a radical new means of financing a merger can be

[20] The trade-off was first analysed by Williamson (1968) and is further considered in the Introduction to this volume.

[21] There are also, of course, problems on the cost side: how precise are the plans of the parties involved? Would they be achieved anyway if merger were prevented?

considered difficult ones to judge in an objective and consistent manner in a public forum.[22] This difficulty is reflected in apparent inconsistencies from report to report and in dissenting opinions within the Commission.

Second, the procedures which enable the Commission to consider thoroughly and afresh the repercussions of a highly leveraged bid, for example, hamper it in other ways. The structure of the inquiries draws out the particular rather than general facts of the case in question, allows participants to dictate the agenda of the investigation, and down-grades cross-referencing between reports.

Third, these matters are seen to be problems particularly in the Commission's handling of competition. Here the Commission repeatedly has to confront questions such as how we can judge the state of competition in a market and what is an unacceptable restriction of competition. Yet although the same issues come up repeatedly—market definition, effects of potential competition—it is hard to trace the Commission's reasoning from report to report, or even to perceive that it regards such continuity as an important matter.

4. Conclusions

Rather than repeat the conclusions of Sections 2 and 3, this section will concentrate on three themes—scope, predictability, and, to a lesser extent, timing—pertaining to the overall operation of merger policy. The *scope* of British policy is clearly perceived as an important issue, as is reflected in the 1984 Tebbit guidelines. The legislation clearly entitles the Commission to consider issues not involving competition: the question is which, if any, of these matters can be dealt with effectively in this way? Is it a requisite part of a regional policy to have controls on mergers, or can regional policy objectives be secured in a more direct way? Over what set of industries is review of foreign investment appropriate? There has been doubt about the effectiveness of merger policy in these areas, and they do not seem to form part of current objectives. However, new 'public interest' issues do arise on occasion—witness the highly leveraged bid for Allied Lyons—and it may well be appropriate to retain the current flexible procedure against similar

[22] To these could be added the general concern with disclosure and the more recent problem of merger financing. An earlier specific example was *Eagle Star/Sunley/Grovewood*, which examined the effects of a building society taking over property companies at the time of the secondary banking crisis.

I would not classify all the disputes about managerial efficiency in the same way. However, in several of these there was evidently doubt about the suitability of the individuals involved to take charge of their targets, for example *Alan J. Lewis/Illingworth Morris* and the Lonrho/House of Fraser cases. This would seem a broad public interest objective, paralleled in company law.

contingencies in future. For this reason, it looks unlikely that the predictability of policy in this area could be greatly increased.

There remains the question of whether policy should extend to consideration of the merger process more generally. There is considerable evidence that the market for corporate control does not function smoothly. Is it then appropriate for the Commission to try to separate valuable takeovers from those based on speculative motives and poorly thought-out plans? Indeed should many more mergers be subject to this test, and the test made easier for the Commission by reversing the burden of proof?[23] Although such a case can be made, the problem is that it entails the Commission becoming involved in what are very public and often very bitter disputes between companies, with no guarantee that its expertise in such matters will go unchallenged. Indeed in the more recent cases such as *Taubman/Sothebys* and *Lonrho/House of Fraser* (1985), the Commission itself seems to have been aware of this fact, and to have stepped back from acknowledging that there are public interest issues with which it should be involved. There is also a possible alternative to merger policy in this area, which is to displace the merger process by improving internal monitoring of companies' performance, an issue discussed in the Introduction and by King, both this volume.

There is little doubt that merger policy should extend to the effects of mergers on competition, and it is here that the matter of *predictability* holds more force. The question is essentially whether standards can be set out in advance, or whether the details and refinements of each issue have to be considered for each case. I have suggested above that the Commission's procedures, more suited to broad public interest investigations, overemphasize the specific at the expense of what is general. This could be changed by directly requiring the Commission to refer to its previous decisions, perhaps by making a general reference on horizontal mergers to allow the Commission to clarify its own rules. For further reasons given below, I suggest instead that the OFT be brought more directly into proceedings, taking on a role before the Commission.[24] There would then be a clear advocate of competition and less reliance on the arguments of the parties involved. The OFT would have a strong incentive to draw out the

---

[23] Reversal of the burden of proof has been considered by Meeks (1977) and O'Brien (1978). See also George (this volume).

[24] The role of the OFT, or to be precise the Director General, in merger policy is less developed than in other areas of competition policy. In the field of restrictive practices he is charged with taking cases to the Restrictive Practices Court, and has some discretion to allow non-significant agreements. With monopolies, he makes the references to the Commission in almost all cases, and negotiates and monitors undertakings which result. Under the 1980 Competition Act, he is charged with the preliminary investigation of anticompetitive practices: although this may only be the prelude to reference to the Commission, in many cases the investigation ends here.

common themes and to force the Commission to confront the key issues directly. At present the Commission returns to matters it has acknowledged in previous reports, but attempts little quantification and thus leaves it unclear why the balance between them may have shifted since a previous similar case.

In the conclusions to Section 2, I made further suggestions on the referral stage of policy which complement the recommendations above. It seems anomalous that the Secretary of State should be able to prejudge events by not referring a merger which has been shown to give rise to concern on competitive grounds. I suggested that the referral decision be taken out of his hands, although it may be appropriate for him to retain responsibility for public interest references of the type described above. The OFT would be in charge of taking on cases involving competition, and as part of this would have to clarify its decisions at the current reference stage.

Turning now to the question of *timing*, it is clear that a reference may be a handicap to a bidding company in that it gives at least 6 months for share prices to alter adversely and new bidders to arrive on the scene. I think that the answer to this lies more in the arguments on predictability than in any direct attempts to compress the Commission's investigation into a period shorter than 6 months. The Commission has a lot of issues to cover, and has to prepare its findings for public scrutiny. In any particular case, the recommendations above suggest closer scrutiny of the relevant issues rather than the reverse. However, the point is that the proposals aim to develop clear standards, and that once these exist, the number of cases will diminish. With a standard in place, any inquiry then becomes essentially a matter of establishing how the facts of the case correspond to the standards. In most instances, it will be possible for the parties to the merger to resolve such questions. Realizing that a merger proposal would infringe the standards would result in the proposal not being made. Only difficult or novel cases would then require consideration before the Commission. Of course, it may be possible in advance of any reference to reorganize some proposals so that they do not infringe the standards. In this sense the recommendations here merely continue a recent development in existing policy.

On the question of what the standards might be, I shall be less committal. However, for horizontal mergers it seems there are two positions one can take. First, one could essentially identify competition with market concentration, and set thresholds in terms of market shares (or of some more complete index of concentration). This would give a very predictable policy. There has, however, been growing doubt in the economics literature that this is an appropriate stance.[25] Second, one can inquire more directly into the effects of a particular merger on the state of competition within

[25] See the references in Fairburn and Geroski (this volume).

that industry. Rather than simply measuring the outcome of the current state of competition—the firms' market shares—this involves inquiring somewhat more closely into why those market shares arise and what this entails. Do we see only a few firms each with large market share because there are extensive scale economies in production, meaning that to produce efficiently for the industry one has to be large in relation to it? Are current firms' reputations in the eyes of consumers a valuable asset which cannot readily be duplicated? If such factors are present, mergers between such competitors should not be allowed, since they have the likely effect of raising price with the consequent loss to society. That market processes might in time rectify matters through new firms entering the industry is not a suitable defence. Such adjustments take time and use up resources, and the incumbent firms will have been placed in a stronger position to defend themselves. Finally, trade-offs with decreased costs should not generally be attempted.

Vertical mergers have typically proved more difficult to evaluate. It seems clear that the only effective inquiry to pursue here is into the underlying economic effects.

These are admittedly somewhat vague criteria, and at a disadvantage to market share standards in terms of predictability. However, market shares are one step away from the problem, and in detailed examination of an industry this will become apparent. The proposed criteria also allow one to get to grips with situations in which market shares are clearly misleading. Furthermore, they are the type of factors which the Commission currently employs, as was shown in Section 3, although less emphasis is placed here on outright market dynamics.

Finally I should note that the emphasis in this section is on the proposals as a means of dealing with perceived problems with current policy—anomalies in referral decisions, uncertainty as to policy standards, etc.—rather than on the particular details of the proposals. Although they seem a feasible means of developing policy from existing arrangements, considerably more attention must yet be given to changes to the law and the institutions of policy before they could be implemented.

8

Merger Policy in the US

GEORGE HAY*

with the assistance of

ROD NYDAM†

Merger policy in the United States has undergone radical transformation during the past decade.[1] The most visible manifestation of that transformation is the large number of major horizontal acquisitions that have taken place in recent years, acquisitions that would have been regarded as unthinkable under the standards of the 1960s and 1970s, yet seem to be greeted with indifference by the present enforcement authorities.

It may be tempting to ascribe these events to politics; that is, the product of a *laissez-faire* economic policy that is likely to be reversed as soon as the current Administration leaves office. However, such a view would be mistaken. Changes in merger policy are part of a fundamental reorientation of American thinking about antitrust based on the widespread adoption of economics as the guiding principle of antitrust analysis. This is not to say that antitrust policy in general, and merger policy in particular, in a future Democratic Administration would be indistinguishable from current policy.

---

* Professor of Law and Economics, Cornell University.

† Cornell Law School 1987.

[1] The Antitrust Section of the American Bar Association has recently published an extraordinarily comprehensive analysis of merger policy, including a history of merger enforcement from the passage of the Sherman Act to the present. Many of the ideas presented in the current paper are treated in much greater detail in that monograph. The reader interested in further detail is urged to consult it. See *Horizontal Mergers: Law and Policy*, ABA Antitrust Section, Monograph 12 (1986). The present paper focuses on horizontal mergers. Efforts to apply the antitrust laws to conglomerate mergers were abandoned more than a decade ago, and vertical mergers are thought to raise competitive concerns only in the most extraordinary circumstances.

However, it is highly unlikely that the United States will return to the restrictive merger policy of the 1960s and early 1970s, no matter which party is in charge of antitrust enforcement.

While all aspects of antitrust have been affected by the increased emphasis on economic analysis, the impact on merger policy has been especially significant. There are two reasons. The first is that economists' thinking about the links between industrial concentration and the danger of monopolistic pricing has itself undergone considerable transformation. It is no longer the prevailing view that increased concentration in an industry necessarily raises substantial concerns that the industry will be able to exact supranormal profits. Whether or not one shares this relaxed attitude about the dangers of concentration, there is no dispute that the current thinking has direct and obvious consequences for merger policy.

The second reason that merger policy has been particularly influenced by the increased reliance on economic analysis is that, from a procedural perspective, merger policy is carried out differently from most other branches of antitrust. American antitrust is conducted primarily in what can be called the judicial mode; that is, as a general rule, antitrust activity gets underway when a plaintiff files a lawsuit against a defendant. The plaintiff in an American antitrust action may be the federal government; both the Justice Department and the Federal Trade Commission have jurisdiction to enforce the antitrust laws. (Congress, which favoured competition among business entities, apparently also favoured competition among federal agencies in enforcing the law.) However, by far the majority of American antitrust cases are filed by private plaintiffs, typically a competitor or a dealer of the defendant firm or firms. Indeed, in most years, the federal government has accounted for less than 10 per cent of all antitrust cases filed in federal courts.

As a consequence, the attitude of the Justice Department (or the Federal Trade Commission), however strongly committed to economic analysis as the guiding principle of antitrust and to economic efficiency as the sole or, at least, most important goal of antitrust, has at best only a limited impact on the bulk of antitrust activity. Private plaintiffs need be motivated by nothing more than the prospect of monetary damages (which are automatically trebled in the American system), and changes in the general thinking about the proper goals of antitrust or the proper way to analyse an alleged infraction are relevant only in so far as they affect the private plaintiff's likelihood of success.

This would be of no great importance if changes in the 'conventional wisdom' about antitrust translated rather directly into the way that plaintiffs' claims are evaluated in the judicial process. But another relevant aspect of American antitrust is that any individual case is tried before one of several hundred federal judges and frequently involves a lay jury. The judge is unlikely to be a specialist in antitrust matters since, depending on the district, the typical judge may see an antitrust case only once in 3 or 4 years. The jury is even less likely to be knowledgeable about antitrust matters or even about economics, with university education being the exception, rather than the norm, for a juror. Hence, changes in the prevailing antitrust 'philosophy' work their way into the case law slowly and with great diversity; and so long as the case law is in flux, plaintiffs have an incentive to challenge even conduct that virtually all economists would agree is highly unlikely to be anticompetitive.

Mergers, however, represent a pocket of antitrust in which the influence of economics has been much more direct. The reason is that, as a practical matter, merger policy is not conducted in the judicial mode. All mergers of even modest dollar amounts must be reported in advance to the Justice Department and the Federal Trade Commission (FTC).[2] While, in principle, the Justice Department can prevent a merger only by filing an antitrust case and going through the normal judicial process, in fact if the Justice Department announces its intention to challenge a proposed merger, in almost all cases the parties to the transaction will either call it off or restructure the transaction to obtain Justice Department blessing, since it is generally impractical for the acquiring firm to hold an offer open for the time it will take for the litigation process to run its full course.[3]

If, on the other hand, the Justice Department decides not to challenge the proposed transaction, there is very little threat that the merger will be thwarted by private antitrust action. A firm being acquired in a tender offer normally has no interest in blocking the transaction since its shareholders are being paid a substantial premium for their shares. Competitors will not wish to block the transaction if they think that the merger will result in higher prices and profits for the industry. If competitors claim that the industry will become more competitive, perhaps because the merger will produce efficiencies that will lead to price reductions, they will normally be

---

[2] Traditionally, the Justice Department and the Federal Trade Commission (FTC) have avoided overlapping investigations by using an informal allocation procedure in which a particular merger is assigned to one agency or the other. The assignment is usually based on a particular agency's past experience with the industry involved in the merger, although other factors such as availability of staff may play a role. For the most part, the FTC has used the same procedures and methods as the Justice Department in analysing mergers. The present paper focuses on the Justice Department, but the reader can interpret the discussion as applying to the FTC as well.

[3] If the parties attempt to proceed with the merger, the Justice Department will normally seek a preliminary injunction to prevent the merger from being consummated until a full trial is conducted. If the court denies the preliminary injunction, the parties can consummate the transaction, but then they face the burden of having to unscramble the assets if the Justice Department ultimately prevails.

denied standing to challenge the merger.[4]

The result, then, is that the key decision as far as mergers are concerned is the decision of the Justice Department whether or not to challenge the merger. Because this is essentially an administrative decision, not subject to judicial review or any of the procedures normally associated with administrative action, even radical changes in policy can be implemented very quickly. These changes may not show up in the case-law but will have a significant impact on the numbers and kinds of mergers that will be attempted. In sum, an analysis of present-day merger policy in the US is essentially a study of the decision-making process of the federal antitrust enforcement agencies. This paper attempts to present and explain that process and to assess the impact of the changes that have occurred in the past several years.

Our discussion begins with a brief attempt to place present policy in some historical context.[5] Merger policy in the US effectively began in 1950 with the passage of the Celler-Kefauver Amendment to the 1914 Clayton Act. The original Act was flawed in failing to cover mergers that took the form of asset acquisitions, and firms desiring to merge frequently found little difficulty in arranging for the transaction to fit within the loophole. The Celler-Kefauver Amendment was designed to close the loophole.

However, the congressional debate surrounding the 1950 amendment was not limited to technical considerations, but rather went to the heart of Congress's concerns about the dangers inherent in allowing business consolidations. Of course, there was discussion about the likelihood that increased concentration would lead to high prices. However, Congress also expressed concern about the fate of small businesses if consolidation were to continue, the fact that local ownership and control of resources would be transferred to managers in other parts of the country, and that the increasing concentration of industry would likewise concentrate political power in the hands of a few major corporate decision-makers, with

---

[4] A private plaintiff may sue only for 'antitrust injuries'. Hence a plaintiff in a merger case must claim that he was injured by increased market power resulting from the merger, and as a general matter will be denied standing if he claims he was injured as a result of the increased efficiency of the post-merger firm. See *Brunswick Corp. v. Pueblo Bowl-o-Mat, Inc.* 429 US 477 (1977) and, more recently, *Cargill, Inc. v. Montfort of Colorado, Inc.* 107 S. Ct. 484 (1986), in which the Court described the circumstances under which a private plaintiff can obtain an injunction against a prospective merger.

As yet unresolved by the Supreme Court is the question of whether, after the fact, a private plaintiff may sue for divestiture. The lower courts are split on this issue. Compare *CIA Petrolera Caribe Inc. v. ARCO Caribean*, 754 F.2d 404, 413–14 (1st Cir. 1985) and cases cited therein (divestiture not precluded as an equitable remedy) with *Arthur S. Langenderfer, Inc. v. S. E. Johnson Co.*, 729 F.2d 1050, 1059–60 (6th Cir. 1984) and cases cited therein (stating divestiture is not an available remedy).

[5] Much of what follows is excerpted or condensed from the ABA monograph, op. cit.

references to Nazi Germany as an example of the possible long-term consequences of such a trend.

While Congress clearly expressed the multiple goals it wanted merger policy to address, it gave little in the way of specific guidance about how the courts were to accomplish these goals in the context of evaluating a specific transaction. A merger would be illegal if the effect 'may be substantially to lessen competition or to tend to create a monopoly', with the operational details presumably left to the enforcement agencies and the courts to sort out.

Shortly after the passage of the 1950 amendment, a National Committee to Study the Antitrust Laws was set up under the direction of the Attorney General of the United States. The committee studied all aspects of antitrust enforcement, and in the area of mergers the Committee Report, issued in 1955, provided an early version of a set of merger guidelines for the courts and the enforcement agencies. The report suggested that the following market factors may be helpful in determining the competitive consequences of any particular acquisition:

(a) the character of the acquiring and the acquired company;
(b) the characteristics of the markets affected;
(c) immediate changes in the size and competitive range of the acquiring company and in the adjustments of other companies operating in the markets directly affected; and
(d) probable *long-range* differences that the acquisition may make for companies actually or potentially operating in these markets.

The report went on to discuss these factors in some detail. It did not, however, explain how any of these factors would be applied, evaluated, or balanced in a particular case.

Brown Shoe (1962) was the first merger case decided by the Supreme Court following the 1950 amendment.[6] The Court acknowledged that market share statistics, being the primary index of market power, would be an important piece of data in analysing a merger, but went on to say that 'only a further examination of the particular market—its structure, history, and probable future—can provide the appropriate setting for judging the probable anticompetitive effect of a merger'. Invoking these criteria, the Court struck down a merger between G. R. Kinney Co. and Brown Shoe Co. even though the new company would control only about 5 per cent of the market.

In the wake of *Brown Shoe*, the mid-1960s witnessed a series of government victories in merger cases involving similarly small market

---

[6] *Brown Shoe Co.* v. *United States*, 370 US 294 (1962).

shares. For example, in *United States v. Pabst Brewing Co.*[7] the Court found illegal a merger between brewers accounting for a combined 4.49 per cent of nationwide beer sales, and in *United States v. Von's Grocery*[8] the Court disallowed a merger between two grocery chains accounting for a combined 7.5 per cent of retail grocery sales in the Los Angeles, California metropolitan area. The latter decision provoked a dissent by Justice Stewart with the now famous observation that the only consistency he could find in merger litigation under the antitrust laws is that the government always wins.

At best, these decisions created great uncertainty about how a given horizontal merger would be evaluated by the enforcement agencies and the courts. At worst, the cases suggested a standard of *per se* illegality for virtually all horizontal mergers. Neither outcome was compatible with the empirical research on industrial concentration, which was interpreted to show that the main determinant of competitive behaviour in an industry was the level of concentration, and that anticompetitive effects from concentration were unlikely to be felt unless concentration exceeded certain threshold levels.

The person in charge of the Antitrust Division of the Justice Department at this time was Donald Turner who, in addition to being a distinguished lawyer, carried a PhD in economics, and was thoroughly familiar with and sympathetic to the arguments that merger policy should be less random in its application and that the proper standards should reflect the current economic wisdom, often referred to as the structure–conduct–performance paradigm. Turner's solution was to issue the 1968 Justice Department Merger Guidelines, which laid out a matrix of concentration–market share combinations, and indicated that the government would generally not challenge mergers that fell within the Guidelines. However, if the merger exceeded the threshold set out in the Guidelines, the government would be highly likely to seek to block or undo the transaction.

The 1968 Guidelines left little scope for argument once the market share threshold was exceeded. There was no suggestion that a claim of low entry barriers would be given serious consideration, and foreign competition was not even mentioned. In addition, the Guidelines made it clear that efficiencies would not in general be a defence to an otherwise anticompetitive merger.

Since the market share standards were clearly laid out in the Guidelines, and since the Department would not give serious weight to any defences that might be raised in connection with a merger that exceeded the numerical

---

[7] *United States v. Pabst Brewing Co.*, 384 US 546 (1966).

[8] *United States v. Von's Grocery Co.*, 384 US 270 (1966).

criteria of the Guidelines (one exception being a situation where the firm being acquired was likely to go bankrupt absent the merger), the only area of uncertainty was in the proper definition of the market. The Guidelines did not provide a great deal of assistance on the proper way to measure a market. Hence what little merger litigation occurred primarily involved issues of market definition. Where the government won, it did so because the court accepted the narrower of the alternative definitions that were proposed, and vice versa.

While the potential for flexibility in defining the proper market generated some uncertainty (and produced some rather bizarre markets), as a general matter the Guidelines seemed to work reasonably well. Since the Department's enforcement position was clear and the threat of private merger challenges was remote, businessmen could plan on the assumption that the Guidelines were 'the law'. (As a practical matter, the Federal Trade Commission generally followed the Justice Department criteria.) While some litigation occurred over questions of market definition or because of some uncertainty about how the Department would apply the Guidelines in unusual fact situations, the primary impact of the Guidelines is seen not in the litigated decisions, but in the mergers that could be planned because of confidence that they would survive Justice Department scrutiny, and in the many other mergers that 'didn't happen' because of the near-certainty that they would be challenged. This is a hard impact to measure with any degree of precision, but there is very little dispute among observers of merger enforcement that the Guidelines did work in this way.

Over time, however, discontent about the impact of the 1968 Guidelines began to grow. For one thing, the lack of any coherent standards for defining the proper product and geographic market eventually grew to become something of an embarrassment, as prosecutors and courts wrestled with such weighty questions as whether fresh pies were in the same market as frozen pies, and whether one could make a respectable market out of artificial Christmas trees.[9] But several other areas were seen as raising far more important problems with merger enforcement policy.

First, the confidence of economists in the earlier empirical work that purported to show a strong correlation between concentration and excess prices or profits began to erode rapidly in the wake of a stream of studies that tended either to disprove the existence of any significant relationship or to provide plausible alternative explanations with far more benign connotations. While few economists would have recommended abandoning merger enforcement altogether, the consensus seemed at least to suggest that higher thresholds of concentration would not result in large numbers of seriously anticompetitive mergers.

---

[9] Rowe (1984) p. 1528.

Second, developments in international financial markets which lowered the effective price of most imports in the United States, combined with the growing industrialization of many Far East nations, meant that whether or not foreign competition was properly ignored as generally inconsequential when the Guidelines were first implemented, that competition was a very significant reality by 1980. To measure concentration without including actual imports, or to suggest that concentration in domestic markets raised the risk of higher prices without reference to the possibility of increased imports, was no longer seen as a mere simplification of the analysis without any real consequences for the 'correct' outcome.

Third, the attitude—explicit in the 1968 Guidelines—that horizontal mergers were unlikely to yield efficiencies of any significant magnitude and that claims of efficiency could comfortably be ignored in evaluating mergers was no longer regarded as an acceptable simplification of the evaluation process. The success of the Japanese mega-corporations seemed to suggest that economies of size could be obtained well beyond the rather modest market shares that would trigger a government challenge under the Guidelines, and the inability of domestic firms to attain those efficiencies through merger placed them at a serious disadvantage to their off-shore rivals.

As these developments were coming to a head, the Reagan Administration installed Professor William Baxter of Stanford University Law School as the Assistant Attorney General for Antitrust. While Baxter did not have formal credentials as an economist, those who knew him had no doubt that he was aware of, and fully comfortable with, the new learning in economics, and that he would show no timidity in bringing that learning to bear on all aspects of antitrust enforcement, including merger evaluation.

The first fruit of Baxter's efforts was the 1982 Merger Guidelines. The Guidelines were applied economics throughout, reflecting a consumer orientation with no room for explicit consideration of social or political values, such as protecting small business or maintaining the control of corporate decision-making in local hands. The clear and dominant theme of the 1982 Guidelines was that mergers would be challenged if and only if they increased the likelihood that one or more firms would be able to maintain prices above a competitive level for a sustained period of time.

At the time the Guidelines were issued, the most readily apparent changes from the 1968 version were the substitution of the Herfindahl index[10] for the 4-firm concentration ratio as the measure of market concentration and, after converting from one measure to the other, an increase in the threshold

[10] The Herfindahl index is the sum of the squares of the market shares of each firm in the market. For a monopoly, the Herfindahl index is 10,000 (100 squared). For an industry of 10 firms each with 10 per cent of the market, the Herfindahl index is 1,000.

level of concentration for challenging mergers. The switch to the Herfindahl index, by itself, was not significant, since industries that are concentrated by one measure will almost certainly be concentrated by the other. (In technical terms, the correlation between the two measures for specific industries is very high.) Aside from having to explain to the business press why one would want to square market shares, the major impact of the switch arose from the fact that the 4-firm concentration ratio for most industries is reported in published government statistics and the Herfindahl index is not, nor can it be computed from published data, since the government does not release individual market shares. This led to a significant demand for private data sources that included estimates of individual firm market shares.

Nor was the increase in the threshold, by itself, of great consequence, partly because the 1982 threshold, after making the translation from concentration ratios to Herfindahl indices, did not represent a dramatic increase from the 1968 threshold, and partly because a modest increase in the threshold was fully consistent with the current economic thinking. Hence, while the result of the higher threshold, not surprisingly, was a mini-wave of mergers as firms took advantage of the change to arrange mergers up to the new threshold, this was not regarded with great alarm by most observers.

The most significant impact came from more subtle changes in the Guidelines. The first was the proposed methodology for defining markets and for measuring shares in those markets. The method of the 1982 Guidelines is primarily forward-looking rather than historical, organized around the key question 'what would happen if there were only a *single* seller of product X in the geographic region and he attempted to raise price above the competitive level by, say, 5 per cent?' To what extent would consumers switch to other products (that is, demand substitution); to what extent would producers of closely related products (from a supply-side perspective) be able to switch to making product X and how much would they sell; to what extent would producers of product X in other geographic regions be able profitably to ship into the sales territory of the seller who raised the price, and how many sales would they make?[11]

If on the demand side enough consumers would switch to the substitute product so that the hypothetical price increase would be unprofitable, the relevant product market is redefined to include the substitute, and market shares are measured with respect to the broader market. This approach is not at odds with the traditional methods of defining a market, but improves on those methods by making clear that the ease of substitution is not

[11] For a detailed explanation of the mechanics of the Guidelines and an illustration of how they can be applied in the context of an actual merger, see Hay and Reynolds (1984).

necessarily seen by examining existing patterns of consumer behaviour.

The approach of the 1982 Guidelines to product market definition also contributes to clearer analysis by the focus on the hypothetical single seller, thereby neatly distinguishing the issue of substitute products from that of competition among existing sellers of the product in question. In practice, this turns out to be particularly effective in getting useful answers from the businessman whose inclination, when asked about substitutes in the usual way, is to focus on existing rivals, because that is the reality he faces on a day-to-day basis. Such a response is likely to be interpreted as an admission that there are no effective substitutes for the product itself because, while customers may switch back and forth among the various sellers of the good in question as prices or other terms of sale differ among those sellers, they do not routinely turn to other products. However, when asked how many customers would be lost if he and all other producers (that is, the hypothetical monopolist) were to effect a non-transient 5 per cent price increase, the same businessman is able to imagine a much greater range of possibilities.

The methodology is different for questions of supply substitution and geographic substitution. Here, issues of market definition and market share are intermingled. Producers of related products (from a supply perspective) are awarded 'imputed' market shares based on the degree to which they would switch to the supply of product X in response to a non-transient price increase. Similarly, producers of X in different geographic regions are awarded 'imputed' market shares based on what they could profitably import into the region in question.

The Herfindahl calculations that are used to determine if the concentration threshold will be exceeded are based, not on historical market shares, but on the imputed shares that come out of the 'what if' exercise. The result of these adjustments is that markets that appear concentrated based on actual market shares may well fall below the threshold, and horizontal mergers between firms with large 'actual' shares escape condemnation.

It is important to emphasize that the traditional methodology might have led to the same result. For example, if transport costs between geographic regions were very low, the old methodology might have redefined the market to include the adjacent regions, and market shares would be measured based on overall sales or capacity. But the exercise would be a two-stage process in which the first stage would be a simple binary choice (the market is either the east coast of the US or the entire country) and, whatever is decided at the first stage, the second stage relies on actual historical sales or production capacity. Similarly, if production substitutability were relatively high, the old methodology might have redefined the market to include the substitute, but then concentration calculations would be based on actual sales or capacity of any of the products that are now 'in the market'.

But the two methodologies will not always yield the same results. If, for example, transport costs (and other costs associated with penetrating a new territory) are such that the amount of actual imports is modest and might not expand *too* much even in the face of a local price increase, the old methodology would have defined a local market and only actual historical imports would enter into the market share calculation. Under the 1982 Guidelines, all 'what if' imports will be included, thereby diluting the market shares of the local firms and possibly causing the Herfindahl index to fall below the threshold level in close cases.

The difference between the two methodologies is particularly dramatic with respect to the treatment of imports, not from other regions in the US, but from foreign countries. The 1968 Guidelines never mention the possibility of competition from foreign countries, and the discussion of geographic market definition seems to make it clear that the largest possible market is the entire US. Hence, while actual imports presumably would be counted in measuring market shares, the potential of increased imports would seem not to enter the analysis.

In contrast, the 1982 Guidelines allow specifically for the possibility of imputing market shares to potential foreign suppliers, although the Justice Department will exercise some caution in assessing the likely supply response of specific foreign firms, since they may be subject to additional constraints not present in the purely domestic context. (Changes in exchange rates, tariffs, and general political conditions are given as examples of the factors which may limit the ability of such firms to respond to domestic price increases.) Moreover, in the 1984 revision of the 1982 Guidelines (which was largely an effort to clean up some minor technical ambiguities present in the earlier version), the Department's caution about the supply response of foreign firms was substantially reduced. The consequence is that mergers of very large domestic firms in very concentrated domestic markets will be allowed if the Department believes that a small but significant increase in the domestic price will be likely to induce substantial imports.

The second source of significant change from the 1968 Guidelines is the current treatment of efficiencies for an otherwise anticompetitive merger. The 1968 Guidelines indicated that, absent exceptional circumstances, the Department would not accept the claim that a merger would produce efficiencies as a justification for deviating from the market share criteria. This reflected three interrelated notions about efficiencies:

(a) the Department's adherence to the standards will usually result in no challenge being made to mergers of the kind most likely to involve

companies operating significantly below the size necessary to achieve significant economies of scale;
(b) where substantial economies are potentially available to a firm, they can normally be realized through internal expansion; and
(c) there usually are severe difficulties in accurately establishing the existence and magnitude of economies claimed for a merger.

The hostility to an 'efficiencies defence' was carried through for the most part to the 1982 Guidelines, which indicated that:

> In the overwhelming majority of cases, the Guidelines will allow firms to achieve available efficiencies through mergers without interference from the Department. Except in extraordinary cases, the Department will not consider a claim of specific efficiencies as a mitigating factor for a merger that would otherwise be challenged. Plausible efficiencies are far easier to allege than to prove. Moreover, even if the existence of efficiencies were clear, their magnitudes would be extremely difficult to determine.

Moreover, the Guidelines indicated that, in any event, efficiencies would be considered only in resolving otherwise close cases.

However, probably because of a political flap within the government over the Department's handling of a particular steel industry merger,[12] the 1984 revisions indicate a more receptive attitude toward claims of efficiencies, stating that 'If the parties to the merger establish by clear and convincing evidence that a merger will achieve such efficiencies, the Department will consider those efficiencies in deciding whether to challenge the merger.' Moreover, the Department's contemporaneous comments about the treatment of efficiencies, as well as its handling of specific cases, makes it clear that the evaluation of efficiencies as a possible defence is no longer limited to 'close cases'. Once again, the consequence of this change in policy is that mergers between large companies in very concentrated markets might survive scrutiny, and there is certainly no doubt that many such mergers, which in all likelihood would not even have been proposed during the 1960s and at least into the late 1970s because of the certainty that they would be challenged, have been blessed by the Department under the current Guidelines.

To be clear, it is not necessarily wrong that some mergers between large firms should be allowed, either because the threat of competition (from imports or from substitution on the demand side or the supply side) renders even a large domestic firm without any significant market power, or because the efficiencies to be gained from a merger make it likely that consumers will benefit despite a significant increase in domestic

---

[12] 'Fire smoulders within administration over posture on LTV–Republic merger', 46 *Antitrust & Trade Regulation Report* No. 1156, at 502–3 (15 March 1984).

concentration. Nevertheless, experience with the 1984 Guidelines suggests several areas of concern.

The first area of concern is the standards themselves. Granted that, for reasons stated above, some large horizontal mergers ought to be allowed. But what are the proper criteria for determining when a proposed transaction falls in that category? Earlier, the point was made that after translating from the 4-firm concentration ratio to the Herfindahl index, the threshold in the 1982 and 1984 Guidelines was not that much more lenient than the 1968 threshold.

However, the 1984 Guidelines calculations are not being made with actual market shares but with imputed shares based on the 'what if' scenario, which can be radically different from historical shares. Under such circumstances, is the 1984 threshold perhaps too generous? In addition, given that the imputed shares are merely estimates of what might happen, what is the confidence interval around such estimates, and given the uncertainty inherent in the estimates, should the decision-making process be biased in favour of allowing a merger or in favour of the status quo? This will depend, of course, on the risks perceived in incorrectly blocking a desirable merger as compared with the risks in incorrectly permitting an anticompetitive merger.

A second area of concern has to do with political accountability. When the merger evaluation procedures were based on actual historical sales or market shares, with little weight being given to the possibility of a big influx of competition should prices rise, or to the possibility that efficiencies would offset the anticompetitive consequences of a large merger, it was relatively easy for outsiders (that is, those not in the Department or not parties to the specific transaction) to understand the basis for a decision not to challenge a given transaction. (The basis of a decision *to* challenge a transaction would normally become clear when the complaint was filed, unless the parties called off the transaction. However, the Department is under no obligation to disclose its reasons for *not* challenging a merger.) Under the new procedures, this is no longer the case, since the shares used in the Herfindahl calculations are imputed shares based on the staff's calculations of what would happen in response to a hypothetical price increase. In addition, if a decision is based on claimed efficiencies, there is unlikely to be any practical way for an outsider to verify that the claims are credible or that they justify the proposed merger. Indeed, an outsider cannot even tell generally whether the decision to allow the merger was based on the threat of imports, or on claimed efficiencies, or on anything else, since the Department is not obligated to reveal the basis for its decision.[13] While the potential for abuse in such a system is apparent, the

[13] As a practical matter, the Department, especially in the case of large, highly visible mergers,

solution to the problem is not obvious. Given the large numbers of transactions that the Department evaluates in a given year (most of which raise no significant competition issues), the burden of preparing a formal report on the reasons for the decision not to sue would be extremely burdensome. In addition, the reasons for the decision are not infrequently based on data that would be regarded as highly confidential by the parties to the transaction or other parties who might have supplied data to the Department during the course of the inquiry. Finally, there may be more broadly-based philosophical objections to requiring the prosecutor to reveal the basis for every decision not to prosecute.

A final and related issue of concern is that the inherent flexibility in those procedures has made it extremely difficult to predict how the Department will come out on any specific transaction that is proposed. If one of the main purposes of the 1968 Guidelines was to enable businessmen to plan with confidence about how a given transaction would be received, that ability has been significantly diminished. If so, one has to ask whether the Guidelines serve any useful purpose at all except as a training manual for Justice staff.

Interestingly, as part of a broad antitrust reform package (that would, among other things, detreble damages in all but price-fixing and related cases), the Administration has proposed that the 1984 Guidelines effectively be codified as part of the Clayton Act,[14] thus requiring the courts to follow

---

frequently issues a press release indicating the general basis for its decision but, for the reasons given above, it is still difficult or impossible for the outsider to replicate the analysis and verify that the Department's decision was economically sound.

[14] The proposed Merger Modernization Act ('the Act') achieves its goals in three basic ways. First, the Act amends the first two paragraphs of section 7 to state more precisely the degree of certainty regarding anticompetitive effects that is legally required to prohibit a merger. The Act replaces the 'may be' and 'tend to' language in section 7 with the requirement that there be a 'significant probability' that a merger will be harmful before it will be prohibited. It makes clear that section 7 is not intended to prohibit mergers on the mere possibility, rather than the significant probability, that anticompetitive effects will follow.

Second, the Act makes clear that section 7 is directed against mergers that 'substantially increase the ability to exercise market power'. Market power is defined in the Act as 'the ability of one or more firms profitably to maintain prices above competitive levels for a significant period of time'. The Act thus affirms that section 7 is intended to preserve competition, rather than competitors *per se*. It does so by focusing merger analysis on the increased ability of firms to raise prices to consumers as a consequence of a merger, and away from the mere fact that one or more firms will be eliminated from the market by acquisition.

Third, the Act establishes a sound framework for determining the likely effects of mergers by clearly directing courts to consider the important economic factors that bear on that analysis, and identifies a specific list of factors derived from the Guidelines (including foreign competition and efficiencies) that the courts should take into account.

For a complete presentation of the proposals, see 50 *Antitrust & Trade Regulation Report* No. 1253 (Special Supplement, 20 February 1986).

the Guidelines' approach in deciding merger cases. While this would undoubtedly influence how the courts analysed and decided cases, the overall impact would be confined since, as discussed, relatively few mergers actually reach litigation.

Hence the real significance of the codification may be to bind future administrations in their administrative decision-making process. Whether this is good or not depends on one's degree of satisfaction with the Guidelines. This paper has not attempted to give a final evaluation. At this point, all that can be said is that the new Guidelines have opened up issues that require further discussion, not only in the United States, but in any community that is evaluating how its enforcement or investigatory agent will handle mergers.

9

Merger Policy: Current Policy Concerns

SIR GORDON BORRIE, QC*

On 5 June 1986 the Secretary of State for Trade and Industry announced a review of law and policy on mergers and restrictive trade practices. Mr Channon said that he intended the review to investigate 'both the scope for changes in policy under existing legislation and the desirability of changes in the law'. He called for wide public debate and invited all interested persons to send their views to his Department.

It is necessary for me first to explain the existing framework of law and policy, my own statutory role, and some of the necessary implications of that framework. Although merger controls have operated for more than 20 years and the Director General of Fair Trading has played a part in those procedures since 1973 when the Office of Fair Trading was established, I still encounter a good deal of misunderstanding about how the law actually works.

Secondly, I shall pose some of the questions that I would expect the government's review to address. These must start with questions of strategy—what is the underlying objective of merger policy?—before coming on to questions of procedures and powers, which have attracted perhaps disproportionate attention.

The present machinery of control will be broadly familiar to most readers. It is a play in which three distinct authorities act their three different roles. As put in the guide issued by my Office (Office of Fair Trading (1985); see also Appendix 1): 'In essence, the Secretary of State decides, the Director General advises and the [Monopolies and Mergers] Commission investigates.'

It is my job under the Fair Trading Act to keep myself informed about mergers—actual or prospective—and to advise the Secretary of State on whether a so-called 'qualifying' merger should be investigated by the

---

* Director General of Fair Trading
This contribution formed the text of an address given at the IFS conference on Merger Policy, held in London on 16 July 1986.

Commission. A qualifying merger is one where the gross assets taken over exceed £30 million or where the merged companies would constitute a monopoly as defined by statute because they will together control at least 25 per cent of the UK market. The Act does not invite me to say whether or not a merger should be allowed to take place, and it does not empower me to conduct the sort of detailed examination which under the Act falls to the Monopolies and Mergers Commission. I am supposed to screen all mergers within the size limits of the Act and to conduct a sort of initial sift so as to identify cases calling for investigation.

When a merger is referred to the Commission they then have up to 6 months (extendable by not more than 3 months) for conducting their investigation. They must report to the Secretary of State whether or not they consider that the merger would operate against the public interest: the Act gives a number of pointers but requires the Commission to take into account anything they consider relevant to the public interest.

The Fair Trading Act has been properly described as essentially benevolent towards mergers. Firms under investigation do not have to demonstrate that a merger will be positively beneficial. On a recent case, the Commission said in so many words: 'We discern no material advantages to the public interest arising from the proposed merger; but the question before us is whether the merger may be expected to operate against the public interest and in our view there are not sufficient grounds for such an expectation.' (*Scottish & Newcastle Breweries/Matthew Brown*, para. 7.31.) And the Commission has set itself a high threshold of proof. In another well-known case it expressed it thus:

> The question . . . is not merely whether there is a possibility that the merger will operate against the public interest. If only a possibility were required, hardly any merger would ever be allowed to proceed . . . The question is whether the evidence creates an expectation . . . To put the matter colloquially . . . not 'This may happen' but 'We expect that this will happen'. (*Berisford/British Sugar*, para. 9.40)

It is only where the Commission finds by this test that a merger would operate against the public interest that the Secretary of State has powers to prohibit it or to impose conditions. If the Commission finds that a merger would not operate against the public interest, that is the end of the story. In other words, on a scale ranging from total *laissez-faire* to total regulation, our procedures fall very much nearer the first pole than the second.

There has been an unprecedentedly high level of merger activity over the last 9 or 10 months. In my Office, we have been dealing with more mergers, we have been dealing with bigger mergers, and we have been dealing with mergers that present more intricate questions. In the first 6 months of 1986, my staff examined 165 cases which technically qualified by size or market share for reference to the Commission, together with a number of cases which were found on investigation to fall outside the Act. That is an annual rate of more than 300 qualifying merger cases, compared with 192 which were dealt with in 1985, an increase of 50 per cent. A more significant fact is that within the totals, the number of those more complex cases which call for discussion in the interdepartmental Merger Panel is running at twice the rate of 1985. So far this year, the Secretary of State on my advice has made 10 references to the Commission (see Appendix 2).

At the mechanical level, the procedures have stood up pretty well. There is a general and understandable concern with timing, and sometimes invidious comparisons have been drawn between the time taken in the British system to determine a case and the allegedly speedier procedures in the USA. The facts do not bear this out. The great majority of mergers under the Act are cleared as a result of the initial sift in my Office. The time this takes will depend almost entirely on the date at which the firms provide full information. Once that is available, it would be most unusual for a case to take longer than 3 or 4 weeks. As for the handful of cases which go to the Commission, the time limit of 6 months (or exceptionally the statutory maximum of 9 months) compares more than favourably with the time taken under other jurisdictions. Under US law, for example, the authorities have an initial 30 days within which to decide whether to challenge a notified merger. But this period can be extended if the authorities request further information. If they then make an order or file a suit to prohibit the merger, the proceedings can be protracted, particularly if the initial decision is appealed to higher courts.

In regard to the handful of cases that go to our Monopolies and Mergers Commission, one must not overlook a very obvious point—the trade-off between the two important factors of speed and fairness. Six months may be too long—9 months almost certainly is, save for the most exceptional case—but it must be borne in mind that the duration is very largely a manifestation of firms' wishes to put their cases as well as they can and to know the case they have to answer. At this stage, the lawyers have taken over, which perhaps does not help. But if any public authority is to give soundly based advice on critical and probably irreversible matters of company ownership, then it needs facts on which to assess difficult questions about market definition and to probe easy assertions about such buzz words as efficiency, synergy, and competitiveness. I am not at this point expressing any view on whether such questions should be determined by a public authority rather than by the market or, if so, whether the present institutions are the best for doing so. I simply point out that if society and Parliament decide that a public authority should be involved, then the question of speed is intimately involved both with the question of fairness and with the question of obtaining information.

The issue of timing assumed particular importance in relation to some important mergers earlier this year because of one complication. For various reasons, the British system and our efficient capital markets make it easy to mount hostile take-over bids which appeal over the heads of the board to the proprietors of the company—the shareholders. The hostile bid is not infrequently associated with the contested bid in which two potential acquirers get into a sort of auction. The tactical handling of bids—the attack, the defence, the out-manoeuvring of a rival—has become a highly sophisticated art form in which timing plays an important part. Immense sums of money are at stake and the play is getting dirtier. Each side is likely to play the monopoly card and lobby for a reference to the Commission if it is defending, or vice versa. The City authorities have laid down detailed requirements in their Code for the various stages of a take-over about what each side is free to do in the way of releasing information and so on, with the object of achieving fair and equal treatment for shareholders. Against this background, even the timing of the Secretary of State's announcement about a reference may be vitally important, and there may be pressures on my Office to accelerate—or sometimes decelerate—according to where the tactical advantage lies. The principle that I follow is to do my job as well as I can; that is, to advise the Secretary of State as soon as I have the necessary information. If there is the likelihood of a reference, then I naturally do not want the merger to take place before a reference is made because of the difficulty of unscrambling it should the Commission condemn it. Beyond this, I do not gear my advice to the timing that may be convenient to the parties.

So much for the present task. Now, why is it that there are underlying concerns about merger control, and what are the issues that I would expect the Secretary of State's review to address?

I began by saying that the first set of questions are strategic, and that means they are essentially a matter for political decision. What is the object of intervention? What is the assumption behind any mergers policy? Only then can one sensibly go on to answer the question of whether the present approach is too weak, too strong, or whether we could make the procedure more effective in achieving the objective.

As to the objective, doubts that have been aired in recent months are not all pulling in the same direction. I have said that present powers and procedures can be characterized as benign and minimalist. Although 10 merger investigations in 6 months is high by historical standards, the great majority of transactions go through unimpeded. Furthermore the law is entirely reactive. The procedures were never intended to stand in for the sort of policies that involve powers for a positive manipulative approach to sectors of industry, the approach of an industrial policy in which public authorities plan to achieve a particular optimum structure. Neither I nor the Commission is asked to say whether some alternative solution might be preferable to the proposal actually before us. The aim is merely to identify and stop the positively detrimental, and otherwise let markets and proprietors decide. Similarly, the system is not apt for examining structural and sectoral changes that go beyond the effect of the particular merger on the table. My Office is sometimes asked to consider the domino argument—that the particular merger may be acceptable but will open the floodgates to others which in aggregate would produce an unacceptable level of concentration. As the law stands, I believe this to be irrelevant.

Without going quite to the lengths of seeking to assimilate merger controls to a National Plan, I have the impression that a number of people rather hanker after a system that puts higher barriers in the way of merging firms. They argue that, in some ways, it is now too easy to merge, and indeed the economic evidence suggests that many mergers are a failure. This would seem to point to some legislative change in the burden of proof and a greater number of merger proposals being put under the searchlight of investigation before being allowed to proceed.

Similarly, there has been concern at the short-term view which, it has been said, has boosted many recent take-over bids and mergers. Fuelled by the rise in stock market prices, bidding companies are said to have diverted expenditure from investment in fixed assets or research and development (R & D), to expenditure on acquisitions. It is argued that this is done because of the quicker return, while target companies—even potential target companies—have had to find ways of improving their share prices in the short term, say by cutting back their investment or R & D. In the course of the review, consideration will no doubt be given to this concern, and to any evidence which may support it. Even if there is some substance in it, remedies would be difficult to devise. To take the criticism to its logical conclusion would be to prevent one of the major potential benefits of take-overs, mergers, and the threat of take-overs—a discipline on inefficient management.

Most governments in developed countries feel the need for some power to intervene in relation to mergers. Let us assume therefore that our own review will not lead to the radical conclusion that in the United Kingdom there are never grounds for government to interfere with the decisions of proprietors reached in the market-place. The next question is, what are the grounds for intervention? At present we are operating under the minimalist law which I have summarized and under a policy enunciated in 1984 by Mr Norman Tebbit, who said that he would intervene 'primarily on competition grounds'. I have a number of statutory responsibilities for promoting competition, so I am naturally in favour of a policy of intervention where a merger may significantly restrict competition.

Competition ensures that markets work efficiently. The objective of a competition-based mergers policy is to promote the effective working of markets where, without intervention, the merging firms would be able to exploit in some way or another their market power. There may be reasons why a merger that is in the commercial interests of the bidding company may need to be questioned on public interest grounds other than a reduction in competition, but under current policy such cases are likely to be exceptional. Since Mr Tebbit's statement, I have advised him or his successors as Secretaries of State for Trade and Industry to send 16 mergers to the Commission (see Appendix 2). In all but 4 cases, the main reason for my advice was the likelihood that the merger would restrict competition in the UK.

However, I am aware that some observers are unhappy with what they perceive to be certain consequences of this stress in legislation and policy on the promotion of competition in the UK. One of these criticisms I can dismiss quite briefly. Some have suggested that it entails too narrow a view of the appropriate market and that the UK market should no longer be regarded as distinct from the European Community or even the world. But I think such critics are simply confusing the legal test in the Act (control of 25 per cent of a UK market is a monopoly) with the judgemental question of whether a merger would in fact confer market power. When evaluating a merger (both to establish whether it qualifies for investigation and to assess the effects on competition in the UK market) I do consider, and always have considered, imports into the UK market, both actual and potential. So I do not think there is much new in this point for the review. But I should just add that it is simply not the case that all UK markets are now just part of a larger geographical market. In some cases we are dealing with goods and services that are not traded, and recent merger investigations by the Commission have dealt with such sectors as laundries, retail distribution, building materials, and public houses. Even where manufactured goods are concerned, there can be non-tariff barriers to trade ranging from customer preference to tacit procurement policies.

A more difficult question arises when firms proposing a merger concede that there is some risk of restricting competition in the home market, but point to the benefit expected to accrue from the creation of a firm big enough—they say—to compete in international markets with the giants of other developed countries. The CBI (Confederation of British Industry) has stated that the primary issue for British competition policy is that it should promote the international competitiveness of British firms—an apparently simple statement which wraps up many important but complex economic arguments. A similar argument was raised in relation to a merger proposal recently reported on by the Commission (*GEC/Plessey*). Is it true that the present UK approach gives insufficient weight to the need to create large firms that can meet the R & D and other requirements to compete internationally with their opposite numbers from the USA and Japan? I wonder whether our leading industrialists would really be deterred from pursuing what they considered an important merger, in international trade terms, by the prospect of an investigation; Lord Weinstock has shown that he was not. However, if it were indeed the case that desirable restructuring schemes were being deterred by national laws and procedures, then this would clearly be a matter for consideration in any review.

The argument for scale cannot be accepted uncritically. There is no general correlation between size and export performance. Some giant firms have proved a positive disaster. There are no doubt some circumstances in which size brings quantifiable economies of scale and efficiencies, and the question then may be whether such potential gains should outweigh the risk of monopoly abuse.

Mr Tebbit's statement explicitly recognized the need both to maintain competition at home and to improve competitiveness overseas. The number of cases in which these two objectives conflict is likely to be small. When they arise, they will be critical to our economic performance. How should the conflict be resolved? Under the present legal framework, they should be resolved by the Commission. The intention is that the Commission is to hear the evidence and advise the government. In all probability, the Commission will have to weigh a number of conflicting factors: yes, the merger might restrict competition in the UK market, but against that will be alleged economies of scale and an increase in competitiveness in export markets; yes, the merger might raise prices to consumers, but it is claimed to be the only way to save jobs in an area of high unemployment. The identification of these factors, attributing weight to them, and reaching a judgement on the balance of advantage is the job of the Commission. So where I consider that there is a serious case to answer, I recommend the Secretary of State to invite the Commission to investigate; in other words, to make a reference.

Some observers have suggested that Mr Tebbit's policy statement introduced a bias in favour of conglomerate mergers which is not self-evidently in the public interest. Has life now become somewhat easier for conglomerates, since they can assume from mergers policy of recent years that they face no problems with the authorities? And if so, does it matter? No doubt this is another family of issues for the review.

The point attracted some debate in the early months of the year as part of the issue of so-called 'even-handedness'. When two companies were battling for the same target, was it right that one potential merger should be referred to the Commission when the other was not? In two cases I advised that this should happen. I have heard it suggested that such a decision is unfair to the shareholders. That argument leaves me unmoved, if only because every act of intervention must inevitably involve some interference with proprietorial rights. A more serious argument, which I concede, is that a single reference in the circumstances of a contested bid could mean that a potentially advantageous merger simply does not happen.

There is some such risk in relation to any merger reference. There is, of course, no compulsion on bidders to go through with the Commission's inquiry, and the record shows that about 1 in 3 will drop out at that stage. Of the 10 references so far this year that I mentioned, only 6 have led to a full investigation. In the 4 other cases, the bidder has abandoned or reorganized his plans and the reference has been set aside (see Appendix 2). But the special feature of a contested bid situation is that the referred bidder may not have the option to continue even if he wants to. The shareholders of the target company will often prefer to grasp the bird in the hand and accept an offer that does not entail waiting for the Commission's verdict. In such circumstances, the initial decision to investigate, and thus my own advice, must unavoidably have larger consequences than the legislators envisaged. This has been an unintended result and perhaps a complication of the policy of basing references primarily on competition.

The problem as I see it has nothing to do with fairness or unfairness to shareholders. Indeed it could be argued that a reference when there is another bidder in the wings is less unfair to shareholders than when they have nowhere else to go. The problem is that the contemporary contested bid is a particular and extreme example of the more general fact that during the time it takes to investigate a merger proposal, other things will change. We cannot freeze the status quo so as to guarantee that the parties will have the same options open to them if the Commission clears one of the proposals. There have been cases where a target firm has been acquired by a third party while an earlier bid was under investigation.

Although such cases are few and far between, I would expect the review to consider the present procedural and institutional framework to see if there is any scope for speeding things up. If there is to be intervention at all, it cannot be entirely painless. Could it be quicker or cheaper or more predictable? I am not at all certain that the answer is yes, but it is important that the options be explored. If speed is to be the overriding priority, then perhaps we shall have to consider such radical procedural changes as the compulsory pre-notification of mergers to the authorities so that the essential supporting information is available more quickly.

It will be clear that some developments on the take-over scene have tended to impose new burdens on my own Office. Bidders are desperately anxious to avoid an investigation by the Commission. It is frequently suggested to me that I am competent to take a rounded view of the merger and should therefore refrain from recommending a reference because the benefits so clearly outweigh the detriments. Indeed, I was recently asked by the chairman of a firm involved in a reference why my staff had not continued our dialogue with his company until our concerns had been allayed. I had to explain that I had neither the powers nor the resources to act as a substitute for the Commission. Of course, I am prepared within reason to consider obvious factors which indicate that, although a merger will bring about a high market share, this cannot in fact confer market power or lend itself to abuse. I have already said that I look at competition—and potential competition—from imports as part of my examination of how far the market is 'contestable'. In the same way, I will consider arguments that falling demand, over-capacity, or buyer power will constrain a monopolist. But I cannot take this very far within the time scales of the present institutional framework. And I do not think it is currently feasible to go beyond this into the complex and difficult question of whether an anticompetitive merger is nevertheless necessary because it would improve 'the competitive position of United Kingdom companies in overseas markets' (Mr Tebbit's words). This is indeed a very important question, but it is rarely easy to answer. Under the Fair Trading Act, the proper agency for advising government on it is the Commission, and I am not entitled to usurp its function. It may be that the Secretary of State's review will need to consider this division of power and responsibilities between my Office and the Commission.

I turn to another recent development—the emergence of what might be described as plea bargaining. Firms that think a merger in one shape might present problems will offer a modification instead. This occurred in relation to schemes involving Distillers and Imperial Group. In each case, a bid was referred to the Commission and a merger proposal was thus stopped in its tracks. In each case the bidder—Guinness in one case, United Biscuits in the other—abandoned its first scheme, enabling the Commission to lay the investigation aside. The second scheme was framed in a way which very much modified the anticompetitive features of the first. More recently, Dixons announced an eventually unsuccessful bid for Woolworth and made a similar move. Dixons made it publicly known that if it succeeded, it would not propose to retain Woolworth's Comet chain—the area of the business that raised obvious competition problems. In all these cases, my Office had to consider how tightly these divestment schemes were constructed and the situation that would obtain if they were carried through.

Personally I have found no great difficulty in principle in examining a contingent scheme of this nature on its merits—indeed, I have little alternative as the law stands. I may have to look at two mergers instead of one, and I have to decide how far I can be satisfied that the proposed scheme will stick. Some people have argued that tactics of this sort are intrinsically undesirable and should not be allowed to succeed; in other words, that the mergers should be referred to the Commission as a sort of sanction. I question this on grounds both of law and of policy. If a bidder can in fact construct a scheme in a way that preserves more rather than less competition, what is wrong with that? One objection, perhaps, is that divestment schemes cobbled together in haste might not in fact be conducive to the efficiency of the underlying business. But this is not necessarily the case. In the three cases I have mentioned, I was able to advise the Secretary of State that neither the main merger nor the consequential hiving-off seemed to require examination by the Commission.

Perhaps this is the point at which to repeat that I reject the argument that a bidding company with an outstanding export record should receive special treatment—in other words, its acquisitions should not be investigated despite the fact that they appeared to restrict competition significantly. At the other end of the scale, I would not advise an investigation into a scheme which on merits seemed to pose no problems simply because I wanted to demonstrate disapprobation of the people or tactics involved. In advising on references, I do not regard myself as awarding a Good Conduct Prize or imposing a Bad Order Mark. The intention and words of the Fair Trading Act seem to me to be adequately clear. The object is to obtain an expert and objective analysis of the intrinsic effect of a particular structural change as a basis, if necessary, for intervention to stop it.

From all this, I think it will be clear that the Secretary of State's policy review is going to have to address a wide range of interlocking questions. It must start from the most fundamental—should government intervene? Assuming the answer to be yes or sometimes, it must go on to questions of who, how, when, and why. There is the question of the basic rationale for interfering at all with commercial decisions. Does this go beyond the need to stop monopolistic or anticompetitive mergers; in other words, is British merger policy merely one arm of competition policy, or are there other policy objectives? Some jurisdictions have their own separate institutions for considering questions of foreign ownership. Here they can be considered, if at all, only by so-called 'competition authorities' (leaving aside an unused provision (Chapter 68) in the Industry Act 1975).

In anything short of a totally *laissez-faire* policy, there will need to be procedures and agencies to apply the law. A thorough review must thus address questions of timing, of fairness, of the onus of proof, of the distribution of duties between different agencies, and of their powers. There are doubtless respects in which the present law might be improved. Nevertheless I would like to conclude by drawing attention to one impressive and positive characteristic—the immense flexibility it has shown over 20 years to accommodate changes in government policy and in the external environment.

Ultimately many of the questions I have posed are political questions, the answers to which are likely to reflect a particular political philosophy. The government's review will be addressing questions that are fundamental to the competitiveness of the economy, but to which there may be no very obvious or conclusive answers. That is not an unusual situation in politics or in life. In my own non-political capacity as Director General of Fair Trading, I shall continue to do my job under the existing law in the spirit in which I have described it. I shall await with great interest any restatement of government policy. I shall also wait—for obvious reasons, this wait is likely to be rather longer—for any amendments that may be proposed to the Fair Trading Act that would affect my statutory duties. Whatever changes there are, I trust that they will enhance the possibilities of promoting a vigorous competitive economy.

Appendix 1

The following extracts from the Office of Fair Trading booklet, *Mergers: A Guide to Procedures under the Fair Trading Act 1973*, are Crown copyright and are reproduced by permission of the Controller of Her Majesty's Stationery Office.

EXAMINATION OF MERGERS BY THE OFFICE OF FAIR TRADING

1 This chapter [of the Guide] describes the Office's approach to mergers, sets out the kind of questions which parties to a merger are likely to be asked by the Office and considers the factors taken into account before the Director General tenders his advice.

2 The assumption which underlies the merger provisions is that significant mergers may have economic, social or other effects which go beyond the interests of the shareholders in the merging enterprises and merit examination on the grounds of public interest. The parties do not have to demonstrate that their merger is positively beneficial, merely that it is not likely to be against the public interest. There is no presumption that mergers, as such, are undesirable.

Initial inquiry

3 The initial inquiry carried out by the Office is to establish whether there are doubts about the likely impact of a merger on the public interest which may require detailed independent investigation by the Commission. Each case is looked at on its merits, and no two mergers are identical in all their characteristics. The Office is not an adjudicating body and is not equipped to carry out the sort of in-depth investigation which the Commission can. The Office's job at this stage is to consider aspects in which a merger *might* be detrimental. If there appear to be substantial drawbacks, or if there are genuine doubts about possible drawbacks, it is for the Commission to consider their significance, whether they are outweighed by other positive and beneficial aspects of the merger, and whether the merger as a whole is likely to operate against the public interest.

4 Section 84 requires the Commission to consider whether a merger operates or may operate against the public interest by reference to all matters which appear to them to be relevant and, in particular, by reference to five specific matters, the desirability of:

(a) maintaining and promoting effective competition;
(b) promoting the interests of consumers, purchasers and other users of goods and services in respect of prices, quality and variety of goods and services supplied;
(c) promoting, through competition, reduction of costs, development and use of new techniques and new products and facilitating the entry of new competitors into existing markets;
(d) maintaining and promoting the balanced distribution of industry and employment; and
(e) maintaining and promoting competitive activity in overseas markets.

5 This statutory guidance is not addressed to the Director General, and the Act does not specify the matters to which he has to have regard in advising the Secretary of State under section 76. In carrying out its preliminary evaluation, the Office will nonetheless have regard to the pointers given to the Commission since these may be relevant to the case for reference. It is not possible to publish a few simple rules from which it can automatically be determined whether or not a particular merger will be referred. For example, there is no particular level of market share above which mergers are *certain* to be referred to the Commission.

6 In July 1984, the then Secretary of State announced the results of a review of mergers policy. His statement reaffirmed his intention to make references primarily on competition grounds as part of the Government's general policy of promoting competition within the economy. . . . When the Director General considers his advice to the Secretary of State on a particular merger he naturally takes account of any such statements of the Government's policies.

7 The paragraphs which follow illustrate the matters which are taken into account before the Director General gives advice.

Basic questions

8 The Office addresses two basic questions: 'Does the merger come within the scope of the Act?' (a question of law); and, if so, 'Are there sufficient reasons for seeking an investigation by the Commission?' (a question of judgment). As indicated in paragraph 6 it is concerned in particular with the effects of the merger on competition within the United Kingdom.

Does the merger come within the scope of the Act?

9 The Office first has to decide whether the merger meets the legal definition of a 'merger situation qualifying for investigation' as described in chapter 1 [of the Guide]—for example whether at least one of the enterprises involved in the merger is carried on in the United Kingdom or by or under the control of a body corporate incorporated in the United Kingdom and whether the merger satisfies the size of

assets or share of market criteria. Relevant questions are:

(a) what are the gross assets of the enterprise being taken over or in which an interest is being acquired? As a preliminary step the Office examines the audited accounts as shown in the latest annual reports and accounts of the target company (see paragraph 20 of chapter 1 [of the Guide]);
(b) do the enterprises involved supply or consume similar goods or services and, if so, will they account between them for a quarter or more of the market in the United Kingdom or any substantial part of it? For this the Office normally needs:
i statistics by value or volume of the market in the United Kingdom for each significant category of products which *both* firms produce (or consume)—preferably total United Kingdom production less exports plus imports. Where these figures are not readily available in sufficient detail, the Office can proceed provisionally on the basis of the United Kingdom production figures only;
ii comparable statistics for each firm's output, exports, market share and consumption in each significant category of products. Where precise figures for the total market are not available the Office seeks informed estimates of market share, for example, on the basis of recent market surveys;
iii similar statistics in respect of substantial parts of the United Kingdom if this is relevant.

If neither of the criteria is satisfied, the Office takes no further action. If, however, the Office is satisfied that the merger appears to come within the scope of the Act, it will go on to consider the second basic question.

Are there sufficient reasons for seeking an investigation by the Commission?

10 The Office's approach to this question is not identical in each case. However, there is a general thrust which its enquiries take—beginning with a consideration of the possible effects of the merger on *competition* followed by an examination of *other aspects* of the merger.

Effects on competition

11 Mergers are conveniently classified as 'horizontal', 'vertical' or 'conglomerate', though features of each may be found in many mergers. Mergers between two or more companies producing *similar* goods or services are classed as horizontal. Vertical mergers occur where a company takes over an actual or potential supplier or customer. A merger of two companies which supply unrelated goods and/or services is described as a conglomerate merger. Many large diversified companies operate in the United Kingdom and it is inevitable that many mergers will contain a mixture of horizontal, vertical and conglomerate elements. The nature of the issues which arise, and thus the questions to which the Office will seek answers, will largely depend on the degree to which each of these elements arises.

12 Horizontal mergers can have a direct effect on competition. The Office looks carefully at mergers which may significantly reduce competition in this way,

regardless of the size of the companies or of the markets in which they operate. The Office is likely to be particularly concerned about mergers in a market where one or both of the companies are leading producers, or where there are already a relatively small number of producers. In examining the competitive effects of such mergers, the Office takes account of the degree to which there are substitutes for the product in question, the presence or absence of competition from imports, the extent to which the producers' customers (or suppliers) possess buying (or selling) power, and the ease with which new competitors can enter the market. The Office will not accept at face value the assertion that a market is contestable or is open to potential competition from imports, but will invite those advancing such arguments to substantiate them.

13 Vertical mergers require the Office to consider the risk that opportunities for competitors at either level will be foreclosed. For example, a supplier company which took over one of its customers might be in a position thereafter to require that company to make all its purchases from within the group. Competing suppliers might find themselves excluded from part of their actual or potential market. Moreover, a large integrated corporate organisation might be in a sufficiently powerful position to discriminate in price and availability of supplies in favour of companies within the group, which would thereby have an advantage in competing with companies outside the group. The Office similarly considers the possible effects of a merger in relation to increases in the buying power of the merged companies as purchasers of raw materials or components.

14 Conglomerate mergers have no direct effect on competition. Nevertheless, it is sometimes held that large diversified groups can behave in ways which may have detrimental effects on competition; for example, they may be able to cross-subsidise one activity from the revenue generated by another and thereby restrict or suppress the competition they face from more specialised enterprises. In addition, there may be a risk that investment decisions within a group may not be subject to the same criteria as they would be if capital had been raised externally—in other words, the discipline of the market may not operate. A large conglomerate may be under less pressure to innovate and to compete aggressively in selling its product. There is also a risk—to which the Commission have drawn attention in some of their reports—that information about the performance of its several parts will be lost to the market.

15 The Office will already have been provided with sales information (see paragraph 9). The statistics requested in paragraph 9 will provide some of the basic information that the Office requires in considering the above issues. Annex 4 [of the Guide] outlines further questions which the Office will normally seek to pursue. It is of assistance to the Office, and helps to speed up the consideration of a merger, if firms are able to provide answers to these questions, preferably in advance of any meeting with the Office.

Efficiency

16 The parties to mergers often contemplate an amalgamation because they believe

that the merged company will be more efficient than the two companies run separately. For example, longer production runs may be possible, resulting from rationalisation of plants serving the same geographical area. The Office is always prepared to take account of the efficiency gains from a merger but it is difficult to do so if they cannot be quantified. It appreciates, however, that it is sometimes difficult for companies to be precise about possible savings before a merger takes place. Equally, it is often difficult for the Office to evaluate fully the efficiency arguments in the brief time available for the initial scrutiny. In cases where a significant adverse effect on competition seems likely, the Director General may therefore recommend to the Secretary of State that a merger should be referred to the Commission for a more thorough investigation of the balance between the efficiency and competition effects.

Employment and regional considerations

17 If a merger (or a failure to merge) seems likely to lead to significant decrease in employment—particularly if it is regionally concentrated or expected to be sudden—the Director General will comment on this in giving his advice to the Secretary of State. He will need to be reasonably certain that the effect on employment is not due to some other cause. Existing patterns of employment cannot remain unaltered regardless of changes in the market or in industry itself.

International competitiveness

18 A merger which promotes exports or contributes to import substitution may have a favourable effect on the balance of payments. If this arises from enhanced international competitiveness resulting from the merger it will be considered by the Office when the efficiency gains are evaluated. If the benefits arise from other sources—improved access by one of the companies to overseas marketing networks, for example—these too will be evaluated by the Office. A merger which reduces competition in the United Kingdom may be justified in public interest terms from a strengthening of an industry's international competitiveness. In a case where the effect on competition is likely to be significant it may be felt that investigation by the Commission is the best means of ascertaining how the two effects weigh in the balance.

Foreign ownership

19 It is government policy to welcome inward investment and in normal cases the nationality of the new owners (foreign or British) is immaterial. However, there could be exceptional cases where foreign ownership might affect the public interest—for example, in relation to a sector of strategic importance or in cases where the nationality of the owner might affect export prospects. Such points would need to be considered.

Failing firms

20 The Office is sometimes told that a merger is a rescue operation. It may be intended to deal with over-capacity in an industry. A company may argue that it can no longer survive independently and that the only way to keep the business alive is to sell out to a competitor. The Office may be told that the case is so urgent that an investigation by the Commission would entail closures and loss of jobs. The Office will consider such arguments on their merits, but it should not be assumed that they automatically displace the working assumption that it is for the Commission to evaluate mergers which restrict competition. In such cases the Director General will seek to advise the Secretary of State on the practical effects which a reference could be expected to achieve—particularly in terms of competition and of employment. Firms advancing the failing firm argument will be invited to substantiate it.

Other considerations

21 In order to get a full picture of the merger and its attendant circumstances, the Office will seek the following information:

(a) a description of the transaction and any related arrangements;
(b) a description of the business of the parties (including their position within a group structure), financial information, the location of their places of business, the number of their employees, their export performance and markets, their ownership and shareholding structure, and their management and control practices (much of this will normally be obtainable from the company reports and accounts). In this context it should be noted that irrespective of the formalitics of a merger the Office normally regards an acquisition as being made by the ultimate parent of a group;
(c) the reasons for the merger, and the plans of the acquirer for the target enterprise;
(d) the views of the target enterprise; and
(e) the expected effects of the merger on the industry involved and the public interest. In the case of a contested merger the views of the acquirer and target enterprise on this may differ.

22 The purpose of seeking this information is to allow the Office to set the merger in its proper context, and to ensure that a balanced view can be taken of all its aspects. The Director General can then make a recommendation to the Secretary of State which takes into account not only the likely effect of the merger on competition but any other considerations which may have a bearing on the public interest.

Timing

23 The Office will also need to know the timetable which the parties have in mind for the completion of the merger or, in the case of an already completed transaction, the date on which it took place. Every effort is made to deal with cases promptly so as to avoid disrupting the parties' arrangements but the Director General's primary duty is to obtain the information he needs to give considered advice. As a rough guide, a case can be expected to take about a month from the time the Office has been given

all the necessary material information. Cases are not, however, necessarily dealt with in rotation, and urgent ones will be given priority. For instance, public offers for shares, where it is desirable for a decision to be made before the first closing date, or schemes of arrangement, involving a legal timetable, are likely to be given priority over private transactions or confidential guidance cases, where arrangements are more flexible. Contentious cases, or those which give rise to a number of new and/or significant issues, may take longer.

INFORMATION SOUGHT BY THE OFFICE IN ASSESSING MERGERS

This note indicates the information that the Office of Fair Trading seeks from companies in assessing the impact of a merger on competition. It is helpful if the information is made available before any meeting which might be held with the companies involved and if the source of data is indicated where appropriate.

General

1 Two copies of both companies' (and relevant subsidiaries') latest annual report and accounts.

2 The value of sales and the total annual value of the United Kingdom market for each product (goods or services) where either company accounts for 10 per cent or more of United Kingdom sales.

3 The nature and extent of any vertical links between the companies involved in the merger.

For each *United Kingdom product market where the activities of the merged companies overlap the following information is also sought*

4 The value (and, if appropriate, the volume) of the United Kingdom sales of the merging companies (and their relevant subsidiaries).

5 The annual value of the United Kingdom market.

6 If the market is served regionally, the market share breakdown in any region where the merging companies together account for 25 per cent or more of the value of sales, and an estimate of the overall value of the market in these regions.

7 The names of the significant competitors (including importers) and an estimate of their market shares.

8 Recent trends in:

(a) the total value of the market;
(b) market shares of significant competitors (including imports);
(c) market entry, market exit and other mergers;
(d) the exports of the merging companies; and
(e) total exports from the United Kingdom.

9 A description of any substitutes in terms of product characteristics and price differences.

10 If available, details of each company's profits, turnover and capital employed *in the product market* for the last three years.

11 An estimate of the capital expenditure (including research and development expenditure) which would be required to enter the market on a scale equivalent to significant competitors. An indication of the scale of expenditure on advertising and promotion required to enter the market. Information on other factors which might inhibit entry such as licensing or patent restrictions or the need for access to raw materials.

12 For each of the merging companies, the names of the main customers and an estimate of the percentage of output each purchases.

Appendix 2

References to the Monopolies and Mergers Commission since the 'assets required' threshold was raised from £15 million to £30 million (announced in Mr Norman Tebbit's statement of 5 July 1984 and effective from 26 July 1984)

1985

Imperial Group PLC/Permaflex Ltd
Scottish and Newcastle Breweries PLC/Matthew Brown PLC
British Telecommunications PLC/Mitel Corporation (Canada)
McCorquodale PLC/Richard Clay PLC
Elders IXL Ltd/Allied Lyons PLC
BET PLC/SGB Group PLC

1986

The General Electric Co. PLC/Plessey Co. PLC
* Imperial Group PLC/United Biscuits (Holdings) PLC
* Guinness PLC/The Distillers Company PLC
* J. B. & S. Lees Ltd (subsidiary of Cope Allman International PLC)/Firth Cleveland Steel Strip Ltd (subsidiary of GKN PLC)
Norton Opax PLC/McCorquodale PLC
Tate & Lyle PLC/S. & W. Berisford PLC
* Hillsdown Holdings Ltd/S. & W. Berisford PLC
London International Group PLC/Wedgwood PLC
P & O/European Ferries Group
Ferruzzi Group/S. & W. Berisford PLC

* denotes references set aside by the Secretary of State for Trade and Industry.

10

Merger Policy: Certainty or Lottery?

JOHN SWIFT, QC

1. Discretion and the Development of Rules

Over 20 years ago, by the enactment of the Monopolies and Mergers Act 1965, a legislative and administrative system for the examination of acquisitions and mergers was introduced into the competition law of the United Kingdom. At first sight, it may appear to be a serious failing in that system that the subtitle of my paper—'certainty or lottery?'—is included. The operation of the rule of law is surely inconsistent with the degree of unpredictability of outcome associated with a lottery. Yet there is bound to be uncertainty in any system based on the legislative framework adopted by the United Kingdom in which the 'public interest' is defined so broadly and the discretionary powers of the government are largely unfettered.

There is, I think, in 1986, a greater degree of predictability about the decisions that the law requires to be taken within our system than there was, say, 10 years ago. That is the consequence of the adoption—by the Secretary of State, the Monopolies and Mergers Commission, and the Director General of Fair Trading—of what may be called the 'competition criterion' as the single most important test for determining whether specific mergers call for scrutiny or prohibition. Whether the adoption of that policy, within the existing legislative framework, best serves the efficiency with which the United Kingdom's resources are employed in the supply of goods and services at home and internationally is debatable and is not the subject of this paper. In my view, we have now reached the stage at which (i) the unlikelihood that mergers of a certain kind will be referred to the Commission; (ii) the unlikelihood that the Commission will relax its very strict requirement that mergers must be *proved* to be against the public interest before they should be prohibited; and (iii) the inability to challenge a decision by the Commission that a merger may be expected *not* to operate against the public interest, provide the best opportunity for fundamental review of the kind advocated in October 1985 by Mr David Walker of the Bank of England, in a speech given to the Glasgow Finance and Investment

Seminar on 24 October 1985.

I may add that the Bank of England's concern at the limitations of the 'competition criterion' for assessing the 'public interest' implications of acquisitions was expressed with force and conviction in the recent Commission inquiry on the proposed acquisition of Allied-Lyons PLC by Elders IXL Limited, in which there were no competition issues of any significance. But the issue of the future competitiveness of Allied-Lyons in the industries in which it was a major participant was regarded by the Commission as a public interest issue. The Bank, Allied, and the majority of the other witnesses failed to convince the Commission that the capital gearing and interest cover of the merged concern exposed it to too great a risk of commercial misfortune or distortion of resources away from beneficial new investment. In other words, on 'causation' the Commission found that the damage would not occur. But the finding that the financial strength of a major undertaking in the private sector of the economy was a matter of public and not merely private interest provides a signal to the government that the Commission will not, as it were, 'throw out' future references if made on financial grounds alone.[1]

As stated above, the institutional framework of merger control in the United Kingdom consists of the Secretary of State for Trade and Industry, the Commission, and the Director General of Fair Trading. Their functions are set out in the Fair Trading Act 1973. In the following sections I discuss each in turn.

2. The Secretary of State as Decision-maker

UNFETTERED DISCRETION

Under the Fair Trading Act the Secretary of State has an unfettered discretion *not* to refer any 'merger qualifying for investigation' to the Commission.[2] Thus the Secretary of State may, and occasionally does,

[1] In December 1986 the Secretary of State referred to the Commission the proposed (contested) acquisition of Imperial Continental Gas Association by Gulf Resources (UK), a wholly owned subsidiary of Gulf Resources and Chemical Corporation of the USA, since it appeared to him that the financial arrangements and the possible effect of the merger on users of Calor Gas required investigation. The bid was subsequently abandoned.

[2] A merger qualifies for investigation under a 'market share' test (25 per cent or more of relevant goods or services), or 'size of assets' test (£30 million of assets to be acquired), or both. In all mergers of any economic significance, the Secretary of State's convention is to make the reference on the ground of size of assets, even though in the majority of such cases the reason for making the reference is the likely increase in the market share of the merged concern.

refuse to make a merger reference in circumstances in which the Director General has recommended to him that it would be appropriate to refer. See, for a recent example, the acquisition by the Cannon Group of Thorn-EMI Screen Entertainments which involved an increase in concentration of cinemas. The Director General recommended (as part of his duties under Section 76 of the Fair Trading Act) that a reference should be made, no doubt applying the 'competition criterion' in an already highly concentrated service industry. The Director General presumably considered the economic difficulties of the industry but thought that the concentration was of sufficient significance to merit an investigation. The Secretary of State was probably more concerned with the parlous state of the cinema industry and the prospects for investment and employment.

Similarly, in the exercise of his discretion, the Secretary of State may refer where the Director General has recommended against a reference. Before the 'Tebbit Guidelines' (quoted in full below) were issued, references had been made by Ministers in cases where the competition criterion was wholly absent and the only issue appeared to be the bona fides or respectability of the individual responsible for making the bid: Mr A. Alfred Taubman in his agreed bid for Sotheby's (the contested bid by Knoll International having already been referred to the Commission, again not on competition grounds), and Mr Alan J. Lewis in his bid for the textile company Illingworth Morris.

PRINCIPLES REQUIRED TO AVOID ANARCHY IN THE EXERCISE OF DISCRETION

However, although the Minister's discretion remains unfettered, it should be guided by principles. There is no basic conflict between pragmatism and precedent. The common law thrives on a combination of the two.

The fact of making a reference has or may have serious consequences for the principal parties; also the reference provides a signal to others contemplating a merger of the kind referred; and, more subtly, the government conveys to the Director General *and* to the Monopolies and Mergers Commission the government's areas of concern. One always has to bear in mind that the government has the whip-hand in merger policy in that the Secretary of State alone can prohibit a merger: true, he can only prohibit a merger if the Commission finds that it may be expected to operate against the public interest, but he can, without giving reasons, refuse to accept such conclusions and allow the merger through. See *R v Secretary of State for Trade* Ex p. *Anderson Strathclyde PLC* [1983] 2 All E.R. 233.

THE TEBBIT GUIDELINES:
WHAT THEY SAY AND WHAT THEY DO NOT SAY

The 'Tebbit Guidelines' of July 1984 have been expressly adopted by his successors in that office. As the Minister of State in that Department recently observed, it is worth recalling exactly what Mr Tebbit said in July 1984 in a written answer to a Parliamentary Question:

Apart from the market share and assets test in Section 64 the Fair Trading Act lays down no statutory criteria for references to the MMC [Monopolies and Mergers Commission]. I regard mergers policy as an important part of the Government's general policy of promoting competition within the economy in the interests of the customer and of efficiency and hence of growth and jobs. Accordingly my policy has been and will continue to be to make references primarily on competition grounds. In evaluating the competitive situation in individual cases I shall have regard to the international context: to the extent of competition in the home market from non-United Kingdom sources and to the competitive position of United Kingdom companies in overseas markets.

Three comments are called for. First, the government's reference to 'competition grounds' is left deliberately vague. The government could have made the position clearer as to the effect of the merger on competition: either the possibility of the creation or intensification of a dominant position *or* a risk of serious distortion to the competitive process. One is at least on firm ground in thinking that there is a likelihood of a reference if either of those consequences can reasonably be foreseen.

The second comment is that the government has retained a discretion to refer mergers where the competition criterion is weak or non-existent. The 'public interest' as defined in Section 84 of the Fair Trading Act is extremely wide. For convenience of reference it is worth setting out in full the relevant part of Section 84 of the Act:

84.—(1) In determining for any purposes to which this section applies whether any particular matter operates, or may be expected to operate, against the public interest, the Commission shall take into account all matters which appear to them in the particular circumstances to be relevant and, among other things, shall have regard to the desirability—

(a) of maintaining and promoting effective competition between persons supplying goods and services in the United Kingdom;

(b) of promoting the interests of consumers, purchasers and other users of goods and services in the United Kingdom in respect of the prices charged for them and in respect of their quality and the variety of goods and services supplied;

(c) of promoting, through competition, the reduction of costs and the development and use of new techniques and new products, and of facilitating the entry of new competitors into existing markets;

(d) of maintaining and promoting the balanced distribution of industry and employment in the United Kingdom; and

(e) of maintaining and promoting competitive activity in markets outside the United Kingdom on the part of producers of goods, and of suppliers of goods and services, in the United Kingdom.

So long as the public interest is so defined in the legislation, it is arguable that if the Secretary of State has reason to believe that a merger will produce adverse consequences on an appreciable scale under any of the headings of Section 84 of the Fair Trading Act, it is not for him to apply one of the grounds—the 'competition criterion'—to the exclusion of all others.

Such an argument would appear to have the support of the Commission. In its recently published report on the proposed merger between Elders IXL Limited and Allied-Lyons PLC, the Commission considered 'that Elders' financial arrangements for the acquisition of Allied-Lyons could raise questions of public interest if they were such as to appear to threaten the future of the merged group'. The Commission rejected the *laissez-faire* approach:

. . . there is a view that even if the merged group were to be so extended financially that it collapsed, the normal operation of market forces would ensure the most effective reallocation of resources. Buyers would come forward for the businesses that were viable, and other suppliers would step in to meet the demand for the goods and services previously supplied by those that were not. Natural selection would have ensured the survival of the fittest.

8.23 We recognise that this argument might be applicable in some cases, although there is inevitably a cost involved in both financial and human terms that may be considerable and ought not to be ignored. However, when dealing with a company of the size and importance of Allied-Lyons, account must be taken of the possible detrimental effects on the public interest if the company were to become financially over-extended. In this case these might include the weakening of a major competitor in the national brewing industry which could lead to damage to its suppliers and customers, to substantial disruption to trade and industry, job losses on a serious scale, and the possible loss to the United Kingdom of markets—including the home market—to overseas suppliers.

There is as yet no 'financial criterion' to set alongside the 'competition criterion' in determining whether or not merger references will be made to the Commission. But the Commission's firm rejection of 'natural selection' enables the Secretary of State to develop the 'financial criterion' after taking into account the views of the Bank of England and the Stock Exchange. In its report, the Commission referred to the guidelines suggested by Allied-Lyons (paragraph 6.64 of the report) which the Secretary of State may also find worthy of incorporation into any financial 'guidelines' adopted as a result of the Elders/Allied inquiry.

The third comment on the Tebbit Guidelines is an attempt to clarify the reference to the 'international context' in which the competitive situation in individual cases is evaluated. The Guinness offer for Distillers is a case in point. A merger between Guinness and Distillers (announced in January 1986) would have produced a pro forma market share in the supply of Scotch whisky in the United Kingdom of about 35 per cent. It was common knowledge that Distillers's market share had dropped from about 65 per cent to about 15 per cent in 20 years, and that other brands, including retailers' own brands, had been successfully marketed. Indeed, the most successful was Bell's Special, acquired in 1985 by Guinness. But, above all, 90 per cent of Distillers's production of Scotch whisky was destined for overseas markets. Within the 'international context' therefore the future use of Distillers resources in overseas markets—its competitiveness—was a matter of real importance, and appeared to some as a factor that should outweigh the increase in United Kingdom market share. Notwithstanding the reference to the 'international context', which might reasonably have been taken as an important check on the utility for reference purposes of pro forma domestic market shares, the Guinness/Distillers bid was referred. It was only after Distillers had entered into an agreement with Whyte & Mackay to divest the merged group of certain Scotch whisky brands and thus substantially reduce its domestic pro forma market share of Scotch whisky that the Secretary of State gave clearance to the new proposals.

There is, of course, a tension between two 'public interest' objectives. The first is to ensure that the United Kingdom user or consumer is not adversely affected in price or range of goods and services in the event of a substantial pro forma increase in market share. If the companies merging are in substantial and effective competition with imports, it can always be inferred that the strength of international competition is the consumer's best safeguard against any use of increased power associated with increased market share. But the second objective looks to the efficiency with which United Kingdom resources can be used in international markets—to promote or maintain investment in the UK. If the merger would lead to increased concentration as between UK *producers* of goods, especially those in which research and development or design innovation is important, the second objective may take precedence over the first. It would be helpful, if or when the Secretary of State reviews the Tebbit Guidelines, to include a more reasoned analysis of the relevance of international trade than a single cross-reference to the 'international context'.

DECISION-MAKING UNDER SECTION 73 OF THE FAIR TRADING ACT

As stated above, the Secretary of State may decide not to prohibit a merger even if the Commission concludes that the merger may be expected to operate against the public interest. He may also accept the Commission's conclusions but substitute remedies different from those recommended by the Commission. Thus in the British Telecom (BT)/Mitel merger (Commission report published in January 1986) the Secretary of State decided that the proposed merger could proceed, subject to conditions similar to those proposed by the Commission. He concluded, however, that competition in the UK market for telecommunications equipment would be sufficiently protected by imposing a ceiling on Mitel's marketing to and through BT rather than imposing a complete prohibition on such marketing.

3. The Commission as a Decision-making Body

THE RELEVANT FUNCTIONS OF THE COMMISSION

Once the merger reference has been made to the Commission, now in the majority of cases accompanied by a cryptic statement from the Department of Trade and Industry that the merger may give rise to issues of competition in some specific product market, the public interest issues fall to be considered by a panel of, usually, six members of the Commission headed by the Chairman or one of the Deputy Chairmen of the Commission.

The Commission has to decide whether there is indeed a merger situation qualifying for investigation; if so, whether it operates or may be expected to operate *against* the public interest (specifying the adverse effects); if so, whether to recommend to the Secretary of State that the merger should be prohibited or whether the public interest could be safeguarded by the giving of undertakings; at any stage of its inquiry, whether a proposal to merge the relevant businesses has been abandoned.

DECISIONS ON JURISDICTION

As to the first consideration above—jurisdiction—there is usually little room for argument. Problems can arise where a merger reference has been made on the ground that it appears to the Secretary of State that a person has acquired an ability materially to influence the policy of the target company (deemed to be 'control' under the Fair Trading Act), but discussion of those matters falls outside the scope of this paper.

DECISIONS ON THE PUBLIC INTEREST

The areas of difficulty, for one seeking to predict the outcome of a Commission Inquiry, are the second and third considerations above; I deal with the fourth separately because the Commission's decision-making here gave rise to a recent unsuccessful challenge in the High Court.

The importance of the competitive structure of markets

Section 84 of the Fair Trading Act, cited above, does not even provide an exhaustive list of public interest issues since the matters covered under the sub-paragraphs are illustrative only. However, some degree of order and consistency has emerged, at least in the *priorities* and in the *method* of arriving at decisions. As to the priorities, analysis of Section 84 shows that the primary area of concern is the potential adverse effect of the merger on the competitive process within the relevant product market: either through a reduction of competition as *between* the merged or to-be merged enterprises, or some other likely distortion. That is not the exclusive area of concern; indeed, as the Commission concluded in its report on the Elders/Allied merger, the future competitiveness of firms in home and international markets may also be adversely affected by a merger in which issues of competition as between the relevant enterprises do not arise to any material degree.

Assuming that a 'merger situation' creates the possibility of a restriction of competition *as between* the enterprises that fall under common control or is otherwise anticompetitive in effect, the Commission has to decide whether that causes a 'detriment' to the public interest. The first aspect is one of materiality; the second is one of causation.

Materiality

It is predictable that in a measurement of the effects of a merger on competition, materiality starts with an analysis of market shares and, because of its wide powers for obtaining information (see, for example, Section 85 of the Fair Trading Act), the Commission invariably produces in its reports analyses of sales by value or volume which are more accurate than the estimates of those participating in the relevant markets.

However, there is no rule or practice whereby in a 'horizontal' merger a combined market share of 40 to 45 per cent or above would be deemed to be prima facie against the public interest and a market share falling below that level would be deemed to give rise to no adverse effects on the competitive process. Just as in conditions of full and open competition an apparent 'oligopoly' may not operate against the public interest (see Commission report on the supply of tampons), so an increase in pro forma market share (that is, adding together the pre-merger market shares of the two companies) to fairly high levels may not operate against the public interest if external forces are strong enough to prevent the merged concern acting in a potentially exploitative or anticompetitive manner (see, for example, the recent Commission report on the proposed merger between Norton Opax PLC and McCorquodale PLC).

Thus inevitably the Commission is drawn into an analysis of conditions of competition in relevant markets in order to attempt to *predict* the outcome under the usually hypothetical change in market structure which it is required to examine. At this stage, even for the 'insiders' (that is, the companies principally concerned in the inquiry and their advisers) it may become very difficult to predict the Commission's own predictions, the more so when it is almost impossible to gauge the effect of evidence or argument on the Commission panel throughout the period of the inquiry. I do not regard that as a failure of the system: these are generally 'difficult cases' in which the Secretary of State found it necessary to intervene and the potential acquirer considered the risk worth taking; the panel is bound to be impressed by evidence which is an amalgam of many different views from different angles on how the competitive process is working or may be expected to work under a changed structure. It is, however, fair to say that where a merger is agreed, the Commission loses the opportunity of having the case against the merger presented with the vigour and with the attention to detail to be expected in a contested merger where the future independence of the target company may be strenuously defended.

Thus on 'materiality' the Commission's conclusions will depend on its judgement of the effects of the change in market structure on price, availability, range of goods or services, innovation, levels and direction of research and development, employment, and other matters which may be adversely affected by the merger. The higher the combined market share and the more difficult the barriers to entry, the more likely it will be that the Commission will conclude that there is a *materially* adverse effect on the competitive process; similarly if a dominant firm acquires one of a small number of its suppliers (see Commission report on the merger between British Telecom and Mitel). So far, on 'materiality' I have confined my comments to the effects of a merger on competition within one or more relevant markets. I have done so because that is the main emphasis of every reference made by the Secretary of State in accordance with the 'competition criterion', and *most* references are made on that ground. Before I consider the predictability of Commission reports on other aspects of the public interest, I must deal with the issue of 'causation' or, as it is sometimes referred to, 'burden of proof'.

Causation

Under Section 69 of the Fair Trading Act, the Commission is required to report on the question of whether the creation of a merger situation operates or may be expected to operate against the public interest. There is no presumption that mergers operate in or against the public interest, but UK legislation requires that if a person is to be prohibited from making an offer to buy somebody else's business, there must be specific reasons why it would be against the public interest for him to do so. Plainly any analysis of the public interest has to compare two hypothetical positions: the future assuming the merger takes place, and the future assuming no merger. That involves a degree of prediction as to the future behaviour of the merged concern and others affected by its conduct. Some consequences may be certain, others less predictable, even speculative. The Commission has imposed on itself a severe discipline. 'To put the matter colloquially, the required conclusion is not, "This may happen", but "We expect that this will happen".' (Report on S & W Berisford Ltd and British Sugar Corporation Ltd.) In other words, if the risk is that as a result of the merger, prices will be materially higher (a detriment of considerable magnitude) the Commission cannot evaluate that risk without undertaking an analysis of probability.

It is plain, therefore, that when a merger reference has been made on the competition criterion (the more especially when the Commission's attention has been drawn by the Secretary of State to the specific product market in which competition may be diminished), the Commission's tests of materiality and 'foreseeability' or 'likelihood' are capable of sound application—economic theory, or at least that branch concerned with industrial economics, providing helpful signals along the way. Thus it should not matter which Commission panel is selected by the Chairman of the Commission to carry out the inquiry.

Weighing benefit and detriment

But there are two problems for which *ad hoc* and thus significantly unpredictable solutions have to be found. The first problem is the recognition that in certain circumstances detriments to the competitive process may be outweighed by benefits or *neutralized* by undertakings as to the future management of the merged concern. The second problem is that Section 84 of the Fair Trading Act is not limited to public interest issues created by a reduction of competition as between the merging enterprises, or as between the merged concern and third parties.

Faced with these problems, the Commission appears to have found its own solution, though it is barely articulated in the reports. As to the first problem, the Commission's strict test as to foreseeability puts a very great burden on those seeking to justify a materially anticompetitive merger: normally once the materiality test has been satisfied—and most obviously in contested mergers—it is extremely difficult to persuade the Commission that the benefits may be expected to outweigh the detriments; moreover, the Commission has shown itself generally unsympathetic to the offer of undertakings to prevent the occurrence of the predicted adverse consequences (the British Telecom/Mitel report was exceptional and depended on special facts).

The supposedly rational acquirer

As to the second problem, one has to recall that almost 20 years ago a conglomerate merger (Rank/de la Rue) was held to be against the public interest because the Commission concluded that de la Rue's efficiency would be seriously jeopardized by the departure of individuals in senior managerial positions, whereas in the absence of the contested acquisition those individuals would have stayed on. It is almost inconceivable that such an argument would prevail today. But those contentions, clearly resistable when they rely on the performance of supposedly irreplaceable individuals, still raise a genuine fear that there will be 'bad' mergers which the Stock Exchange system is incapable of identifying and yet raise *no competition problems*. I say, with no serious criticism of the Commission, that it is very difficult for them to know fools from wise men or knaves from honest men in the relatively short period for which they become acquainted. Merger inquiries are not Department of Trade inquiries, nor are they civil or criminal trials. The Commission must go back to the statute from which it derives its authority: the statute deals with 'enterprises', businesses the performance and conduct of which will inevitably be determined by the conditions of the market within which they compete, but also by the quality of their management. In many contested mergers the management of the target company may be convinced that the motives of the acquirer are those of financial opportunism (a well-known expression in Stock Exchange defence documents), or that the method of financing the acquisition is irresponsibly risky, or that the acquirer is inefficient, or too small, or too high-handed with employees, or connected with firms of dubious reputation, or an asset-stripper, and so forth. Indeed, it may all be true and the merger may turn out to be calamitous or at best unproductive—merely exchanging different ownership for a price which yields greater rewards to those financing it than to those who have a continuing stake in its commercial success: shareholders, employees, customers, suppliers.

However, it is one thing to admit the possibility that these adverse consequences *may* happen, even having accepted that they *will not* happen if the merger were not to take place. It is another matter to devise a system by which these 'non-competition' issues can be verified and evaluated. The solution adopted by the Commission (again barely articulated as such in their reports) is to assume that (in the absence of something equivalent to 'mala fides') the management of the merged concern will act rationally and responsibly in the conduct of the business of the merged concern and will, in competition with other enterprises, seek to raise profits and earnings per share. Thus, if the acquirer were to dispose of substantial parts of the company to be acquired (Elders/Allied Lyons) that would appear to raise no problem for the Commission, even if it involved the sale of foreign assets to foreign purchasers. The public interest detriment would be too remote to be identified as material. If the target company were more experienced than the acquirer in certain product or geographical markets, so be it: the acquirer would act rationally so as to use the skills available to the merged concern rather than ignore them (Norton Opax/McCorquodale). If the share price of the target company looked embarrassingly high for the acquirer to make a bid without incurring an irresponsibly and dangerously high level debt, so be it: the acquirer's banks could be relied upon to put up the money only if they were convinced that no harm would be suffered by the merged concern (even if the merged concern had to undergo some major surgery in the mean time) (Elders/Allied Lyons).

Conclusions

In any kind of analysis directed at predicting what the Commission may do, one has to simplify complex matters. The tasks for the Commission are often difficult: those who suggest that the Commission should report within say a 2- or 3-month period should recognize that there may be a substantial cost to be paid, which may outweigh the benefit to the parties of knowing what they can or cannot do. However, as in the case of the functions of the Secretary of State, I have sought to indicate the manner in which the Commission itself is deciding 'cases' with a view to identifying the real public interest issues as soon as is practicable and to minimising the degree of unpredictability inherent in the process.

ABANDONMENT OF MERGER PROPOSALS

The Commission is also decision-taker in the event that in the course of reference to the Commission, the acquirer abandons the proposals that were referred but indicates an intention to make new proposals involving a merger of some, but not all, of the activities of the two companies. The position is that if the arrangements that were originally proposed by a take-over bidder had been replaced by new arrangements proposed by the bidder which were significantly different from the original proposals, the Commission was entitled to find that:

> the proposal to make arrangements such as are mentioned in the reference had been abandoned and to exercise its power under S75(5) [of the Fair Trading Act] to lay the reference aside. It was a question of fact, to be determined by the Commission, whether an amended or revised bid amounted to new arrangements or merely an amended form of the existing arrangements.

See *R v Monopolies and Mergers Commission* Ex p. *Argyll Group* [1986] 2 All E.R. 257.

4. The Director General of Fair Trading as a Decision-maker

The functions of the Director General of Fair Trading in relation to mergers consist those which are expressly provided for in the Fair Trading Act and those which are incidental thereto. As to the former, the Director General is under a *duty* to keep himself informed about actual and prospective mergers and to make recommendations to the Secretary of State for or against a referral to the Commission. Moreover, the Secretary of State is under a duty to 'take account' of any advice given to him by the Director General with respect to a report of the Commission. As to the functions incidental thereto, the Director General operates in conjunction with the Secretary of State a 'confidential guidance' system and may also seek the views of a 'Mergers Panel' consisting of other interested government departments. The confidential guidance system is intended to assist those contemplating an acquisition as to the likely attitude of the Secretary of State: 'no reference', 'reference', or 'cannot say'. I am not sure as to the usefulness of this procedure. It is plainly unworkable in the difficult, border-line cases; and, as I have sought to indicate above, there is a greater degree of predictability as to the Secretary of State's decisions than is sometimes assumed, thus rendering 'confidential guidance' unnecessary in clear cases.

As to the 'predictability' of the Director General's recommendation to the Secretary of State under Section 76 of the Fair Trading Act (to refer or not), the principal test adopted is that described above—whether there appears to be sufficient 'cause for concern' as to the operation of the competitive process in an economically relevant product market to justify a reference. If there is, a reference should be recommended *even if* another person has arrangements in contemplation for the acquisition of the same 'target' company which will not be referred to the Commission.

Thus in the battle for control of the Distillers Company PLC, Argyll PLC (the major food retail group) was first to bid. Following the recommendation of the Director General, the Secretary of State decided *not* to refer. Then it was the turn of Guinness to make a bid for Distillers. But in the previous year Guinness had acquired Bell's, which supplied the largest selling Scotch whisky brand in the UK—Bell's Extra Special. No reference had been made of that merger, because Guinness was not then in the Scotch whisky market. The dilemma for the Director General was clearly serious: if the Guinness/Distillers bid were referred to the Commission—and it was an agreed merger—that would effectively rule Guinness out of play for 6 months, during which time Argyll or a third party could continue to make offers to Distillers's shareholders. Moreover, although the combined Bell's/Distillers pro forma UK market shares of Scotch whisky were about 35 per cent, supply in the UK accounted for only about 10 per cent of total Distillers production. Nevertheless, the competition criterion was the decisive factor. The reference was made. Despite the clamour that the decision was unfair, the Secretary of State refused to reconsider his decision not to refer the Argyll/Distillers merger.

Now Guinness had a problem to solve.

In the resolution of that problem we can see the three decision-making processes at work. At first sight it looked as if the Guinness bid for Distillers was doomed. Chapter 4 of the Mergers Guide (Office of Fair Trading (1985))—said to be a clear and concise guide to the law on mergers and 'how it is interpreted by the Monopolies and Mergers Commission and the other responsible bodies'—suggested that once the reference to the Commission had been made, the Commission could only be released from its obligation to produce a report if the bidding company satisfied the Commission that it no longer had any intention of seeking to take over the other company.

However, on closer examination of the relevant provisions of the Act, it appeared that there was no authority for such a suggestion. The Act is concerned with the 'enterprises' that come under common control. What if Guinness had agreed to sell its interests in Bell's *before* making a bid for Distillers? It seemed highly unlikely that in such circumstances a merger reference would have been made. Was there then any difference if Guinness were to agree to dispose of, not Bell's, but part of Bell's and part of the activities of the business of Distillers, so that the enterprises that would come under common control would be different from those originally contemplated? It appeared not. Thus Guinness abandoned the proposal that had given rise to the reference. The Chairman of the Commission accepted that there had been an abandonment within the meaning of Section 75(5) of the Act, a decision which was upheld by the Court of Appeal (see above), therefore setting Guinness free to make a new offer to Distillers's shareholders.

However, there remained two further hurdles: would the Director

General regard the new proposals as sufficiently different from the old proposals as to cause him to recommend that there should not be a new reference; and even if he did, would the Secretary of State agree?

Since the steps taken by Guinness, by United Biscuits (agreed pre-sale of Golden Wonder nuts and snacks business), and by Dixons (contested pre-sale of F. W. Woolworth's 'Comet' business) have been referred to, erroneously, as 'plea bargaining', it may be helpful to spell out what has to be done before the authorities (Director General and Secretary of State) can be satisfied that no reference should be made on the competition criterion by reason of a decision by the bidder to dispose of one or more relevant businesses (either his own, or the target's, or both).

Firstly, the bidder has to identify the *problem area*. A reference to the Commission can kill a bid and the bidder is, in my view, entitled to be told by the Office of Fair Trading (OFT) where the 'cause for concern' is. In the case of Guinness, the 'cause for concern' was the combined pro forma market share in the supply of Scotch whisky in the UK. Unless the OFT is prepared to co-operate, the bidder has to play a guessing game, which is plainly absurd.

Secondly, the exercise has to be *feasible*: can the enterprises be identified, and if so can one or more of them be readily divested as a business or part of a business? Where the cause for concern arises in a segment of a broader market, it may be impracticable for the bidder, especially in a contested bid, to identify the business to be divested with sufficient precision to allay the suspicions of the OFT.

Thirdly, is the divestment *material*? It is fallacious to think that a merger will necessarily be referred unless the proposed divestment has the effect of bringing the pro forma market share of the merged businesses below 25 per cent. On the other hand, the bidder has to establish to the satisfaction of the Director General that there is no reasonable prospect of any 'cause for concern' on competition grounds, and an agreement which reduces the market shares to about or below 25 per cent might be of considerable relevance to the exercise of that judgement. Materiality is at all times a question of fact and degree, and it should not be assumed that the 'market share' test is the only test on materiality.

Fourthly, is there a serious risk that even after divestment the bidder will not be in *active competition* with the divested business? It is possible to envisage circumstances in which the enterprise to be divested remains so dependent upon the merged concern that it cannot carry out its business policies in full and direct competition with the merged concern, for fear of prejudicing its commercial position, or generally that it prefers a 'cosy' relationship. Thus the manner in which, if at all, the merged concern is to trade with the diverted business is a matter for close investigation.

Fifthly, is there a serious risk that the divested business will be *less competitive* generally under the new owners than were it to remain part of the enterprise to be acquired? Divestment is not simply a formula to reduce a combined pro forma market share below the level at which a reference would otherwise be made. Divestment should secure, and if possible enhance, the competitiveness and future efficiency of the relevant divested business.

Sixthly, there has to be an *agreement* in existence for the disposal of the relevant business to a credible buyer, conditional only upon the success of the bid for the target company (whether recommended or contested): otherwise the fourth and fifth points above cannot be tested. Moreover, an undertaking to dispose of a business in the future will not be acceptable.

For my part, I see no harm in the evolution of mergers policy along the lines I have described. It has the advantage that one can seek to discuss and resolve problems with the 'executive' first—the OFT and Secretary of State—but if they want the system to work they must be prepared to take *final* decisions and not just 'reference' decisions. If everything were to be regarded as 'too difficult' to be resolved at the primary stage of investigation, then there would be no point even in embarking upon the six steps that I have outlined. Everything would go to the Commission. But I sense in the developments of 1986 a recognition that the OFT and Secretary of State *will at least if they are asked* extend their decision-making functions to a speedy reconstruction of the relevant industry without the benefit of a full Commission inquiry.

5. Summary

(1) Merger policy—including decision-taking by Secretary of State, Commission, and Director-General—is more predictable than is generally acknowledged.

(2) The Tebbit Guidelines need to be amplified at least in the following respects:
(a) to describe what the competition criterion is and to what extent the Secretary of State is influenced by domestic pro forma market shares (which may be an unhelpful guide to conditions of competition generally, and specifically in international markets).
(b) to recognize the existence of the financial criterion and to describe the circumstances in which it is likely to be applied;
(c) to indicate whether, in the absence of the 'competition criterion' or the 'financial criterion', references are likely to be made *other than* where the national interest may be considered to be affected.

(3) The Commission's reports and methods of carrying out new inquiries

now provide clear signals to the principal parties (and to the Secretary of State and the Director General) that:
(a) the potential effect of the merger on the distortion of the competitive process is the primary issue for investigation;
(b) the tests of materiality and causation in establishing that a merger may be expected to operate *against* the public interest are strict;
(c) if a detriment to the competitive process is established, it is difficult to prove that any benefits of the merger will outweigh the detriments;
(d) on issues other than 'competition issues' it is, again, difficult to prove that the purpose or effect of the merger—assuming rationality on the part of the acquirer—will be to cause effects adverse to the public interest; although in respect of the 'financial criterion' the Commission will require proof from the acquirer that the financial arrangements are prudent and are not likely to weaken the merged group and reduce its ability to contribute to the competitive process in a beneficial manner.

(4) The Director General's operation, in conjunction with the Secretary of State, of the procedures for 'confidential guidance' needs to be clarified.

(5) The Office of Fair Trading's booklet *Mergers: A Guide to the Procedures under the Fair Trading Act 1973* requires amendment to take account of the decision of the Court of Appeal in *R v Monopolies Commission* Ex p. *Argyll.*

11

Do we Need a Merger Policy?

KENNETH GEORGE*

1. Introduction

There has been growing concern recently over the level of merger activity in the UK. Several factors have contributed to this concern. In one or more of the recent take-over battles, some alarm has been expressed about the size of the bid, the method of finance, foreign ownership, and the over-emphasis on short-term considerations to the neglect of longer-term effects on industrial structure and efficiency. This concern about merger activity is, of course, not new. Some economists have, over a long period, been critical of our permissive merger policy; more widespread concern has flared up at times of intense merger activity such as occurred in the late 1960s and early 1970s, and now again in the mid-1980s. However, this concern is not shared by everyone. Indeed it is possible to make out a case, using theoretical and empirical evidence, for not having an antimerger policy, or at the very least for suggesting that we should not be over-concerned about the present level of merger activity and the present state of merger policy. Section 2 presents this case which, for simplicity, is put under the heading 'arguments for abandoning antimerger policy'. Section 3 presents the case for retaining merger policy, and Section 4 suggests some changes to the present UK policy approach.

2. Arguments for Abandoning Antimerger Policy

There are several points that can be made in developing the case for the abandonment of antimerger policy.

---

* Head of Department of Economics, University College, Swansea. Professor George was a member of the Monopolies and Mergers Commission from 1978 until 1986.

An earlier version of this paper was presented as the Fifth Roll Lecture on Economic Policy at the University of Southampton on 8 May 1986. The author is grateful to Steve Littlechild for comments on an earlier draft of this paper.

The most familiar arguments are those having to do with the advantages of scale. Merger proposals are invariably supported by claims of efficiency as a result of large-scale production or large-scale distribution and marketing. In the case of multi-product firms, emphasis is frequently placed on 'economies of scope' resulting from joint production and marketing, and the sharing of overhead costs. The advantages of size should not be under-estimated. For instance, in the manufacture of motor car engines for mass-produced cars, optimum size consists of a production line producing about 600,000 units a year on a two-shift basis, and two of Europe's largest car manufacturers, Peugeot and Renault, have seen fit to set up a joint venture in the manufacture of car engines. However, in the context of merger activity it is the market advantages of large firms that should perhaps be emphasized most, because they are more likely to be realized than are technical economies of scale. Furthermore, it has to be recognized that in many markets UK firms face intense international competition and have to compete with large overseas firms which have substantial marketing strength. Arguments concerning the marketing advantages of size were prominent in the Guinness and Argyll bids for Distillers, and also in the Hanson and United Biscuits bids for the Imperial Group.

Although mergers have undoubtedly been responsible for a big increase in industrial concentration, there is no convincing evidence that this has in general been accompanied by an increase in market power. In part, this is due to a simultaneous increase in international competition; indeed, many mergers may have occurred as a response to this increased competition (Curry and George (1983)). Increased concentration may also go hand in hand with greater diversification, so that large firms meet in head-on competition over a wider range of products. This is particularly noticeable in the high street, where structural change has resulted not only in the greater concentration of sales, but also in the diversification of the activities of the leading retailers. Lack of evidence of any general increase in market power is also reflected in UK statistical studies of the effects of mergers. Most of these have found that, for the majority of mergers studied, there has been a small decline in post-merger profitability (see, for instance, Meeks (1977) and Kumar (1984)). Even where this has not been so and where merging firms have been able to improve their post-merger profitability, the tendency in this direction has been weak (see Cosh, Hughes, and Singh (1980)). On balance, UK empirical work suggests that mergers have not had a strong impact on profitability either way. Although there are well-known difficulties of inferring changes in efficiency and market power from figures of profitability, the evidence is consistent with the conclusion that, in recent years at least, UK mergers have not as a rule enhanced market power.

One of the worries about mergers is that by committing managerial resources, they might have an adverse effect on new investment. In addition the pressure to invest may be reduced if merger increases the degree of monopoly. On the other hand, a reduction in competitive pressure may improve the balance between safety and competition and thereby improve business expectations. Mergers may also result in a market structure in which there is more oligopolistic rivalry, including rivalry in the creation of new capacity.[1] In the UK, what little work has been done on these more dynamic effects is mildly reassuring. Meeks (1977), in a study of the period 1964–71, found that active acquirers had also invested more heavily than average in new fixed assets. A similar result was found by Kumar (1984) for the period 1967–74, except that when mergers were classified by type it was found that for horizontal mergers there was, on average, some decline in post-merger investment performance.

Next there is the view, backed up by some evidence, that take-overs are an efficient selection mechanism that weeds out inefficient firms, transferring assets to those who are best able to manage them. Singh (1975), for instance, found a tendency for the discipline of the take-over bid to be more severe on firms with low profitability than on those with better profit performance, and also that acquiring firms tend to have better profit and growth performance than those that are acquired. The transfer of assets to more efficient management is a real gain to the economy, and on average take-overs succeed in realizing such gains.

Many of the attempts to estimate the effects of mergers are based on statistical analysis and relate to average outcomes. In some cases mergers will increase market power; in others they may reduce it. A diversity of outcomes will also be found for the effect on managerial efficiency, investment, and so on. It has been argued that because the future is uncertain and industrial structure is constantly adapting itself to changing circumstances, the success rate in predicting the effects of mergers is likely to be low. Since most mergers are likely to be pro-competitive or neutral in their effects, it is best to replace merger control with control of the undesirable conduct of monopolies if and when such conduct appears (see Littlechild (1978)). This is the conclusion that tends to emerge from the approach to competition of economists such as Schumpeter, Hayek, and Demsetz. This Austrian or 'competitive process' school of thought argues that the standard approach to competition is based on a static analysis which gives a false view of the complex interrelationships between structure, conduct, and performance. Competition is in fact a dynamic process;

---

[1] This effect of mergers may be particularly likely where merger produces a market structure of more evenly matched rivals. Emphasis on this aspect of the competition between oligopolists goes back at least to Duesenberry (1958).

mergers are an important part of this process, and to prevent mergers is to protect firms, thereby impeding the competitive process.[2]

Two recent developments—one theoretical, the other practical—add weight to the case for abandoning merger policy. The theoretical point is the emphasis given to the threat of new entry in recent developments in the industrial economics literature. The extreme version of the economics of potential competition is the perfectly contestable market, a concept developed by Baumol, Panzar, Willig, and their colleagues in the United States (Baumol, Panzar, and Willig (1982)). In a perfectly contestable market there is perfectly free entry and absolutely costless exit. Entry is perfectly free because entrants do not suffer any disadvantage as compared with incumbents; exit is costless because an entrant does not incur any sunk costs. One of the important insights of the theory is that even with perfect contestability, incumbent monopolists or oligopolists may be able to prevent entry and perpetuate their positions of dominance, but only by behaving virtuously; that is, by offering to the consumers the benefits that competition would bring. Baumol (1982) suggests that this offers what may be a new insight on antitrust policy. 'It tells us that a history of absence of entry in an industry and a high concentration index may be signs of virtue not of vice. . . .' Baumol is careful to point out that the perfectly contestable market is a theoretical construct which may not correspond to any real world market. Indeed the assumptions of the theory have been criticized as being so at odds with reality that the theory can be of little practical value for policy purposes (Shepherd (1984)). Yet there is no doubt that the theory, and in particular the way in which it highlights the beneficial effects of the threat of entry, have been influential, and may have important repercussions for merger policy. As Hay (1985) has stated, 'If the threat of entry is as important an influence on the behaviour of incumbent firms as is suggested by the emphasis given it in the recent literature, the implications for merger policy are potentially quite significant'. The revision of the US Merger Guidelines in 1982 and 1984 certainly gave much greater weight to entry conditions than had previously been the case. Hay (1985) comments that this increased emphasis on potential competition could have a 'quite dramatic' impact, 'allowing mergers to go forward even where existing market shares are extremely high'.

The other development is the, currently fashionable, willingness of predators to divest themselves of part of their assets in order to avoid a merger reference. Had it been successful in acquiring the Imperial Tobacco Group, United Biscuits would have sold the Golden Wonder snack food division of Imperial in order to reduce the merged company's share of the snack foods market to below 25 per cent. In announcing its take-over bid

---

[2] For a more detailed discussion, see George (1985).

for Distillers, Guinness said that it would sell several brands of whisky in order to avoid creating a dominant position in the UK market. Indeed the Chief Executive of Guinness is reported to have said that the proposed divestment was in the public interest because it would stimulate competition in the UK market. Dixons, in announcing its take-over bid for Woolworth, said that it would dispose of the Comet electrical chain which was acquired 2 years ago by Woolworth, in order to avoid any possible reference to the Monopolies and Mergers Commission.

These divestment strategies are seen by some commentators as evidence of a serious weakness in current merger policy, and as evidence that companies are outsmarting the Office of Fair Trading. However, UK merger policy has been criticized for failing to focus sharply enough on competition issues, and for failing to lay down clear and predictable rules for deciding on merger references. Merger references are now decided largely on competition grounds, and the factor most likely to trigger a reference is a combined market share for the merged company of 25 per cent or over. Most economists regard simple and predictable rules as advantageous in the competition policy game. When such rules are laid down, it can confidently be predicted that firms will respond strategically to them.

The main point, however, is that if firms are *prepared* to divest themselves of activities in order to avoid a reference, the government ought to be prepared to *enforce* divestment as part of a policy towards the anticompetitive behaviour of dominant firms. We would then have the makings of a serious argument for doing away with merger policy altogether, in favour of concentrating on an effective policy towards the abuse of dominant positions including, where appropriate, enforced divestments.

3. The Case Against Abandoning Merger Policy

The case for abandoning merger policy and relying entirely on antimonopoly policy would be most appealing if the evidence suggested that the majority of large mergers resulted in significant efficiency gains, if there were no feasible alternative to mergers as a means of securing these gains, and if we could indeed rely upon an effective policy for dealing with the anticompetitive behaviour of large firms.

On the association of efficiency and size, although it is undoubtedly the case that economies of scale are important in many sectors, some of the benefits, in particular those associated with technical economies of scale, may not be secured by merging two or more sub-optimal sized firms. There has been a tendency to associate efficiency with size, irrespective of *how* large size is attained—internal expansion is often a more certain way of benefiting from scale economies than is acquisition.

As to the view that take-overs are efficient in weeding out inefficiency, the UK evidence is again rather mixed. As mentioned in Section 2, Singh's (1975) study of mergers over the period 1955–60 found a general tendency in this direction, but it was rather weak. There was a great deal of overlap between the profit performance of acquired and non-acquired firms, and the probability of being acquired within a particular time period was noticeably higher than average only for firms with a *very* poor profit performance. A later study covering the period 1967–9 found that in 'only nine of the fourteen individual industries was the average profitability of acquiring firms greater than that of the firms they acquired', and that in general there was 'little difference in the average profitability of the two groups of firms' (Cosh, Hughes, and Singh (1980)).

Concern over the efficiency of stock market selection has been highlighted by the short time horizons that seem to have been adopted in recent take-over battles. Several aspects of this emphasis on the short term are worth mentioning.

In the first place, the euphoria of a stock market boom and the feverish merger activity that accompanies it is itself propelled by short-term forces which may be a poor guide to long-term efficiency. Secondly, during the course of a stock market boom, the share prices of some firms will move ahead of others. We do not have anything like a complete explanation of why particular firms do well in this respect while others lag behind. However, firms that are in the middle of a process of rationalization or that have committed themselves to long-term investments may be particularly vulnerable. In the GKN/AE merger reference, for instance, AE argued that the low price of its shares was due to low dividend payments resulting from the priority it had given to investment in rationalization, modernization, and research and development. Hepworth's bid for Steetley came at a time of reorganization and rationalization when Steetley's profits and share prices were depressed. Similarly, Dixons's bid for Woolworth came at a time when Woolworth was in the middle of a modernization and rationalization programme. Measures to improve long-term competitiveness may therefore expose a firm to a take-over bid, so that to avoid the latter, long-term competitiveness might have to be sacrificed in favour of measures that increase short-term profits and share prices.

A third observation is that particular take-over battles can be won and lost on the basis of quite small differences in the share prices of the predator companies. These differences may owe more to the relative skills of the contestants in winning the support of the financial institutions than to any deep assessment of the relative merits of competing bids.

Fourthly, there is an important defensive element in many acquisitions, which suggests that many take-overs would not have occurred but for the fact that the acquiring company itself felt threatened. This defensive element appears in much of the recent merger activity, including the unsuccessful attempt by Imperial Tobacco to merge with United Biscuits following the Hanson bid; the successful attempt by Distillers to merge with Guinness following the Argyll bid; and the Allied-Lyons acquisition of the Hiram Walker wines and spirits division following the take-over threat from Elders (IXL).

Finally, mention should be made of the practice whereby a predator indemnifies a merchant bank in respect of any losses suffered in disposing of shares bought on its behalf. Morgan Grenfell was so indemnified by United Biscuits in the battle for the Imperial Group. Hanson Trust complained that if both bids failed, Imperial's share price might well fall substantially, resulting in losses to those who bought shares during the take-over battle. However, the fear of such losses is removed by indemnification arrangements, so that an element of moral hazard is introduced. The result is to give a further impetus to the merchant banks' search for short-term profit from take-over activity.

All this is not to deny that the threat of take-over has an important role to play in encouraging efficiency. Indeed in many cases this threat is the most important element of contestability. But though the threat of take-over should not be removed, take-overs themselves are not always the only way or the best way of improving the efficient use of existing assets. For even if a take-over does succeed in improving financial management, marketing, and productivity (and experience tells us that this is not always so), it takes time for these improvements to be realized. Over much the same time span, it may be possible to achieve broadly the same measure of improvement by the infusion of new management into a firm without change of ownership. For example, not so many years ago Guinness would have been widely regarded as a sleepy, poorly managed company, but under a new chief executive its image and its performance have been transformed. Distillers, Imperial Tobacco, and Woolworth are all examples of companies that have been badly managed but in which new top management brought about substantial improvements. Clearly in the case of Distillers and Imperial Tobacco the City was not sufficiently impressed with the progress that had been made, but this had more to do with the opportunity for short-term gains from take-over on a booming stock market than with an assessment of the relative long-term effects on efficiency of take-over and internal growth.

Assessment of the future prospects of a company subject to a take-over bid has been an important part of merger investigations conducted by the Monopolies and Mergers Commission.

In its report on the take-over bids for the Royal Bank of Scotland, the Commission said:

If we had thought that Royal Bank Group needed better management or additional capital which could be obtained only by a merger, or that it had poor long term prospects as an independent concern, we might well have been persuaded that in the circumstances of the case a merger would not be expected to operate against the public interest. (*Hongkong and Shanghai Banking Corporation/Standard Chartered/Royal Bank of Scotland*, para. 12.40)

In investigating Hepworth's take-over bid for Steetley, the Commission found that:

Steetley is confident that . . . it can continue without the merger . . . well able to compete with foreign manufacturers and to generate funds sufficient to finance research and to develop new products. . . . There was . . . no doubt of the confidence in Steetley's future expressed to us in the company's evidence through the present Chairman, and we have no reason to think that confidence is misplaced . . . (*Hepworth/Steetley*, para. 10.40)

And as a final example, in the report on the GKN/AE merger, the Commission concluded:

It is clear that in striking the balance between the detriments to be expected from the merger and the claimed advantages, much depends on our assessment of AE's prospects of competing successfully without the merger. We see little evidence that AE is in need of rescue or that it cannot compete successfully by itself. (*GKN/AE*, para. 8.34)

In these cases, and in others that could be cited, importance was attached to the quality of management in the company under threat of take-over, and to evidence that management (sometimes as a result of new blood) was putting right past weaknesses. There is no doubt that companies are often far too slow in eliminating inefficiency and in recognizing the need for change, and for this, ultimate responsibility rests with the shareholders. The large institutional shareholders, who are, or certainly should be, well informed and who play such a prominent role in take-over battles, are particularly to blame, in many cases, for not using their voting power to bring about management changes in non-bid situations. There will, of course, be a division of opinion on the matter of judging managerial competence and on the pros and cons of a take-over bid, as indeed there has been in some of the cases that have come before the Commission. What is important, however, is that the alternatives are carefully examined and that due consideration is given to the prospects of a potential victim continuing as a successful independent concern.

Turning to the views of the competitive process school, there is no doubt that economists such as Demsetz in the US and Littlechild in the UK make a valuable contribution in emphasizing the importance of time, uncertainty, and the tendency for market structures to adapt to changing circumstances. However, it is perfectly possible to accept these points while disagreeing with the suggestion that it might be best to replace merger control with the control of the undesirable conduct of monopolies if and when such conduct appears.

A general point worth making is that to view competition as a dynamic process taking place under conditions of uncertainty is not in itself sufficient reason for being complacent about the dangers of monopolization and anticompetitive conduct. For instance, Downie's (1958) analysis of the competitive process suggests that unrestrained market forces will tend to lead to increasing levels of monopolization and to a growing incidence of collusion between large firms.

More specifically, a difficulty in accepting any down-grading of merger policy is that the evidence on the effects of mergers, both in cross-section statistical studies and in case studies, is not very reassuring. True, statistical studies show that the effect of mergers on profitability, even where it has been adverse, has not been quantitatively very large. But there is very little evidence in the UK to suggest that mergers have had a particularly beneficial effect on resource allocation. Case studies have come to a similar conclusion. For instance, a detailed study of 9 mergers that occurred in the late 1960s concluded that 'society has not attained any extensive resource savings as a result of these mergers over and above what could have been achieved without them' (Cowling *et al.* (1980)).

As to the argument that mergers increase competitiveness, this is often the case but it is not always so. It is not a convincing argument when internal growth is a feasible alternative for the acquiring firm, or when merger eliminates an effective competitor, or when it weakens potential competition. We know from case studies that these effects of mergers do occur, especially with mergers involving large firms, which are the ones most relevant to policy. For example, all three considerations played a part in the Monopolies and Mergers Commission's recommendation that the proposed merger between General Electric and Plessey should not be allowed.

It might be argued that the doubts that have been expressed so far would be dispelled if there were an effective monopoly policy for dealing with the abuse of market power. Are there any problems in placing greater reliance on antimonopoly policy? What is needed, it should be made clear, is not only effective machinery for dealing with monopoly, but also the ability to identify anticompetitive and cost-raising activities.

In principle there is no difficulty in devising effective machinery for dealing with monopoly so that policy has a noticeable effect. In practice, however, successive governments have shown no great enthusiasm for introducing a strong monopoly policy. The Director General of Fair Trading has a duty under Section 2 of the 1973 Fair Trading Act to collect information about market structure and business conduct, and generally keep under review commercial activities in the UK. Information gathered in the course of these duties, together with complaints received from firms and members of the public, forms the basis on which a decision is made about whether to refer a monopoly for investigation. However, it is not easy to uncover anticompetitive behaviour, and the parties who are most aware of it—that is, the customers and competitors of dominant firms—do not have sufficient incentive to complain. As Sharpe (1985) has pointed out, 'no independent private remedy exists and even if a practice is condemned in strong terms no retrospective remedy exists. The incentive to draw the existence of anti-competitive practices to the attention of the Office [of Fair Trading] is therefore weak'. Consequently the rooting out of anticompetitive behaviour is, within existing policy, likely to fall short of being satisfactory, and not surprisingly it is possible to find examples of firms persisting in conduct which has previously been condemned or which indeed is illegal under the terms of restrictive practices legislation. For example, in April 1986 a price-fixing cartel of 15 petrochemical companies, including ICI and Shell, was fined £35 million by the European Commission for breaking EEC competition law.

There are three other points that can usefully be made about the weaknesses of existing monopoly policy. The first is that, apart from one or two minor instances, the structural remedy of divestment has not been used. As mentioned earlier, a willingness to enforce divestment is a prerequisite to the weakening or abandonment of merger policy. The second observation is that the UK authorities have been very slow in referring monopolies for investigation even in those cases where dominant positions have existed for many years. In their study of the effects of 8 monopoly inquiries, Shaw and Simpson (1985) concluded that 'the problem with the MMC [Monopolies and Mergers Commission] investigations was that they often came too late to have a significant impact.' The weakness of monopoly policy, together with the fact that the erosion of dominant positions by market forces often occurs very slowly, suggests that we should wherever possible prevent such dominance being created by merger activity. The third point is that all the problems of controlling the conduct of single firm dominance apply, if anything, with even more force to policy towards oligopoly.

The problems of devising an effective monopoly policy, however, are not only those of devising a set of rules that will have a noticeable effect. There is also the problem of ensuring the desired effect; that is, of directing policy at those business practices that are unambiguously anticompetitive or efficiency-reducing. If recent theoretical developments in industrial economics may be said to have weakened the case for merger policy, they have also blurred the policy implications of dominant firm behaviour. This is demonstrated in Schmalensee's recent survey of the relevant literature (Schmalensee (1987)). Rules designed to modify the conduct of dominant firms or to hasten their decline typically have ambiguous effects on efficiency and welfare. This applies, for instance, to policies directed at limiting price discrimination, the restrictions imposed by firms on their customers, and policies aimed at facilitating new entry. When innovative activity is taken into account, even policies aimed at reducing high prices have unclear effects, because if this reduces short-run profitability there may be adverse effects on the incentive to invest in innovation.

It has been argued that the analysis of business conduct in some of the recent literature is based on some rather contrived situations and may lead to 'impotent policy agnosticism' (see Geroski and Jacquemin (1984)). It is certainly the case that the simplifying assumptions of the theoretical literature are sometimes so drastic that the analysis offers little or no assistance in the formulation of policy. However, even when it is possible to discover exceptions to a general rule that are not fanciful, this does not render the rule useless. It is not difficult, for example, to think of cases where free entry is likely to have an adverse effect on efficiency and welfare, but this does not detract from the usefulness of adopting a general presumption in favour of reducing barriers to new competition.

More problematic is the fact that some aspects of dominant firm behaviour are likely in general to be welfare-enhancing and yet at the same time difficult to disentangle from anticompetitive behaviour. Indeed they may be both welfare-enhancing and anticompetitive. In particular there are the arguments most forcefully presented by Demsetz (1982) and Okun (1980), both of whom have emphasized the importance to the firm of a reputable history, and that a good reputation creates customer attachments, which in turn encourage the firm to take a long view.[3]

Okun uses his customer attachments model to explain why manufacturing prices are not highly sensitive to changes in demand. As he points out, price inflexibility means that prices will generally be in excess of marginal cost, and this may entail a certain amount of welfare loss. However, there are benefits to be considered in the form of lower shopping costs for customers and more efficient production scheduling for firms.

Related to these ideas is the concept mentioned earlier of the balance between safety and competition; that is, the degree of competition that businessmen consider tolerable for conducting business on a long-term basis. Too much competition, like too much monopoly power, may be harmful to long-run performance. Considerations such as this may have something to do with explaining the similar market concentration patterns that are observed in many industries in countries of widely different sizes.

The problem therefore in relying entirely on policies aimed at modifying the behaviour of dominant firms is that once dominant firms are created,

---

[3] Customer attachments are also emphasized in Duesenberry (1958).

there is bound to be great difficulty in devising a policy for dealing with them. We have a lot of evidence from case studies, including Monopolies and Mergers Commission investigations, to show that monopolists have substantial advantages over new entrants and small competitors, advantages related to such factors as complex technologies, financial power, access to distribution channels, and customer attachments. However, theory does not give clear guidance on the extent to which these advantages should be condemned and the behaviour of monopolists modified, and where we can agree on what constitutes anticompetitive behaviour, it is not always easy to unearth it. Furthermore it is doubtful whether the authorities are ever likely to adopt a vigorous policy of divestment.

This leads to the conclusion that, while we should not give up our surveillance of anticompetitive behaviour by dominant firms, more is likely to be gained by focusing attention on the creation of dominant positions. Dominance can be created by internal growth or by merger. It may be indirectly acquired as the by-product of innovative activity or it may be directly sought after in order to reduce competition and earn monopoly rent. There is no clear correspondence between merger and the search for monopoly rent on the one hand, and internal growth and innovative activity on the other, if for no other reason than that innovative activity includes innovation in management techniques which may be spread more rapidly by acquisition. But at the very least, mergers, as compared with internal growth, are a quicker and safer way of gaining positions of market power without necessarily any accompanying efficiency gains. Internal growth, on the other hand, is more likely to be solidly based on long-term efficiency gains and innovation.

The case for maintaining merger policy may be summarized as follows.

First, the stock market is an imperfect selection mechanism which gives too much weight to short-run profit opportunities and too little to longer-term forces that shape efficiency.

Second, although the majority of mergers are not likely to be anticompetitive, many are, especially those involving large firms. Mergers have certainly been important historically in creating positions of market dominance, and some of these positions have been firmly entrenched over long periods and associated with anticompetitive conduct, including strategic entry deterrence.

Third, there is little prospect of devising an effective monopoly policy that would justify the weakening or abandonment of merger policy.

Finally, although the results of cross-section statistical studies do not lead to strong conclusions either way, these studies cover large populations, whereas those relevant to policy are, in the main, confined to a relatively small number of mergers involving large companies. As far as these are concerned, the author's limited experience as a past member of the Monopolies and Mergers Commission suggests that it *is* possible to disentangle the market power and efficiency gain motives for mergers, and thus that it is possible to improve upon completely unregulated merger activity.

4. Suggestions for Reform

The balance of theoretical and empirical evidence suggests that there is a need for merger policy. At the same time, however, it does not point to the need for a *radical* change in terms of the severity with which mergers are treated in the UK. Nevertheless some worthwhile changes could be made to UK policy.

MERGER GUIDELINES

At present, a merger reference can be made where a merger creates or enhances a monopoly (defined as 25 per cent of the relevant UK market) or where the value of the assets taken over exceeds £30 million. Firms are not obliged to notify the Office of Fair Trading (OFT) of an intended merger, but normally do so, because they can obtain confidential guidance as to whether or not a reference is likely. The Director General of the OFT is advised by the Mergers Panel—an interdepartmental committee with representatives of all interested government departments—and the Director General in turn advises the Secretary of State whether or not to refer a merger to the Commission. This advice is usually taken but not invariably so. There are cases where important references have been vetoed, and also where a reference has been made in spite of advice to the contrary. For instance, in 1979 the Secretary of State decided not to accept the Director General's advice that the merger between Thorn Electrical Industries and EMI be referred, and in 1982 decided to refer A. J. Lewis's bid for Illingworth Morris against the advice of the Director General. Other examples of insignificant mergers that have been referred are the bids for Sotheby's (1983) and the proposed merger of two manufacturers of snuff (1985)![4]

The procedures for vetting mergers should be strengthened by setting guidelines for defining take-over bids that would automatically be challenged by the OFT. Such a challenge need not necessarily lead to a full investigation by the Commission, but where a reference is not made, the

[4] The latter lapsed after the reference was made to the Commission.

OFT should publish a report explaining the reasons for its decision. Whether a bid is referred or not, the onus of proof should be on the bidder to demonstrate benefit, a point that will be returned to later.

One of the main reasons for adopting guidelines is to create greater certainty for the business community in relation to the application of policy. For this reason they should be based on readily understood structural measures—market shares and concentration levels relating to UK sales, thus allowing for imports. A minimum market size should also be specified in order to eliminate trivial references. The 1978 Green Paper *A Review of Monopolies and Mergers Policy* (Department of Prices and Consumer Protection (1978)) suggested the following possible set of guidelines for horizontal and vertical mergers:

(a) *horizontal mergers:* any merger which increased the combined companies' share of the UK market for a particular product or service to 25 per cent or more; except where:
(i) the size of the UK market concerned was less than £4 million; or
(ii) the value of the gross assets of the acquired company was less than £1 million;

(b) *vertical mergers:* any merger where either the acquiring or the acquired company has a 25 per cent or greater share of the UK market for a particular product or service, and the merger involved the acquiring company taking over a significant supplier or customer.

Structural guidelines of this sort would need to be supplemented by a number of key factors which affect the significance of concentration and market share data. One such factor is the rate of growth of the market. Where demand is expanding rapidly, internal growth will be an inducement to investment in capacity extensions and in research and development. In a declining industry, on the other hand, particularly one with a highly competitive market structure, there may be serious obstacles to the internal growth of firms and the case for mergers may be strong. Such an industry may be characterized by chronic excess capacity because of the slow adjustment of capacity to demand, an aged capital stock, and generally poor quality management. In such a situation, a merger can improve efficiency by encouraging the scrapping of old machines and investment in new ones, by reducing the uncertainty associated with excess capacity, and by increasing the proportion of the industry's assets under the control of efficient managers. In these circumstances mergers will frequently involve the acquisition of firms that are 'failing', and the particular circumstances of a case may be sufficiently clear for a decision not to refer to be arrived at speedily.

It is not possible to devise a set of guidelines that would suit all conceivable merger situations, and so allowance would need to be made for exceptional cases. Here, however, policy should 'err' on the side of making exceptions of cases that fail to meet the concentration tests rather than the other way round. In particular it is desirable to protect 'effective competitors', a matter which will be considered below.

The adoption of guidelines would have the advantage of creating greater certainty for the business community in relation to the application of policy. It would also assist in achieving greater consistency in applying the policy. It is at the pre-referral stage of merger policy that the greatest scope exists for a 'consistent approach', because by their very nature the cases that are referred should be the ones where the pros and cons are more finely balanced and where therefore it is more difficult to reach a clear verdict.

THE PUBLIC INTEREST

The public interest is defined very widely for the purposes of monopoly and merger investigations. The Commission is instructed to take into account 'all matters which appear to them in the particular circumstances to be relevant . . .', and among other things shall have regard to the desirability:

(a) of maintaining and promoting effective competition . . .

(b) of promoting the interests of consumers, purchasers and other users

(c) of promoting, through competition, the reduction of costs, the development and use of new techniques and new products and facilitating new entry

(d) of maintaining and promoting the balanced distribution of industry and employment . . .

(e) of maintaining and promoting competitive activity in markets outside the United Kingdom.

The guidelines have been criticized for being too wide and for forcing the Commission into considering matters about which it is not well qualified.

The regional dimension of the public interest has featured in a number of recent references, particularly *Lonrho/House of Fraser* (1981), the take-over bids for the Royal Bank of Scotland, and *Charter Consolidated/Anderson Strathclyde*. In the first of these, the claim by House of Fraser that the merger would have an adverse effect on the Scottish economy was dismissed by the Commission as not having sufficient weight. In the other two cases the majority view on the Commission was that a merger would result in significant damage to the economy of Scotland. In both cases emphasis was placed on the loss of employment that would ensue as a result of the change in status of the acquired company, from being independent to being a subsidiary of a large group. Regional problems are, of course, important, and there is evidence that suggests that development is adversely affected if a region has a high proportion of its business in the form of branch factories or subsidiaries of companies whose headquarters are located elsewhere. The problem, however, is that these considerations do not fit happily within a competition policy that is supposed to apply to the whole of the United Kingdom. In any case regional problems can, and should, be dealt with more effectively with the aid of more appropriate policy weapons such as grants, loans, and other regional incentives.

The same point can be made about the balance of payments effects of mergers. Once more the claims and counter-claims made in evidence to the Commission are more than usually speculative and difficult to assess. In the report on car parts,[5] for instance, the UK car manufacturers and importers argued that the termination of the exclusive buying of replacement parts imposed by them upon franchised dealers would have an adverse effect on imports and the balance of payments. However, representatives of the car components industry contested the view that they would be unable to compete with foreign suppliers. Once again the important consideration is that more powerful and reliable weapons than competition policy are available for dealing with the balance of payments. Interestingly, in the car parts report the Commission concluded that

> even if it were established that the components industry and other industries dependent on it needed protection against foreign competition, the desirability of providing it and the method of doing so should be matters of considered government policy and should not be left to the operation of an anti-competitive practice adopted to further sectional commercial interest.

There is a fairly widespread view that the open-ended approach to defining the objectives of competition policy is a fundamental weakness in enforcement decision-making. A possible solution would be to restrict the relevant matters in merger references to those that are contained in paragraphs (a), (b), and (c) of Section 84(1) of the 1973 Act and which are summarized in (a) to (c) above.

If the Commission is to continue to be asked to investigate mergers in which the major issues relate to regional or to balance of payments problems, it would be better for these to be treated as special cases outside the main stream of merger references. The Enserch/Davy reference, for instance, would not have occurred on the basis of a concentration/market share guideline approach because there was no question of any detriment arising out of reduced competition. The reference might have been made, however, on the basis of extraordinary circumstances relating to the national interest and to export markets.

It has also been suggested that the Commission should not be concerned with the efficiency consequences of a merger. However, unless the

---

[5] *Car Parts*, HC 318 (1981–82), HMSO, London.

benefit–cost approach to mergers is to be abandoned altogether, it is essential that the likely efficiency consequences of mergers be taken into account, but this is not to say that the present method of handling matters relating to efficiency is entirely satisfactory.

The present position, in the case of a report that a proposed merger may be expected to operate against the public interest, is that the Commission shall 'specify particular effects, adverse to the public interest, which in the opinion of the Commission [the proposed merger] may be expected to have'. There are three matters relating to this instruction that merit discussion. First, a problem has arisen over the wording, *effects* [which the merger] *may be expected to have*. Second, the onus of proof is on the Commission to find adverse effects and not on the company to demonstrate benefit. Third, the Commission has to specify *particular* adverse effects.

EXPECTED EFFECTS OF MERGERS

In arriving at an adverse finding, the Commission has to conclude that a merger may be expected to have certain adverse effects. In the Charter Consolidated/Anderson Strathclyde reference the majority, in their assessment of the public interest, concluded that the merger should not be allowed to proceed, but their recommendation was not accepted by the Secretary of State. His decision may have been influenced by a point made in the Note of Dissent to the effect that the majority case was based merely on possibilities and risks, and not 'in terms of definitely foreseen results'. The majority did indeed refer to 'likelihoods', 'risks', and 'probabilities', but such terms are also used in other merger reports where the mergers were blocked—Enserch/Davy, where a whole section of the concluding chapter comes under the heading 'Possible disadvantages of the proposed merger', and Lonrho/House of Fraser, where references are made to the risks involved in allowing the merger to proceed. Furthermore the majority report in the Anderson Strathclyde reference did conclude that the merger may be *expected* to have an adverse effect upon management effectiveness and labour relations; that it *would* affect employment; that it *would* detract from the dynamism of business in the region; and that it *may be expected to have* an adverse effect upon employment.

In analysing the effects of a merger, it is not possible to speak in terms of definitely foreseen results apart, that is, from the immediate impact on firm size and market shares. In any merger reference, the Commission is faced with choosing between alternative pictures of the future, and none of these pictures can be definitely foreseen. It is most unlikely to have been the intention of Parliament to make such a fine distinction between what is 'expected to happen' and a 'real and substantial risk' of something happening or something being 'most likely' to happen. In an uncertain world these statements amount to much the same thing. The problem that arose in the Charter Consolidated/Anderson Strathclyde case has only occurred once, but it would be just as well to take advantage of any reform of merger policy to remove this particular ambiguity.

THE ONUS OF PROOF

The case for reversing the burden of proof was considered in 1978 by the Green Paper *A Review of Monopolies and Mergers Policy*, and rejected in favour of a neutral position. The arguments presented in the Green Paper are not convincing. There would be no need as the document suggested to reverse the general presumption that mergers are not against the public interest. The majority of mergers would, as at present, be cleared quickly. How many would be challenged would depend on exactly how the guidelines are drawn up, and of course only a proportion of those above the threshold, set in terms of market share/concentration data, would be referred to the Commission. The document goes on to argue that reversing the burden of proof

> would be a strong deterrent against bringing forward merger proposals above the threshold even though they might be desirable in the national interest. The much severer treatment of merger proposals above the threshold (choice of which would inevitably be arbitrary) would tend to distort companies' approach to mergers as those below the threshold came to be regarded as in some way better than those above it, and it cannot be assumed that the outcome would be the most favourable to the public interest.

However, the choice of mergers for referral based on the use of guidelines could not possibly be more arbitrary than present UK practice. Furthermore the severer treatment of merger proposals above the threshold is exactly what should be aimed for. If we are not prepared to accept that, a priori, the greatest danger to competitive behaviour comes from the most highly concentrated industries, there is not much of a basis left for policy. As to *deterring* large mergers, that again is a desirable outcome. There would be a strong disincentive to companies to come forward with merger proposals that rested on flimsy arguments. However, it would not deter merger proposals being made where the parties concerned felt that they had a convincing case. This is as it should be.

Reversing the onus of proof would not mean that large mergers would automatically be banned. It is important, especially in an open economy, that each case be treated on its merits and that due consideration be given to the arguments in favour of large size. It would, however, improve the quality of information supplied by firms to the Commission. It may be argued that reversing the onus of proof is impracticable because acquiring companies have only the most general ideas of the benefits that an acquisition may bring. Perhaps this explains why so many mergers fail. The fact is that, as matters stand, acquiring firms do not have a strong enough incentive to research an acquisition before proceeding with a bid. On economies of scale, for instance, the evidence presented to the Commission often amounts to little more than an assertion that a larger company would be better able to compete in home and overseas markets. A bidding company should be better informed than anyone else about the pros and cons of an acquisition, because it should have given careful thought to the key issues before launching a bid. It would seem reasonable therefore to expect it to be able to 'demonstrate' benefit. Changing the onus of proof would be in the interest of acquiring firms as well as in the interest of better policy. For it would be a powerful inducement to such firms to consider acquisitions more carefully and to produce better evidence.

SPECIFIC ADVERSE EFFECTS AND EFFECTIVE COMPETITORS

In order to recommend that a merger not be allowed to proceed, the present position is that the Commission has to specify particular adverse effects. There is often some difficulty in doing this with conviction, and mergers have been blocked on what, to some observers, have appeared to be trivial or irrelevant grounds. In Lonrho/House of Fraser and Charter Consolidated/Anderson Strathclyde, for instance, emphasis was placed on the adverse effects the merger was expected to have on managerial efficiency. However, in these two cases and others such as Enserch/Davy, Hepworth/Steetley, GKN/AE, and the bids for the Royal Bank of Scotland, a factor that influenced members of the Commission was either that the threatened company was efficient or that it was showing clear signs of improved performance. However, since a merger cannot be blocked simply on the grounds that the company to be acquired is efficient, the Commission may be forced to argue that the efficiency of the acquired company, the acquiring company, or both may be expected to be impaired as a result of the acquisition.

It would be far more satisfactory if the Commission were able to recommend that a merger be stopped on the grounds that it would result in the elimination of a company that, on the evidence available, may be expected to have a successful and independent future. This would not be a radical change since, as the examples in Section 3 make clear, the protection of effective competitors has in a number of cases formed a major part of the Commission's reasons for recommending against a merger. Such a change would also be in the spirit of existing legislation. The wording of Section

84(1)(c) of the 1973 Fair Trading Act is that the Commission should have regard to the desirability 'of promoting, *through competition*, the reduction of costs and the development and use of new techniques . . .' (emphasis added). In other words, there would seem to be a presumption against the acceptance of arguments that these desirable goals are to be achieved by structural changes that are likely to lead to an enhancement of market power, at least if a viable and more competitive alternative is available. The preservation of effective competitors must be good for the maintenance of effective competition.

THE RELEVANCE OF OTHER POLICIES

Finally, it should be emphasized that in deciding on the most appropriate merger policy, consideration should be given to macroeconomic performance and policy. If we have a low growth rate compared with other countries, UK firms will fall behind their overseas competitors in terms of investment, research and development expenditures, etc. They will tend increasingly to look to investment overseas and to take-overs at home in order to protect their positions. It is easier to justify a strong antimerger policy if there are successful macroeconomic policies in place that increase the opportunities for new investment by internal growth. For growth is an important aspect of safety that encourages firms to invest in new capacity and that reduces the importance of take-overs in maintaining competitive positions.

12

Myths and Merger Policy

STEPHEN LITTLECHILD*

1. Introduction

The last formal review of UK merger policy, conducted by a working group of senior government officials under the chairmanship of Mr Hans Liesner, was published as a Green Paper in May 1978 (Department of Prices and Consumer Protection (1978)). The Green Paper recognized that mergers could have numerous beneficial effects, with respect to economies of scale, innovation, productive efficiency, and improvements in technology and management. But it also saw cause for concern, summarized in four main propositions based on economic theory and empirical evidence.

(a) Aggregate concentration has been rapidly increasing in Britain and mergers have contributed at least half the increase;

(b) high concentration in particular industries confers market power and allows excess profits;

(c) mergers are often unprofitable and yield few efficiency gains; and

(d) merger policy is important to prevent dominant firms adopting practices that restrict competition.

In the light of these four propositions, the Green Paper argued that 'a more critical approach to mergers should be adopted'. It recommended that 'the policy should be shifted to a neutral approach', in contrast to the present presumption that mergers are not generally harmful. Other critics, essentially relying on the same four economic propositions, have argued for

---

* Professor of Commerce, University of Birmingham. Professor Littlechild has been a member of the Monopolies and Mergers Commission since 1983.

The author is grateful for comments from Rosemary Clarke, P. Dodd, J. E. Franks, Sir Alan Neale, M. Wright, and B. S. Yamey, and especially discussions with M. E. Beesley, but none of these is to be held responsible for the views expressed herein. The useful monograph by Chiplin and Wright (1987), published after this paper was written, contains additional evidence and references.

more severe forms of merger control. These range from putting the onus on the merging firms to prove that benefits will follow, to a complete prohibition of specified classes of mergers.

It will be argued in this paper that developments in economic theory and empirical evidence that have taken place since 1978 (some of which were available before 1978 but not fully appreciated then) necessitate a substantial revision in the Green Paper's characterization of the benefits and detriments of mergers. As to benefits, less emphasis nowadays would be placed on economies of scale and more on the gains from putting existing assets to better use. Kay (1986) observes that the present merger boom differs from previous ones in precisely this respect. (Hence the greater proportion of contested mergers, as rival managers compete for control.) The reasons for mergers are not fully known: it is difficult to explain the extreme fluctuations in merger activity in terms of swings, either in economies of scale or scope or in management inefficiency, and several other explanations for merger have been proposed (Hughes (this volume), Jensen (1986a), King (1986)). Nevertheless the evidence that on average there *are* benefits to merger has been strengthened, as will be discussed below.

The Green Paper's four propositions concerning detriments of mergers are more vulnerable. None of them can now be maintained with the clarity and confidence with which they were advanced in 1978. At best, they need to be heavily qualified; but some are no longer true, if indeed they ever were. For the most part, they are simply myths. It follows that the economic case for stricter merger control is severely weakened, if indeed it can be advanced at all.

Bearing in mind the difficulty of identifying and estimating costs and benefits *ex ante*, some have argued for abandoning merger control altogether, instead putting the emphasis on *ex post* monitoring of anticompetitive practices (Beesley (1973)). Others have pointed out the drawbacks of this approach (George (this volume)).

It is not argued here that *no* form of merger control is required. It is increasingly recognized that the main threat to the competitive market process derives from barriers to entry. Mergers may be a means of creating or raising entry barriers, thereby enabling monopoly power to be more extensively exploited. Where this is likely, investigation is appropriate. It may be possible and desirable to modify the barriers, or to specify safeguards under which a merger may proceed. In some cases, however, prohibiting the merger may be the least unsatisfactory means of protection against monopoly.

The evidence and analysis presented in this paper suggest that, in so far as present policy embodies the presumption that mergers are generally not harmful, it is right to do so. Rather than an increase in the scope or severity of merger control, a more narrow focusing on those few but problematic mergers involving barriers to entry is indicated. This can easily be done within the present legal framework by a modification in the Secretary of State's merger policy statement.

An examination of referred mergers since 1980 suggests that the effect of this modification might be to reduce the number of mergers referred by between one-quarter and one-half. If the Monopolies and Mergers Commission found the 'barriers to entry' criterion persuasive, the number of investigated and non-abandoned mergers found against the public interest might also fall, but only slightly as a proportion of the reduced number of mergers referred. Such reductions in referrals and adverse verdicts would be beneficial in several respects.

2. Myth 1: Aggregate Concentration and Mergers

It was a widely held fear in the late 1970s that concentration was relentlessly increasing, fuelled by 'merger mania'. This fear seems to have prompted the then Secretary of State, Mr Roy Hattersley, to order the review of merger policy. The Green Paper confirmed the fear. 'Aggregate concentration . . . has been rapidly increasing in Britain in the post-war era' (pp. 11–12) and 'Since the late 1950's mergers have contributed at least half the increase in concentration' (p. 15). In his foreword to the Green Paper, Mr Hattersley stated that 'The increasing concentration of industrial power is the most obvious indication of the need to re-examine our competition policy'.

Calculations by Prais (1976) were presented showing that the share of the 100 largest enterprises in UK manufacturing output rose steadily from 16 per cent in 1909 to 41 per cent in 1968. Prais (1974, pp. 284–5) had earlier estimated that 'At the current rate of increase one might guess that the hundred largest manufacturing enterprises will be responsible for two-thirds of net output in manufacturing within another decade' (that is, by 1983). The Green Paper also presented later calculations by Prais (1977) showing that the share of the largest 100 firms was 39 per cent, 40 per cent, and 41 per cent in the three years 1970, 1971, and 1972 respectively. Because of a change in census statistics, these figures were not entirely comparable to those of the earlier years, but they suggested that the trend was continuing.

Subsequent evidence shows that the trend came to a halt. The share of the 100 largest firms reached 42.2 per cent in 1974 but remained slightly below that level thereafter (Mann and Scholefield (1986) Table 1). A recent study of the whole economy (not just the manufacturing sector) finds that 'the share of the top 100 firms in aggregate concentration has been declining since the mid-1970's' (Hughes and Kumar (1984a)).

Similar results obtain for concentration in individual industries. The

5-firm concentration ratio, averaged over 93 comparable industries, increased dramatically from 1958 to 1968, but only slightly during the early 1970s. Since then it has been declining, apparently at an increasing rate (Mann and Scholefield (1986)).

The Green Paper summarized four studies which calculated that mergers accounted for between one-third and two-thirds of the increase in concentration during the 1950s and 1960s. It noted a further study which attributed *all* the increase in concentration to mergers (and, indeed, calculated that concentration would have fallen in the absence of mergers).

But since the 1960s the pattern of mergers has undergone a striking change. There are proportionately fewer horizontal mergers and more diversifying (conglomerate) mergers. The Green Paper noted (p. 16) that in the late 1960s diversification accounted for about 7 per cent of mergers (by value of assets), whereas by the early 1970s this had risen to 29 per cent. This proportion has now risen to 40 per cent in the 1980s and hit 54 per cent in 1985 (Hughes (this volume)). The corresponding proportion of horizontal mergers fell from 89 per cent in the late 1960s to about 66 per cent throughout the 1970s, to 57 per cent in the 1980s and 42 per cent in 1985. The significance of this change is that whereas horizontal mergers increase concentration within an industry, diversifying mergers typically do not.

There have been other important changes in the pattern of merger activity. An increasing proportion of what are classed as mergers are not in fact the joining of two hitherto independent companies, but the sale of a subsidiary by one company to another. Such transfers have increased from around 20 per cent by number and 13 per cent by value in the period 1968–73, to around 28 per cent by number and 20 per cent by value in the period 1979–85 (Hughes (this volume)). There has also been a remarkable growth of management buy-outs during the 1980s—the three largest in 1985 and 1986 averaging about £100 million each, and the largest to date being £273 million (Chiplin and Wright (1987), Wright and Coyne (1987)). Sales of subsidiaries and management buy-outs do not necessarily increase concentration, either in individual markets or in aggregate, and may well decrease it.

A survey of recent studies casts doubt on the earlier claims concerning the extent to which mergers increase aggregate concentration (Hughes (this volume)). Merger booms during the 1960s in the USA, and during the period 1968–73 in the UK, changed aggregate concentration hardly at all. The explanation for concentration is evidently more complex.

The Green Paper did not explain how aggregate concentration (in the UK as a whole) would adversely affect consumers. Indeed, it acknowledged that the concept does not reflect the importance of imports, which provide a source of competition to rival domestic production. International trade has been increasing since the 1970s. It has been calculated that the influence of imports on average 5-firm industry concentration was almost 2½ times as great in 1977 as in 1958 (Utton and Morgan (1983)), and that this influence has persisted and indeed grown during the early 1980s (Mann and Scholefield (1986)). It is not clear that aggregate concentration has any useful bearing on merger policy.

3. Myth 2: Concentration and Profits

The Green Paper argued that high concentration in particular *industries* would have detrimental effects:

> the market power arising from high concentration may permit excess profits to be made. (p. 14)

> It is widely held that one consequence of high concentration is the ability of some firms to restrict output and obtain abnormally high profits. . . . In a survey of the very extensive US literature on the subject, Weiss (1974) concluded that a statistically significant relationship existed between the degree of concentration and profits. (p. 71)

The Green Paper admitted that 'For the UK recent research (Gribbin 1977) tends to confirm US results but the relationship is if anything weaker and emerges with less clarity' (p. 71). Recent surveys confirm this view: 'The results of studies based on UK data are mixed, and in general less favourable to the profitability concentration hypothesis than the studies for the US' (Yamey (1985) p. 128). 'There is no evidence that concentration had a positive effect on the average level of, or the (linear) trend in, profit margins in this period [1970–6]' (Clarke (1984) p. 66).

Moreover, even the evidence for a concentration–profits relationship in the USA was debatable in 1978. The survey by Weiss was published in a conference volume which contained a companion paper by Demsetz surveying the same extensive US literature. Demsetz (1974, p. 174) concluded that 'more studies reveal a positive correlation between profits and concentration than do not. There are enough of those that fail to show such a correlation, however, that the policymaker ought not suppose that conclusive evidence of this statistical relationship exists.'

There has been much research since the mid-1970s, which has yielded sometimes conflicting evidence and interpretations, but the balance of evidence now rejects the claim that higher concentration leads to higher profit. Apparently positive relationships between concentration and profits have not been sustained in studies with later and better data (Schwartzman (1959) and Bodoff (1975) for the US and Canada; Cowling and Waterson (1976) and Hart and Morgan (1977) for the UK). Any remaining concentration–profits relationship can be better explained by the greater profitability of larger firms in more concentrated industries (Demsetz (1973), Carter (1978); but see Clarke, Davies, and Waterson (1984) for the UK), by the association between increases in concentration and reductions in costs (Peltzman (1977), Lustgarten (1979)), or indeed by purely random growth processes (Mancke (1974)). (These and many other papers are referenced in Yamey (1985).) We have already noted that calculations of industry concentration do not take into account the increasing importance of foreign trade.

The present state of knowledge (at least in the USA) has been summarized as follows (Brozen (1982) pp. 10–11). First, accounting profits are positively related to concentration only in some years, not all years. Second, the efficiencies of large size and superior performance are the major reasons for high concentration. Third, the largest firms in almost all industries are more productive than smaller firms in the same industries; this circumstance, and not concentration, caused the positive concentration–profit relationship in those years in which it occurred. Fourth, the concentration–profitability relationship weakened or disappeared when other causes were admitted into the design of regressions. Fifth, profitable industries (both concentrated and diffused) were shown to be profitable because of temporary disequilibria (due to unanticipated changes in demand or cost) which disappeared as competition led to adjustments towards long-run equilibria.

Many US economists, lawyers, and politicians favoured a policy of deconcentration during the 1950s and 1960s. In 1968 a Task Force on Antitrust Policy appointed by President Johnson recommended that any industry in which the 4 biggest firms persistently accounted for 70 per cent or more of its output should be compulsorily broken up by reducing the size of all firms with more than 15 per cent of the market. By the late 1970s this enthusiasm had waned, and the signatories to the Task Force report had recanted. One of them—Professor William Baxter, subsequently appointed Assistant Attorney General for Antitrust at the Department of Justice—explained that 'the state of the economic art has changed somewhat since 1968' (quoted in Brozen (1982, pp. 388–9) and Yamey (1985, p. 128)). The relaxation of US merger guidelines during the 1980s is one reflection of this change in view (Hay (this volume)).

4. Myth 3: Mergers, Profitability, and Efficiency

The Green Paper summarized available studies as follows: 'Mergers are often found to be unprofitable by those carrying them out and little in the way of efficiency gains seemed to be realised. . . . it is difficult to find empirical support for the proposition that mergers tend in general to *raise* business efficiency' (pp. 104–5).

Among the motives for merger, the Green Paper noted the search for advantages of size with respect to economies in research, production, distribution, and marketing, and for the various financial benefits arising from the tax system. It also drew attention to 'managerial behaviour of a different kind', associated with growth maximization rather than profit maximization (p. 100), and claimed that 'the increasing divorce between the ownership and control of firms provides an incentive for growth by acquisition' (p. 17).

Managerial theories of the firm never satisfactorily explained how sales or growth maximizers could survive against a profit maximizer. There is enough evidence that a number of the latter are around. With the use of leveraged bids, pure size is no longer an adequate defence against take-over, as witness the Elders IXL/Allied-Lyons bid.

It is no longer accepted uncritically that in fact there is, or ever was, a separation between ownership and control. Demsetz (1983) has shown that US top managers have a substantial proportion of their own wealth in their companies' shares. The incidence of share incentive schemes is also much more widespread nowadays, which has been attributed to the 1978 Finance Act (Hanson (1987)). The Institute of Directors reports that 'more than half the UK's company directors now have some performance-related element in their pay. Recent studies indicate this figure will rise 5–10 per cent next year' (*Director*, November 1986, reported in *The Times*, 3 November 1986).

It is now better understood how take-overs can protect shareholders even where ownership may be dispersed among many small and passive shareholders. The stock market is not just a means of raising funds; it is also a 'market for corporate control', in which alternative management teams compete for the right to manage a company's resources (Manne (1965)). This competition between management teams protects shareholders by limiting divergence from shareholder wealth maximization: inefficient managements are vulnerable to a take-over bid. So, too, are corporations whose internal control mechanisms are too slow, costly, or clumsy to bring about the restructuring required by changes in technology or market conditions (Jensen (1986a)).

This is not to argue that the capital market is perfect. The transactions costs of take-over inevitably leave some margin for managerial discretion. It takes time to acquire and interpret relevant information. There may be a 'free-rider' problem whereby shareholders refuse to sell because they think that the shares will be worth more than a bidder is offering, so the bidder fails to gain control (Grossman and Hart (1980)). There are not always several teams of able and enterprising managers lining up to take over from every flaccid management. Bidders as well as victims may be seeking empires, perks, or quiet lives. Not all, or even most, diversifying mergers are necessarily for the best. Some companies may benefit by escaping rather than embracing take-over. Suggestions have therefore been made for improvements or alternatives to the market for corporate control (Kay (1986), King (this volume)). Despite all this, the present market for corporate control provides more adequate protection for shareholders than any other known device. The threat of take-over acts as a spur to efficiency. Any reduction in this threat would affect not only those mergers actually proposed, but potentially *all* companies whether envisaging merger or not.

The Green Paper placed considerable emphasis on studies of post-merger profitability using accounting data, which found that mergers tended to reduce profits. The most important of these was the influential study by Meeks (1977), which had then just been published, based on a sample of 213 larger quoted companies that merged in the period 1964–72.

> After adjusting for the accounting bias and the level of profits experienced by the industry to which the merged company belonged, the profits of the combined company were compared with the profits of the acquiring and acquired firms in the three years before the merger. Profitability fell on average after the merger. Only in the year of the merger was there an increase in average profits and too much weight cannot be attached to this finding because measurement problems are especially acute in that year. But in all subsequent years including the seventh average profits were lower than before the merger with over half the merged firms experiencing a decline. (p. 18)

The Green Paper noted that 'these conclusions on post-merger profitability have to be interpreted bearing in mind that many mergers have increased the market share of the enlarged company' (p. 19). This combination of increased market power and reduced profitability cast severe doubt on the claim that mergers tended to increase business efficiency. A recent US study has shown a similar decline in accounting measures of post-merger profitability (Ravenscraft and Scherer (1986b)). However, Cosh, Hughes, and Singh (1980) found suggestions of an increase in post-merger profitability in the UK.

The Green Paper acknowledged that the accounting studies of merger profitability 'are subject to many limitations and have been variously criticised' (p. 18). Awareness of these limitations has become more acute since 1978, and criticisms have become more explicit (notably Fisher and McGowan (1983)), to the extent that the accounting approach has more or less been abandoned in favour of the study of share prices.

> The accounting studies [of merger profitability] are in the minority since they are fraught with problems. First it is not clear what accounting criteria should be used to judge success, nor how long after the acquisition researchers need to look. Second it is extremely difficult to isolate the component of performance due to the acquisition, particularly when looking only at annual consolidated accounts, and when the majority of acquisitions are small relative to the size of the acquiror.

Third, it is very difficult to control for what would have happened in the absence of the acquisition. Fourth, accounting numbers are notoriously difficult to compare, both over time and across companies, particularly given the obfuscating effects of different post-merger accounting treatments. Finally, it is almost impossible to translate changes in accounting numbers into statements about the value of the deal, and its impact on shareholder wealth.

For these and many other reasons, the accounting studies on merger profitability have been unconvincing and inconclusive. Instead, most researchers now look directly at share price histories. In an efficient stock market, the news of a bid will be rapidly evaluated and incorporated in the share prices of both the acquiror and the acquiree. Share price changes around the time of the announcement therefore provide a direct measure of the market's assessment of the value of the move to the bidder, to the victim, and to the two parties combined. (Marsh (1986))

Marsh refers to forty or fifty such studies, notably the survey by Jensen and Ruback (1983), which yield 'a broadly consistent picture'. US studies indicate that acquired (target) firms in successful take-overs experience abnormal share price gains averaging 20 per cent in agreed mergers and 30 per cent (50–60 per cent after 1975) in hostile bids. Share price increases for acquirer firms are much smaller, averaging 4 per cent for hostile bids and zero for agreed mergers. Only one study (Dodd (1983)) records a loss. The significance of these results is as follows.

Quite simply, if acquirees' shareholders gain, and if (at worst) acquirors' shareholders do not lose, there must therefore be net gains to shareholders from acquisitions. Put another way, acquisitions have historically allowed companies to reap economic and efficiency gains. (Marsh (1986) p. 12)

What is the evidence for the UK? Franks, Broyles and Hecht (1977) found significant positive gains to acquirees and no offsetting losses to acquirers in the brewing industry during 1955–72. Firth (1979, 1980) found any gains to acquirees more than offset by losses to acquirers over 1969–75. Barnes (1984) found small gains to acquirers for 39 mergers in 1974–6, but greater losses during the subsequent 6 months. Dodds and Quek (1985) used a larger sample for the same period and found similar results to Franks *et al*. The latest and most comprehensive study (Franks and Harris (1986a)), of nearly 1,900 acquisitions over the period 1955–85, shows large bid premiums to acquirees (averaging 22 per cent) and modest gains to acquirers (averaging 1 per cent). The gains are larger for the 6-month period surrounding the bid (30 per cent and 7 per cent respectively). Evidently there are net gains overall, as in the USA. Australian evidence presents a similar picture (Dodd and Officer (1986)).

It might be conjectured that the profitability of mergers derives in part from (expected) price increases consequent upon greater monopoly power. However, this seems not to be the case, since companies in the same industry, which might be expected to benefit from such a reduction in competition, do not experience positive abnormal share price increases (Jensen and Ruback (1983)).

The proper interpretation of the share price changes is nonetheless not entirely clear. If there is competition between potential sellers of companies as well as potential buyers, why should the lion's share of the gains go to acquirees? To some extent the gains to acquiree shareholders reflect a premium paid for control of the company, without any implication that the incumbent management is inefficient (Hughes (this volume)).

How accurately do changes in share prices reflect the discounted value of future gains from merger? There are some indications of systematic reductions in post-merger share prices of bidding firms. This is puzzling: one would not expect the stock market systematically to over-estimate future efficiency gains. An alternative explanation is that acquirers time mergers to follow favourable performance in their own share prices (Franks and Harris (this volume)). On this latter argument, acquirers' profit and share price performance would have declined anyway, even in the absence of the merger. Profit performance immediately before the merger is thus an inappropriate bench-mark for judging efficiency. (This might also explain Meeks's accounting data results.) If the performance of other firms is taken as the relevant bench-mark, there is evidence that 'subsequent to mergers, acquiror shareholders match or slightly outperform the market in general' (Franks and Harris (1986a) p. 25).

The precise nature and extent of the gains from merger are thus debatable. Investors in the stock market do not seem to share the enthusiasm of companies doing the acquiring, but on average they judge the effect on both bidder and target to be positive rather than negative. Thus, despite the reservations, the overall picture has changed significantly since 1978, when a few accounting studies constituted all the available evidence on profitability and efficiency of mergers.

> . . . those who would argue that acquisitions are a vice rather than a virtue should recognise that the balance of evidence is currently against them. There is evidence of net gains to shareholders, and no countervailing evidence of losses to other groups. The onus of proof, therefore, lies with the critics of mergers. Indeed, those who are pressing for greater restraint on merger activity run the risk of making the market for corporate control less efficient. (Marsh (1986))

We may note in passing that recent studies have exploded a great many other myths about take-over. It is widely believed that take-over bidders focus on short-term results at the expense of sound long-term growth. However, merging firms in the UK show higher post-merger growth rates of assets than do non-merging firms (Cosh, Hughes, and Singh (1980)) and, on average, merger leads to a small increase in investment (Kumar (1984)). In the US, acquired companies typically do no research and development or less than half the industry average, and their ratio of capital expenditure to earnings is also below the industry average; this implies that companies are not made more vulnerable to take-over by taking a longer-term view (Jarrell and Lehn (1985), Pound, Lehn, and Jarrell (1986); see also Jensen (1986a)).

5. Myth 4: Practices of Dominant Firms

Stricter merger control is often advocated on the grounds that 'prevention is better than cure' (for example, George (this volume)). The Green Paper was sympathetic to this argument: 'certain practices of dominant firms are directly aimed at restricting competition and are unlikely to benefit consumers' (p. 22), so given the difficulty of dealing with dominant firms, merger policy is 'important to prevent the further development of such situations' (pp. 33–4).

The Green Paper reviewed the 32 Monopolies (and Mergers) Commission reports, issued from 1959 to 1977, on monopolies and oligopolies in the supply of goods. Eight practices were identified which were sometimes but not always found against the public interest, and another 6 practices which 'might reasonably be presumed to be against the public interest under any normal circumstances. In general terms they are those which serve as entry barriers to preserve the position of the leading firms' (p. 74). Two of these 6 practices—namely tie-in sales and full-line forcing—were singled out in a companion Green Paper as 'likely almost invariably to operate against the public interest' (Department of Prices and Consumer Protection (1979) p. 56). It was proposed that they be prohibited *per se* following a general reference to the Commission. For present purposes it will be sufficient to assess whether the need to prevent these two practices provides any justification for stricter merger control.

The 1978 Green Paper's objection to these two practices was twofold. 'Full-line forcing and tie-in sales reflect the ability of multi-product firms to carry over a dominant position from one market into another and serve as an entry barrier to other firms who produce the tied good or other items in the line.' (p. 75.)

These explanations of tie-ins were once standard. But they are no longer tenable. The 'leverage' theory—that monopoly power can be carried over from one market to another—is false because monopoly profit can only be extracted once. The customer cares about the *total* price paid. A monopolist can take its profits *either* on the tying good *or* on the tied good, but it cannot take the same profit twice. If it extracts monopoly profit on punch cards or photocopying ink (to use the classic cases), it can no longer charge a monopoly price for the computer or photocopying machine.

The more plausible explanation for such tie-ins is that they are a form of price discrimination (Posner (1979) p. 929). A customer's usage is broadly correlated with willingness to pay, so a charge based on usage (punch cards or ink) will extract more consumer surplus. Tie-in sales are thus not intended to monopolize the tied good market, but are rather a means of extracting a greater monopoly profit from the tying good than would otherwise be legally or commercially possible. And as the Green Paper acknowledged, discriminatory behaviour 'can be undesirable [but] will not always be against the public interest. Thus, monopolistic price discrimination increases the size of the market as well as the profits of the monopolist' (p. 21).

Nor are such tie-ins a barrier to entry in the tied good market: the monopolist would be quite happy to purchase cards or ink from a new competitor who could produce them more cheaply than the monopolist itself.

Different explanations of tie-ins seem more plausible in other cases—for example, to control the quality of supplies so as to protect the reputation of the machine. This argument was accepted by the Commission in the case of Rank Xerox materials and parts (but not paper and ink). Here again, the aim is not to extend monopoly to the tied good market. Nor is it to erect an entry barrier: reliable and cheaper new supplies and processors will increase rather than decrease monopoly profits on the tying good and render the tie no longer necessary. Prohibiting the tie may jeopardize the quality of service. (For yet other explanations of tie-ins, see Scherer (1980) pp. 582–5.)

In its 1981 report on tie-in sales and full-line forcing, the Monopolies and Mergers Commission found no clear examples of ties used to extend monopoly power from one product to another (with one possible exception), and reaffirmed that materials and spares tied to machines (for example, copiers) might be justified on technical grounds. It found no widespread consumer objection to ties. Full-line forcing was rare, and in the one clear case (pharmaceutical wholesaling) was generally accepted as necessary. The Commission concluded that tie-in sales were by no means always against the public interest.

Many of the other practices hitherto viewed with hostility or suspicion by economists, and by the Green Paper, have been re-examined by Chicago economists 'through the lens of price theory' (Posner (1979)). The general thrust of their argument is that, despite initial appearances, these practices are typically *not* anticompetitive or exclusionary in the sense of extending monopoly power to new markets, or erecting entry barriers there, or driving out competitors. Such practices would be unprofitable (and unlikely to be persisted in by companies that wrongly supposed they would deter entry). The practices actually adopted are a means to increase profit either by price discrimination or by reducing transactions costs, but this is not necessarily, or even generally, against the interests of consumers. The case for stricter merger control as a means of preventing the emergence of such practices is correspondingly weakened.

6. Barriers to Entry

We have shown that the four propositions on which the 1978 Green Paper based its argument for a more critical approach to mergers have subsequently been shown to be false or no longer true. However, this is not to argue that mergers may not, in some circumstances, pose a threat to competition and need to be investigated and prevented on that account. It is therefore necessary to establish the nature of competition in order to identify which mergers might threaten it.

From the 1930s to the early 1970s, the static concept of 'perfect competition' was widely used as a bench-mark for appraising the efficiency of markets. It is now increasingly recognized (as it was by Adam Smith and the Austrian economists) that competition needs to be seen as a process of rivalry taking place over time (McNulty (1967), Kirzner (1973), Littlechild (1986)). In this view, the extent of competition is related not to the number of competitors in the market but to the ease of entry into the market. Barriers to entry are the ultimate source of monopoly power. Where potential suppliers who would like to compete are prevented from doing so, existing suppliers are able to earn abnormally high profits by raising price, lowering quality, resisting innovation, and in general failing to meet the wishes of consumers.

It must immediately be admitted that the definition, identification, and measurement of entry barriers are fraught with difficulty and the subject of dispute. Three of the four barriers proposed by Bain (1956)—namely capital requirements, product differentiation, and economies of scale—are now largely discredited (Stigler (1968), Brozen (1969)), although sunk costs still command respect (Dixit (1982), Beesley (1986)).

Advertising is no longer generally regarded as a barrier to entry. It is increasingly seen as a means of competition and indeed of entry itself (Brozen (1974)). It is the *prohibition* of advertising which hinders the entry and growth of new competitors. Current UK (and US) policy towards the professions reflects this view.

Similarly, reputation is more appropriately interpreted not as a barrier, but as a means of *overcoming* the barrier generated by the cost of transmitting and acquiring information. Prohibiting mergers where reputation is important will discourage the building up of such reputation; this can ease entry in the short term, but only at the expense of discouraging activities (for example, the maintenance of quality) that are beneficial to customers in the longer term (Demsetz (1982), George (this volume)).

Other barriers allegedly erected by dominant firms themselves are of doubtful importance. As the previous section indicated, many practices that *seem* anticompetitive are not designed to deter entry. Nor do they have that effect. Shaw and Simpson (1986) found that, following Monopolies and Mergers Commission monopoly investigations, there was a statistically significant but modest decline in the market share of leading firms, and an even pattern of gains and losses by second-rank firms. But this pattern was equally found in a control group of markets investigated by the National Board for Prices and Incomes (NBPI). Abandoning so-called anticompetitive practices (in the Commission group but not in the NBPI control group) apparently had no effect on growth of competitors. A set of eight case studies confirmed that 'the MMC [Monopolies and Mergers Commission] criticisms and recommendations, and the resulting undertakings given to government, had only a minor impact on the process of competition' (Shaw and Simpson (1985) p. 95).

Sole ownership of an input necessary to production is a more substantial barrier. Potential entrants are forced to use inferior inputs or to compete via different products: the competitive process is diverted although not destroyed. A case can be made that sole ownership secured as a result of competition is not always undesirable, because the resulting monopoly profit may be a necessary incentive to discover and supply a new product or introduce a new technology (Kirzner (1973)). Monopoly is a market alternative to patents as a means of internalizing the social benefits of a public good. But in any actual case, the advantages claimed for sole ownership would have to be carefully scrutinized and weighed against the disadvantages.

The most fundamental and undeniable barrier to entry—what Bain called an *absolute* barrier—is that established and enforced by government. Examples are statutory monopolies, licences, quotas, patents, and copyright. All these restrict and distort competition.

Not all barriers are necessarily undesirable: creating a barrier means that some lose but others gain, and the gainers may include classes of consumers whom it is desired to protect. Or it may be thought that consumers in general will benefit (for example, from the longer-term incentive to innovate provided by patents and copyright) despite the short-term restrictions on price competition. But in many cases, perhaps most, statutory barriers to entry serve only to protect privileged incumbents, at the expense of consumers and potential competitors. The problem is to decide which barriers to entry (that is, which sets of property rights) are, on balance, socially beneficial (von Weizsäcker (1980), Demsetz (1982)).

What is the relationship between mergers and entry barriers? It is to be assumed that firms fully exploit whatever monopoly power they derive from existing barriers to entry. A merger is a source of concern if it increases this monopoly power. *Attention is therefore drawn to those cases where a merger creates or increases barriers to entry.* A merger may also facilitate the better exploitation of existing barriers where, before the merger, commercial or legal costs of collusion outweigh the benefits of collusion to the parties concerned. In the light of the foregoing discussion of the various types of entry barrier, potentially the most serious case is where a merger increases the ability of the firms involved to influence government to erect or raise some form of barrier in their favour.

An implication for merger policy follows immediately. Where there are no significant barriers to entry, and where the merger does not create any, there is prima facie no need for a merger investigation on competition grounds. But where there *are* significant barriers to entry—more particularly, where the merger would create or increase them—there is a prima-facie case for a Commission investigation. The outcome of this investigation cannot be specified in advance. It may be possible and desirable to remove or reduce the barriers to entry; or certain other conditions might be imposed as a condition of approving the merger, in order not to increase the barriers; or it may be necessary to prohibit the merger. The appropriate solution will depend upon the circumstances of each particular case.

7. Entry Barriers and Referred Mergers

What role do entry barriers presently play in UK merger policy? From 1980 to 1986, there were 46 mergers referred and either abandoned or reported on. In 15 of those mergers—one-third of the number referred—barriers to entry may be identified in the Commission report (see Table 12.1). As noted earlier, there is inevitably a large element of subjectivity in the identification of a barrier. Here, a merger is classified as having an entry barrier if government licensing or purchasing was involved (for example, casinos, TV, pubs, banking, telecoms, and defence), although this may or may not have played a major role in the eventual verdict. One entry barrier based on economies of scale and reported difficulties of new entrants was also included, despite the earlier remarks on the definition of entry, because the Commission laid great stress on this in its report (GUS/Empire Stores). (For the abandoned mergers, the existence or otherwise of barriers was deduced from other reports in which the same or similar companies were involved.)

Table 12.2 cross-classifies mergers according to existence of entry barriers and outcome. Of those mergers where the Commission gave a verdict, about half were judged against the public interest and half not. But where

Table 12.1. Barriers to entry in referred mergers, 1980–6

Year	Merger	Acquired assets (£m.)	Commission verdict[a]	Nature of barrier
1980	Hiram Walker/Highland Distilleries	33	A	Reputation; capital costs
	Berisford/BSC	339	U d	Sugar beet quotas
	Grand Met/Coral	113	ab	Casino licensing
1981	European Ferries/Sealink	169	A	Port facilities
	Hong Kong & Shanghai/Royal Bank of Scotland	487	A d	Bank of England recognition
	Standard Chartered/ Royal Bank of Scotland	487	A d	Bank of England recognition
1982	ICI/Holden	17	Na	Technology
	GUS/Empire Stores	53	A	Scale economies; failure of entrants
1983	Pleasurama/Trident TV	22	A d[b]	Casino licensing
	Grand Met/Trident TV	22	A d	Casino licensing
1984	Scottish & Newcastle/ Cameron	52	ab	Tied houses; licensing laws
1985	Scottish & Newcastle/ Matthew Brown	65	Na	Tied houses; licensing laws
	BT/Mitel (C$464m.)	300	U d	Licensing telecom operators
	Elders/Allied Lyons	1 910	Na	Tied houses; licensing laws
1986	GEC/Plessey	576	A d	Ministry of Defence 'Buy British' policy; patents

[a]Key to Commission verdict:

A	against public interest;
Na	not against public interest;
U	allowed subject to undertakings;
d	dissenting opinion;
ab	abandoned.

[b]Subsequent merger of Pleasurama and Trident TV not referred, 20 February 1985.

there were *no* entry barriers, over two-thirds were found not against the public interest, whereas if there *were* entry barriers, less than a quarter were so held. Thus entry barriers do seem to make a difference to the verdict, even though influence is not always acknowledged in the text of the report.

Table 12.2. Analysis of mergers referred to the Commission, 1980–6

	Outcome of Commission reference			Total
	Abandoned	Not against	Against	
No entry barriers	8	16	7	31
Entry barriers	2	3	10	15
Total	10	19	17	46

Source: Commission reports from 1 January 1980 to 30 December 1986.

Nearly one-quarter of all mergers referred were abandoned. The proportion of mergers abandoned was twice as high where there were no entry barriers as where there were. Calculations not reported here show that the abandoned merger typically involved a smaller target company: the value of the assets to be acquired was under £100 million for 90 per cent of abandoned mergers, compared with 55 per cent of non-abandoned mergers; the value was under £25 million for 50 per cent of abandoned mergers compared with 20 per cent of others.

Of the 10 adverse verdicts where there were entry barriers, the 2 Royal Bank of Scotland judgements were mainly based on non-competition grounds. In a further 2 cases (GUS/Empire Stores and Hiram Walker/Highland Distillers) the judgements did not turn on entry barriers as strictly defined in the preceding section. The Commission's decision may be interpreted as arguing that the merger would increase the height or exploitation of barriers in the remaining 6 cases: Berisford/British Sugar, European Ferries/Sealink, BT/Mitel, GEC/Plessey, and the 2 Trident TV mergers.

8. Recommendations for Policy

In order to use the resources of the Commission most effectively, with the minimum of disruption and disincentive to the economy, the analysis of the previous sections suggests that it would be sensible to use barriers to entry more explicitly as a criterion for referral.

Several commentators have called for merger guidelines, presumably of a quantitative nature along US lines. The latter are couched in terms of concentration ratios, which (it has been argued above) do not provide an adequate basis for assessing potential monopoly power. Moreover the definition and interpretation of the US guidelines have changed noticeably since their first introduction in 1968, and it is not clear how predictable they presently are (George (1985), Hay (this volume)).

Could alternative guidelines be devised based on barriers to entry? It seems doubtful whether they could be defined sufficiently precisely and unambiguously to be useful. Nevertheless, attention could be drawn to the importance of entry in a straightforward way.

Present policy on referring mergers is embodied in the statement of 5 July 1984 by the then Secretary of State for Trade and Industry, Mr Norman Tebbit.

> I regard mergers policy as an important part of the Government's general policy of promoting competition within the economy in the interests of the customer and of efficiency and hence of growth and jobs. Accordingly my policy has been and will continue to be to make references primarily on competition grounds. In evaluating the competitive situation in individual cases I shall have regard to the international context: to the extent of competition in the home market from non-United Kingdom sources and to the competitive position of United Kingdom companies in overseas markets. (Quoted in Office of Fair Trading (1985) p. 44)

The proposed approach is fully consistent with this policy. International competition in the home market is a particularly important type of entry. But the significance of entry barriers does need to be spelled out more explicitly—and, by implication, the absence of threat to competition posed by mergers that do not create or increase entry barriers. An addition along the following lines might suffice: 'In evaluating the competitive situation in individual cases I shall have regard to *conditions of entry* and to the international context: *to natural or artificial barriers which prevent the entry or growth of competitors*, to the extent of competition in the home market from non-UK sources . . ., etc.'

9. Effects of Recommended Policy

What effect would this modification have had? Pending evidence on the actual effect (if any) of the 1984 policy statement, this can only be conjecture. Suppose explicit attention had been drawn to barriers to entry in the Secretary of State's policy statement, that it had been issued before 1 January 1980, and that as a result the Office of Fair Trading gave greater weight to barriers in its initial screening. It is unlikely that only those 15 mergers with entry barriers would have been referred. The stated policy is to make references *primarily* on competition grounds but not *exclusively* so. As a first approximation, assume that the mergers referred would also have included, of those with no entry barriers, the 7 subsequently found against the public interest, plus 2 where a minority report found against the public interest, plus from 0 to 8 of the subsequently abandoned mergers. Assume no additional mergers would have been referred. Then between 24 and 32 mergers would have been referred, a reduction of between 14 and 22 on the original 46. By extrapolation, the policy amendment suggested would imply a reduction of between one-quarter and one-half in the number of mergers referred (all of the non-referred mergers being cases where no significant entry barriers could be identified).

The Commission is bound by statute, not by the Secretary of State's policy statement on referrals and subsequent action. Any change in the Commission's attitude would presumably reflect a longer-term change in its view of economic analysis and evidence. Again, we can only speculate how a greater emphasis on entry barriers (as opposed to concentration, say) might have altered Commission judgements over this period. We assume no change in the Commission's evaluation of non-competition considerations.

It seems unlikely that there would have been any change in verdict on any of the 19 mergers found not against the public interest. Of the 7 mergers found against the public interest where there were no barriers, 1 involved foreign ownership (Enserch/Davy), but in the remaining 6 cases a change in verdict seems possible. Of the 10 cases found against the public interest where there were barriers to entry, a changed verdict is plausible in 2 cases (GUS/Empire Stores and Hiram Walker/Highland Distilleries), where it is not clear that the merger would have increased either the height or exploitation of the existing barriers. In sum, a changed verdict might have been plausible for 8 cases. This would have reduced the number of adverse verdicts from 17 to 9, a reduction from one-half to one-quarter of the original 36 non-abandoned references. But if the number of references were reduced from 46 to between 24 and 32, the proportion adverse would be reduced only slightly.

The hypothetical overall result is shown in Table 12.3 (assuming no further modification in number of mergers referred).

10. Benefits of Proposed Policy

The proposed modification in policy would have several benefits.

First, the effectiveness of competition policy would be increased by focusing the Department of Trade and Industry, the Office of Fair Trading, and the Monopolies and Mergers Commission more precisely on entry conditions as determining the threat to competition.

Table 12.3. Hypothetical effect of modified merger policy, 1980-6

	Outcome of Commission reference			Total
	Abandoned	Not against	Against	
No entry barriers	0 - 8	8	1	9 - 17
Entry barriers	2	5	8	15
Total	2 - 10	13	9	24 - 32

Second, there would be a modest but worthwhile saving in both public and private costs of operating UK competition policy. A reduction of between 14 and 22 referrals over 7 years, valued at say £0.5 million per referral, would represent an average saving of over £1 million per annum. These are financial outlays; the figure would be significantly higher if the opportunity cost of executive time were taken into account.

Third, a number of potentially beneficial mergers are presently being referred, and subsequently prevented or abandoned, on erroneous competition grounds. No less than a third of all mergers referred involved no entry barriers and were found not against the public interest. Half as many again were abandoned, even though they probably involved no entry barriers. The change in criterion would enable the benefits of these mergers to be realized.

Fourth, a reduction in referrals could increase the effectiveness of the stock market in its function as a market for corporate control. This is because of the 'free-rider' problem (Grossman and Hart (1980, 1981)).

> . . . an investigation reduces the incentive for bidders to gather and process information about prospective acquisitions, if the possibility of investigation increases the likelihood that private information collected by the bidder will be revealed to other potential bidders.
>
> Furthermore, the delays accompanying an investigation (regardless of the outcome) may permit other companies to become bidders, thereby reducing the prospective profits of first processing the information. (Franks and Harris (this volume))

Franks and Harris suggest that current Commission activity is not likely to create large disincentives for gathering information, but that an increased number of investigations (for example, following a change in the burden of proof) could do so. However, even the present level of activity may be a disincentive where a reference is thought likely.

Fifth, parallel bids might present a less substantial problem. Where there are no barriers to entry, there is less likelihood of either being referred; if there are barriers, then both bids are likely to be referred. There would still be a difficulty if one bid would raise the barriers to entry and another not.

Adoption of the proposed policy would encourage public recognition that socially undesirable mergers are a very small subset of all mergers, and that the real problem is barriers to entry. It was noted above that, of the 10 adverse verdicts where there were entry barriers, 2 did not turn on competition issues and in 2 others the existence of the alleged barrier was questionable. This suggests that only about 6 mergers over the last 7 years are likely to have had significant adverse effects on competition. UK competition policy has reduced undesirable barriers to entry in airlines, buses, telecommunications, energy, the City, and the professions, with strikingly successful results. Merger policy too could be orientated in this direction, as argued by economists and policy-makers in the USA and the EEC (Brozen (1982) p. 406, Brozen (1986)). The continued critical examination of barriers to entry throughout the economy is likely to be more effective in promoting competition than an increase in the number of mergers investigated and prevented.

Appendix: The Commission's Merger Reports

1966

Jan	The British Motor Corporation Ltd and the Pressed Steel Company Ltd. HC 46 (1965–66)
May	Ross Group Ltd and Associated Fisheries Ltd. HC 42 (1966)
Aug	The Dental Manufacturing Co Ltd or the Dentists' Supply Co of New York and the Amalgamated Dental Co Ltd. HC 147 (1966)

1967

Jan	Guest, Keen and Nettlefolds Ltd and Birfield Ltd. Cmnd 3186
May	British Insulated Callender's Cables Ltd and Pyrotenax Ltd. HC 490 (1966–67)
Sep	United Drapery Stores Ltd and Montague Burton Ltd. Cmnd 3397

1968

July	Barclays Bank Ltd, Lloyds Bank Ltd and Martins Bank Ltd. HC 319 (1967–68)
July	Thorn Electrical Industries and Radio Rentals Ltd. HC 318 (1967–68)

1969

June	Unilever Ltd and Allied Breweries Ltd. HC 297 (1968–69)
June	The Rank Organisation Ltd and The De La Rue Company Ltd. HC 298 (1967–68)

1970

Nov	British Sidac Ltd and Transparent Paper Ltd. HC 154 (1970)

1972

July	Beecham Group Ltd and Glaxo Group Ltd, The Boots Company Ltd and Glaxo Group Ltd. HC 341 (1971–72)

1973

Oct	British Match Corporation Ltd and Wilkinson Sword Ltd. Cmnd 5442

1974

Apr	Davy International Ltd and The British Rollmakers' Corporation Ltd. HC 67 (1974)
June	Eagle Star Insurance Company Ltd and Bernard Sunley Investment Trust Ltd and Grovewood Securities Ltd. Cmnd 5641
July	Charter Consolidated Investments Ltd and Sadia Ltd. HC 345 (1974)
July	The Boots Company Ltd and House of Fraser Ltd. HC 174 (1974)

1975

June	Dentsply International Incorporated and AD International Ltd. HC 394 (1974–75)
July	The NFU Development Trust Ltd and FMC Ltd. HC 441 (1974–75)
Aug	H Weidmann AG and BS & W Whitely Ltd. Cmnd 6208

1976

May	Amalgamated Industrials Ltd and Herbert Morris Ltd. HC 434 (1975–76)
Oct	Eurocanadian Shipholdings Ltd and Furness Withy and Company Ltd and Manchester Liners Ltd. HC 639 (1975–76)

1977

Feb	Babcock and Wilcox Ltd and Herbert Morris Ltd. HC 175 (1976–77)
Mar	Pilkington Brothers Ltd and UKO International Ltd. HC 267 (1976–77)
May	BP/Century Oil. Cmnd 6827
Aug	The Fruehauf Corporation and Crane Fruehauf Corporation Ltd. Cmnd 6906

1978

Feb	Smith Bros Ltd and Bisgood, Bishop & Co Ltd. HC 242 (1977–78)
May	Rockware Group Ltd, United Glass Ltd, Redfearn National Glass Ltd. HC 431 (1977–78)

1979

Mar	Lonrho Ltd and Scottish and Universal Investments Ltd and House of Fraser Ltd. HC 262 (1978–79)
July	FMC Corporation, Merck & Co, Inc, Alginate Industries Ltd. HC 175 (1979–80)
Sep	The General Electric Company Ltd and Averys Ltd. Cmnd 7653

1980

Aug	Hiram Walker-Gooderham & Worts Ltd and the Highland Distillers Company Ltd. HC 743 (1979–80)
Oct	Blue Circle Industries Ltd and Armitage Shanks Group Ltd. Cmnd 8039

1981

Jan	Compagnie Internationale Europcar and Godfrey Davis Ltd. HC 94 (1980–81)
Mar	S & W Berisford Ltd and British Sugar Corporation Ltd. HC 241 (1980–81)
Jun	British Rail Hovercraft Ltd and Hoverlloyd Ltd. HC 374 (1980–81)
Sep	Enserch Corporation and Davy Corporation Ltd. Cmnd 8360
Dec	European Ferries Ltd, Sealink Ltd. HC 65 (1981–82)
Dec	Lonrho Ltd and House of Fraser Ltd. HC 73 (1981–82)

1982

Jan	The Hongkong and Shanghai Banking Corporation, Standard Chartered Bank Ltd, The Royal Bank of Scotland Group Ltd. Cmnd 8472
June	BTR Ltd and Serck Ltd. HC 392 (1981–82)
Sep	Imperial Chemical Industries PLC and Arthur Holden & Sons PLC. Cmnd 8660
Oct	Nabisco Brands Inc and Huntley & Palmer Foods PLC. Cmnd 8680
Dec	Charter Consolidated PLC and Anderson Strathclyde PLC. Cmnd 8771

1983

Jan	The Great Universal Stores PLC and Empire Stores (Bradford) PLC. Cmnd 8777
May	The Sunlight Service Group PLC and Johnson Group Cleaners PLC and Initial PLC and Johnson Group Cleaners PLC. Cmnd 8868
May	Linfood Holdings PLC and Fitch Lovell PLC. Cmnd 8874
Aug	The Enterprises of Alan J. Lewis and Illingworth Morris PLC. Cmnd 9012
Aug	London Brick PLC and Ibstock Johnsen PLC. Cmnd 9015
Sep	A. Alfred Taubman and Sotheby Parke Bernet Group PLC. Cmnd 9046
Dec	Pleasurama PLC and Trident Television PLC and Grand Metropolitan PLC. Cmnd 9108

1984

Feb Hepworth Ceramic Holdings PLC and Steetley PLC. Cmnd 9164
Mar Trafalgar House PLC and the Peninsular and Oriental Steam Navigation Company. Cmnd 9190
Mar Guest, Keen and Nettlefolds PLC and AE PLC. Cmnd 9199

1985

Jan The Dee Corporation PLC and Booker McConnell PLC. Cmnd 9429
Feb The British Electric Traction Company PLC and Initial PLC. Cmnd 9444
Mar Lonrho PLC and House of Fraser PLC. Cmnd 9548
Nov Scottish & Newcastle Breweries PLC and Matthew Brown PLC. Cmnd 9645

1986

Jan British Telecommunications PLC and Mitel Corporation. Cmnd 9715
May BET Public Limited Company and SGB Group PLC. Cmnd 9795
Aug The General Electric Company PLC and The Plessey Company PLC. Cmnd 9867
Sep Elders IXL Ltd and Allied Lyons PLC. Cmnd 9892
Sep Norton Opax PLC and McCorquodale PLC. Cmnd 9904
Dec The Peninsular and Oriental Steam Navigation Company and European Ferries Group PLC. Cm 31.

References

Aaronovitch, S. and Sawyer, M. C. (1975a), *Big Business*, London: Macmillan.

—— and —— (1975b), 'Mergers, growth and concentration', *Oxford Economic Papers*, **27**, 136–55.

Adams, J. W. and Heimforth, K. (1986), 'The effect of conglomerate mergers on changes in industry concentration', *Antitrust Bulletin*, Spring.

Alchian, A. A. and Demsetz, H. (1972), 'Production, information costs and economic organisation', *American Economic Review*, **62**, 777–95.

—— and Kessel, R. A. (1962), 'Competition, monopoly, and the pursuit of pecuniary gain', in *Aspects of Labour Economics*, Princeton: National Bureau of Economic Research.

Alexander, G. J., Benson, P. G., and Kampmeyer, J. M. (1984), 'Investigating valuation effects of announcements of voluntary corporate sell-off', *Journal of Finance*, **39**, 503–17.

American Enterprise Institute (1985), *Proposals Affecting Corporate Takeovers*, Washington DC: American Enterprise Institute.

Appelbaum, E. (1982), 'The estimation of the degree of oligopoly power', *Journal of Econometrics*, **9**, 283–94.

Appleyard, A. R. (1980), 'Takeovers: accounting policy, financial policy and the case against accounting measures of performance: a synopsis', *Journal of Business Finance and Accounting*, **7**, 541–54.

Arrow, K. (1974), *The Limits of Organisation*, New York: Norton.

Bain, J. S. (1951), 'Relation of profit rate to industry concentration: American manufacturing, 1936–1940', *Quarterly Journal of Economics*, **65**, 293–324.

—— (1956), *Barriers to New Competition: Their Character and Consequences in Manufacturing Industries*, Cambridge, Mass.: Harvard University Press.

—— (1959), *Industrial Organisation*, New York: John Wiley.

Baker, J. B. and Bresnahan, T. F. (1985), 'The gains from merger or collusion in product-differentiated industries', *Journal of Industrial Economics*, **33**, 427–44.

Bank of England (1983), 'The composition of company boards in 1982', *Bank of England Quarterly Bulletin*, **23**, 66–8.

—— (1985), 'The boards of quoted companies', *Bank of England Quarterly Bulletin*, **25**, 233–6.

—— (1986), 'Performance of large companies', *Bank of England Quarterly Bulletin*, **26**, 390–2.

Barnes, P. A. (1978), 'The effect of a merger on the share price of the attacker', *Accounting and Business Research*, **8**, 162–8.

—— (1984), 'The effect of a merger on the share price of the attacker, revisited', *Accounting and Business Research*, **15**, 45–9.

—— (1985), 'UK building societies: a study of the gains from merger', *Journal of Business Finance and Accounting*, **12**, 75–91.

—— and Dodds, J. C. (1981), 'Building society mergers and the size-efficiency relationship: a comment', *Applied Economics*, **13**, 531–4.

Baumol, W. J. (1959), *Business Behaviour, Value and Growth*, New York: Macmillan.

—— (1982), 'Contestable markets: an uprising in the theory of industry structure', *American Economic Review*, **72**, 1–15.

——, Panzar, J. C., and Willig, R. D. (1982), *Contestable Markets and the Theory of Industrial Structure*, New York: Harcourt Brace Jovanovich.

Beesley, M. E. (1973), 'Mergers and economic welfare', in *Mergers, Takeovers and the Structure of Industry*, IEA Readings 10, 73–80.

—— (1986), 'Commitment, sunk costs and entry to the airline industry: reflections on experience', *Journal of Transport Economics and Policy*, **20**, 173–90.

Berle, A. A. and Means, G. C. (1932), *The Modern Corporation and Private Property*, New York: Macmillan.

Berry, C. H. (1975), *Corporate Growth and Diversification*, Princeton: Princeton University Press.

Black, F. (1986), 'Noise', *Journal of Finance*, **41**, 529–43.

Board of Trade (1969), *Mergers: A Guide to Board of Trade Practice*, London: HMSO.

Bodoff, J. (1975), 'Monopoly and price revisited', in Y. Brozen (ed.), *The Competitive Economy*, Morristown, NJ: General Learning Press.

Boesky, I. F. (1985), *Merger Mania*, London: The Bodley Head.

Bolton (1971), *Small Firms: Report of the Committee of Inquiry on Small Firms*, Cmnd 4811, London: HMSO.

Bork, R. H. (1978), *The Antitrust Paradox: A Policy at War With Itself*, New York: Basic Books.

Borooah, V. K. and van der Ploeg, F. (1986), 'Oligopoly power in British industry', *Applied Economics*, **18**, 583–98.

Boswell, J. (1972), *The Rise and Decline of Small Firms*, London: Allen and Unwin.

Boudreaux, K. J. (1975), 'Divestiture and share price', *Journal of Financial and Quantitative Analysis*, **10**, 619–29.

Bradburd, R. M. and Over, A. M. (1982), 'Organizational costs, "sticky" equilibria and critical levels of concentration', *Review of Economics and Statistics*, **64**, 50–8.

Bradley, M., Desai, A., and Kim, E. (1983), 'The rationale behind interfirm tender offers: information or synergy', *Journal of Financial Economics*, **11**, 183–206.

Brealey, R. and Myers, S. (1981), *Principles of Corporate Finance*, New York: McGraw-Hill.

Brooks, D. and Smith, R. (1963), *Mergers Past and Present*, London: Acton Society Trust.

Brown, S. J. and Warner, J. B. (1980), 'Measuring security price performance', *Journal of Financial Economics*, **8**, 205–58.

—— and —— (1985), 'Using daily stock returns: the case of event studies', *Journal of Financial Economics*, **14**, 3–31.

Brozen, Y. (1969), 'Competition, efficiency and antitrust', *Journal of World Trade Law*, **3**, 659. Reprinted in Y. Brozen (ed.) (1975), *The Competitive Economy: Selected Readings*, Morristown, NJ: General Learning Press.

—— (1974), 'Entry barriers, advertising, and product differentiation', in H. J. Goldschmid, H. M. Mann, and J. F. Weston (eds.), *Industrial Concentration: The New Learning*, Boston: Little, Brown & Co.

—— (1982), *Concentration, Mergers and Public Policy*, New York: Macmillan.

—— (1986), 'European competition policy', presented at the symposium 'Economic Policy in the Market Process: Success or Failure' in Slot Zeist, The Netherlands, 19 January (forthcoming in Proceedings).

Brudney, V. and Chirelstein, M. A. (1978), 'A restatement of corporate freezeouts', *Yale Law Journal*, **87**, 1354–76.

Buckley, A. (1972), 'A profile of industrial acquisition in 1971', *Accounting and Business Research*, **2**, 243–52.

Bull, A. and Vice, A. (1961), *Bid for Power*, London: Elek Books.

Burns, M. R. (1977), 'The competitive effects of trust-busting: portfolio analysis', *Journal of Industrial Economy*, **85**, 717–39.

—— (1983), 'An empirical analysis of stockholder injury under S.2 of the Sherman Act', *Journal of Industrial Economics*, **31**, 333–62.

Butler, R. and Carney, M. G. (1983), 'Managing markets: implications for the make-buy decision', *Journal of Management Studies*, **20**, 213–31.

Cable, J. R. (1977), 'A search theory of diversifying merger', *Récherches Economiques de Louvain*, September.

Calvo, G. A. and Wellisz, S. (1978), 'Supervision, loss of control and the optimum size of the firm', *Journal of Political Economy*, **86**, 943–52.

Carter, J. R. (1978), 'Collusion, efficiency and antitrust', *Journal of Law and Economics*, **21**, 435–44.

Caves, R. E. (1968), 'Market organisation, performance, and public policy', in R. E. Caves (ed.), *Britain's Economic Prospects*, London: Allen and Unwin.

——, Khalilzadeh-Shirazi, J., and Porter, M. E. (1975), 'Scale economies in statistical analyses of market power', *Review of Economics and Statistics*, **57**, 133–40.

—— and Porter, M. E. (1977), 'From entry barriers to mobility barriers: conjectural decisions and contrived deterrence to new competition', *Quarterly Journal of Economics*, **91**, 421–34.

——, ——, Spence, A. M., and Scott, J. T. (1980), *Competition in the Open Economy: A Model Applied to Canada*, Cambridge, Mass.: Harvard University Press.

—— and Pugel, T. (1980), *Intra-industry Differences in Conduct and Performance: Viable Strategies in U.S. Manufacturing Industries*, Monograph Series in Finance and Economics, New York University Graduate School of Business Administration.

Chandler, A. (1977), *The Visible Hand: The Managerial Revolution in American Business*, Cambridge, Mass.: Harvard University Press.

Channon, D. F. (1973), *The Strategy and Structure of British Enterprise*, London: Macmillan.

Charkham, J. P. (1986), *Effective Boards*, London: Institute of Chartered Accountants.

Chiplin, B. (1986), 'Information technology and personal financial services', in R. L. Carter, B. Chiplin, and M. K. Lewis (eds.), *Personal Financial Markets*, Oxford: Philip Allan.

—— and Wright, M. (1980), 'Divestment and structural change in UK industry', *National Westminster Bank Review*, February, 42–51.

—— and —— (1982), 'Competition policy and state enterprises in the UK', *Antitrust Bulletin*, **27**, 921–56.

—— and —— (1987), *The Logic of Mergers*, Hobart Paper 107, London: Institute of Economic Affairs.

Clarke, R. (1984), 'Profit margins and market concentration in UK manufacturing industry: 1970–76', *Applied Economics*, **16**, 57–72.

—— (1985), *Industrial Economics*, Oxford: Basil Blackwell.

—— and Davies, S. W. (1982), 'Market structure and price–cost margins', *Economica*, **49**, 277–87.

—— and —— (1983), 'Aggregate concentration, market concentration and diversification', *Economic Journal*, **93**, 182–92.

——, ——, and Waterson, M. (1984), 'The profitability–concentration relation: market power or efficiency?', *Journal of Industrial Economics*, **32**, 435–50.

Coase, R. H. (1937), 'The nature of the firm', *Economica*, New Series, **4**, 386–405.

Colenutt, D. W. and O'Donnell, P. P. (1978), 'The consistency of Monopolies and Mergers Commission merger reports', *Antitrust Bulletin*, **20**, 51–82.

Comanor, W. S. and Wilson, T. A. (1967), 'Advertising, market structure and performance', *Review of Economics and Statistics*, **49**, 423–40.

—— and —— (1979), 'The effect of advertising on competition: a survey', *Journal of Economic Literature*, **17**, 453–76.

Conn, R. L. (1985), 'A re-examination of studies that use the capital asset pricing model methodology', *Cambridge Journal of Economics*, **9**, 43–56.

Cosh, A. D. (1975), 'The remuneration of chief executives in the UK', *Economic Journal*, **85**, 75–94.

——, Hughes, A., Kumar, M. S., and Singh, A. (1985a), 'Institutional investment company performance and mergers: empirical evidence for the UK: a report to the Office of Fair Trading', mimeo, Cambridge.

——, ——, ——, and —— (1985b), 'Conglomerate organisation and economic efficiency: a report to the Office of Fair Trading', mimeo, Cambridge.

——, ——, and Singh, A. (1980), 'The causes and effects of takeovers in the UK: an empirical investigation for the late 1960's at the micro-economic level', in D. C. Mueller (ed.), *The Determinants and Effects of Mergers*, Cambridge, Mass.: Oelschlager, Gunn and Hain.

——, ——, and —— (1986), 'Financial institutions, investment management and corporate takeover in the UK', paper presented to the ESRC Industrial Economics Study Group, Nottingham University, 17 April.

Cowling, K., Stoneman, P., Cubbin, J., Cable, J., Hall, G., Domberger, S., and Dutton, P. (1980), *Mergers and Economic Performance*, Cambridge: Cambridge University Press.

—— and Waterson, M. (1976), 'Price–cost margins and market structure', *Economica*, **43**, 267–74.

Coyne, J. and Wright, M. (eds.) (1986a), *Divestment and Strategic Change*, Oxford: Philip Allan.

—— and —— (1986b), 'Buy-outs and corporate strategy', in *International Management Development Review*, Brussels: Management Centre Europe.

—— and —— (1986c), *Review of UK Management Buy-outs, 1985*, London: Venture Economics.

Cragg, J. and Malkiel, B. (1982), *Expectations and the Structure of Share Prices*, Chicago: University of Chicago Press.

Cubbin, J. S. and Geroski, P. (1987), 'The convergence of profits in the long run: inter firm and inter industry comparisons', *Journal of Industrial Economics*, **35**, 427–42.

—— and Hall, G. (1979), 'The use of real cost as an efficiency measure—an application to merging firms', *Journal of Industrial Economics*, **28**, 73–88.

Curry, B. and George, K. D. (1983), 'Industrial concentration: a survey', *Journal of Industrial Economics*, **31**, 203–55.

Cyert, R. M. and March, J. G. (1963), *A Behavioural Theory of the Firm*, Englewood Cliffs, NJ: Prentice-Hall.

Davies, J. R. and Kuehn, D. A. (1977), 'An investigation into the effectiveness of a capital market sanction on poor performance', in A. P. Jacquemin and H. W. de Jong (eds.), *Welfare Aspects of Industrial Markets*, Leiden: Martinus Nijhoff.

Davies, P. L. (1976), *The Regulation of Take-overs and Mergers*, London: Sweet and Maxwell.

Davies, S. (1979), 'Choosing between concentration indices: the iso-concentration curve', *Economica*, **46**, 67–75.

Davis, G. (1986), 'Strategic trading: rationalisation in US brewing', in J. Coyne and M. Wright (eds.), *Divestment and Strategic Change*, Oxford: Philip Allan.

de Angelo, H., de Angelo, A., and Rice, E. (1984), 'Going private: minority freeze-outs and stockholder wealth', *Journal of Law and Economics*, **27**, 367–402.

Demsetz, H. (1973), 'Industry structure, market rivalry, and public policy', *Journal of Law and Economics*, **16**, 1–9.

—— (1974), 'Two systems of belief about monopoly', in H. J. Goldschmid, H. M. Mann, and J. F. Weston (eds.), *Industrial Concentration: The New Learning*, Boston: Little, Brown & Co.

—— (1982), 'Barriers to entry', *American Economic Review*, **72**, 47–57.

—— (1983), 'The structure of ownership and the theory of the firm', *Journal of Law and Economics*, **26**, 375–90.

Department of Prices and Consumer Protection (1978), *A Review of Monopolies and Mergers Policy: A Consultative Document*, Cmnd 7198, London: HMSO.

—— (1979), *A Review of Restrictive Trade Practices Policy*, Cmnd 7512, London: HMSO.

Dickson, V. A. (1982), 'Collusion and price-cost margins', *Economica*, **49**, 39–42.

Dixit, A. (1982), 'Recent developments in oligopoly theory', *American Economic Review*, Papers and Proceedings, **72**, 12–17.

Dodd, P. (1983), 'The market for corporate control: a review of the evidence', *Midland Corporate Finance Journal*, Summer.

—— and Officer, R. R. (1986), 'Takeovers: the Australian evidence', draft, 1 June, presented at the Centre for Independent Studies Conference, Sydney, 13 June.

Dodds, J. C. and Quek, J. P. (1985), 'Effect of mergers on the share pricc movement of the acquiring firms: a UK study', *Journal of Business Finance and Accounting*, **12**, 285–96.

Donsimoni, M.-P., Geroski, P. A., and Jacquemin, A. P. (1985), 'Concentration indices and market power: two views', *Journal of Industrial Economics*, **32**, 421–34.

Downie, J. (1958), *The Competitive Process*, London: Duckworth.

Duesenberry, J. S. (1958), *Business Cycles and Economic Growth*, London: McGraw-Hill.

Dugger, W. (1983), 'The transactions cost analysis of Oliver E. Williamson: a new synthesis?', *Journal of Economic Issues*, **17**, 95–114.

Duhaime, I. M. and Baird, I. S. (1985), 'The role of business unit size in divestment decision-making', mimeo, University of Illinois.

—— and Grant, J. H. (1984), 'Factors influencing divestment decision-making: evidence from a field study', *Strategic Management Journal*, **5**, 301–18.

Easterbrook, F. H. (1984), 'The limits of antitrust', *Texas Law Review*, **63**, 1–40.

Ellert, J. C. (1976), 'Mergers, antitrust law enforcement and shareholder returns', *Journal of Finance*, **31**, 715–32.

Elliott, D. C. and Gribbin, J. D. (1977), 'The abolition of cartels and structural change in the United Kingdom', in A. P. Jacquemin and H. W. de Jong (eds.), *Welfare Aspects of Industrial Markets*, Leiden: Martinus Nijhoff.

Ellis, T. S. (1971), 'A survey of the government control of mergers in the United Kingdom', *Northern Ireland Legal Quarterly*, **22**, 251–300 and 459–97.

Elster, J. (1984), *Sour Grapes*, Cambridge: Cambridge University Press.

Evans, D. S. and Grossman, S. J. (1983), 'Integration', in D. S. Evans (ed.) *Breaking Up Bell: Essays on Industrial Organization and Regulation*, New York: North-Holland.

Evely, R. A. and Little, I. M. D. (1960), *Concentration in British Industry*, Cambridge: Cambridge University Press.

Fairburn, J. A. (1985), 'British merger policy', *Fiscal Studies*, **6**, 1, 70–81.

Fama, E. (1980), 'Agency problems and the theory of the firm', *Journal of Political Economy*, **88**, 288–307.

Firth, M. (1976), *Share Prices and Mergers*, Farnborough: Saxon House/Lexington Books.

—— (1978), 'Synergism in mergers: some British results', *Journal of Finance*, **33**, 670–2.

—— (1979), 'The profitability of takeovers and mergers', *Economic Journal*, **89**, 316–28.

—— (1980), 'Takeovers, shareholder returns and the theory of the firm', *Quarterly Journal of Economics*, **94**, 235–60.

Fisher, F. M. and McGowan, J. J. (1983), 'On the misuse of accounting rates of return to infer monopoly profits', *American Economic Review*, **73**, 82–97.

Fothergill, S. and Gudgin, G. (1982), *Unequal Growth*, London: Heinemann Educational Books.

Francis, A. (1980), 'Company objectives, managerial motivations and the behaviour of large firms: an empirical test of the theory of managerial capitalism', *Cambridge Journal of Economics*, **4**, 349–61.

Franks, J. R., Broyles, J. E., and Hecht, M. J. (1977), 'An industry study of the profitability of mergers in the United Kingdom', *Journal of Finance*, **32**, 1513–25.

—— and Harris, R. S. (1986a), 'The role of the Mergers and Monopolies Commission in merger policy: costs and alternatives', *Oxford Review of Economic Policy*, **2**, 4, 58–78.

—— and —— (1986b), 'Shareholder wealth effects of corporate takeovers: the UK experience 1955–85', London Business School and University of North Carolina at Chapel Hill Working Paper.

——, ——, and Mayer, C. P. (1987), 'Means of payment in takeovers: results for the UK and US', Centre for Economic Policy Research, Discussion Paper 200.

Friedman, M. (1953), 'The methodology of positive economics', in *Essays in Positive Economics*, Chicago: University of Chicago Press.

Galai, D. and Masulis, R. W. (1976), 'The option pricing model and the risk factor of stock', *Journal of Financial Economics*, **3**, 53–81.

Gale, B. T. and Branch, B. S. (1982), 'Concentration versus market share: which determines performance and why does it matter?', *Antitrust Bulletin*, **27**, 83–105.

Garvin, D. A. (1983), 'Spin-offs and the new firm formation process', *California Management Review*, **25**, 3–20.

Geithman, F., Marvel, H., and Weiss, L. (1981), 'Concentration, price and critical concentration ratios', *Review of Economics and Statistics*, **63**, 346–53.

George, K. D. (1985), 'Monopoly and merger policy', *Fiscal Studies*, **6**, 1, 34–48.

Geroski, P. A. (1981), 'Specification and testing the profits-concentration, price and critical concentration ratios', *Economica*, **48**, 279–88.

—— (1982a), 'Interpreting a correlation between profits and concentration', *Journal of Industrial Economics*, **30**, 305–18.

—— (1982b), 'Simultaneous equations models of the structure-performance paradigm', *European Economic Review*, **19**, 145–58.

—— (1983), 'Some reflections on the theory and application of concentration indices', *International Journal of Industrial Organization*, **1**, 79–84.

—— (1984), 'On the relationship between aggregate merger activity and the stock market', *European Economic Review*, **25**, 223–33.

—— (1987), 'Do dominant firms decline?', in D. A. Hay and J. S. Vickers (eds.), *The Economics of Market Dominance*, Oxford: Basil Blackwell.

—— and Jacquemin, A. P. (1984), 'Dominant firms and their alleged decline', *International Journal of Industrial Organization*, **2**, 1–27.

—— and —— (1986), 'The persistence of profits: a European comparison', mimeo, Louvain la Neuve.

—— and Knight, K. G. (1984), 'Corporate merger and collective bargaining in the UK', *Industrial Relations Journal*, **15**, 51–60.

—— and Masson, R. T. (1987), 'Dynamic market models in industrial organization', *International Journal of Industrial Organization*, **5**, 1–13.

——, Phlips, L., and Ulph, A. (1985), 'Oligopoly, welfare and competition: some recent developments', *Journal of Industrial Economics*, **33**, 369–86.

——, Ulph, A. M., and Ulph, D. T. (1987), 'A model of the crude oil market in which conduct varies over time', *Economic Journal*, Supplement, **97**, 77–86.

Gist, P. and Meadowcroft, S. A. (1986), 'Regulating for competition: the newly liberalised market for private branch exchanges', *Fiscal Studies*, **7**, 3, 41–66.

Givoly, D. and Palmon, D. (1985), 'Insider trading and the exploitation of inside information: some empirical evidence', *Journal of Business*, **58**, 69–87.

Goddard, J. B. and Smith, I. J. (1978), 'Changes in corporate control in the British urban system, 1972–77', *Environment and Planning*, Series A, **10**, 1073–84.

Goldberg, L. G. (1973), 'The effect of conglomerate mergers on competition', *Journal of Law and Economics*, **16**, 137–58.

—— (1974), 'Conglomerate mergers and concentration ratios', *Review of Economics and Statistics*, **56**, 303–9.

Gollop, F. and Roberts, M. (1979), 'Firm interdependence in oligopolistic markets', *Journal of Econometrics*, **10**, 313–31.

Gorecki, P. K. (1975), 'An inter-industry analysis of diversification in the UK manufacturing sector', *Journal of Industrial Economics*, **24**, 131–46.

Gort, M. (1969), 'An economic disturbance theory of mergers', *Quarterly Journal of Economics*, **83**, 624–42.

Goudie, A. and Meeks, G. (1982), 'Diversification by merger', *Economica*, **49**, 447–59.

Gough, T. J. (1979), 'Building society mergers and the size–efficiency relationship', *Applied Economics*, **11**, 185–94.

—— (1981), 'Building society mergers and the size–efficiency relationship: a reply', *Applied Economics*, **13**, 535–8.

Graham, J. (1979), 'Trends in UK merger control', *Trade and Industry*, 14 September.

Gratton, C. and Kemp, J. R. (1977), 'Some new evidence on changes in UK industrial market concentration 1963–68', *Scottish Journal of Political Economy*, **24**, 177–81.

Greer, D. F. (1986), 'Acquiring in order to avoid acquisition', *Antitrust Bulletin*, Spring.

Gribbin, J. D. (1974), 'The operation of the Mergers Panel since 1965', *Trade and Industry*, 17 January.

—— (1977), 'Postwar revival of competition as industrial policy', Government Economic Working Paper 19.

Griffin, J. M. and Wiggins, S. N. (1986), 'Takeover raids: financial structure and managerial discipline', mimeo, Texas A & M University.

Grinyer, P. H. and Spender, J. C. (1979), *Turnaround: The Fall and Rise of the Newton Chambers Group*, London: Associated Business Press.

Gripaios, P. (1977), 'The closure of firms in the inner city: the south-east London case 1970–75', *Regional Studies*, **11**, 1–6.

Grossman, S. J. and Hart, O. D. (1980), 'Takeover bids, the free-rider problem and the theory of the corporation', *Bell Journal of Economics*, **11**, 42–64.

—— and —— (1981), 'The allocational role of takeover bids in situations of asymmetric information', *Journal of Finance*, Papers and Proceedings, **36**, 253–70.

—— and —— (1986), 'The costs and benefits of ownership: a theory of vertical and lateral integration', *Journal of Political Economy*, **94**, 691–719.

Hague, D. and Wilkinson, G. (1983), *The IRC: An Experiment in Industrial Intervention*, Hemel Hempstead: George Allen and Unwin.

Hakansson, N. H. (1983), 'Changes in the financial market: welfare and price effects and the basic theorems of value conservation', *Journal of Finance*, **37**, 977–1004.

Halpern, P. (1983), 'Corporate acquisitions: a theory of special cases? A review of event studies applied to acquisitions', *Journal of Finance*, **38**, 297–317.

Hamlin, A. P. (1986), *Ethics, Economics and the State*, Brighton: Wheatsheaf Books.

Hannah, L. (1974), 'Takeover bids in Britain before 1950: an exercise in business pre-history', *Business History*, **16**, 65–77.

—— (1976), *The Rise of the Corporate Economy*, London: Methuen. Second edition, 1983.

—— and Kay, J. A. (1977), *Concentration in Modern Industry*, London: Macmillan.

—— and —— (1981), 'The contribution of mergers to concentration growth: a reply to Professor Hart', *Journal of Industrial Economics*, **29**, 305–13.

Hanson, C. (1987), 'Employee profit-sharing: Weitzmania and wild-goose chases', *Economic Affairs*, **7**, 2, 10–14.

Harcourt, G. C. (1965), 'The accountant in a golden age', *Oxford Economic Papers*, **17**, 66–80.

Hart, P. E. (1975), 'Moment distributions in economics', *Journal of the Royal Statistical Society*, Series B, **138**, 423–34.

—— (1979), 'On bias and concentration', *Journal of Industrial Economics*, **27**, 211–26.

—— (1980), 'Lognormality and the principle of transfers', *Oxford Bulletin of Economics and Statistics*, **42**, 263–7.

—— (1981), 'The effects of mergers on industrial concentration', *Journal of Industrial Economics*, **29**, 315–20.

—— and Clarke, R. (1980), *Concentration in British Industry, 1935–75*, Cambridge: Cambridge University Press.

—— and Morgan, E. (1977), 'Market structure and economic performance', *Review of Economics and Statistics*, **25**, 177–93.

——, Utton, M., and Walshe, G. (1973), *Mergers and Concentration in British Industry*, Cambridge: Cambridge University Press.

Hassid, J. (1975), 'Recent evidence on conglomerate diversification in the UK manufacturing sector', *Manchester School of Economic and Social Studies*, **43**, 372–95.

Hay, G. A. (1985), 'Competition policy', *Oxford Review of Economic Policy*, **1**, 3, 63–79.

—— and Reynolds, R. (1984), 'Competition and antitrust in the petroleum industry: an application of the Merger Guidelines', in F. Fisher (ed.), *Antitrust and Regulation: Essays in Honor of John J. McGowan*.

Healey, M. J. (1982), 'Plant closures in multi-plant enterprises—the case of a declining industrial sector', *Regional Studies*, **16**, 37–51.

Hearth, D. P. and Zaima, J. K. (1986), 'Divestiture, uncertainty and shareholder wealth: evidence from the USA', *Journal of Business Finance and Accounting*, **13**, 71–86.

Heath, J. B. (1961), 'Restrictive practices and after', *Manchester School of Economic and Social Studies*, **29**, 173–202.

Heiner, R. (1983), 'The origin of predictable behaviour', *American Economic Review*, **73**, 560–95.

Helm, D. R. (1984a), 'Enforced maximisation: competition, evolution and selection', D.Phil. thesis, Oxford.

—— (1984b), 'Predictions and causes: Hicks and Friedman on method', *Oxford Economic Papers*, Supplement, **36**, 118–34.

—— (1986), 'The economic borders of the state', *Oxford Review of Economic Policy*, **2**, 2, i–xxiv.

Herman, E. S. (1981), *Corporate Control Corporate Power*, Cambridge: Cambridge University Press.

Hicks, J. R. (1935), 'The theory of monopoly: a survey', *Econometrica*, **3**, 1–20. Reprinted in J. R. Hicks (1983), *Classics and Moderns: Collected Essays on Economic Theory, Volume III*, Oxford: Basil Blackwell.

—— (1982), 'Limited liability: pros and cons', in T. Orhnial (ed.), *Limited Liability and the Corporation*, London: Croom Helm. Reprinted in J. R. Hicks (1983), *Classics and Moderns: Collected Essays on Economic Theory, Volume III*, Oxford: Basil Blackwell.

Hill, C. W. L. (1984), 'Profile of a conglomerate takeover: BTR and Thomas Tilling', *Journal of General Management*, **10**, 34–50.

—— (1985), 'Diversified growth and competition: the experience of 12 large UK firms', *Applied Economics*, **17**, 827–47.

—— and Pickering, J. F. (1986a), 'Conglomerate mergers, internal organisation and competition policy', *International Review of Law and Economics*, June, 6.

—— and —— (1986b), 'Divisionalization, decentralization and performance of large UK companies', *Journal of Management Studies*, **23**, 26–50.

Hindley, B. (1972), 'Recent theory and evidence on corporate merger', in K. Cowling (ed.), *Market Structure and Corporate Behaviour: Theory and Empirical Analysis of the Firm*, London: Gray-Mills.

—— and Richardson, R. (1983), 'United Kingdom: an experiment in picking winners—the Industrial Reorganisation Corporation', in B. Hindley (ed.), *State Investment Companies in Western Europe: Picking Winners or Backing Losers?*, London: Macmillan.

Hirschey, M. (1986), 'Mergers, buyouts and fakeouts', *American Economic Review*, Papers and Proceedings, **76**, 317–22.

Hirschleifer, J. and Riley, J. (1979), 'The analytics of uncertainty and information', *Journal of Economic Literature*, **17**, 1375–421.

Hite, G. L. (1986), 'Discussion on Klein', *Journal of Finance*, **41**, 696–8.

—— and Owers, J. E. (1983), 'Security price reactions around corporate spin-off announcements', *Journal of Financial Economics*, **12**, 409–36.

Hitiris, T. (1978), 'Effective protection and economic performance in U.K. manufacturing industry', *Economic Journal*, **88**, 107–20.

Holland, D. M. and Myers, S. C. (1979), 'Trends in corporate profitability and costs', in R. Lindsay (ed.), *The Nation's Capital Needs: Three Studies*, New York: Committee for Economic Development.

Holtermann, S. E. (1973), 'Market structure and economic performance in U.K. manufacturing industry', *Journal of Industrial Economics*, **22**, 119–40.

Hope, M. (1976), 'On being taken over by Slater Walker', *Journal of Industrial Economics*, **24**, 163–79.

Hughes, A. (1976), 'Company concentration, size of plant, and merger activity', in M. Panic (ed.), *The UK and West German Manufacturing Industry, 1954–72*, London: NEDO/HMSO.

—— (1978), 'Competition policy and economic performance in the UK', in NEDO, *Competition Policy*, London: HMSO.

—— (1986), 'Investment finance, industrial strategy and economic recovery', in P. H. Nolan and S. H. Paine (eds.), *Rethinking Socialist Economics*, Cambridge: Polity Press.

—— (1987), 'Small firms, merger activity and competition policy', in J. Barber and J. S. Metcalfe (eds.), *Barriers to the Growth of Small Firms in the UK*, London: Croom Helm, forthcoming.

—— and Kumar, M. S. (1984a), 'Recent trends in aggregate concentration in the UK economy', *Cambridge Journal of Economics*, **8**, 235–50.

—— and —— (1984b), 'Recent trends in aggregate concentration in the UK economy: revised estimates', *Cambridge Journal of Economics*, **8**, 401–2.

—— and —— (1985), 'Mergers, concentration and mobility amongst the largest UK non-financial corporations 1972–82: a report to the Office of Fair Trading', mimeo, Department of Applied Economics, Cambridge.

——, Mueller, D. C., and Singh, A. (1980), 'Hypotheses about mergers', in D. C. Mueller (ed.), *The Determinants and Effects of Mergers*, Cambridge: Oelschlager, Gunn and Hain.

—— and Singh, A. (1980), 'Mergers, concentration, and competition in advanced capitalist economies: an international perspective', in D. C. Mueller (ed.) (1980), *The Determinants and Effects of Mergers*, Cambridge: Oelschlager, Gunn and Hain.

—— and —— (1987), 'Takeovers and the stock market', *Contributions to Political Economy*, forthcoming.

Jacquemin, A. P. and de Jong, H. W. (1977), *European Industrial Organisation*, London: Macmillan.

Jain, P. C. (1985), 'The effect of voluntary sell-off announcements on shareholder wealth', *Journal of Finance*, **40**, 209–24.

Jarrell, G. A. and Lehn, K. (1985), 'Institutional ownership, tender offers and long-term investments', Office of the Chief Economist, Securities and Exchange Commission, Washington DC.

Jay, J. (1986), 'Argyll recounts the cost', *Sunday Times*, 21 December, 27.

Jensen, M. C. (1986a), 'The takeover controversy: analysis and evidence', *Midland Corporate Finance Journal*, **4**, 2, 6–32.

—— (1986b), 'Agency costs of free cash flow, corporate finance and takeovers', *American Economic Review*, Papers and Proceedings, **76**, 323–9.

—— and Meckling, W. H. (1976), 'Theory of the firm: managerial behaviour, agency costs and ownership structure', *Journal of Financial Economics*, **3**, 305–60.

—— and Ruback, R. S. (1983), 'The market for corporate control: the scientific evidence', *Journal of Financial Economics*, **11**, 5–50.

Johnston, Sir A. J. (1980), *The City Take-over Code*, Oxford: Oxford University Press.

Jones, C. S. (1985), 'An empirical study of the role of management accounting systems following takeover or merger', *Accounting Organisations and Society*, **10**, 177–200.

Kahneman, D., Slovic, P., and Tversky, A. (1983), *Judgement under Uncertainty: Heuristics and Biases*, Cambridge: Cambridge University Press.

—— and Tversky, A. (1979), 'Prospect theory: an analysis of decisions under risk', *Econometrica*, **47**, 263–91.

Kay, J. A. (1976), 'Accountants, too, could be happy in a golden age: the accountant's rate of return and the internal rate of return', *Oxford Economic Papers*, **28**, 447–60.

—— (1986), 'The role of mergers', IFS Working Paper 94, July.

—— and Mayer, C. P. (1986), 'On the application of accounting rates of return', *Economic Journal*, **96**, 199–207.

Keane, S. M. (1983), *Stock Market Efficiency: Theory, Evidence, and Implications*, Bath: Philip Allan.

Keynes, J. M. (1921), *A Treatise on Probability*, London: Macmillan.

—— (1936), *The General Theory of Employment, Interest and Money*, London: Macmillan.

Khalilzadeh-Shirazi, J. (1974), 'Market structure and price–cost margins in United Kingdom manufacturing industries', *Review of Economics and Statistics*, **56**, 67–76.

King, M. A. (1986), 'Takeovers, taxes and the stock market', mimeo, London School of Economics.

—— and Roell, A. A. (1987), 'The regulation of take-overs and the stock market', mimeo, London School of Economics.

Kirzner, I. M. (1973), *Competition and Entrepreneurship*, Chicago: University of Chicago Press.

Kitching, J. (1967), 'Why do mergers miscarry?', *Harvard Business Review*, November–December, 84–101.

—— (1974), 'Why acquisitions are abortive', *Management Today*, November, 52–7, 148.

Klein, A. (1986), 'The timing and substance of divestiture announcements: individual, simultaneous and cumulative effects', *Journal of Finance*, **41**, 685–95.

Klein, B. (1983), 'Contracting costs and residual claims', *Journal of Law and Economics*, **26**, 367–74.

Knoeber, C. R. (1986), 'Golden parachutes, shark repellents and hostile tender offers', *American Economic Review*, **76**, 155–67.

Krattenmaker, T. G. and Salop, S. C. (1986), 'Anticompetitive exclusion: raising rivals' costs to achieve power over price', *Yale Law Journal*, **96**, 209–93.

Kudla, R. J. and McInish, R. S. (1981), 'The microeconomic consequences of an involuntary corporate spin-off', *Sloan Management Review*, **22**, 41–6.

Kuehn, D. A. (1975), *Takeovers and the Theory of the Firm*, London: Macmillan.

Kumar, M. S. (1984), *Growth, Acquisition and Investment*, Cambridge: Cambridge University Press.

—— (1985), 'Growth, acquisition activity and firm size: evidence from the United Kingdom', *Journal of Industrial Economics*, **33**, 327–38.

Kwoka, J. E. (1979), 'The effect of market share distribution on industry performance', *Review of Economics and Statistics*, **61**, 445–53.

—— (1981), 'Does the choice of concentration measure really matter?', *Journal of Industrial Economics*, **20**, 445–53.

—— and Ravenscraft, D. J. (1986), 'Co-operation v. rivalry: price–cost margins by line of business', *Economica*, **53**, 351–63.

Landes, W. M. and Posner, R. A. (1981), 'Market power in antitrust cases', *Harvard Law Review*, **94**, 937–96.

Lawton, P. (1984), 'Demergers: an assessment', *The Company Lawyer*, **5**, 17–26.

Leigh, R. and North, D. J. (1978), 'Regional aspects of acquisition activity in British manufacturing industry', *Regional Studies*, **12**, 227–45.

Levine, P. and Aaronovitch, S. (1981), 'The financial characteristics of firms and theories of merger activity', *Journal of Industrial Economics*, **30**, 149–72.

Levy, H. and Sarnat, M. (1970), 'Diversification, portfolio analysis and the uneasy case for conglomerate mergers', *Journal of Finance*, **25**, 795–802.

Little, I. M. D. and Rayner, A. G. (1966), *Higgledy Piggledy Growth Again*, Oxford: Basil Blackwell.

Littlechild, S. C. (1978), *The Fallacy of the Mixed Economy*, Hobart Paper 80, London: Institute of Economic Affairs. Second edition, 1986.

Loomes, G. and Sugden, R. (1982), 'Regret theory: an alternative theory of rational choice under uncertainty', *Economic Journal*, **92**, 805–48.

Lorenz, P. (1979), *Investing in Success: How to Profit from Design and Innovation*, London: Anglo-German Foundation for the Study of Industrial Society.

Lustgarten, S. (1979), 'Gains and losses from concentration: a comment', *Journal of Law and Economics*, **22**, 183–90.

Lye, S. and Silberston, A. (1981), 'Merger activity and sales of subsidiaries between company groups', *Oxford Bulletin of Economics and Statistics*, **43**, 257–72.

Lyons, B. R. (1981), 'Price–cost margins, market structure and international trade', in D. Currie, D. Peel, and W. Peters (eds.), *Microeconomic Analysis*, London: Croom Helm.

——, Kitchen, P. D., and Hitiris, T. (1979), 'Effective protection and economic performance in U.K. manufacturing industry: comments and reply', *Economic Journal*, **89**, 926–41.

McNulty, P. J. (1967), 'A note on the history of perfect competition', *Journal of Political Economy*, **75**, 395–9.

Malatesta, P. H. (1986), 'Measuring abnormal performance: the event parameters approach using joint generalized least squares', *Journal of Financial and Quantitative Economics*, **21**, 27–38.

Mancke, R. B. (1974), 'The causes of inter-firm profitability differences: a new interpretation of the evidence', *Quarterly Journal of Economics*, **84**, 181–93.

Mann, M. and Scholefield, T. (1986), 'Recent trends in UK concentration', in *Issues in UK Competition Policy—A Discussion Document*, London: Confederation of British Industry.

Manne, H. G. (1965), 'Mergers and the market for corporate control', *Journal of Political Economy*, **73**, 693–706.

Markham, J. W. (1955), 'Survey of the evidence and findings on mergers', in G. J. Stigler (ed.), *Business Concentration and Price Policy*, New York: National Bureau of Economic Research.

—— (1973), *Conglomerate Enterprise and Public Policy*, Boston: Harvard Graduate School of Business Administration.

Marris, R. L. (1964), *The Economic Theory of 'Managerial' Capitalism*, London: Macmillan.

—— and Mueller, D. C. (1980), 'The corporation, competition and the invisible hand', *Journal of Economic Literature*, **18**, 32–63.

Marsh, P. (1980), 'Valuation of underwriting agreements for UK rights issues', *Journal of Finance*, **35**, 693–716.

—— (1986), 'Are profits the prize of the prey or the predator?', *Financial Times: Mergers and Acquisitions*, May.

Martin, S. (1979), 'Advertising, concentration and profitability: the simultaneity problems', *Bell Journal of Economics*, **10**, 639–47.

—— (1980), 'Entry barriers, concentration and profits', *Southern Economic Journal*, **46**, 471–88.

—— (1983), *Market, Firms and Economic Performance*, New York: New York University Graduate School of Business Administration.

Marx, K. (1971), *Capital: A Critique of Political Economy Vol. III*, London: Lawrence and Wishart.

Massey, D. B. and Meegan, R. A. (1978), 'Industrial restructuring versus the cities', *Urban Studies*, **15**, 273–88.

—— and —— (1979), 'The geography of industrial reorganisation: the spatial effects of restructuring the electrical engineering industry under the IRC', *Progress in Planning*, **10**, 155–237.

Mayshar, J. (1983), 'On divergence of opinion and imperfections in the capital market', *American Economic Review*, **73**, 114–28.

Meade, J. S. (1968), 'Is the "New Industrial State" inevitable?', *Economic Journal*, **78**, 372–92.

Meadowcroft, S. A. and Thompson, D. J. (1986), 'Empirical analysis of returns to pre-merger shareholdings', mimeo, Institute for Fiscal Studies.

—— and —— (1987), 'Partial integration: a loophole in competition law', *Fiscal Studies*, **8**, 1, 24–47.

Meeks, G. (1977), *Disappointing Marriage: A Study of the Gains from Merger*, Cambridge: Cambridge University Press.

Meeks, J. G. and Meeks, G. (1981), 'Profitability measures as indicators of post merger efficiency', *Journal of Industrial Economics*, **29**, 335–44.

—— and Whittington, G. (1976), 'The financing of quoted companies in the United Kingdom', Background Paper 1, Royal Commission on the Distribution of Income and Wealth, London: HMSO.

Melicher, R. W., Ledolter, J., and D'Antonio, L. J. (1983), 'A time series analysis of aggregate merger activity', *Review of Economics and Statistics*, **65**, 423–30.

Mennel, W. (1962), *Takeover*, London: Lawrence and Wishart.

Merrett Cyriax Associates (1971), *Dynamics of Small Firms*, Research Report 12, Committee of Inquiry on Small Firms, London: HMSO.

Miles, J. A. and Rosenfeld, J. D. (1983), 'The effect of voluntary spin-off announcements on shareholder wealth', *Journal of Finance*, **37**, 1597–606.

Miller, E. (1977), 'Risk, uncertainty and divergence of opinion', *Journal of Finance*, **32**, 1151–68.

Millward, N. and McQueeney, J. (1981), 'Company takeovers, management organization and industrial relations', Department of Employment, Manpower Paper 16, London: HMSO.

Mirrlees, J. (1976), 'The optimal structure of incentives and authority within an organisation', *Bell Journal of Economics*, **7**, 105–31.

Montgomery, C. A., Thomas, A. R., and Kamath, R. (1984), 'Divestiture, market valuation and strategy', *Academy of Management Journal*, **27**, 830–40.

Moon, R. W. (1968), *Business Mergers and Take-over Bids*, London: Gee & Co.

Mueller, D. C. (1969), 'A theory of conglomerate mergers', *Quarterly Journal of Economics*, **83**, 643–59.

—— (1986), *Profits in the Long Run*, Cambridge: Cambridge University Press.

Myers, S. and Majluf, N. (1984), 'Corporate financing and investment decisions when firms have information that investors do not have', *Journal of Financial Economics*, **13**, 187–221.

Nelson, R. L. (1959), *Merger Movements in American Industry 1895–1956*, Princeton: Princeton University Press.

Nerlove, M. (1968), 'Factors affecting differences among rates of return on investment in individual common stocks', *Review of Economics and Statistics*, **50**, 312–31.

Newbould, G. D. (1970), *Management and Merger Activity*, Liverpool: Guthstead.

Newman, M. (1978), 'Strategic groups and the structure–performance relationship', *Review of Economics and Statistics*, **60**, 417–27.

Nickell, S. and Metcalf, D. (1978), 'Monopolistic industries and monopoly profits or, are Kellogg's cornflakes overpriced?', *Economic Journal*, **88**, 254–68.

O'Brien, D. P. (1978), 'Mergers—time to turn the tide', *Lloyds Bank Review*, October, 32–44.

——, Howe, W. S., and Wright, O. M., with O'Brien, R. J. (1979), *Competition Policy, Profitability and Growth*, London: Macmillan.

Office of Fair Trading (1985), *Mergers: A Guide to the Procedures under the Fair Trading Act 1973*, London: HMSO.

Okun, A. M. (1980), *Prices and Quantities: A Macroeconomic Analysis*, Oxford: Basil Blackwell.

Opie, R. (1982), 'Merger policy in the United Kingdom', in K. J. Hopt (ed.), *European Merger Control: Legal and Economic Analyses on Multinational Enterprises, volume 1*, Berlin: Walter de Gruyter.

Oster, S. (1982), 'Intra-industry structure and the ease of strategic change', *Review of Economics and Statistics*, **64**, 376–83.

Pass, C. L. and Sparkes, J. R. (1980), 'Control of horizontal mergers in Britain', *Journal of World Trade Law*, 135–59.

Payne, P. L. (1967), 'The emergence of the large-scale company in Great Britain, 1870–1914', *Economic History Review*, **20**, 519–42.

Peltzman, S. (1977), 'The gains and losses from industrial concentration', *Journal of Law and Economics*, **20**, 229–64.

Penrose, E. (1959), *The Theory of the Growth of the Firm*, Oxford: Blackwell.

Phillips, A. (1972), 'An econometric study of price-fixing, market structure and performance in British industry in the early 1950's', in K. Cowling (ed.), *Market Structure and Corporate Behaviour*, London: Gray-Mills.

Pickering, J. F. (1974), *Industrial Structure and Market Conduct*, London: Martin Robertson.

—— (1980), 'The implementation of British competition policy on mergers', *European Competition Law Review*, 177–98.

—— (1983), 'Causes and consequences of abandoned mergers', *Journal of Industrial Economics*, **31**, 267–81.

Porter, M. (1979), 'The structure within industries and companies performance', *Review of Economics and Statistics*, **61**, 214–28.

Porter, R. (1983), 'A study of cartel stability: the Joint Executive Committee, 1880–1886', *Bell Journal of Economics*, **14**, 301–14.

Posner, R. A. (1975), 'The social costs of monopoly and regulation', *Journal of Political Economy*, **83**, 807–27.

—— (1976), *Antitrust Law: An Economic Perspective*, Chicago: University of Chicago Press.

—— (1979), 'The Chicago School of anti-trust analysis', *University of Pennsylvania Law Review*, **127**, 925–48.

Pound, J., Lehn, K., and Jarrell, G. (1986), 'Are takeovers hostile to economic performance?', *Regulation*, September/October, 25–30, 55–6.

Prais, S. J. (1974), 'A new look at the growth of industrial concentration', *Oxford Economic Papers*, **26**, 273–88.

—— (1976), *The Evolution of Giant Firms in the United Kingdom*, Cambridge: Cambridge University Press.

—— (1977), 'Mergers and the public interest', *Financial Times*, 7 November, 9.

—— (1980), 'Industrial concentration: the role of statistical theories (a comment on Mr Sawyer's note)', *Oxford Bulletin of Economics and Statistics*, **42**, 269–72.

—— (1981), 'The contribution of mergers to industrial concentration: what do we know?', *Journal of Industrial Economics*, **29**, 321–9.

Pratten, C. F. (1970), 'A case study of a conglomerate merger', *Moorgate and Wall Street*, Spring, 27–54.

Radner, R. (1985), 'The internal economy of large firms', *Economic Journal*, Supplement, **96**, 1–22.

Ravenscraft, D. J. (1983), 'Structure–profit relationships at the line of business and industry level', *Review of Economics and Statistics*, **61**, 214–28.

—— and Scherer, F. M. (1986a), 'Divisional sell-off: a hazard function analysis', in *Mergers, Sell-offs and Economic Efficiency*.

—— and —— (1986b), 'The profitability of mergers', Bureau of Economics, Federal Trade Commission Working Paper 136, January.

Rees, R. (1984), 'A positive theory of the public enterprise', in M. Marchand, P. Pestieau, and H. Tulkens (eds.), *The Performance of Public Enterprises*, Amsterdam: North-Holland.

Rhoades, S. R. (1985), *Power, Empire Building and Mergers*, Mass.: Lexington Books.

Roberts, M. (1984), 'Testing oligopolistic behaviour: an application of the variable profit function', *International Journal of Industrial Organization*, **2**, 367–83.

Roell, A. (1986a), 'Allocative effects of takeovers under UK rules', London School of Economics Working Paper.

—— (1986b), 'The regulation of take-overs', paper presented to the LSE conference on the Economics of Takeovers, mimeo, London School of Economics.

Rose, H. B. and Newbould, G. D. (1967), 'The 1967 takeover boom', *Moorgate and Wall Street*, Autumn, 5–24.

Rosenfeld, J. D. (1984), 'Additional evidence on the relation between divestiture announcements and shareholder wealth', *Journal of Finance*, **39**, 1437–48.

Rowe, F. M. (1984), 'The decline of antitrust and the delusions of models: the Faustian Pact of law and economics', *Georgetown Law Journal*, **72**, 1511 ff.

Rowley, C. K. (1968), 'Mergers and public policy in Great Britain', *The Journal of Law and Economics*, **11**, 75–132.

Salinger, M. (1984), 'Tobins q, unionization and the concentration–profit relationship', *Rand Journal of Economics*, **15**, 159–70.

Samuels, J. M. (1971), 'The success or failure of mergers and takeovers', *Journal of Business Policy*, Spring.

Sawyer, M. C. (1979), 'The variance of logarithms and industrial concentration', *Oxford Bulletin of Economics and Statistics*, **41**, 165–81.

—— (1980), 'The variance of logarithms and industrial concentration: a reply', *Oxford Bulletin of Economics and Statistics*, **42**, 273–8.

Scherer, F. M. (1980), *Industrial Market Structure and Economic Performance*, second edition, Chicago: Rand McNally.

—— (1984), 'Mergers, sell-offs and managerial behaviour', paper presented to the Eleventh EARIE Conference, Fontainebleau, August.

Schipper, K. and Smith, A. (1983), 'Effects of recontracting on shareholder wealth: the case of voluntary spin-offs', *Journal of Financial Economics*, **12**, 437–67.

Schmalensee, R. (1977), 'Using the H-index of concentration with published data', *Review of Economics and Statistics*, **59**, 186–93.

—— (1982), 'Another look at market power', *Harvard Law Review*, **95**, 1789–816.

—— (1985), 'Do markets differ much?', *American Economic Review*, **75**, 341–51.

—— (1986), 'Interindustry studies of structure and performance', in R. Schmalensee and R. D. Willig (eds.), *Handbook of Industrial Economics*, Amsterdam: North-Holland, forthcoming.

—— (1987), 'Standards for dominant firm conduct: what can economics contribute?', in D. A. Hay and J. S. Vickers (eds.), *The Economics of Market Dominance*, Oxford: Basil Blackwell.

Schwartzman, D. (1959), 'The effect of monopoly on price', *Journal of Political Economy*, **67**, 352–62.

Securities and Exchange Commission (1985), 'Institutional ownership, tender offers, and long-term investments', mimeo, Office of the Chief Economist, Securities and Exchange Commission, Washington DC.

Shackle, G. (1949), *Expectations in Economics*, Cambridge: Cambridge University Press.

Sharpe, T. A. E. (1985), 'British competition policy in perspective', *Oxford Review of Economic Policy*, **1**, 3, 80–94.

Shaw, R. and Simpson, P. (1985), 'The Monopolies Commission and the process of competition', *Fiscal Studies*, **6**, 1, 82–96.

—— and —— (1986), 'The persistence of monopoly: an investigation of the effectiveness of the UK Monopolies Commission', *Journal of Industrial Economics*, **34**, 355–72.

Shepherd, W. G. (1972), 'Structure and behaviour in British industries with U.S. comparisons', *Journal of Industrial Economics*, **21**, 35–54.

—— (1984), '"Contestability" vs. competition', *American Economic Review*, **74**, 572–87.

Shiller, R. J. (1981), 'Do stock prices move too much to be justified by subsequent changes in dividends?', *American Economic Review*, **71**, 421–36.

Shleifer, A. (1986), 'Do demand curves for stocks slope down?', *Journal of Finance*, **41**, 579–90.

Shoemaker, P. (1982), 'The expected utility model: its variants, purposes, evidence and limitations', *Journal of Economic Literature*, **20**, 529–63.

Simon, H. A. (1955), 'A behavioural model of rational choice', *Quarterly Journal of Economics*, **69**, 99–118.

—— (1976), 'From procedural to substantive rationality', in S. Latsis (ed.), *Method and Appraisal in Economics*, Cambridge: Cambridge University Press.

Singh, A. (1971), *Takeovers: Their Relevance to the Stock Market and the Theory of the Firm*, Cambridge: Cambridge University Press.

—— (1975), 'Takeovers, economic "natural selection", and the theory of the firm: evidence from the post-war UK experience', *Economic Journal*, **85**, 497–515.

Slater, M. (1980), 'The managerial limitation to the growth of firms', *Economic Journal*, **90**, 520–8.

Smith, I. J. (1979), 'The effect of external takeovers on manufacturing employment change in the northern region between 1963–73', *Regional Studies*, **13**, 421–37.

—— (1986), 'Takeovers, rationalization and the northern region economy', *Northern Economic Review*, Winter 1985/6.

—— and Taylor, M. J. (1983), 'Takeover, closure and the restructuring of the UK ironfoundry industry', *Environment and Planning*, Series A, **15**, 639–61.

Solomon, E. and Laya, J. (1967), 'Measurement of company profitability: some systematic errors in accounting rate of return', in A. A. Robicheck (ed.), *Financial Research and Management Decisions*, New York: John Wiley.

Solow, R. M. (1971), 'Some implications of alternative criteria for the firm', in R. L. Marris and A. J. B. Wood (eds.), *The Corporate Economy*, London: Macmillan.

Spicer, B. H. and Ballew, V. (1983), 'Management accounting systems and the economics of internal organisation', *Accounting, Organisations and Society*, **8**, 73–96.

Steer, P. S. and Cable, J. (1978), 'Internal organization and profit: an empirical analysis of large UK companies', *Journal of Industrial Economics*, **27**, 13–30.

Steiner, P. O. (1975), *Mergers: Motives, Effects, Control*, Ann Arbor: University of Michigan Press.

Stigler, G. J. (1951), 'The division of labour is limited by the extent of the market', *Journal of Political Economy*, **59**, 3, 185–93.

—— (1968), *The Organization of Industry*, Chapter 6, Homewood, Ill.: Irwin.

Stoneman, P. (1978), 'Merger and technical progressiveness: the case of the British computer industry', *Applied Economics*, **10**, 125–39.

Strickland, A. and Weiss, L. (1976), 'Advertising, concentration and price-cost margins', *Journal of Political Economy*, **84**, 1109-21.

Sturgess, B. and Wheale, P. (1984), 'Merger performance evaluation: an empirical analysis of a sample of UK firms', *Journal of Economic Studies*, **11**, 4.

Summers, L. H. (1986), 'Does the stock market rationally reflect fundamental values?', *Journal of Finance*, **41**, 591-601.

Sutherland, A. (1969), *The Monopolies Commission in Action*, Cambridge: Cambridge University Press.

Swann, D., O'Brien, D. P., Maunder, W. P. J., and Howe, W. S. (1974), *Competition in British Industry*, London: Allen and Unwin.

Teece, D. J. (1980), 'Economies of scope and the scope of the enterprise', *Journal of Economic Behaviour and Organisation*, **1**, 223-47.

Thompson, R. S. (1982), *The Diffusion and Performance Impact of the Multidivisional Form in the UK*, PhD thesis, University of Newcastle upon Tyne.

Tzoannos, J. and Samuels, J. M. (1972), 'Takeovers and mergers: the financial characteristics of companies involved', *Journal of Business Finance*, **4**, 3, 5-16.

Utton, M. A. (1971), 'The effects of merger on concentration in UK manufacturing industry 1954-65', *Journal of Industrial Economics*, **20**, 42-58.

—— (1972a), 'Some features of the early merger movements in British manufacturing industry', *Business History*, **14**, 51-60.

—— (1972b), 'Mergers and the growth of large firms', *Oxford Bulletin of Economics and Statistics*, **34**, 189-97.

—— (1974), 'On measuring the effects of industrial mergers', *Scottish Journal of Political Economy*, **21**, 13-28.

—— (1975), 'British merger policy', in K. D. George and C. Joll (eds.), *Competition Policy in the UK and EEC*, Cambridge: Cambridge University Press.

—— (1979), *Diversification and Competition*, Cambridge: Cambridge University Press.

—— (1986), *Profits and the Stability of Monopoly*, Cambridge: Cambridge University Press.

—— and Morgan, A. D. (1983), *Concentration and Foreign Trade*, Cambridge: Cambridge University Press.

von Weizsäcker, C. C. (1980), 'A welfare analysis of barriers to entry', *Bell Journal of Economics*, **11**, 399-420.

Walshe, G. (1974), *Recent Trends in Monopoly in Great Britain*, Cambridge: Cambridge University Press.

Waterson, M. (1980), 'Price cost margins and successive market power', *Quarterly Journal of Economics*, **94**, 135-50.

—— (1984), *Economic Theory of the Industry*, Cambridge: Cambridge University Press.

Weisbach, M. S. (1986), 'Outside directors, monitoring, and the turnover of chief executive officers: an empirical analysis', mimeo, MIT.

Weiss, L. W. (1974), 'The concentration-profits relation and antitrust', in H. J. Goldschmid, H. M. Mann, and J. F. Weston (eds.), *Industrial Concentration: The New Learning*, Boston: Little, Brown & Co.

Whish, R. (1985), *Competition Law*, London: Butterworth.

White, L. (1976), 'Searching for the critical concentration ratio: an application of the switching of regimes technique', in S. Goldfield and R. Quandt (eds.), *Studies in Non-linear Estimation*, Boston: Ballinger.

Williamson, O. E. (1963), 'Managerial discretion and business behaviour', *American Economic Review*, **53**, 1032–57.

—— (1968), 'Economies as an anti-trust defense: the welfare trade-offs', *American Economic Review*, **58**, 18–36. Reprinted with corrections in C. K. Rowley (ed.) (1972), *Readings in Industrial Economics*, London: Macmillan.

—— (1971), 'The vertical integration of production: market failure considerations', *American Economic Review*, **61**, 112–23.

—— (1975), *Markets and Hierarchies: Analysis and Anti-trust Implications*, New York: Free Press.

—— (1977), 'Economies as an antitrust defence revisited', *University of Pennsylvania Law Review*, **125**, 699–736. Reprinted in A. P. Jacquemin and H. W. de Jong (eds.) (1977), *Welfare Aspects of Industrial Markets*, Leiden: Martinus Nijhoff.

—— (1983), 'Vertical merger guidelines: interpreting the 1982 reforms', *California Law Review*, **71**, 604–17.

Wilson, H. (1980), *Report of the Committee to Review the Functioning of the Financial System*, London: HMSO.

Winter, S. G. (1964), 'Economic "natural selection" and the theory of the firm', *Yale Economic Essays*, **4**, 225–72.

Wood, A. J. B. (1971), 'Diversification, merger and research expenditure: a review of empirical studies', in R. L. Marris and A. J. B. Wood (eds.), *The Corporate Economy*, London: Macmillan.

Wright, M. (1985), 'Divestment and organisational adaptation', *European Management Journal*, **3**, 85–93.

—— (1986a), 'Demergers', in J. Coyne and M. Wright (eds.), *Divestment and Strategic Change*, Oxford: Philip Allan.

—— (1986b), 'The make-buy decision and managing markets: the case of management buy-outs', *Journal of Management Studies*, **23**, 443–64.

—— and Coyne, J. (1985), *Management Buy-outs in British Industry*, London: Croom Helm.

—— and —— (1986), *Management Buy-outs in 1985*, Nottingham/London: Centre for Management Buy-out Research/Venture Economics.

—— and —— (1987), *Review of UK Management Buyouts 1986*, London: Venture Economics.

——, Coyne, J. and Mills, A. (1987), *Spicer and Pegler's Management Buy-outs*, Cambridge: Woodhead-Faulkner.

—— and Thompson, R. S. (1986), 'Vertical disintegration and the life cycle of industries and firms', *Managerial and Decision Economics*, **7**, 141–4.

—— and —— (1987), 'Divestment and the control of divisionalised firms', *Accounting and Business Research*, 259–67.

Yamey, B. S. (1985), 'Deconcentration as antitrust policy: the rise and fall of the concentration ratio', *International Review of Economics and Business*, **32**, 2, 119–40.

Yarrow, G. K. (1976), 'On the predictions of managerial theories of the firm', *Journal of Industrial Economics*, **14**, 267–79.

—— (1985), 'Shareholder protection, compulsory acquisition and the efficiency of the takeover process', *Journal of Industrial Economics*, **34**, 3–16.

Young, S. and Lowe, A. V. (1974), *Intervention in the Mixed Economy*, London: Croom Helm.

Index